Introduction

21ST Century Business has been written with students and teachers in mind. It covers every area of the syllabus and includes the experience and hindsight gained from nine past Leaving Certificate exams and incorporating all the styles of exam questions asked. The syllabus is treated so thoroughly that additional teacher notes are not required.

The book is written using clear and student-friendly English. All concepts are thoroughly explained in a way that is totally accessible to students of all ability levels, yet sufficiently detailed for Higher Level students to achieve an A1. The theory is backed up throughout with clear, concise and familiar real-world examples to reinforce learning.

The book contains many "evaluations" to prepare Higher Level students for this important question. The marketing chapter, for example, evaluates the marketing and promotional mixes of several brand leaders. All the laws on the course are evaluated.

Each chapter contains a large bank of homework questions at both Ordinary and Higher Levels, covering every style of question examined in the Leaving Certificate. Every chapter includes at least one ABQ so that Higher Level students can practise this essential question.

I would like to express my gratitude to Greg O'Connor for reviewing the contents and for his advice which helped to improve the book so much. I am extremely grateful to Pádraig Hanratty for his excellent editorial assistance – the numerous proofreadings, meetings and "beyond the call of duty" work – all were very much appreciated. The process of writing a book is a lengthy and all-consuming one. Heartfelt thanks to Diarmuid Furlong for his patience and advice throughout the entire process.

WILLIAM MURPHY

Published by
C J Fallon
Ground Floor – Block B
Liffey Valley Office Campus
Dublin 22

First Edition May 2008

Higher Level Business

The exam consists of three sections to be answered as follows:

Section	Contents	Instructions	Marks	Areas covered
1	10 short questions	Answer any 8	20%	Units 1 – 7
2	Applied Business Question	This question is COMPULSORY and all three parts MUST be answered	20%	The areas examinable rotate every 5 years. 2009 Units 1, 2 and 3 2010 Units 2, 3 and 4 2011 Units 3, 4 and 5 2012 Units 4, 5 and 6 2013 Units 5, 6 and 7
3	Part 1 contains 3 questions Part 2 contains 4 questions	You must answer FOUR questions from the 7 given, as follows: *Two* from Part 1 and *Two* from Part 2 OR *One* from Part 1 and *Three* from Part 2	60%	Part 1 questions come from units 1, 6 and 7 of the course Part 2 questions come from units 2, 3, 4 and 5 of the course

Ordinary Level Business

The exam consists of two sections to be answered as follows:

Section	Contents	Instructions	Marks	Areas covered
1	15 short questions	Answer any 10	25%	Units 1 – 7
2	Part 1 contains 3 questions Part 2 contains 5 questions	You must answer FOUR questions from the 8 given, as follows: *Two* from Part 1 and *Two* from Part 2 OR *One* from Part 1 and *Three* from Part 2	75%	Part 1 questions come from units 1, 6 and 7 of the course Part 2 questions come from units 2, 3, 4 and 5 of the course

Dedication

This book is dedicated to my parents, Katherine and William Murphy.

Contents

CHAPTER 1

People In Business

Who are the Main Stakeholders in Business?

A business is an organisation set up to provide goods and services to customers. Businesses affect a lot of people. For example, imagine your local supermarket closed down. This would affect many people.

The supermarket employees would lose their jobs; you the customer would have to find somewhere else to shop; the supermarket owner would lose her livelihood; the suppliers, for example the bread and milk companies that sold to the supermarket, would lose sales; and the government would no longer receive taxes from the supermarket.

In other words, *lots* of people are affected by how a business is run. These people are called **stakeholders**.

 ▶ These are the main stakeholders in any business:

1. Entrepreneur
2. Investor
3. Employer
4. Employee
5. Producer
6. Consumer
7. Service Provider
8. Interest Group

Role of the Entrepreneur in a Business

An entrepreneur is a person who spots an opportunity (a gap in the market) and takes the initiative to set up a business to make money from that opportunity.

For example, Gillian Bowler noticed in the 1970s that package holidays to Spain were becoming increasingly popular but no company sold package holidays to Greece. Having been to Greece many times, she thought that Irish people would like it there and decided to set up her own travel agency, called Budget Travel, selling package holidays to Greece.

The entrepreneur takes a big risk when setting up the business. She takes a financial risk because if the business is a failure, she will lose the money she invested in it. She also takes a personal risk because if the business fails, she may lose her self-esteem and self-confidence.

Gillian Bowler took a risk when setting up Budget Travel. She resigned her job and took out a bank loan to set up the business. Had it failed, she would have been unemployed and unable to repay the bank.

Entrepreneurs are willing to take these risks, however, because they expect the business to be a success and they expect to make a profit.

Budget Travel prospered and Gillian Bowler became very wealthy when she later sold the business.

Examples of Entrepreneurs

In the 1970s, Bill Gates predicted that computers would be used in every office and home in the future. So he set up Microsoft, a company that makes computer software.

Anita Roddick was so frustrated that no business sold small sizes of cosmetics in simple packaging that she set up her own business, called The Body Shop, to do so.

During a trip to the United States, Brody Sweeney noticed how successful the sandwich shop Subway was. Realising that there were no Subways in Ireland (at that time), he set up his own sandwich business in 1988 called O'Briens Sandwich Bars.

Role of the Investor in a Business

An investor is a person who gives the money (called capital) to the entrepreneur that she needs to set up and run her business, in exchange for a return on investment.

The investor can lend money (called debt capital) to the entrepreneur, which he expects to be paid back with interest.

- ▶ Ulster Bank gave Gillian Bowler a loan of approximately €127 to set up Budget Travel. So Ulster Bank was an investor in Budget Travel.

▶ Bank of Ireland loaned Brody Sweeney IR£21,000 (approx €27,000) to open his first O'Briens Sandwich Bar. Thus, Bank of Ireland was an investor in Brody's business.

Alternatively, the investor can give the entrepreneur the capital in return for a share (part-ownership) in the business. This is called equity finance. In this case, the return the investor receives is an annual share of the profits, called a dividend. The investor can sell his share later.

▶ To get the money to open her second shop, Anita Roddick sold a half share in her business to an investor for Stg£5,000 (€7,500).

Examples of investors include banks that give loans to entrepreneurs, and government agencies such as Enterprise Ireland that give grants to the entrepreneur to help her set up her business.

Note:

Can you see how the entrepreneur and investor depend on each other? The entrepreneur depends on the investor for the capital to start her business. The investor depends on the entrepreneur to make the business a success and pay him a decent return on investment.

Role of the Employer in a Business

An employer is a person who hires others to work for her. An entrepreneur may become an employer when her business begins to grow and she cannot do all the work herself or because she does not have certain skills that are essential for running the business. For example, she may employ a computer graduate to design the business's website and look after its computer system if she is not skilled at computers.

The employer rewards the employee for the work he does. The employer can reward the employee financially with pay, bonuses and commission, and non-financially with more holidays.

An example of an employer is Aer Lingus. It hires pilots to fly its planes.

Role of the Employee in a Business

An employee is a person who works for an employer in return for a wage. He carries out the essential tasks needed to make the business a success, which the employer cannot or will not do.

When some Microsoft workers saw the worldwide success of the Sony PlayStation, they thought of the idea of Microsoft developing a games console. They worked on their idea, presented it to their boss and this led to Microsoft launching the Xbox.

An example of an employee is a pilot in Aer Lingus. He flies planes for the airline in return for a wage.

Note:

Can you see how the employer and employee depend on each other? The employer depends on the employee to do all the work needed to make the business a success. The employee depends on the employer for a wage.

Role of the Manager in a Business

A manager's job is to run the business and make sure that it achieves its objectives. The manager must use the resources of the business (such as people, money, equipment and so on) in the best possible way so that the business is a success.

A successful manager must be able to lead and motivate her employees and communicate effectively with them and with all the other stakeholders in the business.

An example of a manager is the Chief Executive Officer of Ryanair, Michael O'Leary. Ryanair started with just one route in 1985. Michael O'Leary proceeded to turn the company into one of the world's most successful airlines.

Role of the Producer in a Business

A producer is a business that makes finished products to sell to consumers. Producers are manufacturers who take raw materials and use a manufacturing process to turn them into a finished product.

Producers use the four factors of production to make a product: land (raw materials from nature), labour (employees), capital (man-made things such as machines) and enterprise (ideas).

For example:
- ○ Cadbury takes milk and other ingredients and turns them into chocolate.
- ○ Tayto takes potatoes and turns them into crisps

Role of the Consumer in a Business

A consumer is a person who buys goods or services from the entrepreneur for his own personal use. In this way, the consumer provides the entrepreneur with a market for her product and thus a profit.

The consumer also provides the entrepreneur with market research information, by telling the entrepreneur what he likes and dislikes in a product. The entrepreneur can use this information to make products that consumers like and thus make even more profit for herself.

For example, when parents pay for childcare for their children, they are consumers.

Note:

Can you see how the producer and consumer depend on each other? The producer depends on the consumer to buy her products so that she can make a profit. The consumer depends on the producer to make the products he needs and wants such as medicines, dishwashers and so on.

Role of the Service Provider in a Business

A service provider is a business that offers a range of valuable supports to an entrepreneur. For example, a bank enables the entrepreneur to deposit her money safely and pay for goods with cheques and laser cards.

Other examples include:

eircom   Provides the entrepreneur with communications (phone and Internet) services.

Solicitor   Provides the entrepreneur with legal advice if she is sued and defends her if the case comes to court.

Service providers operate in the tertiary sector of the economy. They don't extract materials out of nature (primary sector). Unlike producers, they don't make a finished product (secondary sector). Instead, they do a range of helpful things for the entrepreneur.

For example, DHL provides the entrepreneur with a courier service that will deliver parcels and documents for the entrepreneur all over the world.

Role of Interest Groups in a Business

An interest group is an organisation of people who come together and campaign for a common goal. By joining forces, they have more power, more money and more talents at their disposal and so are more likely to be listened to by the decision-makers.

They might use tactics such as organising negative publicity and boycotts of businesses that they are campaigning against. They lobby politicians to bring out laws that will meet their demands.

For example, Greenpeace is an environmental interest group. When Shell Oil attempted to dump an old oil rig into the sea, Greenpeace organised a massive consumer boycott of the company. Shell lost so much money that it gave in to the pressure and agreed to dispose of the oil rig properly in a safe environmental way.

Many different interest groups operate in Ireland. Some, such as the Irish Business and Employers Confederation (IBEC) and the Irish Small and Medium Enterprises (ISME), are set up specifically to help businesses. These interest groups try to help entrepreneurs by lobbying the Minister for Finance to do something positive for businesspeople in his budget (for example, lower business taxes).

Others, such as the Irish Congress of Trade Unions (ICTU), fight for the rights and interests of Irish workers. Irish farmers too have interest groups that fight for them – the Irish Farmers Association (IFA) and the Irish Creamery Milk Suppliers Association (ICMSA). Consumers are represented by the Consumers Association of Ireland.

Relationships Between Stakeholders

All the different stakeholders (parties) in a business have a relationship with each other. This relationship can be described under four headings as follows:

1. Co-operative Relationship

This means that the parties in business have the same objective and so they work together and help each other in order to achieve their goals. Working together produces better results than if they worked alone or against each other. They both do well out of the co-operation. The following are examples of co-operative relationships:

- If a business is going through a bad patch, employers and employees might work together to save the business. The employees agree to a pay cut until the business is back on its feet and the employer agrees to give them shares instead of pay. In this way, both win in the long term because the business does not go bankrupt but continues to provide profits and jobs. This happened in Aer Lingus.

- The Body Shop promotes the cause of Amnesty International, a human rights interest group. Both benefit from this co-operation. The Body Shop increases sales because consumers are impressed that it cares about more than money. And Amnesty International benefits from free, high-profile publicity in main streets in major cities throughout the world.

- In the 1990s Ford and Mazda (two car producers) had a co-operative relationship. They formed a strategic alliance to develop a new car (Ford Fiesta/Mazda 121). They shared the costs of developing the new car between them. And, by sharing ideas, they were able to come up with the best possible car.

2. Competitive Relationship

This means that one party in business wants to be more successful than another. Only one of them can win and so they fight against each other and become rivals. The following are examples of competitive relationships:

- ▶ Two employees may compete within a business for a promotion. Each will try to work harder and try to impress the boss in order to get the promotion.

- ▶ Employees and employers can compete. Employees want job security, whereas the employer may want to make redundancies to save money. For example, ESB announced in 2007 that it wanted to close down three old power stations. The employees' union said that it would not let this go ahead.

- ▶ Ryanair and Aer Lingus compete with each other to win customers. When one announces a low fare, the other fights back with a lower fare. When one organises an ad campaign, the other fights back by running an ad campaign showing that it is better. This is called comparative advertising.

3. Dependent Relationship

This means that the parties in business need each other in order to be successful. They cannot achieve their goals on their own. They rely on the other party to provide them with what they need so that they can be a success. The following are examples of dependent relationships:

- ▶ Consumers and producers depend on each other. Consumers need producers to make the products they need or want, such as headache tablets, washing machines, designer clothes and so on. Producers depend on consumers to buy the products they make so that they can make a decent profit from their business.

- ▶ Without a loan from Bank of Ireland (investor), Brody Sweeney (entrepreneur) would not have been able to set up O'Briens Sandwich Bars. Without Brody and successful entrepreneurs like him, Bank of Ireland would not make a return on its investment.

> **Note:**
>
> Read through this chapter again to see examples of how other parties in business depend on each other.

4. Dynamic Relationship

This means that the relationship between the stakeholders in business is constantly changing. Sometimes it is competitive and sometimes it is co-operative. The following are examples of dynamic relationships:

- There is fierce competition between Coke and Pepsi, with each trying to beat the other to win customers (increase market share). They do this by developing new products and ideas. However, when Pepsi received a letter offering to sell it Coke's secret recipe, Pepsi immediately notified Coke of this, enabling Coke executives to contact the FBI and have the culprit arrested.

- Competing businesses in a town might work together once a year to organise a town festival to bring more people to the area.

- People's roles in business change over time as well. When employees buy shares in the business, their role changes. They become investors in the business as well as employees.

Contract Law

Definition of Contract

A contract is a legally binding agreement between two or more people that is enforceable in law. This means that if one person breaks the agreement, a judge can order her to pay compensation or force her to carry out the contract as originally agreed.

Example
- Anne had a contract to sell her house to Peter for €420,000. The sale is to take place on 1st February.
- Peter then sells his old house and books a removal firm for 1st February to bring his furniture to the new house.

- On 31st January, Anne changes her mind and refuses to sell to Peter.
- Because it is a contract, Peter can take Anne to court on the grounds that he has suffered because she broke the contract.
- In court, the judge could force Anne to sell the house to Peter because they had a contract.

Essential Elements of a Contract

How do you know whether an agreement you make with someone is a contract? The answer is that an agreement is only a contract if it contains *all* of the following elements of a contract:

1. Offer
2. Acceptance
3. Consideration
4. Intention to Contract
5. Capacity to Contract
6. Consent to Contract
7. Legality of Form
8. Legality of Purpose

1. Offer

An offer is made when one person asks another to enter into a deal with her. To be a valid offer, she must set out all the terms of the deal clearly, completely and without any conditions attached.

She must communicate the offer to the other person. She can do this either by speaking it, by writing it or by her conduct. For example, you are offering to buy the groceries at the supermarket when you place them on the conveyor belt. An offer can be withdrawn at any stage before the other person accepts it.

Note:

Do not confuse an offer with an **invitation to treat**.

- In Irish law, an advertisement, a price tag, a shop display or goods on a shelf are not legal offers. They are invitations to treat.

- They are an indication that the seller of an item would like to receive offers for it. They are a guide to the price the seller is willing to consider and may possibly accept if offered. But they are not legal offers that the seller must accept.

- The customer is the one who *asks* to buy the goods at the price shown. He makes the offer. The seller can then accept or reject this offer.

Example

■ Liam sees a new sports car in a car dealership with a price tag of €125. He goes into the showroom and says he'll buy the car for €125. The salesperson refuses to sell it to him for €125, saying that the price shown is a mistake. The correct price is €125,000. Does the salesperson *legally* have to sell the car to Liam for €125?

Answer

■ If Liam had a contract with the shop to buy the car for €125, then the shop has to sell it to him for €125. The first thing you need for a contract is an offer. Did the car dealer offer the car to Liam for €125?

No. The price displayed on the car is not an offer. It is an invitation to treat. Because there is no offer, there is no contract, so there is nothing Liam can do. It was Liam who made the offer and the car dealer can refuse his offer.

Termination of an Offer

A person can withdraw an offer at any time *before* the other party accepts it. An offer also ends if a deadline set for acceptance passes. For example, if you don't accept an offer from the CAO on time, you lose that college place. Finally, all offers end after a reasonable time. So, if you are offered a job and don't bother to reply, you're not entitled to that job five years later.

2. Acceptance

Acceptance means that the other person agrees precisely to all the terms of the deal without any conditions. They can accept by speaking, putting it in writing or by conduct. For example, the supermarket accepts your offer to buy the groceries when the shop assistant scans them.

The person must accept *all* the terms of the deal exactly as set out and cannot change them. To do so is called a counter offer. Making a counter offer is an automatic rejection of the offer and the end of that contract.

Example

■ David interviews Yvonne for a job in his business. He is very impressed with her qualifications and offers her the job with pay of €40,000 a year. Yvonne tells him she'll think about it. Two days later she tells him she'll take the job if he increases the pay to €45,000.

David tells her he can't afford this and that he'll look for someone else for the job. At this point, she says "OK, I'll take the €40,000." David is annoyed by her greedy attitude and refuses to give her the job. She tells him he must give her the job because she has a letter from him offering it to her.

Does David legally have to give the job to Yvonne?

　　　　　　　　Yes　　　　No　　　　(Circle correct answer)

Explain your answer

Answer

■ If Yvonne had a contract with David for the job, then he has to give her the job. The first thing you need for a contract is an offer. David *did* offer the job to Yvonne with pay of €40,000 a year.

The second thing you need for a contract is acceptance. Did Yvonne agree to all the terms of David's offer precisely and without conditions?

No.

She said she'd take the job if he gave her €45,000. This is a counter offer. She did not agree to his terms exactly. Remember he offered her €40,000. In Irish law, she said no to David's offer when she made the counter offer. If there is no acceptance, there is no contract and therefore there is nothing she can do.

3. Consideration

Consideration means the payment that one person gives to the other as part of the agreement. For an agreement to be a contract there must be consideration and it must be real and valuable.

There must be a *quid pro quo*. In other words, both sides must get something out of it. In the supermarket example, you get the groceries and the supermarket gets your money. (The supermarket gives you the groceries as consideration; you give it the cash as consideration.)

Example

■ Eoin asks Aoife out on a date. She agrees and they arrange to meet on Friday at 8.00pm. Eoin doesn't turn up on Friday. Is Aoife entitled to compensation because Eoin broke his promise?

Answer

■ If Aoife had a contract with Eoin, then she is entitled to compensation. The first thing you need for a contract is an offer. There was an offer when Eoin asked her out on the date. The second thing you need is acceptance. There was acceptance when Aoife said yes. The third thing you need is consideration. Did Aoife receive any payment for agreeing to go on the date?

No. Because there is no consideration, there is no contract, so there is nothing Aoife can do.

4. Intention to Contract

Intention to contract means that both parties to the agreement must mean it to be a legally binding contract. They fully understand at the time they make the agreement that it is a legally binding contract and that they will end up in court if they break their promise.

For example, in Irish law, agreements between family members for non-business transactions are not contracts because there is no intention in them. If Paul promises to wash his mother's car and then doesn't, she can't sue him. No matter how tough his mother is, Paul still wouldn't expect to end up in front of a judge for not washing the car for her.

However, agreements between businesspeople are always contracts because the businesspeople always intend them to be legally binding.

Example

Try this one yourself in your copy.

■ Alan's mother asks him to clean the kitchen for €7. Alan agrees to do it this afternoon. His mother pays him the €7. Alan does not clean the kitchen as promised.

Is his mother entitled to compensation because Alan broke his promise?

Answer

■ If Alan's mother had a contract with him, then she is entitled to compensation. For a valid contract, the following elements of a contract must be present in the agreement:

Offer	(Yes)	No	*"Alan's mother asks him to clean the kitchen"*
Acceptance	Yes	No	
Consideration	Yes	No	
Intention	Yes	No	

There is no contract because there is no _____. Therefore there is nothing Alan's mother can do.

5. Capacity to Contract

Capacity to contract means that a person has the legal ability and power to make a legally binding contract.

All people and businesses have the capacity to make a contract except the following:
- ▶ People under 18 (except for necessities).
- ▶ People who are mentally incapacitated because they are drunk, on drugs or insane.
- ▶ Diplomats, who cannot make contracts because they have diplomatic immunity.
- ▶ Company directors when they do something beyond their authority (as set out in the company's memorandum of association). This is known as directors acting *ultra vires*.

Because these people do not have the capacity to contract, any such agreements they make are not legal contracts.

6. Consent to Contract

For a contract to be valid, both parties must give their real permission to enter into it. They must know exactly what they're getting into (there can't be any mistakes or lies) and they cannot be forced into agreeing to the deal against their will.

In a real-life case, the former chairperson of a company threatened the CEO that he would have him killed if he did not buy his shares. The CEO bought the shares but later tried to get out of the contract. The judge let him out of the contract because he had been forced into it against his will.

7. Legality of Form

This means that certain contracts must be drawn up in a certain way (form) if they are to be legal contracts.

For example, when you are buying a house from someone, you must have the agreement in writing. Otherwise, it is not a valid contract, even if there is offer, acceptance, consideration, intention, capacity and consent. The seller can pull out at any time up to when you both sign the written contract.

Hire purchase contracts (whereby you buy something and pay for it in instalments) must also be in writing if they are to be legal contracts.

8. Legality of Purpose

This means that legally binding contracts can only be for legal transactions. Agreements to commit a crime will not be upheld in court, regardless of how many of the other elements of a contract are present in the agreement.

For example, a judge will not award compensation to a bank robber whose getaway driver did not turn up as promised.

Termination of a Contract

A contract can come to an end in a number of ways:

1. Performance

When both sides carry out their duties under the contract exactly as originally agreed, the contract is ended. For example, Paula signed a contract to sell her shares in AIB to Diane for €15,000. When Diane gives the €15,000 to Paula and Paula gives the shares to Diane, the contract is terminated.

2. Agreement

A contract is terminated if all the parties involved in it voluntarily agree to end it. They may agree to end it because the terms of the contract allow them to get out of it if they give each other notice. For example, most employment contracts contain a clause allowing either the employer or the employee to end the contract by giving the other a month's notice.

They might agree to end because they agree on a better deal for both parties. For example, a young footballer who scores eight goals in the World Cup might agree with his club to end his one-year contract with the club early so that they can sign a new five-year deal. The club wants to keep him and the player gets more money. Both are happy to end the original contract.

3. Frustration

A contract comes to an end if some unforeseen event such as the death or bankruptcy of one of the parties to it occurs, which makes it impossible to carry out the contract.

For example, a singer has a contract with a pub owner to perform at his pub one night. The night before the gig, the singer dies. The pub owner cannot sue the singer for not turning up. Through no one's fault, the contract was frustrated.

4. Breach of Contract

A contract is terminated as soon as one of the people involved breaks their part of the deal. If the person breaks a condition in the contract, it is terminated immediately. A condition is an essential and fundamental part of the contract. If a warranty in the contract is broken, the contract is not ended. A warranty is a term of a contract that is not essential and fundamental to it.

For example, if a football player misses a training session, this is a breach of a warranty. He has not terminated his contract. However if he misses a match, it is a breach of a condition. The contract is terminated and his club can sue him.

Remedies for Breach of Contract

Breach of contract means that one party to the contract fails to perform it exactly as agreed. If a person breaks a contract, she can be taken to court where the judge can award the following to the innocent person:

1. Damages

The judge can order the person who broke the contract to pay financial compensation to the innocent party to compensate him for what he has lost and suffered as a result of the other person's breach.

This remedy can help to solve the conflict over the breach because the innocent person does not lose out financially as a result of the breach. Any money he lost is returned to him and he may receive extra money for any inconvenience caused to him.

For example, a singer agrees to give a concert in Dublin. The promoter starts to organise the event and pays the singer an advance of €250,000. The singer pulls out of the concert at the last minute. The promoter takes her to court for breach of contract. The judge could order the singer to pay the promoter €400,000 in compensation for money lost and inconvenience.

2. Specific Performance

The judge can order the person who breaks the contract to carry out her side of the deal exactly as originally agreed in the contract.

This remedy can help to solve the conflict over the breach because the innocent person does not suffer at all as a result of the breach. The judge orders the contract to be carried out in full as the parties originally promised. The innocent person gets exactly what he contracted for.

In the concert example, the judge could order the singer to perform in Dublin at a later date.

3. Rescind the Contract

The judge can order that the contract be cancelled. He sets the contract aside and returns the two parties involved to exactly the same position they were in before they entered the contract. A judge would rescind a contract that has been frustrated.

This remedy can help to solve the conflict over the breach because the innocent person is returned to the situation he was in before he entered into the contract at all. He is no better and no worse off after the breach.

In the concert example, if the reason the singer could not perform was that she had become seriously ill, the judge might rescind the contract. The singer would have to pay the promoter back the €250,000 advance and then the contract is set aside. It no longer exists (similar to an annulment). Both the singer and the promoter are left as they were before they entered into the contract.

Ordinary Level Questions

EXAM SECTION 1 (25%) - SHORT ANSWER QUESTIONS [10 marks each]

1. List the main parties involved in business.

2. Explain the role of the entrepreneur in business.

3. Outline the role of investors in business and give two examples of investors.

4. Write out what the following letters stand for: IBEC   ICTU   IFA

5. Column 1 is a list of business terms. Column 2 is a list of possible explanations for these terms. Match the two lists by placing the letter of the correct explanation under the relevant number below. One explanation has no match.

Column 1	Column 2: Explanations
1. Consumer	a) A person who provides the entrepreneur with the capital needed to start and run the business
2. Entrepreneur	
3. Interest Group	b) A business that does useful things for others
4. Investor	c) A person who spots an opportunity and sets up a business to make money from that opportunity
5. Producer	
6. Service Provider	d) A business that manufactures finished goods from raw materials
	e) A person who buys goods and services for her own personal use
	f) An organisation of people sharing the same goal who come together and campaign to achieve that goal
	g) A person who works for another in return for a wage

1	2	3	4	5	6
E	C	B	A	D	B

6. Indicate whether each of the following A, B, C, D and E are true or false.

	Sentence	True or False
A	An example of a co-operative relationship in business is when employees go on strike to win a pay rise. *Competitive*	*False*
B	IBEC is an interest group that fights for the rights and interests of business people.	*True*
C	Consumers depend on producers to make the products they need.	*True*
D	All the people affected by how a business is run are called shareholders. *Stakeholders*	*False*
E	Service providers operate in the tertiary sector of the economy.	

7. Outline the role of interest groups in business and give two examples of interest groups.

8. Explain the role of the consumer in business.

9. Outline how employers and employees depend on each other.

10. Indicate whether each of the following (A, B, C, D and E) is true or false.

	Sentence	True or False
A	Breach of contract is when a person breaks her side of a contract.	*True*
B	Consideration means agreeing to an offer exactly.	*False*
C	Specific performance is a remedy for breach of contract.	*True*
D	A contract is terminated by frustration.	*True*
E	Shops must, by law, always sell products at the price displayed.	*True*

11. List four elements of a valid contract.

12. Define "consent to contract".

13. List four ways that a contract can be terminated and outline any one of them.

14. Outline three remedies for breach of contract.

15. Column 1 is a list of business terms. Column 2 is a list of possible explanations for these terms. Match the two lists by placing the letter of the correct explanation under the relevant number below. One explanation has no match.

Column 1
1. Condiseration
2. Capacity to Contract
3. Contract
4. Offer
5. Intention
6. Consent to Contract

Column 2: Explanations
a) When one person asks another to enter into a deal with him
b) When a judge orders a person who broke a contract to carry it out exactly as set out in the contract
c) When both parties to a contract are in agreement and there is no undue pressure on either party
d) When the parties to a contract have the ability and right to make a contract
e) When some benefit or value moves from one party to a contract to the other
f) A legally binding agreement between two or more people
g) When both parties to an agreement mean it to be a legally binding contract

1	2	3	4	5	6
E	D	F	A	G	C

EXAM SECTION 2 (75%) – LONG QUESTIONS

1. Distinguish between "producers" and "service providers". (10 marks)

2. Describe the relationship that exists between an entrepreneur and an investor. (15 marks)

3. Describe the relationship that exists between a producer and a consumer. (15 marks)

4. Describe the relationship that exists between an employer and an employee. (15 marks)

5. Explain the term "competitive relationship" and outline two examples of competitive relationships in business. (20 marks)

6. Explain the term "co-operative relationship" and outline two examples of co-operative relationships in business. (20 marks)

7. Explain the term "interest group" and use an example to illustrate your answer. (10 marks)

8. Name two stakeholders in a business and explain the role of one of them. (15 marks)

9. Explain the terms "offer" and "acceptance". (20 marks)

10. Distinguish between "capacity to contract" and "consent to contract". (15 marks)

Higher Level Questions

EXAM SECTION 1 (20%) - SHORT ANSWER QUESTIONS [10 marks each]

1. Name and give an example of three stakeholders in a business.

2. Complete this sentence: The role of an investor in a business is to…

3. Illustrate your understanding of the term "service provider".

4. Distinguish between "employer" and "employee".

5. Define "consumer".

6. Column 1 is a list of business terms. Column 2 is a list of possible explanations for these terms. Match the two lists by placing the letter of the correct explanation under the relevant number below. One explanation has no match.

Column 1	Column 2: Explanations
1. Co-operative Relationship	a) Applying pressure to a person by contacting them and meeting with them to persuade them to make the decision you want them to make
2. Dynamic Relationship	b) The stakeholders in business work against each other and try to beat each other so that only one of them wins
3. Debt Capital	c) Money that an entrepreneur receives from an investor in return for handing over a share of her business
4. Equity Capital	d) The stakeholders in business work together and help each other to achieve their goals
5. Lobbying	e) Money that an entrepreneur borrows from an investor
	f) The relationship between the stakeholders in business is constantly changing over time

1	2	3	4	5

7. Illustrate your understanding of the term "entrepreneur".

8. Which stakeholder in a business do you feel is the most important? Explain your choice.

9. What is an "interest group"? Name two interest groups.

10. The following table shows three types of stakeholder and four functions. For each function, tick (✓) the type of stakeholder that is *most* likely to match that function.

	Consumer	Employee	Investor
Provides entrepreneur with market research information			
Provides entrepreneur with capital			
Provides entrepreneur with income			
Provides entrepreneur with free advertising when they tell friends how good the product is			

11. Illustrate your understanding of the term "consent to contract".

12. Distinguish between "legality of purpose" and "legality of form".

13. Sam sees a diamond necklace in a jeweller's shop window with a price tag of €10. She goes into the shop and asks to buy it for €10. The assistant refuses, saying that the tag is an error. The price should read €10,000.
Is Sam legally entitled to buy the necklace for €10?

Yes   No   (Circle correct answer.) Explain your answer.

14. Brenda and Andrew are friends. Brenda offers to help Andrew study for his Business test. Andrew accepts and invites Brenda over to his house at 6.00pm that night. Brenda never showed up. Andrew subsequently failed his test.
Is Andrew entitled to sue Brenda?

Yes   No   (Circle correct answer.) Explain your answer.

EXAM SECTION 2 (20%) – APPLIED BUSINESS QUESTION – 80 MARKS
ABQ1

Encanta Ltd.

Aoife Byrne established her furniture-making business, Encanta Ltd., seven years ago after graduating from design college. She got a lot of help and advice from Enterprise Ireland at the time, including a grant to help her pay for the factory and equipment she needed. The rest of the money she needed came from a friend who agreed to invest in return for shares in Encanta Ltd.

Over the years, the business has developed well and Aoife now employs 12 full-time staff. Aoife is tough on her staff. Recently, they have started to complain about the relatively low pay and bad conditions they receive. Aoife told them that if they didn't like it, they could leave. In recent months, six employees have left and Aoife had to spend a lot of time recruiting and training their replacements.

Aoife's business is also encountering other problems. She is losing sales to competitors from Eastern Europe. Aoife asked her customers why this was happening and they told her that the Eastern European furniture makers offered better, more up-to-date and more affordable designs. To make better designs, the business needs an injection of capital. Aoife has told her investor that she will not be paying any dividends for the foreseeable future. She wants to reinvest all the profits in the business to pay for the production technology to make better furniture. Her investor is not happy with this.

(A) Outline, from the above information, the main stakeholders in Encanta Ltd.   (20 marks)

(B) Describe two co-operative relationships that are present above.   (20 marks)

(C) Evaluate how the business might do better if Aoife had a less competitive relationship with her stakeholders.
Support your answer with reference to the above text.   (40 marks)

ABQ2

Urlar Ltd.

Patrick Hudson set up his own carpet-making business, Urlar Ltd., 12 years ago. Thanks to the building boom in Ireland, the business has flourished and now supplies a range of local builders and property developers throughout the Connacht region. Patrick's customers appreciate his flexibility and willingness to go the extra mile to supply them with exactly what they need, when they need it. Patrick now employs 20 full-time and 8 part-time staff in the business.

One of Patrick's customers, a building firm called Zeus Ltd, is refusing to take delivery of and pay for a quantity of carpet (worth €500,000) it ordered from Patrick. It says that it no longer requires the carpet and would prefer wooden floors for the apartment block it is building. It has asked Patrick to return the €10,000 deposit it paid him when it ordered the carpet.

Patrick is angry because he has already made the carpet. He has checked his files and has a written order for the carpet from Zeus Ltd. and copy of a letter he sent them thanking them for their order and telling them that he would have the carpet for them in two weeks time.

(A) Identify, with illustrations from the above information, four stakeholders in Urlar Ltd. (20 marks)

(B) You are Patrick's legal advisor. Explain to him exactly why he has a contract with Zeus Ltd to supply them with the €500,000 carpet. Support your answer with reference to the above text. (30 marks)

(C) Evaluate the legal remedies that a judge might award Patrick if he takes Zeus Ltd. to court for breach of contract. (30 marks)

EXAM SECTION 3 (60%) - LONG QUESTIONS

1. Illustrate the role of entrepreneurs in business. (10 marks)

2. Describe important aspects of the relationship between employers and employees in business. (15 marks)

3. Explain the relationship between investors and entrepreneurs in business. (15 marks)

4. Outline the importance of consumers for an entrepreneur. (15 marks)

5. "All relationships in business are competitive."
   Do you agree with this statement?
   Support your answer with two reasons and examples. (20 marks)

6. Analyse one competitive and one co-operative relationship between the stakeholders in a business. (20 marks)

7. Explain the essential elements of a valid contract. (20 marks)

8. Outline and illustrate what is meant by "invitation to treat".   (15 marks)

9. Explain the methods by which a contract may be terminated.
   Give examples.   (20 marks)

10. Evaluate the remedies for breach of contract.   (20 marks)

CHAPTER 2

Consumer Conflict

Causes of Consumer Conflicts

Whenever a consumer buys goods or services, a basic rule applies called *caveat emptor* or "Let the buyer beware". It means that consumers are expected to be cautious and use their common sense. They should check out a product before buying it.

A prospective house buyer should get a survey done on a house before he buys it. You should try on a pair of shoes before you buy them. You should bring a sample of the paint home to make sure it matches your carpet before you order 10 tins of it.

However, even if consumers are careful, conflict can still arise:

- ○ Poor quality products or services.
- ○ Over-priced products or services.
- ○ Bad customer service.

Non-Legislative Methods of Solving Consumer Conflicts

This means that the consumer and the shop try to solve the conflict themselves or with the help of others, but without reference to the laws of Ireland or to any legal agency.

1. Negotiation

Negotiation is a process of bargaining to try to reach a mutually acceptable solution to the conflict.

The first step in consumer conflict resolution is for the consumer to go back to the

shop where he bought the item and set out his position clearly. He should explain the problem with his purchase and set out what he would like the shop to do to solve the problem.

The shop will then set out its position in relation to the complaint. It might agree to the customer's request to solve the problem or decide to offer an alternative solution Or it might reject the complaint totally.

The consumer and the shop must continue talking until they reach a compromise. This is a solution that they can both live with. It normally involves both giving up something to the other.

2. Consumers' Association of Ireland

The Consumers' Association of Ireland (CAI) is an interest group for consumers. Its aims are to make sure that consumers get good quality products and services and good value and that consumers know their rights.

Any consumer who experiences a problem with goods or services he has bought can contact the CAI. The CAI will give the consumer expert advice on his rights and on how to solve the problem.

The CAI publishes a magazine called *Consumer Choice*. It publishes articles about consumers' rights and helps consumers to make good buying decisions.

The CAI lobbies the government about consumer issues such as consumer laws and the availability of consumer advice services.

Legislative Methods of Solving Consumer Conflicts

This means that you try to solve the conflict by referring to the laws of Ireland or by using a legal organisation.

1. Sale of Goods and Supply of Services Act, 1980

Consumers have a number of **rights** under this law:
1. When a consumer buys *goods*, the goods must be:
    (a) **Of merchantable quality**. This means that they must be of an acceptable standard, taking into account what is said about them, what they are supposed to do, their durability and their price.

(b) **Fit for their purpose.** This means that the goods must do what they are expected to do. For example, a washing machine must wash clothes.

(c) **As described.** This means that the product must be *exactly* as described on the packaging or in the brochure or orally by a salesperson, and must not be misleading.

(d) **Identical to any sample shown.**

If the goods do *not* satisfy the above rules, the consumer is entitled to a remedy.

◉ If the fault is a major one and is discovered soon after the purchase, the consumer is entitled to a full refund, provided he complains promptly.

◉ The consumer may decide to accept a replacement product instead.

◉ If the goods have been used for some time or the consumer delays in making a complaint, the best he can expect is a repair or a partial refund.

2. When a consumer buys *services*, he has the right to expect that:
   (a) The supplier is qualified and has the necessary skill to provide the service.
   (b) The supplier must provide the service with proper care and diligence.
   (c) Any materials the supplier uses are of good quality.
   (d) Any goods sold as part of the service are of merchantable quality.

If the service does *not* satisfy the above rules, the consumer is entitled to a remedy.

◉ If the fault is a major one and is discovered soon after the purchase, the consumer is entitled to a full refund, provided he complains promptly.

◉ The consumer may decide to accept a replacement service instead.

◉ If the service was obtained some time ago or the consumer delays in making a complaint, the best he can expect is a repair or a partial refund.

3. The retailer is always legally responsible for solving the consumer's complaint. He cannot tell the consumer it's not his problem and to contact the manufacturer. The consumer bought the goods from the retailer. He has a contract with the retailer. The retailer must sort out the complaint.

4. The retailer cannot put up any sign that gives the impression that a consumer has no legal rights. It is illegal to display the following signs.

NO REFUNDS

CREDIT NOTES ONLY

NO REFUNDS ON SALE ITEMS

5. Guarantees cannot take away a consumer's basic legal rights against the retailer. They can only give extra protection to the consumer. It gives him the choice of having the goods fixed by the manufacturer under the guarantee or getting the retailer to deal with the complaint under the Sale of Goods and Supply of Services Act, 1980.

Sale of Goods and Supply of Services Act, 1980

EVALUATION OF THE SALE OF GOODS AND SUPPLY OF SERVICES ACT, 1980

This law does a good job of protecting consumers because:

1. It ensures that consumers get their money back if the product or service they buy is not up to legal standards. While the law cannot do away with faulty products, it can ensure that consumers do not lose any money if they buy a faulty product.

2. Furthermore, consumers cannot be fooled into thinking they must accept a credit note by retailers who put up signs to that effect. By banning such signs, this law especially protects those consumers who do not know their rights.

Questions from National Consumer Agency - www.consumerconnect.ie

Question 1

You take your "great bargain" gadget out of the box when you get home from the sales. But it doesn't work. The sales assistant points to signs saying "Strictly no refunds". Do you...

(a) Go away empty handed?

(b) Demand a refund anyway – and complain to the National Consumer Agency?

(c) Call the Gardaí?

Question 2

You buy a jumper but a day later you notice the sleeve is torn. When you bring it back, the shop has no more jumpers in your size. It offers a refund, but only at a lower price because the sales are now on. Do you...

(a) Accept the lower price?

(b) Refuse to take the lower amount, as the jumper is faulty?

(c) Accept another jumper that you don't like?

Question 3

You plug in your new kettle and it doesn't work. You return it to the shop and ask for a refund. The assistant says that the shop only give credit notes. Do you...

    (a)   Say fair enough, take the credit note and spend it in the shop?

    (b)   Complain to the International Kettle Manufacturers' Association?

    (c)   Insist that the shop gives a refund?

Question 4

You give a friend a vacuum cleaner as a wedding present. But it's faulty. Who should bring it back to the shop?

    (a)   Your friend

    (b)   You

    (c)   The mother-in-law

Question 1

> **The correct answer is B.**
> Signs such as "No money refunded" or "No liability accepted for faulty goods" can give the impression that you don't have certain consumer rights but a shop using this kind of statement may be committing an offence, for which it can be prosecuted.

Question 2

> **The correct answer is B.**
> Yes, the price that the jumper is sold at in the sale is irrelevant here. You bought a faulty jumper and under consumer law, as there is no replacement, you are entitled to a refund of what you paid. And you should show your receipt as proof of what you paid.

Question 3

> **The correct answer is C.**
> Get your money back. You don't have to take a credit note.

Question 4

> **The correct answer is B.**
> Consumer rights apply to the person who buys the vacuum cleaner, not to anyone who receives it as a gift.

2. Consumer Information Act, 1978

This law offers consumers protection from
businesses that lie to them and try to mislead them.

Consumer Information Act, 1978

1.   It is against the law for a seller to tell lies about
     a **product or service**.

     ▶   For example, a shop might lie about the
         weight of a product or where it was made.
         A one-hour photo shop might routinely
         take three hours to process films.

It is also against the law to mislead people about a product or service by giving them
the wrong impression about it.

     ▶   For example, a picture of harps and shamrocks on a package might mislead
         people into believing that the contents are Irish made and, unless the
         package says otherwise, this may amount to applying a false trade
         description.

Furthermore, it is against the law for any business to have such goods in its
possession.

2.   It is against the law for a seller to tell lies or mislead people about the **price** of a
     product or service. The price shown must be the total price (with no hidden
     extras). The seller cannot lie or mislead people about the current price, a previous
     price or a recommended price.

Examples

▶   A shop in Balbriggan, Co. Dublin pleaded guilty to breaking the Consumer
    Information Act 1978 by displaying the price of Edam cheese at €2.79, whereas
    the scanned price was €2.89.

▶   If a top of a range car is displayed and is accompanied by a price-tag for the basic
    model in the range, consumers may be misled as to the price of the model
    displayed.

▶   A shop might offer a "free gift" with a product, while raising the price of the
    product for the duration of the offer. For example, a supermarket in Galway was
    prosecuted for displaying the price of Palmolive Hand Soap at €2.99 for two ("Buy
    one, get one free"), whereas the price charged was €5.98 for two.

WAS €80
NOW €8

*This is only legal if the product actually was on
sale at €80 for at least 28 consecutive days (in a
row) in the previous 3 months.*

3. It is illegal to publish a false or misleading advertisement which would deceive consumers and which is thereby likely to cause loss, damage or injury to them.

   ▶ For example, if a chain store advertises goods at a certain price, that price should apply in all its stores unless the ad makes it clear that the price applies only in certain stores.

EVALUATION OF THE CONSUMER INFORMATION ACT, 1978

This law does a good job of protecting consumers because:

1. Consumers get fair and honest information about what they are buying and the price they will have to pay. They cannot be fooled.
2. If they *are* lied to or mislead, the law ensures that this never happens again and that the shop is punished.

3·1. National Consumer Agency (formerly the Director of Consumer Affairs)

The National Consumer Agency was set up by the Irish government under the Consumer Protection Act 2007. Its job is to:

(a) Inform consumers of their rights.
It does this in a number of ways. It publishes a shoppers' rights card, which explains consumers' rights to them. It runs a consumer phone service whereby consumers can ring its office and get advice about any consumer problems. And it has a website (www.consumerconnect.ie), which provides lots of consumer information.

Evaluation: The National Consumer Agency is very worthwhile because having a good understanding of consumer rights empowers Irish consumers to make informed consumer choices and encourages them to seek quality products and services.

(b) Investigate breaches of consumer laws.
It investigates businesses that break consumer law. It has the power to enter the business premises, take evidence, bring the Gardaí and apply to the courts for search warrants.

Evaluation: The National Consumer Agency is very worthwhile because it has real power to investigate businesses that break the law.

(c) Make sure that all businesses obey consumer legislation.
It has the power to issue on-the-spot fines to businesses that break the law about price displays. It can "name and shame" businesses that break consumer law by publishing their details in its Consumer Protection List. It can apply to the courts for a prohibition order to stop shops from engaging in illegal practices. And it has the power to refer cases to the Director of Public Prosecutions (DPP).

Evaluation: This is a good thing because if Irish consumers *are* lied to or misled, there is a government-backed organisation, the National Consumer Agency, that will ensure that this never happens again and that the shop is punished.

(d) Conduct research into consumer issues.
It carries out research to find out what the most important issues to Irish consumers are, what areas of consumer law need improving and what areas consumers need more information about.

Evaluation: This is very useful because the National Consumer Agency's research will ensure that the government and consumers are aware of the latest consumer scams. This helps to ensure that consumers will not be fooled.

(e) Be an advocate for consumers.
This means that the National Consumer Agency promotes and protects the interests of consumers. It informs the government of consumers' problems so that these can be sorted out by law. It advises the government of the impact of any new laws on Irish consumers. It consults with other agencies to assess the impact of their decisions on consumers.

Evaluation: This is very beneficial because Irish consumers have a powerful organisation, the National Consumer Agency, to stand up for them and ensure their welfare is protected.

3·2. The Director of Consumer Affairs

The office of the Director of Consumer Affairs was set up under the Consumer Information Act, 1978. **This office was abolished in 2007.** The role has been taken over by the National Consumer Agency. The Director of Consumer Affairs had a very similar role to the National Consumer Agency. Her role was to:

(a) Inform consumers of their rights.
She did this by publishing information leaflets that explained consumers' rights to them. She ran a consumer phone service whereby consumers could ring her office and get advice about any consumer problems. She had a website which provided lots of consumer information.

(b) Promote better standards of advertising.
She regularly checked a variety of advertisements to make sure that they didn't break the Consumer Information Act, 1978 rules which state that ads cannot lie or mislead consumers. If she found such an ad, she had the power to insist that it was changed or taken down altogether.

(c) Investigate consumer complaints and take businesses to court and prosecute them if they told lies or misled consumers about their products, their prices or in any of their advertisements

(d) She conducted regular surveys around Ireland to make sure that consumers were not ripped off. She publicised her findings. For example, she conducted surveys concerning publicans putting up their prices when important rugby, soccer, hurling and football matches were being played in stadiums near their pub. She named and shamed such publicans.

4. Small Claims Court

A consumer who cannot sort out a dispute with a business can take the business to the Small Claims Court. The aim of the Small Claims Court is to handle consumer claims easily, quickly and cheaply without involving a solicitor.

The consumer cannot sue for an amount more than €2,000. The consumer fills in a special application form outlining the complaint and pays a small fee (€15) to the local District Court. Alternatively, he can take his case electronically using Small Claims Online (www.smallclaims.ie).

If the business contests the claim, both sides are brought together for a meeting by the Small Claims Registrar to try to solve the dispute. This meeting is as informal as possible and private. The Small Claims Registrar may question both parties to clarify the issue.

If the Small Claims Registrar cannot solve the complaint, she will bring the case to the District Court for a hearing. The District Court hearing is held in public. Evidence must be given under oath and each party can be cross-examined by the other. Witnesses can be summoned to attend.

The judge listens to all the evidence and makes her ruling. If she rules in the consumer's favour, the shop has four weeks to pay the compensation awarded by the judge.

EVALUATION OF THE SMALL CLAIMS COURT

The small claims court is effective because:

1. It ensures that all consumers can get justice easily, quickly and cheaply without involving a solicitor.

2. Every consumer in Ireland can get justice locally. They do not have to travel to Dublin. Their nearest Small Claims Court is located in their local District Court.

3. Small claims online is an excellent service because anyone in Ireland can take a case anywhere and at any time at their convenience.

5. The Ombudsman

If a consumer thinks that she has been unfairly treated by any of the following **public bodies**, and she has tried to sort it out herself, then the Ombudsman can look into the complaint on her behalf.

Office of the Ombudsman
Oifig an Ombudsman

- Government departments
- Local authorities
- An Post
- Health Services Executive (HSE)

The Ombudsman operates as follows:

PROCEDURE	EXAMPLE
1. The consumer makes a complaint to the Ombudsman in writing, by phone, by e-mail or by calling into the office in person. There is no fee for this service.	1. Peter writes to the Ombudsman informing her that he has been refused unemployment benefit and that negotiation has not worked with the Department of Social and Family Affairs.
2. The Ombudsman investigates the complaint. She can go to the public body's offices. She can look at any documents she wants and can interview any member of staff.	2. The Ombudsman calls to the Department of Social and Family Affairs. She demands to see Peter's file. She then interviews the civil servant working on Peter's case. She discovers that the civil servant has made a mistake, in thinking that Peter had resigned from his job when in fact he was made redundant because of a downturn in the IT sector.

3. The Ombudsman considers all the evidence but only has the power to make a **recommendation**. Her findings are not legally binding. The public body does *not* have to obey her. But, if it does disobey her, she will include this in the report she makes to Dáil Éireann every year.	**3.** The Ombudsman tells the Department that it has made a mistake and recommends that it should pay Peter his unemployment benefit immediately. Although it does not have to, the Department agrees to this.

EVALUATION OF THE OMBUDSMAN

The Ombudsman is very effective because:

1. The service she provides is free of charge. This saves people in conflict with a public body a lot of money because they don't have to bring the public body to court.

2. It would be very intimidating for an ordinary person to take on a public body, such as a powerful government department. But the Ombudsman has the legal power to take on the public body and investigate the person's complaint thoroughly and get to the truth of the matter.

Ordinary Level Questions

EXAM SECTION 1 (25%) – SHORT ANSWER QUESTIONS [10 marks each]

1. List three reasons why consumers might have conflicts with the businesses they buy from.

2. Explain the term *caveat emptor*.

3. Outline one non-legislative solution to a conflict a consumer has with a shop.

4. List two provisions of the Sale of Goods and Supply of Services Act, 1980.

5. Column 1 is a list of business terms. Column 2 is a list of possible explanations for these terms. Match the two lists by placing the letter of the correct explanation under the relevant number below. One explanation has no match.

Column 1	
1. Consumers' Association of Ireland	4. Small Claims Court
2. Merchantable Quality	5. Ombudsman
3. National Consumer Agency	6. Negotiation

Column 2: Explanations
a) Helps consumers who have problems with certain public bodies
b) Non-legislative solution to consumer conflict involving direct discussions between the consumer and the shop
c) Consumers must be cautious and check products out before they buy them
d) Organisation set up by the government to be an advocate for consumers
e) Voluntary interest group representing consumers
f) A product must be of a reasonable standard
g) Sorts out consumer conflicts in the District Court

1	2	3	4	5	6
E	F ✓	D ✓	G ✓	A ✓	B ✓

6. Indicate whether each of the following (A, B, C, D and E) is true or false.

	Sentence	True or False
A	The law that states that consumers are entitled to a refund is called the Consumer Information Act, 1978.	~~True~~ False ✓
B	All products sold by a business must be as described by the salesperson.	~~False~~ True ✓
C	Signs such as "no refunds" are illegal.	True ✓
D	The Sale of Goods and Supply of Services Act, 1980 states that it is illegal to mislead consumers about the price of a product.	False ✓
E	The Ombudsman investigates complaints against the Gardaí.	~~True~~ False ✓

7. Indicate by means of a tick (✓) the law relevant to each statement.

	Sale of Goods and Supply of Services Act, 1980	Consumer Information Act, 1978
Guarantees cannot remove a consumer's right to a refund.	✓	
The retailer has to sort out a customer's complaint.	✓	
Services must be supplied by skilled and qualified persons.	✓	
It is illegal to tell lies or mislead people about a product.		✓

8. Outline the function of the Small Claims Court.

9. List two functions of the National Consumer Agency.

10. Outline three remedies available to a consumer who buys a faulty product.

EXAM SECTION 2 (75%) – LONG QUESTIONS

1. Name two non-legislative solutions to consumer conflict and
    explain one of them.   (15 marks)

2. Explain three legal rights of consumers under the Sale of Goods and
    Supply of Services Act, 1980.   (15 marks)

3. Explain three legal duties of retailers under the Sale of Goods and
    Supply of Services Act, 1980.   (15 marks)

4. Explain three legal duties of service providers under the Sale of Goods and
    Supply of Services Act, 1980.   (15 marks)

5. Using examples, explain what the Consumer Information Act, 1978 says about
    information supplied by businesses concerning (i) products and (ii) prices. (20 marks)

6. Outline the role of the National Consumer Agency.   (20 marks)

7. Explain how a consumer can take a case to the Small Claims Court. (20 marks)

8. Outline three advantages of the Small Claims Court for consumers. (15 marks)

9. Distinguish between "merchantable quality" and "fit for purpose". (10 marks)

10. Distinguish between the Consumers' Association of Ireland and
    the National Consumer Agency.   (10 marks)

Higher Level Questions

EXAM SECTION 1 (20%) – SHORT ANSWER QUESTIONS [10 marks each]

1. Illustrate your understanding of the term *caveat emptor*.

2. Identify two reasons for conflict between consumers and businesses and describe one
    non-legislative solution to the conflict.

3. Complete this sentence: The role of the Consumers' Association of Ireland is to…

4. When consumers buy products, the products must meet four standards. List these four
    standards.

5. Complete this sentence: When a consumer buys services, she has the right to expect
    that…

6. Name the law that protects consumers from false and misleading descriptions. List two
    of its main provisions.

7. Outline two functions of the National Consumer Agency.

8. Using examples, distinguish between non-legislative and legislative solutions to
    consumer conflict.

9. Complete this sentence: The role of the Small Claims Court is to…

10. Define Ombudsman.

EXAM SECTION 2 (20%) – APPLIED BUSINESS QUESTION – 80 MARKS

Nolan Ltd.

Gemma Nolan set up her t-shirt business, Nolan Ltd., two years ago after graduating from fashion college. She buys the t-shirts from a manufacturer in Wexford and then prints various designs on them. Gemma sells t-shirts with standard designs and custom designs (for hen nights, for example).

Although the business initially proved successful, Gemma has begun to notice an increasing number of problems. Recently, some customers demanded their money back after their t-shirts had shrunk in the wash. They complained that they were told by Gemma that the t-shirts were safe to tumble dry. Gemma informed them that it was a factory error and gave the customers the manufacturer's address in Wexford. These complaints prompted Gemma to put signs up in her shop stating "'Refunds at Owner's Discretion".

Gemma's business is also encountering other problems. A British t-shirt printing chain recently opened a branch in the same shopping centre as Gemma. In order to win customers back, Gemma has started a new promotion campaign. She now offers "3 t-shirts for the price of 2". She put up posters in the shop window proclaiming "Our t-shirts are 100% Irish". She hands out flyers at the entrance to the shopping centre with the slogan "Our t-shirts last longer than all others".

(A) Discuss whether Gemma is meeting her obligations under the Sale of Goods and Supply of Services Act, 1980. (30 marks)

(B) Advise Gemma how the provisions of the Consumer Information Act, 1978 may affect her new promotion campaign. (30 marks)

(C) Evaluate the impact on Gemma's business if some of the unhappy customers complain to the National Consumer Agency. (20 marks)

EXAM SECTION 3 (60%) – LONG QUESTIONS

1. Illustrate how the concept of *caveat emptor* protects businesses. (10 marks)

2. Explain two non-legislative solutions to consumer conflict. (20 marks)

3. Explain the provisions of the Consumer Information Act, 1978. Illustrate your answer with relevant examples. (20 marks)

4. Describe the impact of the National Consumer Agency on business in Ireland. (20 marks)

5. Evaluate the role of the Small Claims Court in dealing with consumer conflict. (25 marks)

6. Under the terms of the Sale of Goods and Supply of Services Act, 1980 explain the rights of consumers when buying goods. (20 marks)

7. "In Ireland, the government is not the friend of the consumer." Do you agree with this statement? Support your answer with two reasons and examples. (20 marks)

CHAPTER 3

Industrial Relations Conflicts

Causes of Industrial Relations Conflicts

The term **industrial relations** refers to the relationship between employers and employees. It covers issues such as how they communicate with each other, work together and generally get along with each other. Industrial relations in a business can be good or bad. They may be bad if pay is low and working conditions are bad.

Importance of Good Employer-Employee Relationships

Good industrial relations bring the following benefits:

1. Employees will be happier in their work and so employee morale is increased. If the employees are happy with their employer, their willingness to do their best for the business increases. Thus employee morale increases.

2. Employees will put in extra effort at their job. Thus employee productivity increases.

3. Employees are more likely to stay in the job because they are happy there. Thus labour turnover (the rate at which employees leave the business) and absenteeism (employees taking days off) will decrease. This saves the business money recruiting, selecting and training replacement employees.

4. The employer will delegate work to the employees because she trusts them. She will also give them power to make decisions for the good of the business (called employee empowerment). This means that the employees make a useful contribution to the success of the business.

5. There will be less chance of strikes. Strikes are bad for the business (loss of reputation, loss of sales and so on) and for the employees (no wages).

Pay Claims

Employees can make four different pay claims. In other words, employees might ask for a pay rise for four different reasons.

PAY CLAIM	EXPLANATION
Comparability Claim	Employees ask for a pay rise because other employees doing similar work got one. For example, if checkout assistants in Superquinn got a pay rise, then Dunnes Stores checkout employees might ask their employer for a pay rise.
Relativity Claim	Sometimes the pay of certain employees is linked to the pay of other employees, even though they do totally different jobs. For example, a TD's salary is linked to that of the civil service. So if civil servants get a pay rise, TDs will ask for one.
Productivity Claim	Employees ask for a pay rise to compensate them for having to work harder or cope with changes introduced by the employer.
Cost of Living Claim	Employees ask for a pay rise because they can't afford to live on the wages they get. They can't afford to buy things because the prices of goods and services they buy are increasing (inflation).

Industrial Action

If the conflict between an employer and employees cannot be resolved, the employees might take industrial action.

INDUSTRIAL ACTION	EXPLANATION
Official Strike	Employees hold a secret vote to see whether a majority wants to go on strike. If so, they then give their employer seven days notice of the strike. The union tells the employees to stop working and pays them strike pay. An official strike is legal in Ireland.
Unofficial Strike	This is when employees go on strike without having a secret vote and/or without giving their employer a week's notice. The union does not recognise the strike. An unofficial strike is illegal.

Wildcat Strike	This is a type of unofficial strike. Employees go on strike without any notice at all. They literally walk off the job. This is illegal
All Out Strike	All the employees in the firm go on strike, even though only some are in dispute with the employer. ICTU permission is needed.
Political Strike	Workers protest against the government by stopping work. This is illegal. *You are entitled to protest against the government but you cannot leave work to do it. It's not fair to punish your employer for something the government does.*
Sympathetic Strike	A group of employees not involved in the dispute goes on strike to show its support for the disputing workers. For example, teachers might go on strike to support striking nurses. This is illegal.
Work-to-Rule	To hurt their boss, employees carry out their work following all rules to the letter. They do their basic job and nothing else. They are completely inflexible and refuse to do any extras to help the employer. This slows down production. Because the employees do not stop working as a protest, they still get paid. For example, in 2007, Irish nurses went on a work-to-rule. They did their regular nursing duties but refused to answer phone calls or use computers. This caused a lot of inconvenience for hospital managers.
Overtime Ban	Employees refuse to do any overtime. This is an especially effective way to put pressure on the employer when the business is very busy.
Lockout	The employer excludes employees from the firm. They are not sacked. They are just refused entry to work.

Non-Legislative Methods of Solving Industrial Relations Conflicts

This means that the employer and employees try to solve the conflict themselves or with the help of others but without reference to the laws of Ireland or to any legal agency.

1. Negotiation

Negotiation is a process of bargaining to try to reach a mutually acceptable solution to the conflict.

The first step in industrial relations conflict resolution is direct negotiations between the employer and the employees. Both parties sit down together to discuss the issue. The employees may be represented by their trade union. The employer may be represented by management.

Each side sets out its position. They state what they think is the problem and how they want to solve it. They discuss the issue and try to reach a solution that they can both accept. This may involve compromise. Both sides may have to give up something to the other in order to reach an agreement.

When both sides agree on a deal, it is called a **collective agreement**. However, it is not legally binding.

Trade Unions

A trade union is an interest group that represents employees' views and interests. Employees pay an annual subscription (fee) to join the union. They then enjoy all the benefits of being in a trade union.

One example of a trade union is SIPTU (Services, Industrial, Professional and Technical Union). SIPTU is the largest trade union in Ireland and represents well over 200,000 workers.

Functions/benefits of a Trade Union

- The union will fight to get **better pay and working conditions** for the union members. The union may have professional negotiators who will bargain with the employer on behalf of the union members. These professional negotiators may get a better deal for the members than if each employee negotiated for herself.

- If an individual employee has a **dispute** with her employer, the union will take up her case. She does not have to negotiate with the employer. The union will represent her and negotiate on her behalf. The union will pay any legal bills necessary to fight for her rights.

▶ The trade union will represent the employees at the **National Pay Agreements** involving all the social partners. It will listen to its members and tell the Irish Congress of Trade Unions (ICTU) what its members think. ICTU will use this information to negotiate a deal that gives Irish trade union members what they want.

▶ The trade union will fight to **protect its members' interests**. It will use its strength to fight to keep their jobs. If members do lose their jobs, the trade union will fight to get them the best redundancy payment possible. If union members are in a dispute, the union will publicise their cause and put the employees' side forward. For example, when Irish nurses went on strike previously, the Irish Nurses Organisation (INO) put posters up on billboards all over Ireland showing the importance of nurses, in order to get public sympathy behind the nurses.

Union members (i.e. employees) elect a SHOP STEWARD to represent them.

Shop Steward

A shop steward is a spokesperson elected by employees as their official union representative in the workplace. Her functions are to:

(a) Recruit new members for the union.

(b) Represent members in negotiations with management.

(c) Keep members up to date with information from union head office.

(d) Inform union head office of members' concerns.

Irish Congress of Trade Unions

ICTU is an interest group representing almost all the trade unions in Ireland. By speaking for almost the entire Irish trade union movement, ICTU has a lot of power and ensures that Irish workers are listened to.

The Functions of ICTU

▶ **National Pay Agreement Negotiations**

ICTU negotiates on behalf of Irish workers at the government-held National Pay Agreements. It tries to secure the best possible pay deal for Irish workers. For example, in the current national agreement, "Towards 2016", ICTU negotiated a 10% pay rise over 27 months for all Irish workers.

▶ **Give permission for all-out strikes**

If *all* the workers in a business want to go out on strike, they need permission from ICTU. For example, if the pilots are on strike in Aer Lingus and all the other workers in various unions in Aer Lingus want to go on strike as a protest, they can only do so with ICTU's permission.

▶ **Settles disputes between unions**

If two unions are having a dispute, ICTU will mediate in the dispute to help them sort out their differences.

▶ **Provide training to unions**

ICTU will train shop stewards and other union officials in the skills needed to run a union properly, such as negotiation skills, employee rights and so on.

▶ **Promote the cause of the trade union movement**

ICTU speaks for well over 750,000 workers on the island of Ireland. It uses PR (public relations) techniques to put forward the arguments of workers and to win public support for workers. It also makes submissions to the Minister for Finance every year to do something in the budget for working people.

N.B.

Only when direct negotiation between employer and employees has failed can they approach the following:

2. Conciliation

Conciliation means that the two parties in a dispute ask an independent outsider, called a conciliator, to help them solve their problems. The conciliator encourages both sides to meet and talk out their problems. She tries to get them to reach a mutually acceptable, negotiated solution to their problem.

She may even suggest a formula to them to solve the conflict that she thinks is the fairest solution possible. *But she does not tell them what they must do.* The employer and employees can accept or reject the solution. In other words, it is not binding on either the employer or the employees.

3. Arbitration

Arbitration is when the employer and employees ask an independent person, called an arbitrator, to investigate the dispute and make a ruling, like a judge, to solve the problem. The arbitrator listens to both sides' arguments, investigates the dispute and gives his judgement as to how the dispute should be solved. *He tells them what to do to solve the dispute.*

Both the employer and the employees agree in advance whether they are going to accept the arbitrator's ruling or not. If they agree to accept it in advance, it is called binding arbitration. This means that both sides will obey the ruling of the arbitrator, no matter what it is.

Legislative Methods of Solving Industrial Relations Conflicts

This means that the employer and employees try to solve the conflict by referring to the laws of Ireland or by using a legal organisation.

1. Industrial Relations Act, 1990

1. Trade Dispute

This law states that employees can take industrial action only in a dispute related to their jobs. This is called a trade dispute.

A trade dispute is defined as a dispute between employers and employees in connection with the employment or non-employment of employees and the terms and conditions of the job.

LEGIMATE TRADE DISPUTE	ILLEGAL TRADE DISPUTE
Pay and conditions of employment. Employees are entitled to take industrial action if they are arguing with their employer about their wages, overtime rates, number of holidays and working conditions of the job.	**Disputes over closed shop agreements.** A "closed shop" is where workers have only one choice of union to join. The management will speak only to that union.
Dismissal or suspension of an employee. Employees are entitled to take industrial action if they disagree with their employer about a fellow employee getting the sack or being disciplined by means of a suspension.	**Political issues.** Workers are entitled to protest against the government but they cannot leave work to do it. It's not fair to punish their employer for something the government does. It's illegal under this law.

LEGIMATE TRADE DISPUTE	ILLEGAL TRADE DISPUTE
Employer refuses to recognise the union. Employees are entitled to take industrial action if their employer refuses to speak to their trade union.	Disagreement between management and employees about how the business should be run (e.g. disputes over pricing policy) is not a valid cause for industrial action.
Discrimination. Employees are entitled to take industrial action if their employer treats some workers less favourably than other workers.	
Duties required of employees. Employees are entitled to take industrial action if they disagree with their employer about the things she asks them to do. If they feel it is not in their job description, they are entitled to protest.	

2. Secret Ballot & Week's Notice

If employees want to go on strike, they must first:

- ■ Have a secret ballot*, and if a majority vote for strike they must
- ■ Give their employer one week's notice before they actually go on strike.

- ● *A secret ballot means that the workers must hold a vote. The vote cannot be a show of hands in public. It must be private.
- ● Each worker is given a voting paper with the option to vote YES or NO for the strike. Each worker fills in her voting paper in private and then places it into a sealed voting box. She does not identify herself anywhere on the voting paper.
- ● The reason for a secret ballot is to make sure that employees are not intimidated by others into voting a certain way.

3. Primary Picketing

If employees have the secret ballot and give their boss seven days' notice of the strike, they are allowed to picket peacefully outside their employer's business. This is called primary picketing.

Picketing involves the employees protesting outside their employer's business premises by walking around outside it. They often carry placards. The aim of picketing is for the employees to draw attention to and get public sympathy for their case and to discourage customers from entering the business.

The picketing must be peaceful, with no intimidation or obstruction.

4. Secondary Picketing

The employees can picket outside the premises of another employer only if he is helping their boss to break their strike. This is called secondary picketing.

Example

Dunnes Stores cashiers are out on strike. The company cannot open the shops because there is no one to take the money. Dunnes is losing a lot of money and is about to give in to the cashiers' demands for more pay when Superquinn sends over some of its cashiers to operate Dunnes Stores' cash registers. Because Superquinn interfered in their strike, Dunnes Stores' workers can now protest outside Superquinn as well.

5. Striking Workers cannot be sued/stopped/arrested

Employees cannot be sued by their employer for damages (e.g. loss of profits) caused by the strike and peaceful picketing, provided that they had the secret ballot and gave the week's notice. Neither can the employer of striking employees go to court to get a judge to stop the employees picketing provided that they had the secret ballot and gave the week's notice. The Gardaí cannot arrest or move on employees who are picketing legitimately and peacefully.

6. Labour Relations Commission

This law set up the Labour Relations Commission (*See following pages*).

EVALUATION OF
THE INDUSTRIAL RELATIONS ACT, 1990

This act does a good job of protecting employees because it ensures:
1. They have the legal right to protest against an employer who will not give in to their legitimate demands. Furthermore, they can protest legally against any other business that tries to frustrate their strike. Thus, they can put pressure on their employer to get their own way.

2. Irish employees cannot be bullied into striking against their will. This law ensures that all ballots to strike are secret so that employees cannot be intimidated by others.

3. Irish workers are legally protected from being arrested or sued by their boss if they go on strike, provided they hold a secret ballot and give their boss one week's notice.

2. Labour Relations Commission

The Labour Relations Commission (LRC) was set up under the Industrial Relations Act, 1990. The aim of the LRC is to:

(a) Promote better industrial relations.

(b) Help solve industrial disputes.

It consists of seven members: a chairperson, two employee representatives, two employer representatives and two government representatives.

Functions of the Labour Relations Commission

○ It provides a conciliation service.

An Industrial Relations Officer at the LRC helps disputing employers and employees to sort out their differences by encouraging them to talk to each other and negotiate a solution to their problem themselves. She offers advice and assistance and even possible solutions but she does not tell them what to do.

Evaluation: Over 80% of all cases referred to for conciliation are settled by conciliation. Furthermore, conciliation is a free service to both the employer and the employees.

○ It provides an industrial relations advisory service and advises employers and employees on how to behave in order to have good industrial relations. The LRC provides free and professional advice to both employers and employees on how to get on better.

Evaluation: This is a very useful service because the LRC's advice helps to prevent industrial disputes.

○ It draws up codes of practice to be used by employers and employees in certain industrial relations situations. Codes of practice are generally accepted rules designed to minimise problems in employment. For example, there is a code of good practice that sets out the correct procedures to follow to address bullying in the workplace.

Evaluation: Following the codes of practice will lead to a better relationship and less disputes.

◐ It conducts research into industrial relations and monitors current developments in industrial relations. This means that it tries to develop new ways of solving disputes and solve new problems that arise in industrial relations.

Evaluation: This is a good thing because research helps the LRC to identify possible future problems in industrial relations and to come up with solutions to them before they arise.

◐ It provides the services of the **Rights Commissioners**.

LRC Rights Commissioners

A Rights Commissioner works for the LRC. She investigates disputes involving a single employee or a small group of employees. She can only deal with disputes about unfair dismissal, suspension, maternity leave and disciplinary procedures, and both the employer and the employee must agree to the involvement of the Rights Commissioner.

The Rights Commissioner will invite the employee and the employer in for a private hearing of the case. She will ask each side to present its case and may question each side. Each party is allowed to comment on what the other has said and to ask questions. Both the employer and the employee may bring witnesses.

The Rights Commissioner will try to reach a mutually acceptable settlement to the dispute. If the employer and the employee cannot agree on a settlement, the Rights Commissioner issues a recommendation on the dispute. Either the employer or the employee can appeal this recommendation to the Labour Court (or the Employment Appeals Tribunal if the dispute is about unfair dismissals).

EVALUATION OF LRC RIGHTS COMMISSIONERS

I think that Rights Commissioners are effective because:

1. A single employee who feels that she is being victimised has a place to go to get justice. The case is heard in private, so her privacy is protected. This results in less distress to an employee who has already been victimised by her boss.

2. There is an incentive for both the employee and the employer to use the Rights Commissioner's services. They are free and any recommendation is not legally binding so neither has anything to lose.

3. Labour Court

The Labour Court was established to provide a free service for solving industrial relations problems. It is not a court of law. It is an industrial relations tribunal. It hears both sides in a case and then issues a recommendation setting out its opinion on the dispute and how it should be solved.

It is the court of last resort. Cases should be referred to the Labour Court only when all other efforts to resolve the dispute have failed.

Because of the voluntary nature of Irish industrial relations resolution procedures, the Labour Court's recommendations are not legally binding except in the cases of breaches of the Employment Equality Act, 1998.

The Labour Court consists of a chairperson and three employer representatives and three employee representatives.

Functions of the Labour Court

- To investigate industrial disputes and issue non-binding recommendations to solve them. The court asks the employer and the employees to firstly submit their case in writing. At the actual hearing, the court has the power to summon witnesses and make them give evidence under oath.

  Evaluation: The Labour Court does a good job in dealing with industrial relations conflict because it has the power to get to the truth in the conflict and therefore make fair recommendations that both sides can agree on.

- To hear appeals from an employer or employee against the recommendation an Equality Officer previously made on their discrimination case under the Employment Equality Act, 1998. The Labour Court considers the matter again and makes a legally binding judgement on the matter.

  Evaluation: The Labour Court does a good job in dealing with industrial relations conflict because it deals with workplace discrimination very thoroughly in that its ruling must be followed in discrimination cases.

- To interpret Labour Relations Commission's codes of practice. This means that the Labour Court gives its opinion as to the correct interpretation of the Labour Relations Commission's codes of good practice. It also investigates any breaches of the Labour Relations Commission's codes of good practice by either the employer or the employees.

  Evaluation: The Labour Court does a good job in dealing with industrial relations conflict because investigating breaches of codes of practice ensures that employers and employees obey best industrial relations practice.

▶ To register collective agreements made between employers and employees. Registering agreements in this way makes them legally binding on both sides. Then, if either party breaks its side of the agreement, the other party can take it to the Labour Court to have the matter investigated.

Evaluation: I think that the Labour Court does a good job in dealing with industrial relations conflict because it gives both sides in an industrial dispute the confidence of knowing that the agreement they reached cannot be broken once the Labour Court registers it.

4. Unfair Dismissals Act, 1977/93

This law protects workers from being unfairly sacked. It states that every sacking is unfair and therefore illegal unless the employer can prove that it was fair. However, the law only applies to employees with one year's continuous service and who are aged between 16 and normal retiring age in the job.

Reasons for Fair Dismissal

The reasons for fair dismissal (i.e., the reasons you *can* be sacked) are set out in this law as follows:

1. **Incapable of doing the job**
    An employee can be sacked because she physically cannot do the work expected of her because of lateness, absenteeism, persistent absence through illness and so on.

2. **Not qualified**
    An employee who lied about his qualifications and who does not in fact have the qualifications needed to do the job can be sacked.

3. **Incompetent**
    An employee who consistently fails to meet the standards of work expected of him can be sacked. For example, a football manager whose team loses every match can be sacked.

4. **Misconduct**
    An employee who engages in illegal or inappropriate activity at work can be sacked. Such activities include stealing, fighting, drunkenness and so on.

5. **Redundancies**
    An employee can be sacked if his employer has to make him redundant because the business is going through a bad time and she cannot afford to keep him on.

Reasons for Unfair Dismissal

The reasons for unfair dismissal (i.e., you *cannot* be sacked for these reasons) are set out in this law as follows:

1. **Pregnancy**

    An employee cannot be sacked just because she is pregnant or because of matters relating to her pregnancy such as giving birth, breastfeeding, going to ante-natal classes, taking maternity leave and so on.

2. **Union activities**

    An employee cannot be sacked just because he is in or is about to join a trade union or because he engages in trade union activities either in work or outside of work.

3. **Beliefs**

    An employee cannot be sacked just because of his religious or political beliefs.

4. **Race**

    An employee cannot be sacked just because of the colour of her skin or her ethnic background.

5. **Suing boss**

    An employee cannot be sacked just because she is suing her employer or is a witness in a case against her employer.

6. **Traveller**

    An employee cannot be sacked just because he is a member of the travelling community.

7. **Sexuality**

    An employee cannot be sacked just because of his sexual orientation.

What to Do if You are Unfairly Dismissed

If an employee feels that she has been unfairly sacked, she can take a case against her employer to a Rights Commissioner at the Labour Relations Commission (see earlier) or to the Employment Appeals Tribunal.

The Rights Commissioner or the Employment Appeals Tribunal will investigate the dispute. However, remember that it is up to the *employer* to prove that the dismissal was fair. The employer will have to prove that she followed correct procedures. In other words, she gave the employee appropriate warnings, investigated all allegations against the employee, allowed the employee representation at the investigation and took adequate time to reach a decision.

Employment Appeals Tribunal (EAT)

- ■ The EAT is an independent body set up to investigate infringements of employees' rights in an informal, quick, fair and inexpensive way.
- ■ The EAT hears the case and makes a judgement on the case. This judgement is final and can only be appealed through the courts.

Redress for Unfair Dismissal

If the employee wins her case for unfair dismissal, she is entitled to one of the following types of redress:

Re-instatement	■ The employee is given her old job back with exactly the same pay and conditions. ■ She is also entitled to full back pay from the date she was unfairly sacked. ■ And she is entitled to any improvements in pay and conditions (e.g. pay rises) that occurred since she was unfairly dismissed.
Re- engagement	■ The employee is given her old job back or a different but reasonably suitable job. ■ But she is not entitled to back pay from the date she was sacked. ■ This remedy is often used where the employee contributed to the dismissal, even though it is still an unfair dismissal.
Compensation	■ The employee is paid an amount of money by her former employer as compensation for the financial loss she suffered as a result of the unfair dismissal. ■ There is no compensation for stress or hurt. ■ The maximum compensation is 2 years pay.

Example

Martin was employed as a Grade VI secretary working for Ms. Doyle, the Finance Director, in a bank. His salary was €600 gross per week. His boss sacked him when Martin tried to organise a trade union in the bank. Martin immediately took a case for unfair dismissal against his boss and four weeks later he won his case. He will be awarded one of the following:

Re-instatement
- ■ Martin is given back his old job in the bank – Grade VI secretary, working for Ms. Doyle, on €600 per week.
- ■ He also gets €2,400 for loss of earnings while unfairly sacked (€600 a week for four weeks).

Re-engagement
- Martin is given a job as Grade VI secretary to Mr. Cregan, the Marketing Director of the bank, on €600 per week.
- But he does not get €2,400 back pay.

Compensation
- Martin gets compensation of €6,000 made up from €2,400 for loss of earnings to the date of winning the case and €3,600, based on the Rights Commissioner's estimate that it will take him another six weeks to find a new job.

Constructive Dismissal

This is where an employee resigns from his job because of his employer's conduct towards him. His employer deliberately makes his life so miserable that he is effectively forced to resign. He is treated so badly by the employer that he cannot take it any longer and resigns from the job. This too is illegal.

The employee can take a case against the employer to a Rights Commissioner (see earlier). But, in the case of constructive dismissal, it is the *employee* must prove that he was forced to resign.

Unfair Dismissal	Constructive Dismissal
Employee is sacked by the boss.	Employee resigns because of alleged bullying by the boss.
Employer must prove the case.	Employee must prove the case.

EVALUATION OF THE UNFAIR DISMISSALS ACT, 1977/93

This act does a good job of protecting employees because:

1. Employees cannot lose their livelihood for spurious reasons such as their employer not liking them. The employer has to have a legitimate reason and has to prove she had a legitimate reason to sack an employee.
2. Any worker who is unfairly sacked can win back her job or compensation by taking a case to a government-backed organisation such as the LRC's Rights Commissioners. This is a free service and, even better, there is no obligation on the employee to prove anything. So she has nothing to lose and everything to gain from taking a case against her former employer.
3. Employees are protected from nasty bosses who make their working lives miserable and bully them out of their job (constructive dismissal). They are entitled to take a case and get their job back or compensation.

5. Employment Equality Act, 1998

Discrimination

1. This law prohibits discrimination at work. It defines discrimination as treating one person less favourably than another person is, has been, or would be treated in a similar situation on any of the following nine grounds:

    ### Gender
    It is illegal to treat men, women or transsexual employees less favourably than each other.

    ### Marital Status
    It is illegal to treat single, married, divorced, separated or widowed employees less favourably than each other.

    ### Family Status
    It is illegal to treat employees who are parents, employees without children or employees caring for relatives less favourably than each other.

    ### Age
    It is illegal to treat younger or older employees less favourably than each other.

    ### Disability
    It is illegal to treat employees who are physically, intellectually or emotionally disabled less favourably than able-bodied employees.

    ### Race
    It is illegal to treat employees of different skin colour, nationality or ethnic origin less favourably than each other.

    ### Sexuality
    It is illegal to treat gay, lesbian, bisexual or heterosexual employees less favourably than each other.

    ### Religious Beliefs
    It is illegal to treat employees of different religions or no religion less favourably than each other.

    ### Traveller
    It is illegal to treat traveller employees less favourably than settled employees.

2. This law makes it illegal to discriminate:
    - When hiring, training and promoting employees.
    - In conditions of employment.
    - In advertising for employees.

3. This law makes "equal pay for equal work" a legal requirement. Employees doing the same, similar or work of equal value must be paid the same.

4. Positive discrimination is allowed to promote equal opportunities. This means that employers can take steps to help the nine categories of employees to achieve full equality in the workplace.

5. This law set up the Equality Authority.
    Its functions are to:
    (a) Eliminate discrimination in the workplace.
    (b) Promote equal opportunities at work for people who fall into any of the nine categories.
    (c) Draw up codes of practice to help with (a) and (b) above.
    (d) Give the public information about the Authority's progress in achieving its aims.

Director of the Equality Tribunal

This law set up the office of the **DIRECTOR OF THE EQUALITY TRIBUNAL** (previously called the Director of Equality Investigations).

▶ The Director of the Equality Tribunal was set up by the Employment Equality Act, 1998 to investigate cases of employee discrimination in the workplace. Discrimination means treating an employee less favourably than others under the following nine grounds: gender, family status, marital status, age, disability, race, traveller, religion and sexuality. Victims of such discrimination must complain to the Director within six months of the discrimination.

Evaluation: This is a good thing because there is a government official who will investigate an employee's discrimination for free and make sure that this discrimination does not continue.

▶ If the discrimination is not very serious, the Director will refer the case to an Equality Mediation Officer, who will investigate it informally and in private. The Equality Mediation Officer tries to reach a solution to the case that both the employer and the employee are happy with.

Evaluation: This is a good thing because the employee's discrimination case is kept totally confidential, which saves the employee from any further stress from having her case publicised.

▶ If the discrimination is serious, the Director will refer the case to an Equality Officer who will investigate it formally. The Equality Officer calls both parties in, listens to their evidence and then makes a ruling on the matter.

Evaluation: This is a good thing because the employee knows that his case will be investigated very thoroughly and that it will be treated very seriously and that the ruling made will be independent and fair.

▷ It is the Director herself who makes the final decision in all cases. Her ruling *must be obeyed*. She has the power to end the discrimination immediately and to award compensation to the employee of up to two years' pay (three years' back pay in equal pay cases).

Evaluation: This is a good thing because the employee can get a lot of compensation for her suffering and is assured that she will receive it because the Director's ruling is legally binding.

Example

A teacher was awarded €127,000 by an Equality Officer when she didn't get the job of principal in an all boys' school in Co. Wicklow. The interviewers asked her why she thought a woman was suitable to be a principal of an all boys' school. After the interview, the Chairman of the Board of Management was heard to say in the staffroom: "She is a good woman, but a woman in the position in an all boys' school wouldn't be appropriate."

EVALUATION OF THE EMPLOYMENT EQUALITY ACT, 1998

This act does a good job of protecting employees because:

1. It ensures that they cannot be treated badly by prejudiced bosses who would discriminate against them. All workers regardless of beliefs, colour, creed, sexuality or personal circumstances must be treated equally.
2. This law deliberately sets out to help nine categories of persons who have historically been the victims of workplace discrimination. Thus, this law attempts to right the wrongs done to them by encouraging their hiring and promotion in businesses.
3. There is a government-backed official, the Director of the Equality Tribunal, who will fight for a worker who has been discriminated against. Unlike many such officials this Director's ruling must be obeyed.

Ordinary Level Questions

EXAM SECTION 1 (25%) – SHORT ANSWER QUESTIONS [10 marks each]

1. List four reasons for industrial relations conflict.

2. Column 1 is a list of business terms. Column 2 is a list of possible explanations for these terms. Match the two lists by placing the letter of the correct explanation under the relevant number below. One explanation has no match.

Column 1	Column 2: Explanations
1. Productivity Claim	a) Employees protest against the government by going on strike.
2. Cost of Living Claim	b) Employees protest against their employer by stopping work following a secret ballot and seven days' warning to their employer.
3. Comparability Claim	c) Employees walk off the job in protest with no notice at all.
4. Official Strike	d) Employees demand a pay rise to compensate them for inflation.
5. Lockout	e) Employees demand a pay rise to compensate them for working harder.
6. Wildcat strike	f) The employer refuses to let employees return to work.
	g) Employees demand a pay rise because others doing the same job got one.

1	2	3	4	5	6
E			B		C

3. Explain the term "trade union" and give two examples.

4. Name three non-legislative solutions to industrial relations conflict and explain any one of them.

5. Outline the role of a shop steward.

6. Indicate whether each of the following (A, B, C, D and E) is true or false.

	Sentence	True or False
A	Employees must vote by show of hands before going on strike.	False
B	Primary picketing means that employees protest at their employer's business by walking around outside.	True
C	The Labour Relations Commission was set up under the Industrial Relations Act, 1990.	True
D	Employees on an official strike cannot be sued by their boss for loss of profits.	True
E	Employees must give their boss seven days' warning before they go on strike.	True

7. Indicate whether each of the following (A, B, C, D and E) is true or false.

	Sentence	True or False
A	Employees can strike because they disagree with the way their boss runs the business.	*False*
B	A Rights Commissioner only deals with disputes involving one worker or a small group of workers.	*True* ✓
C	The Labour Relations Commission provides an arbitration service.	*False*
D	The Labour Court's rulings are always legally binding.	
E	The Labour Court registers agreements between employers and employees to make them legally binding.	

8. List four fair reasons why an employee can be sacked.

9. List four reasons for unfair dismissal.

10. Column 1 is a list of business terms. Column 2 is a list of possible explanations for these terms. Match the two lists by placing the letter of the correct explanation under the relevant number below. One explanation has no match.

Column 1	Column 2: Explanations
1. Industrial Relations Act, 1990	a) Provides an arbitration service to disputing employers and employees
2. Unfair Dismissals Act, 1977/93	b) Organisation that represents the trade union movement in Ireland *ICTU*
3. Employment Equality Act, 1998	c) Makes legally binding rulings on cases of workplace discrimination
4. Labour Relations Commission	d) Makes it illegal for employers to sack employees without a fair reason
5. Labour Court	e) Sets out the legal rules for employees taking industrial action
6. Director of the Equality Tribunal	f) Provides the services of Rights Commissioners
	g) Makes equal pay for equal work a legal requirement

1	2	3	4	5	6
E	*D*	*G*	*A*	*F*	*C*

11. Write out what the following letters stand for: ICTU   SIPTU   LRC

EXAM SECTION 2 (75%) – LONG QUESTIONS

1. Describe two types of industrial action that employees can take.   (10 marks)

2. Your friend has just started working and is thinking about joining SIPTU. Advise her of the benefits of joining a trade union.   (20 marks)

3. Explain three functions of ICTU.   (15 marks)

4. Distinguish between "arbitration" and "conciliation".   (20 marks)

5. Describe the role of the Labour Relations Commission.   (20 marks)

6. Outline three forms of redress available to an employee who has been unfairly dismissed.   (15 marks)

7. List four categories under which workplace discrimination is illegal.   (20 marks)

8. Explain the terms "shop steward" and "trade dispute".   (20 marks)

9. Name two legal organisations that help resolve trade disputes and outline three functions of one of them.   (25 marks)

10. Describe the role of the Director of the Equality Tribunal.   (20 marks)

Higher Level Questions

EXAM SECTION 1 (20%) – SHORT ANSWER QUESTIONS [10 marks each]

1. Complete this sentence: Arbitration involves…

2. The following table shows four causes of industrial unrest. For each cause, tick (✓) whether that cause would constitute a reason for a legitimate trade dispute under the Industrial Relations Act, 1990.

Cause of unrest	Legitimate trade dispute	Illegal dispute
Protest against the government's tax policies	✗	✓
Protest against bad pay and conditions	✓	
Argument over employee suspensions	✓	
Argument about price employer charges for products		✓

3. Distinguish between "primary picketing" and "secondary picketing".

4. What do the letters LRC stand for? Explain its use in business.

5. Outline two functions of a Rights Commissioner.

6. Distinguish between "unfair dismissal" and "constructive dismissal".

7. Column 1 is a list of business terms. Column 2 is a list of possible explanations for these terms. Match the two lists by placing the letter of the correct explanation under the relevant number below. One explanation has no match.

Column 1	Column 2: Explanations
1. Secret Ballot	a) Union representative in a business
2. Shop Steward	b) Treating one person less favourably than another
3. Picketing	c) Independent person makes a ruling to settle a dispute
4. Discrimination	d) Provided by LRC's Industrial Relations Officers
5. Conciliation	e) Vote held in private; required before industrial action can occur
	f) Workers protest by walking outside employer's business premises

1	2	3	4	5
E	A	F	B	D

8. Illustrate your understanding of the term "discrimination".

9. Which employer-employee law do you think is the most important? Explain your choice.

10. Outline two forms of redress that an employee who has been unfairly dismissed may get.

EXAM SECTION 2 (20%) – APPLIED BUSINESS QUESTION – 80 MARKS

Finnie Ltd.

Katherine Finnie has been a major employer in the mid-west. She has a number of factories in the region, employing almost 400 people. In recent years, Katherine has hired a number of workers from the new EU states. Recently, one of these workers, Olga, tried to set up a trade union in the factory. Katherine sacked her immediately to send a lesson to all the others that she would not tolerate unions. Two weeks later, Olga was advised by a friend to contact a solicitor.

Profitability has become an issue for Katherine. The cost of her electricity bills increased 25% in the last year. She spent a lot of money installing new equipment in her factories. She felt let down when her employees asked for a pay rise given all these problems. She knows she pays less than similar factories in Dublin, but she argues the cost of living is lower in the mid-west. Her workers are unconvinced and asked again for a pay rise.

Despite these problems, Katherine considers herself to be a fair employer and prides herself on the fact that she gives every worker with children a Christmas bonus to help them pay for toys and so on. She likes to think that she goes easy on her older workers by not sending them on demanding training courses. "They're for the young ones," she jokes with the older staff members. "Sure, I'd be wasting my money sending you!"

(A)   Outline, from the above information, two non-legislative solutions
      to the pay dispute between Katherine and her employees.   (20 marks)

(B)   Do you think the employees have a point about the pay claim?
      Discuss three reasons why such a claim may be valid.   (20 marks)

(C)   Evaluate how two pieces of industrial relations legislation will impact
      on Katherine.   (40 marks)

EXAM SECTION 3 (60%) – LONG QUESTIONS

1.   Evaluate the benefits of trade union membership to a school leaver
     just about to start work. 3 points.   (25 marks)

2.   Explain how the main provisions of the Industrial Relations Act, 1990
     impact on Irish business.   (25 marks)

3.   Outline how the Labour Relations Commission helps the relationship
     between Irish employers and employees.   (20 marks)

4.   Evaluate how the provisions of the Employment Equality Act, 1998
     protect employees.   (25 marks)

5.   Discuss the importance of the Labour Court in maintaining
     good industrial relations in Ireland.   (20 marks)

6.   Illustrate the importance of ICTU to Irish employees.   (20 marks)

7.   The Unfair Dismissals Act, 1977/93 sets out the following:
     (i) reasons for fair dismissal;
     (ii) reasons for unfair dismissal;
     (iii) redress for employees who have been unfairly dismissed.
     Explain any two of the above.   (25 marks)

8.   Contrast the roles of a Rights Commissioner with that of
     the Director of the Equality Tribunal in solving business conflicts.   (20 marks)

Enterprise

Entrepreneurship

Entrepreneurship (also known as enterprise) involves using your initiative to identify some need and then taking the steps to satisfy that need. It involves taking risks including financial risks (losing money if it fails) and personal risks (losing face if it fails). When you succeed, your entrepreneurship is rewarded. For example, enterprising business people are rewarded by profit.

Role of the Entrepreneur in a Business

An entrepreneur is a person who spots an opportunity (a gap in the market) and takes the initiative to set up a business to make money from that opportunity.

The entrepreneur takes a big risk when setting up the business. He takes a financial risk because if the business is a failure, he will lose the money he invested in it. He also takes a personal risk because if the business fails, he may lose his self-esteem and self-confidence.

Entrepreneurs are willing to take these risks, however, because they expect the business to be a success and they expect to make a profit.

Here are some examples of entrepreneurs:

Bob Geldof set up his own TV production company, Planet 24, when he was angry with the quality of programmes on TV. He set up his own online travel agency, deckchair.com, after he experienced problems booking a family holiday online.

Gillian Bowler noticed in the 1970s that package holidays to Spain were becoming increasingly popular but that no company sold package holidays to Greece. Having been to Greece many times, she thought that Irish people would like it there and decided to set up her own travel agency, called Budget Travel, selling package holidays to Greece.

Jack Odell, an engineer, got the idea for Matchbox toys when his daughter was only allowed to bring toys into school that could fit into a match box.

Anita Roddick was so frustrated that no business sold small sizes of cosmetics in simple packaging, she set up her own business, The Body Shop, to do so.

Enterprise in Other Situations

Enterprise in the...

Home	Parents show enterprise by converting an attic used for storage into a study for their daughter so that she will have a place to study for her Leaving Cert.
Community	Neighbours show enterprise by getting together and organising a committee to clean up their area and entering it in for the Tidy Towns competition.
School	A teacher shows enterprise by organising an after-school drama club and putting on an end-of-year play.
Public Life	The Minister for Finance showed enterprise by bringing out the Special Savings Incentive Accounts in 2001. To encourage people to save, he offered them a 25% bonus on the amount they saved each month. This lead to 1 million Irish people becoming regular savers.

Characteristics of Entrepreneurs

Enterprising people tend to have the following personality traits:

1. **Pro-active**

   Entrepreneurs take positive steps to achieve their goals. They have an idea and take action to get that idea up and running. They do not wait for things to happen to them. They make things happen.

2. **Independent**

   Entrepreneurs like to be in charge. They like working for themselves. They don't like being told what to do. They like to be the ones giving the orders, not taking them.

3. **Self-motivated / Confident**

   Entrepreneurs push themselves to achieve their goals. They are driven and don't need others to inspire them. The drive to do something comes from within themselves.

4. **Self-belief**

   Entrepreneurs believe in themselves and their idea. They do not allow themselves to be put off by what other people think or say. When they suffer setbacks, they don't give up. They believe their business will succeed eventually and they keep at it.

5. **Need for achievement**

   Entrepreneurs have a desire to be a success, to be "somebody". They are ambitious and want to get on in life.

6. **Risk taker**

   Entrepreneurs are not afraid of taking a chance and having a go, even though they might fail. They take sensible risks, ones that have a good chance of success.

7. **Ruthless**

   Entrepreneurs put their business ahead of everything else. If they have a difficult decision to make, they choose the one that's best for the business.

Skills of Entrepreneurs

Skills are particular abilities that you have. Some may be natural to you (innate) and others you may have to learn by practice.

1. **Human relations**

   Entrepreneurs are good with people. They can bring the best out in people and can get them to do what the business needs.

Home	Parents show enterprise by converting the attic into a study for their daughter who is sitting the Leaving Cert. ■ The parents use human relations skills. They persuade the bank manager to give them the loan needed to pay for the conversion.
Community	Neighbours show enterprise by setting up a committee to enter their area in the Tidy Towns competition. ■ The committee members use human relations skills. They persuade as many of their neighbours as possible to volunteer for the clean up.
School	The teacher shows enterprise by getting Transition Year students to put on an end-of-term play. ■ The teacher uses human relations skills. He persuades the students to audition for the play.
Public Life	The Minister for Finance showed enterprise by bringing out the Special Savings Incentive Accounts to encourage Irish people to save more. ■ The Minister used human relations skills. He persuaded An Taoiseach that the idea was a good one and got his permission to run with it.
Business Startup	The entrepreneur shows enterprise by spotting a money-making idea and setting up a business to exploit it. ■ The entrepreneur uses human relations skills. She persuades investors to provide her with the capital she needs to start the business.

2. Time Management

Entrepreneurs are able to successfully complete all the tasks needed to achieve their goals in the time available to them.

Time management involves the following steps:
- Entrepreneurs write down all the tasks they have to do.
- They work out how much time is available to them to get these tasks done.
- If there are too many tasks and not enough time, they prioritise the most important tasks. This means that they do the most important tasks first in the time available.
- In this way, they make sure that all the *important* work is achieved on time.

Home	Parents show enterprise by converting the attic into a study for their daughter who is sitting the Leaving Cert. ■ The parents use time management skills. They draw up a schedule to ensure that the attic is completed before their daughter goes into 6th year.
Community	Neighbours show enterprise by setting up a committee to enter their area in the Tidy Towns competition. ■ The committee members use time management skills. They draw up a schedule ensure that the area is tidied before the Tidy Towns judges call round.
School	The teacher shows enterprise by getting Transition Year students to put on an end-of-term play. ■ The teacher uses time management skills. He draws up a schedule to ensure that the play is cast and fully rehearsed before the end of term.
Public Life	The Minister for Finance showed enterprise by bringing out the Special Savings Incentive Accounts to encourage Irish people to save more. ■ The Minister used time management skills. He drew up a schedule to ensure that idea was ready for the budget in December.
Business Startup	The entrepreneur shows enterprise by spotting a money-making idea and setting up a business to exploit it. ■ The entrepreneur uses time management skills. She draws up a schedule to ensure the shop is decorated, ready and stocked in plenty of time for its opening.

3. Planning

Entrepreneurs set goals for the future and come up with methods, called strategies, to ensure that these goals are achieved.

Home	Parents show enterprise by converting the attic into a study for their daughter who is sitting the Leaving Cert.
	■ The parents use planning skills. They prepare a cash flow forecast (*see Chapter 13*) so they can plan all the money coming into the family and all the money going out. This enables them to see whether there is enough left over to pay for the attic conversion.
Community	Neighbours show enterprise by setting up a committee to enter their area in the Tidy Towns competition.
	■ The committee members use planning skills. They use manpower planning (*see Chapter 9*) to figure out how many volunteers they will need to clean the area. They then plan to recruit as many volunteers as are needed.
School	The teacher shows enterprise by getting Transition Year students to put on an end-of-term play.
	■ The teacher uses planning skills. He prepares a cash flow forecast (*see Chapter 13*) so he can plan all the money coming into the school and all the money going out. This enables him to see whether the school can afford to put on the play.
Public Life	The Minister for Finance showed enterprise by bringing out the Special Savings Incentive Accounts to encourage Irish people to save more.
	■ The Minister used planning skills. He prepared a cash flow forecast (*see Chapter 13*) so he could plan all the money coming into the economy and all the money going out. This enabled him to see whether Ireland could afford to pay for the 25% bonus on people's savings.
Business Startup	The entrepreneur shows enterprise by spotting a money-making idea and setting up a business to exploit it.
	■ The entrepreneur uses planning. She prepares a cash flow forecast (*see Chapter 13*) so she can plan all the money coming into the business and all the money going out. This enables her to see whether the business will be able to pay all its bills and survive.

4. Risk Management

Entrepreneurs come up with a plan to minimise the risks that the business is exposed to. They identify all the risks facing the business – commercial risks (new competition), financial risks (shortage of money) and physical risks (to plant and equipment) and take measures to minimise their impact on the business. These measures can include taking out insurance, employing security and so on.

Home	Parents show enterprise by converting the attic into a study for their daughter who is sitting the Leaving Cert. ■ The parents take out payment protection insurance (*see Chapter 12*) on the loan so that, if they lose their jobs, the loan can be repaid.
Community	Neighbours show enterprise by setting up a committee to enter their area in the Tidy Towns competition. ■ The committee members take out public liability insurance (*see Chapter 12*) so that any volunteers who are injured on the clean up will be compensated by the insurance company.
School	The teacher shows enterprise by getting Transition Year students to put on an end-of-term play. ■ The teacher takes out public liability insurance (*see Chapter 12*) so that any audience members who are injured at the play will be compensated by the insurance company.
Public Life	The Minister for Finance showed enterprise by bringing out the Special Savings Incentive Accounts to encourage Irish people to save more. ■ The Minister made all applicants give their PPS number to minimise the risk of people opening more than the permitted one account.
Business Startup	The entrepreneur shows enterprise by spotting a money-making idea and setting up a business to exploit it. ■ The entrepreneur takes out public liability insurance (*see Chapter 12*) so that any customers who are injured on her premises will be compensated by the insurance company.

5. Decision Making

Entrepreneurs list all the possible solutions to a problem or opportunity and choose the best one for the business.

Entrepreneurs learn how to make good decisions rationally and quickly as follows:

Step 1   Analyse the problem or opportunity.

Step 2   List all the possible solutions.

Step 3   Go through the advantages and disadvantages of each possible solution.

Step 4   Pick the best solution with the most advantages for the business.

Home	Parents show enterprise by converting the attic into a study for their daughter who is sitting the Leaving Cert. ■ The parents research the various builders available and choose the best one they can find.
Community	Neighbours show enterprise by setting up a committee to enter their area in the Tidy Towns competition. ■ The committee members decide who does what job and when is the best time to carry out the clean up.
School	The teacher shows enterprise by getting Transition Year students to put on an end-of-term play. ■ The teacher decides which students get which parts in the play.
Public Life	The Minister for Finance showed enterprise by bringing out the Special Savings Incentive Accounts to encourage Irish people to save more. ■ The Minister decided that a 25% bonus was the right amount to offer savers.
Business Startup	The entrepreneur shows enterprise by spotting a money-making idea and setting up a business to exploit it. ■ The entrepreneur decides which type of business ownership (*see Chapter 15*) to go for (sole trader, private limited company and so on).

6. Reality Perception

Entrepreneurs see situations as they really are and not as they might like them to be. Entrepreneurs realise when things are going wrong and do not fool themselves into thinking otherwise.

Home	Parents show enterprise by converting the attic into a study for their daughter who is sitting the Leaving Cert. ■ The parents use reality perception when they see that the builder is not doing a good job and confront him about it immediately.
Community	Neighbours show enterprise by setting up a committee to enter their area in the Tidy Towns competition. ■ The committee members use reality perception when they realise that not enough neighbours are volunteering for the clean up. They go on a massive recruitment drive to get more locals involved.
School	The teacher shows enterprise by getting Transition Year students to put on an end-of-term play. ■ The teacher uses reality perception when he sees that the lead actor is not working out in the part and replaces him with a better one.
Public Life	The Minister for Finance showed enterprise by bringing out the Special Savings Incentive Accounts to encourage Irish people to save more. ■ The Minister used reality perception. He saw that, despite Ireland's booming economy, all was not well. People were not saving for the future, so he took action to change this.
Business Startup	The entrepreneur shows enterprise by spotting a money-making idea and setting up a business to exploit it. ■ The entrepreneur uses reality perception when she sees that one of her ideas is not going to work and drops it immediately so that she can develop a better one.

Intrapreneur

An intrapreneur is an employee working within a business who shows enterprise. He uses his initiative and thinks of a new idea to help the business he works in.

When some Microsoft workers saw the worldwide success of the Sony PlayStation, they thought of the idea of Microsoft developing a games console. They worked on their idea and this led to Microsoft launching the Xbox.

Art Fry, a worker at 3M, heard about a special glue invented by a 3M scientist. Art thought about uses for the glue and came up with the idea for the Post-it. Post-its are now one of the most popular office products.

ENTREPENEURS	INTRAPRENEURS
Own their own business	Are employees in the business
Take financial and personal risks	Do not take such a high degree of risk

Importance of Enterprise in Business

1. Enterprise is an essential element in setting up a business. It provides the idea and the drive to set up the business in the first place.

2. Enterprise from employees (intrapreneurs) can help the business to increase its sales and/or to reduce its costs (for example, Art Fry's idea of the Post-it made millions for 3M).

3. Enterprise leads to the creation of wealth in the country. Entrepreneurs make profits from their business and their employees earn wages from the business. They spend this money in shops and other businesses. Thus an enterprising economy leads to the creation of more businesses.

4. The taxes the government takes from entrepreneurs and employees can be used to provide grants to help more and more people set up their own businesses.

Importance of Enterprise in the Community

1. Enterprise creates jobs and businesses for local people. The wages or profits they
    receive give them a higher standard of living than they would have if they stayed
    on social welfare. Some unemployed people from Ballymun who set up their
    community enterprise, Greencaps, to provide a porterage service in nearby
    Dublin Airport all benefited in this way.

2. Local people spend the money they make from their job or business in their local
    shops, pubs, restaurants, banks, hotels and so on. This helps these businesses to
    succeed as well. Thus enterprise in the community has a spin-off effect.

3. It creates a new breed of entrepreneurs in the local area. People in the
    community see their friends and neighbours set up businesses and this gives
    them the motivation and courage to set up a business themselves. This leads to
    more wealth in the community.

4. The government receives taxes from the new businesses and also has to pay out
    less on social welfare benefits. This increases the money the government has
    available to spend on local hospitals, schools, Gardaí, roads and so on.

5. Infrastructure in the local area improves. Shops open because people now have
    money to spend. New houses are built to house the workers. Roads are improved
    to make it easier to do business. It transforms the local economy.

Ordinary Level Questions

EXAM SECTION 1 (25%) – SHORT ANSWER QUESTIONS [10 marks each]

1. Explain the term "entrepreneur" and give two examples.

2. Outline two characteristics of an entrepreneur.

3. Column 1 is a list of business terms. Column 2 is a list of possible explanations for these terms. Match the two lists by placing the letter of the correct explanation under the relevant number below. One explanation has no match.

Column 1	Column 2: Explanations
1. Proactive	a) Putting your business ahead of everything else
2. Planning	b) Reducing the chances of bad things happening to the business
3. Risk Management	c) Choosing the best option from a list of alternatives
4. Time Management	d) Setting goals for the future and coming up with strategies to achieve them
5. Decision Making	e) The skill of making things happen
6. Ruthless	f) Doing the most important jobs first
	g) Not being afraid to take a chance

1	2	3	4	5	6
E	D	B	F	C	A

4. Indicate whether each of the following (A, B, C, D and E) is true or false.

	Sentence	True or False
A	An intrapreneur sets up her own business.	False
B	Enterprise is important to Ireland because it creates jobs.	True
C	Risk-taking is a characteristic of entrepreneurs.	True
D	Anita Roddick set up The Body Shop.	True
E	An entrepreneur is an employee who thinks of an idea to help her boss.	False

5. List five skills used by entrepreneurs.

EXAM SECTION 2 (75%) – LONG QUESTIONS

1. What is meant by the term "entrepreneurship"?   (10 marks)

2. Describe four characteristics of enterprising people.   (20 marks)

3. Identify and explain four skills needed by enterprising people.   (20 marks)

4. Your friend has just set up a business in your local area.
    Explain three advantages of this to your community.   (15 marks)

5. Explain, using an example, what is meant by the term "intrapreneur".   (10 marks)

Higher Level Questions

EXAM SECTION 1 (20%) – SHORT ANSWER QUESTIONS [10 marks each]

1. Illustrate your understanding of the term "entrepreneurship".

2. Complete this sentence: The role of an entrepreneur in a business is to…

3. Distinguish between the enterprising characteristics of "self-motivation" and "self-belief".

4. Identify two skills of an entrepreneur and show how they can be used in a school.

5. Column 1 is a list of business terms. Column 2 is a list of possible explanations for these
    terms. Match the two lists by placing the letter of the correct explanation under the
    relevant number below. One explanation has no match.

Column 1	Column 2: Explanations
1. Independent	a) An entrepreneur takes positive steps to make things happen.
2. Need for Achievement	b) An entrepreneur makes decisions that are best for the business. Business needs take priority.
3. Ruthless	c) Entrepreneurs like to be in charge, giving orders, not taking them.
4. Risk taker	d) Entrepreneurs like to be successful.
5. Proactive	e) Entrepreneurs take steps to minimise the risks of bad things happening to the business.
	f) Entrepreneurs are not afraid to take a chance.

1	2	3	4	5
C	D	B	F	A

6. Define "intrapreneur".

7. Explain the term "enterprise". Illustrate its impact on the development of a local
    community.

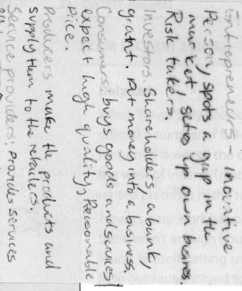

PPLIED BUSINESS QUESTION – 80 MARKS

...d his apprenticeship as a carpenter, he was immediately
...ime jobs in Dublin. Despite protests from friends and family,
...fers so he could set up his own business in his local town in
... persuaded the local bank manager to lend him €50,000,
...wn and bought all the equipment he needed.

...id off but is also resulting in problems for him. He finds that
...s in the day. He is constantly swamped with work and has
...appy with his demanding customers. He looked to hire some
...choose one candidate from among the applicants. He had a
row with an important client who was not happy when her furniture arrived late.

Trevor wants his business to succeed. He is from a deprived area and does not want to
be unemployed like many of the friends he grew up with. He knows the area is run
down with many of the local shops closed and boarded up, but he is optimistic for the
future and wants to stay in the area.

Handwritten annotations on text: inovative, Human relations, risk taker, Decisive, realistic, self confident

(A) Outline the enterprise characteristics displayed by Trevor.   (20 marks)

(B) Describe the contribution that Trevor's business could make to
his local town if it proves successful.   (20 marks)

(C) Evaluate how the business might do better if Trevor improved his
entrepreneurial skills. Support your answer with reference to the above text.   (40 marks)

EXAM SECTION 3 (60%) – LONG QUESTIONS

1. Discuss the importance of enterprise in business.   (20 marks)
2. Describe three skills of an entrepreneur and illustrate their use in public life.   (20 marks)
3. Using examples, distinguish between an entrepreneur and an intrapreneur.   (20 marks)
4. Identify the importance of three entrepreneurial skills in the home.   (20 marks)
5. Using examples, distinguish between risk taking and risk management.   (20 marks)
6. Describe four characteristics of enterprising people.   (20 marks)
7. Describe the impact of enterprise on the development of a local economy.   (20 marks)

CHAPTER 5

Management

Definition of Management

Management is a process that involves a manager working with people and using other resources such as money and equipment to ensure that the business achieves its goals.

The management team of a business consists of a number of people in charge of running the business. The manager in overall control of the business is called the Managing Director (MD), also known as the Chief Executive Officer (CEO).

For example, Ryanair started business in 1985 flying just one route. The CEO, Michael O'Leary, turned the company into one of the world's most successful airlines. Willie Walsh took over as CEO at Aer Lingus just after 9/11. In less than three years he brought the company from the brink of collapse back to profitability.

Management is used in a lot of situations, including business:

In the Home	■ Parents must manage the family budget to make sure that there is enough money to pay for a holiday in the summer.
In the Community	■ A tidy towns committee must manage the effort to make sure that everything is done to make the town as clean as possible.
In School	■ The school principal is a manager. She must run the school. This involves employing teachers, organising the timetable and communicating with teachers, students, parents, the Department of Education and Science and so on.

In Government Departments	■ The Minister for Finance must manage the economy. He must make the best use of the money the country has to benefit all the people of Ireland. ■ He must make sure that there is enough money coming in to the government and not too much going out.
In Business	■ Managers must make sure that employees do their jobs. ■ Managers also make sure that customers are satisfied. ■ Managers have to ensure that the business makes a profit.

Characteristics of Managers

Good managers tend to have the following personality traits:

1. **Decisive**

   Good managers can analyse a situation and quickly come up with an effective solution to deal with it. They can quickly and firmly resolve problems.

2. **Initiative**

   Good managers do not need to be told what to do to. They are able to start things. They can think up new ideas and find solutions to problems themselves.

3. **Good with people**

   Good managers are able to get along with people. They know how to get people on side and get the best out of them to ensure that the business is a success.

4. **Hard worker**

   Good managers put the effort and time into their job. They are not strictly "9 to 5" people. If a problem has to be dealt with, they stay behind and work until it is solved.

5. **Flexible**

   Good managers can change their business methods as situations evolve.

6. **Charismatic**

   Good managers have charisma, the ability to charm people. This makes people respect and like them. Employees are more likely to do what a charismatic manager wants.

Contrast between Enterprise and Management

ENTREPRENEURS	MANAGERS
The entrepreneur sets up the business and answers only to herself. She has ultimate control over the business.	The manager runs the business for the entrepreneur and answers to her.
The entrepreneur takes a big risk (both financial and personal) when setting up the business. She could lose everything she owns if it fails.	The manager doesn't take the same degree of risk. If the business fails, all he will lose is his job.
The entrepreneur comes up with the idea for the business.	The manager ensures that the entrepreneur's ideas are carried out.
The entrepreneur concentrates on the long-term future of the business. She focuses on the "big picture".	The manager concentrates on the day-to-day running of the business. He focuses on the details, such as employee punctuality, productivity and so on.
For example, Richard Branson thinks of the ideas for new business, such as Virgin Galactic (leisure flights to space).	*Branson hires professional managers to run the new business for him so he can then move on to a new project.*

Ordinary Level Questions

EXAM SECTION 1 (25%) – SHORT ANSWER QUESTIONS [10 marks each]

1. Explain the role of a manager in a business. Give two examples of managers.
2. Write out what the following letters stand for: MD CEO
3. List three characteristics of a manager and outline any one of them.
4. Column 1 is a list of business terms. Column 2 is a list of possible explanations for these terms. Match the two lists by placing the letter of the correct explanation under the relevant number below. One explanation has no match.

Column 1	
1. Hard Worker	4. Flexible
2. Initiative	5. Decisive
3. Charismatic	6. Manager

Column 2: Explanations
a)   A person who sets up her own business
b)   A person who can make decisions quickly
c)   A person who can think on her feet
d)   A person with a charm that others warm to
e)   A person who puts in all the hours needed to get the job done
f)   A person who runs a business for the owner
g)   A person who can change her methods when necessary

1	2	3	4	5	6
E		D			

5. Indicate whether each of the following (A, B, C, D and E) is true or false.

	Sentence	True or False
A	A school principal is an example of a manager.	True
B	The job of management is to make sure that a business achieves its goals.	True
C	The manager in overall charge of a business is called the CEO.	True
D	Charisma is the ability to think up solutions to problems quickly.	False
E	A good manager sticks with the methods that have worked in the past and does not change them.	False

EXAM SECTION 2 (75%) – LONG QUESTIONS

Describe three characteristics of a manager.   (15 marks)

Higher Level Questions

EXAM SECTION 1 (20%) – SHORT ANSWER QUESTIONS [10 marks each]

1. Define "management".

2. Illustrate your understanding of the term CEO.

3. The following table shows three actions of a manager and three typical characteristics of successful managers. For each action, tick (✔) the characteristic that is *most* likely to match that action.

	Decisive	Charismatic	Flexible
Manager sacks an employee whom she finds stealing.	✓		
Manager changes the company bonus scheme to motivate workers.			✓
Manager hires a candidate immediately after her interview.	✓		

4. Explain the role of a manager in a business.

EXAM SECTION 2 (20%) – APPLIED BUSINESS QUESTION

Hyland Ltd.

Matthew Hyland worked as a barman in a number of Dublin pubs for many years. During those years, he saved hard. His savings and a very large bank loan helped him to buy his own pub in his native Wexford. Matthew had lots of ideas he wanted to try out in his new business venture. His pub now offers gourmet lunches and dinners and has entertainment at weekends. He offers a bus service to drive customers home at night.

Thanks to Matthew's hard work and great ideas, the pub has become one of the most successful in the county. In fact, it became so busy that he hired a manager, Orla Crowley, to run the pub for him. He prefers to concentrate on new ideas. Already, he is thinking of opening an entertainment venue in Wexford and hopes to attract big names from the world of show business.

Orla runs the pub and is responsible for everything from checking deliveries, which can arrive at 7am, to hiring and firing chefs, bar staff and bus drivers. It can be stressful but Orla always has a smile and a joke for the employees and they really like her. When the ESB warned of power cuts in the area, many businesses chose to close down but Orla bought candles and handed out flyers inviting people to come to a "candlelight music session". It proved to be one of the busiest nights the pub ever had. Because of her success, Orla has been offered a job managing a much bigger bar in Waterford.

(A) Outline the management characteristics shown by Orla in the above situation.   (20 marks)

(B) Contrast the role of Matthew as entrepreneur and Orla as manager.   (30 marks)

EXAM SECTION 3 (60%) – LONG QUESTIONS

1. "Management is not just seen in business." Do you agree with this statement? Support your answer with two reasons and examples. (20 marks)

2. Distinguish between "entrepreneurs" and "managers". (20 marks)

3. Outline four characteristics of successful managers. (20 marks)

CHAPTER 6

Management Skills 1

A manager must have these three skills: **leading**, **motivating** and **communicating**. This chapter examines the first two skills. Chapter 7 looks at communicating.

Management Skill of Leading

Leading (or leadership) is the ability to direct people, give them instructions and make them follow and obey you. In business, good leadership develops a bond between manager and employees and a sense of trust. A manager can lead people using one of the following leadership styles.

1. Autocratic Leadership

The manager makes all the decisions without consulting the employees. He gives orders and expects them to be obeyed without question. The manager uses his position of authority to get employees to do what he wants. He may use fear and threats to get his own way.

Evaluation: This style of leading does not usually produce good results for the manager and is best avoided. Workers resent being treated like this and will become poorly motivated and unwilling to use their initiative.

2. Democratic Leadership

The manager involves employees when making decisions. He invites them to discuss the issues and takes their views into account when making a decision. The manager delegates work to employees because he trusts them. The manager uses reasoned arguments to get employees to co-operate.

Evaluation: This style of leading is much more appropriate for the manager. It achieves better results for him than autocratic leading. This is because employees like to be involved in the business. They like to be listened to. As a result of democratic leading, they will work harder for him, be more motivated and use their initiative.

3. Laissez Faire Leadership

The manager does not interfere with how employees do their work. He gives the employee a goal to achieve and leaves it entirely up to the employee as to how she will work to achieve that goal. The manager **delegates** a lot because he trusts employees and he uses reasoned arguments to get employees to co-operate.

Evaluation: This style of leading is appropriate only when the manager has highly trustworthy employees. It does not work in all situations. Some employees would take advantage of the freedom and others would find it difficult to cope with no one watching over them.

Delegation

An important part of being a leader is delegating work to employees.

Delegation is when a manager gives some of his work to an employee to do for him. The manager gives the employee the authority to carry out the work and will hold the employee responsible for doing a good job. But *ultimate responsibility* lies with the manager.

For example, the Human Resources manager might ask his assistant to interview candidates for an important vacancy in the business, because he doesn't have the time to do it.

The following are required for delegation:

(a) Competent, responsible and trustworthy employees who can cope with the added responsibility of doing the delegated jobs.

(b) A good control system that *immediately* highlights any errors made by the employees who have been delegated to. This will minimise any bad effects on the business.

(c) A manager who is not afraid to delegate and is willing to try it because he knows all the benefits of delegation for himself, the business and the employees.

Advantages of Delegation

1. By delegating the less important work to his employees, a manager has more time to devote to the most important issues in the business. He can give his full attention to solving the business's critical problems.

2. Sharing the work out among the employees through delegation gets the work done faster. This saves the business time and money.

3. Delegating management work to employees is a good way to train them to become managers. This ensures that the business has a steady supply of managers for the future.

4. Delegation makes employees happier because they are more involved in the business. They feel valued when the manager picks them to do a job for him.

Disadvantages of Refusing to Delegate

1. By insisting on doing everything himself and refusing to delegate, the manager becomes swamped with work and may not be able to cope. The stress of the heavy workload can lead to the manager missing important business issues and making costly mistakes.

2. It takes longer for the manager to do all his work alone. The business may miss deadlines as a result.

3. Employees are not trained in management jobs if the manager refuses to delegate. Therefore, the business does not have a pool of well-trained employees to choose from if a management vacancy arises.

4. Employees are unhappy if their manager refuses to delegate to them. They think that he has no faith in their abilities. It damages their self-esteem and lowers morale.

Importance of Effective Leadership

1. **Improved Efficiency**

   A good leader gives clear instructions and directions to his employees. Employees understand and do exactly what is expected of them. Time and other resources are not wasted doing the wrong thing.

2. **Improved Co-ordination**

   An effective leader inspires employees to share his vision for the future of the business.

   Employees believe in the vision and all pull together in the same direction to achieve it. They all work as one for the success of the business.

3. **Employee Retention**

   A good leader delegates tasks to employees. Employees like being trusted and involved in the business and are thus more likely to continue working for the business. It also helps to attract the best employees.

4. **Change**

   A good leader helps a business to change for the better. He acts as a role model for the employees by putting in the effort needed to make the change happen.

This encourages the employees to accept the change as well. When the Irish economy faltered in 2007, the government postponed its pay rise to show people that the economy could not afford massive wage increases.

Management Skill of Motivating

Motivating involves the manager energising employees and providing them with incentives so that they will co-operate and work harder for the business, while finding their work fulfilling.

For example, when you were a baby you could motivate your parents to do anything you wanted. All you had to do was cry. The incentive for your parents to run to you was the peace and quiet once you were happy!

A business example is Microsoft. It has been voted among the 50 best companies to work for in Ireland. It offers bonuses to every employee based on performance at work. Outstanding employees are recognised by the company's Goldstar programme. Those who show extra initiative win cash and shares in the company.

The importance of employee motivation is shown in the case of Radisson SAS Hotels in Ireland (another of the 50 Best Companies to Work for in Ireland). The Human Resources manager said, "There are three very important people we have to look after. First on the list is our staff, because if they're not happy they won't make our guests happy, which means our guests won't come back and then our owners and investors won't be happy. So the starting point for us is our employees and their health, happiness and welfare."

If a manager knew exactly what to offer employees to encourage them to work hard, the business would be a great success. To help managers, there are two main theories on how to motivate employees:

- Theory X and Theory Y   (by Douglas McGregor)
- Hierarchy of Needs   (by Abraham Maslow)

McGregor – Theory X and Y

McGregor said that there are two types of manager – Theory X managers and Theory Y managers. Each type of manager has certain beliefs about employees and these beliefs determine how the manager treats her employees.

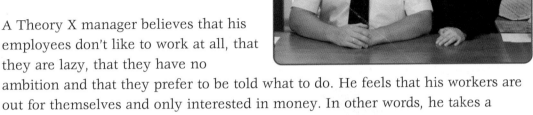

- A Theory X manager believes that his employees don't like to work at all, that they are lazy, that they have no ambition and that they prefer to be told what to do. He feels that his workers are out for themselves and only interested in money. In other words, he takes a pessimistic view of his employees.

- A Theory X manager motivates in two ways. The first is the hard approach, where he keeps a close eye on his workers to make sure that they do their jobs. He uses threats and punishments to keep them in line and make sure they work. The second is the soft approach, where he promises them more money to get them to work harder.

- McGregor said that employees resent being treated like this by Theory X managers. They will become unco-operative and try to do as little work as possible. They will try to get as much money from the manager as possible for the least amount of work.

- A Theory Y manager believes that his employees enjoy working, that they have ambition and want to get on in the business and that they want more responsible and more challenging jobs.

- A Theory Y manager motivates by offering promotions and titles to employees who do well. He praises employees who do good work. He delegates to employees who are good workers.

- McGregor said that Theory Y results in happy, co-operative employees who will work hard. He recommends that managers use Theory Y in their business.

Evaluation: McGregor's Theory X and Y is a good idea about motivation because it makes sense that employees will work harder and make a better contribution to the business if they are treated as responsible and valuable employees.

Maslow's Hierarchy of Needs

Maslow stated that people's needs motivate them. If a manager can learn about employees' needs, he can motivate them by satisfying their needs. Maslow stated that people have five different types of need, which can be arranged in a hierarchy ranging from the most basic human needs to the most sophisticated.

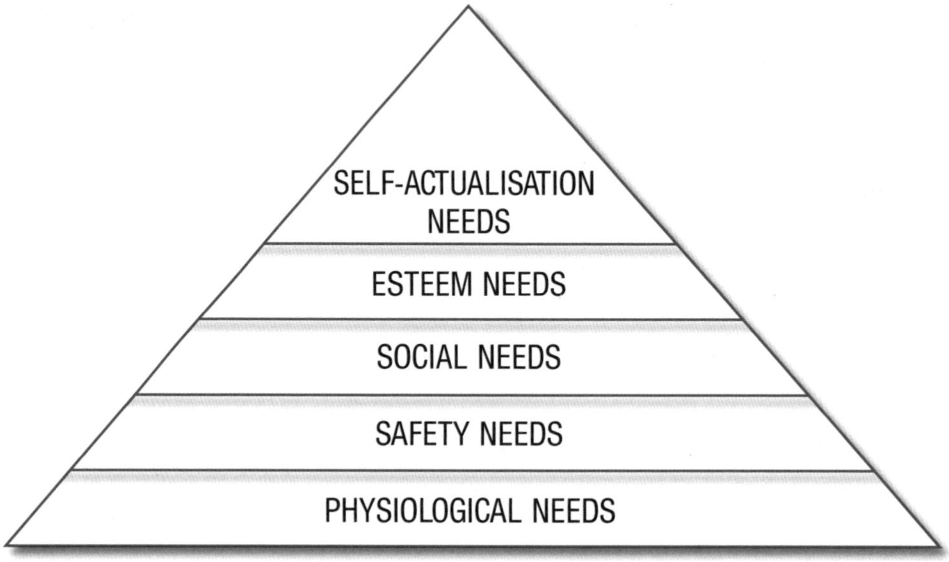

NEED	EXPLANATION	HOW A MANAGER CAN SATISFY THE NEED AND MOTIVATE THE EMPLOYEE
Self-Actualisation	The need to reach your full potential and be the best you can be	More challenging work, share ownership
Esteem	The need for self-respect and respect from others	Praise, awards, promotions
Social	The need for friendship and love	Teamwork, staff parties
Safety	The need to feel safe and secure	Contract of employment
Physiological	The most essential human needs, such as water, food, air and so on	Pay, canteen

○ Maslow stated that everyone starts at the bottom of the hierarchy with the physiological needs. That need is the most important to a person until it is satisfied. For example, a person who is literally starving may steal food. He is not concerned with what his friends might think of him (esteem needs) because he is stuck on physiological needs.

○ Once a need is satisfied, it no longer motivates a person. Satisfying the next need up is what now motivates her. Employees are always motivated to move to the next level.

○ Therefore, it is important for a manager to know which need is dominating each employee. They can be motivated to work harder if the manager can satisfy that need.

Evaluation: Maslow's Hierarchy of Needs provides a good insight into motivation because it tells managers that if they can find out which level each employee is on, they can find suitable ways to motivate her.

However, it is not without its faults. It does not explain why many employees will put up with low pay now in return for the promise of future benefits.

Furthermore, in real life, employees don't just satisfy one need at a time.

Importance of Motivation

Motivating is an essential skill. It helps a manager achieve the business's goals by making every employee willingly play their part in achieving the goals.

1. **Improved Productivity**

   Motivated employees are happier in their jobs and therefore work harder for the business. They are more willing to put in extra effort. This extra effort helps the business to be more successful (see the SAS Radisson case).

2. **Greater Intrapreneurship**

   Highly motivated employees are more likely to co-operate with their managers and offer useful suggestions and ideas to help the business. Microsoft got the idea for Xbox from motivated employees who wanted to see the company beat the Sony Playstation.

3. **Employee Retention**

   Motivated employees are happy and are more likely to stay in their job for a long time. This saves the business a lot of money on recruitment.

4.   **Improved Industrial Relations**
     Motivated employees have a good relationship with management and are more
     likely to talk out any difficulties in a spirit of co-operation rather than going on
     strike.

Ordinary Level Questions

EXAM SECTION 1 (25%) – SHORT ANSWER QUESTIONS [10 marks each]

1.   List the three management skills.

2.   Indicate whether each of the following (A, B, C, D and E) is true or false.

	Sentence	True or False
A	An autocratic leader consults her staff before making a decision.	*False*
B	An autocratic leader uses fear and his position of authority to get his own way.	*True*
C	A democratic leader uses reasoned arguments to get her own way.	*True*
D	A democratic leader trusts his staff and delegates work to them.	*True*
E	A laissez faire leader tells employees what to do and expects them to do it without question.	*False*

3.   Explain what is meant by "delegation" and give one example of delegation in business.

4.   Outline two advantages of delegation.

5.   Column 1 is a list of business terms. Column 2 is a list of possible explanations for these
     terms. Match the two lists by placing the letter of the correct explanation under the
     relevant number below. One explanation has no match.

Column 1	Column 2: Explanations
1. Motivation	a) Human need to reach full potential
2. Theory X	b) Manager assumes employees like work and want to get on
3. Theory Y	
4. Physiological	c) Human need for self-respect and respect from others
5. Esteem	d) Manager assumes employees are lazy and out for themselves
6. Self Actualisation	
	e) Skill of a manager to provide incentives for workers so that they work hard
	f) Basic human needs
	g) Human need for friendship

1 – E
2 – D
3 – B
4 – F
5 – C
6 – A

1	2	3	4	5	6
E	D	B	F	C	A

6. Fill in the blanks in Maslow's Hierarchy of Needs.

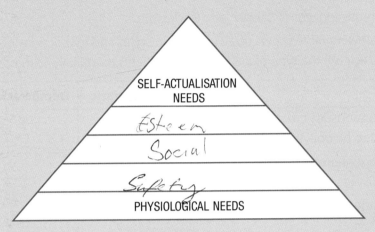

7. Indicate whether each of the following (A, B, C, D and E) is true or false.

	Sentence	True or False
A	A Theory X manager motivates her workers with praise and recognition.	False
B	A Theory X manager's approach will result in unco-operative employees.	True
C	A Theory Y manager motivates his employees with promotions.	~~False~~ True
D	Maslow's theory is called Theory X and Theory Y.	False
E	It is recommended to use Theory X in most business situations.	False

8. Distinguish between "esteem needs" and "social needs".

EXAM SECTION 2 (75%) – LONG QUESTIONS

1. Name three styles of leading and explain any two of them.   (25 marks)
2. What is meant by the term "delegation"?   (10 marks)
3. Describe three benefits for a business of delegation.   (15 marks)
4. Distinguish between "leading" and "motivating".   (10 marks)
5. Describe Theory X and Theory Y.   (15 marks)
6. Describe Maslow's Hierarchy of Needs.   (15 marks)

Higher Level Questions

EXAM SECTION 1 (20%) – SHORT ANSWER QUESTIONS [10 marks each]

1. Distinguish between "autocratic" and "democratic" leaders.

2. Explain the concept of "laissez faire leadership".

3. The following table shows three leadership styles and four actions of leaders. For each action, tick (✔) the type of leadership style that is *most* likely to match that action.

	Autocratic	Democratic	Laissez Faire
Manager issues orders and expects them to be obeyed without question.	✓		
Manager refuses to delegate to employees.	✓		
Manager refuses to consult with employees.	✓		
Manager allows employees to complete tasks as they see fit.			✓

4. Which leadership style do you think is the most appropriate to business? Explain your choice.

5. Illustrate your understanding of the term "delegation".

6. Outline three problems for a manager who does not delegate.

7. Complete this sentence: Delegation helps business because it …

8. Complete this sentence: Motivating helps a business to …

9. Distinguish between a Theory X manager and a Theory Y manager.

10. Illustrate the difference between "safety needs" and "social needs".

EXAM SECTION 2 (20%) – APPLIED BUSINESS QUESTION – 80 MARKS

Purple Ltd.

Entrepreneur

Patsy O'Connor set up her own restaurant business four years after graduating from catering college. The restaurant initially proved a big success and was busy every night, thanks to Patsy's innovative menu and her policy of only buying the freshest ingredients. Recently, however, Patsy has begun to notice problems. A new restaurant opened nearby and is attracting many of her regular customers. She can't think why they would leave her.

Patsy has always worked hard. She regularly puts in 12-hour days at the restaurant. This leaves her exhausted and with little energy for anything else in her life. She has found herself snapping at employees, although she has always been tough on them. To maintain standards in the restaurant, she insists that all employees do exactly what she says and run any problems by her first. To keep employees on their toes, she never praises them but severely reprimands those who make mistakes.

A number of the employees have left the business in recent times, unhappy with the conditions. Patsy can't understand this because she pays well above the going rate. A number of long-serving employees are complaining that there is no career path for them. Patsy dismissed their complaints, telling them that they were lucky to have such well-paid jobs and, if they didn't like it, they could go elsewhere.

(A) Describe Patsy's leadership style. Support your answer with reference to the above text   (20 marks)

(B) Do you think Patsy is a Theory X or Theory Y manager? Support your answer with reference to the above text.   (20 marks)

(C) Evaluate how the business might do better if Patsy improves her skills of leading and motivating.   (40 marks)

EXAM SECTION 3 (60%) – LONG QUESTIONS

1. Discuss the importance of a manager using the correct leadership style in a business.   (30 marks)

2. Evaluate the importance of delegation in a business.   (25 marks)

3. Contrast a Theory X manager with a Theory Y manager.   (20 marks)

4. Explain, using examples, the five categories of needs identified by Maslow.   (15 marks)

5. "Maslow's theory on motivation is still in use today, more than 60 years after he outlined it." Describe and evaluate Maslow's theory.   (25 marks)

CHAPTER 7

Communications

Management Skill of Communicating

Communication involves transferring information from one person to another. The sender turns an idea into a message by using words and/or pictures. She then sends that message through a medium to the receiver, who must interpret the message and act upon it.

There are two types of communications: internal communications and external communications.

Internal Communications

This is communication between two or more people who are all inside the same business. Methods of internal communication include:

- Internal newsletter
- Notice Board
- Internal phone
- Suggestion Box
- Face to face conversations

- E-mail
- Intercom
- Meeting
- Pager
- Memo

Internal communication can be:

Upward   Upward communication moves from a lower to a higher level in the organisation. Employees give information to, ask questions of and make suggestions to management.

Downward   Downward communication moves from a higher to a lower level in the organisation. Managers give orders, reprimands, advice and training to employees.

Horizontal   Horizontal communication moves between people at the same
                    level. The marketing director and the finance director meet to
                    discuss next year's advertising budget.

External Communications

This is communication between the business and other people outside the business.
Examples of external communication include:

Banks   The entrepreneur meets the bank manager to apply for a
                    bank loan.

Suppliers   The production manager sends an order to the supplier for
                    more materials.

Customers   The marketing manager writes back to a customer in response
                    to her complaint.

Government   The entrepreneur sends in her annual tax return to Revenue.

Public Relations   The Public Relations Officer organises a press conference to
                    announce to the media that the business is opening a new factory
                    that will create new jobs.

Methods of external communication include:

- Telephone
- E-mail
- Letter
- WWW
- Press conference
- Video-conferencing

Written, Oral and Visual Communications

	WRITTEN COMMUNICATIONS	ORAL COMMUNICATIONS	VISUAL COMMUNICATIONS
Examples	The written word ■ Business documents such as invoices, orders, quotations and so on. ■ E-mail ■ Fax ■ Letter ■ Memo ■ Reports	The spoken word ■ Face-to-face conversations ■ Intercom ■ Telephone ■ Meeting ■ Conference ■ Video-conferencing	Pictures, symbols, diagrams and maps ■ Bar chart ■ Pie chart ■ Pictogram ■ Break-even chart ■ Line graph ■ Map

	WRITTEN COMMUNICATIONS	ORAL COMMUNICATIONS	VISUAL COMMUNICATIONS
Advantages	1. It provides a permanent record and therefore proof of the communication. Therefore it is especially useful for business contracts. 2. The message can be read and read again to understand any difficult ideas. 3. New technology such as e-mail makes written communication very fast.	1. It is a quick form of communication because you can get an instant response from the receiver. 2. Any problems in understanding can be easily explained there and then. 3. It is personal and therefore good for reaching agreement. 4. It allows emotion and body language to be communicated.	1. It is useful for analysing statistics 2. It makes communication much clearer because pictures are generally easier to understand and easier to remember.
Disadvantages	1. Feedback (getting an answer) is slower than oral communications. 2. There is a risk of information overload. Too much written information can make it difficult for the receiver to understand the message.	1. There is no record of the message, which means there is no proof it took place. 2. Because oral is instant, the message may not be prepared in advance and may come out wrong. 2. The receiver may not listen to the message and miss it.	1. Visual communication is usually not sufficient on its own. To be fully understood, it nearly always has to be accompanied by either of the other two methods.

Bar Charts

■ A bar chart displays the information in the form of bars (rectangles).

■ The bigger the size of each item, the bigger the bar is drawn to represent it.

■ Bar charts are good to show the relative sizes of things.

2007 Ordinary Level – Section 1 (10 marks)

Draw a bar chart to illustrate the following information for FLYNN MOTORS Ltd.

Year	2002	2003	2004	2005	2006
No. of Employees	25	30	40	35	20

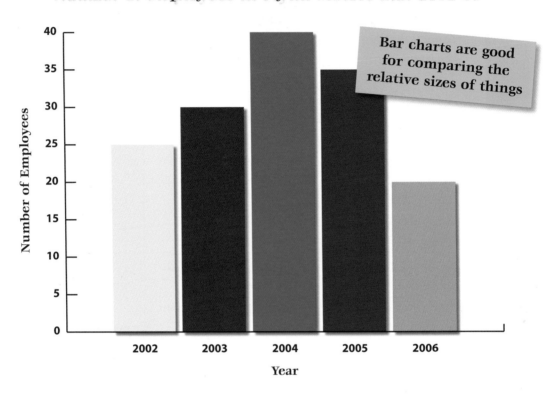

Number of employees in Flynn Motors Ltd. 2002-06

Bar charts are good for comparing the relative sizes of things

Pie Charts

- A pie chart shows the total of the items you are talking about as a circle.
- Fractions of the circle are shaded in to represent the fraction that each item bears to the total.
- Pie charts are a good way of showing fractions and percentages.

Draw a pie chart to illustrate the following information:

Product	DVDs	Washing Machines	TVs	Total Sales
Sales in €'000	25	50	25	100

Sales of Products

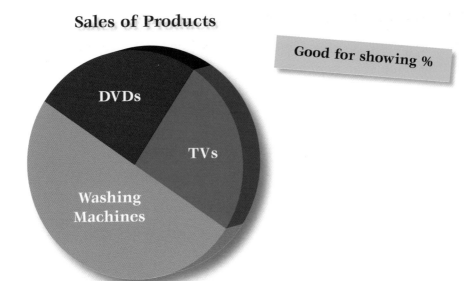

Good for showing %

- One quarter of the pie is shaded "DVDs" because DVD sales are one quarter (25/100) of the total sales.
- One half of the pie is shaded "Washing Machines" because washing machine sales are one half (50/100) of the total sales.
- One quarter of the pie is shaded "TVs" because TV sales are one quarter (25/100) of the total sales.

Pictograms

- A pictogram represents the information in the form of pictures.
- Each picture represents a certain amount of the item in question.
- Pictograms are a good way of showing the relative sizes of the items in question.

Draw a pictogram to illustrate the following information:

	Ulster	Munster	Connacht	Leinster
No. of Employees in Agriculture	5,000	10,000	5,000	30,000

Numbers Employed in Agriculture in Ireland

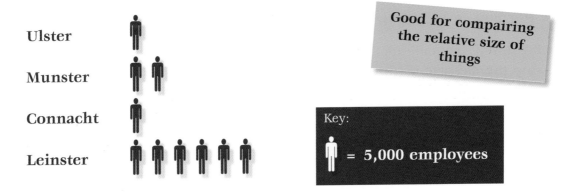

Good for compairing the relative size of things

Key:
👤 = 5,000 employees

Line Graphs

- Line graphs are used to show how the value of an item changes over time.
- The value of an item is plotted as a point.
- The value some time later is plotted as another point.
- The points are then joined by a straight line to show the trend over time.

2005 Ordinary Level – Section 1 (10 marks)

Draw a line graph to illustrate the following information for GHK Ltd:

Year	2000	2001	2002	2003	2004
Sales	€100,000	€150,000	€200,000	€250,000	€200,000

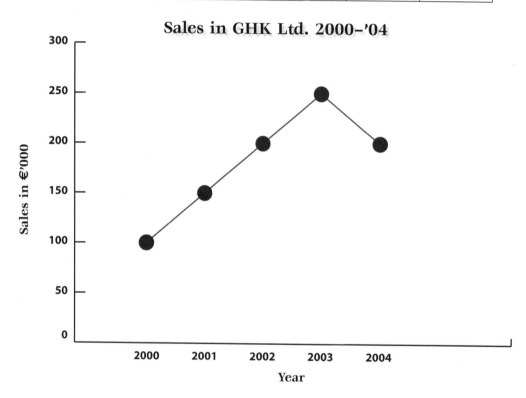

Sales in GHK Ltd. 2000–'04

Barriers to Effective Communication

Barriers to communication are things that **stop the message getting through** the way the sender intended. They stop the receiver understanding the message and acting on it accordingly.

The following are barriers to communication:

Language	■ If the sender uses words in her message that the receiver doesn't understand or if she uses jargon, the receiver may not know what the message is about and won't be able to act on it appropriately. ■ Jargon is a technical language used by people in a specific industry or workplace that only *they* understand.
Prejudice	■ If the receiver has a personal bias against the person sending the message, he might not listen to what she is communicating because of his prejudice against her. Therefore, the message does not get through to him.
Information Overload	■ If the message contains too much information, this can make it very hard for the receiver to take it all in. She might get lost and frustrated with it and she may even tune out and give up trying to understand the message. Long-winded, detailed explanations can make the meaning unclear.
Poor Listening Skills	■ Proper communication involves receiving information as well as giving it. Some people do not listen properly. They may be thinking about what they are going to say next or they may be distracted or bored. Therefore, they cannot receive the information properly and can't act on it appropriately.
Trust	■ If the receiver cannot trust the sender to tell the truth, she will not listen to the message, let alone act on it appropriately. ■ You may not listen to or believe what the other person is saying. For example, the person may have "cried wolf" in the past and is no longer regarded as being trustworthy.
Timing	■ If the message is sent too late, the receiver may be unable to act upon it in time and therefore the communication is useless.

Importance of Good Communication

Good communications is very important for a business. The manager must have good communication skills if she is to communicate effectively with all the people the business comes into contact with. This will help to avoid many problems that could harm the business.

Principle of Good Communication #1: Appropriate Language

An important principle of good communication is to use language appropriate to the receiver and to avoid jargon. This will ensure that the receiver understands the message perfectly and acts on it in the way the business wants.

Example in internal communication

It is important that the manager speaks clearly and simply when giving employees their instructions. If the employees do not understand what the manager says to them (perhaps because she uses jargon), they will not be able to do the job required of them. They will make mistakes and waste time and money for the business as a result.

Example in external communication

It is important that the marketing manager uses clear and unambiguous language when drawing up the company's advertising campaign so that customers understand the product properly and are motivated to buy it.

- For example, Microsoft's Windows Vista product ran into problems in Latvia. The word "vista" means "frumpy woman" in Latvian.

- When Disney was advertising Walt Disney World Resort, it used the phrase "roughly half the size of Rhode Island" to describe its size to American customers. Knowing that this makes little sense out of the USA, it changed it for other markets. In the UK, it changed it to "roughly the size of greater Manchester". In Japan, it changed it to "roughly the size of the subway system".

Principle of Good Communication #2: Read and Write Well

An important principle of good communication is to be able to read and write using good English.

Example in external communication

It is important that the entrepreneur can read and write well when filling in application forms for government grants and bank loans. If the entrepreneur does not give the required information or cannot get her business idea across in words, she may not get the finance she needs for her business.

Principle of Good Communication #3: Send Message in Time

An important principle of good communication is to send the message in plenty of time. If the receiver gets the message too late, she will not be able to act on it in the way the business wanted.

Example in internal communication

It is important that the secretary sends the notice and agenda for a Board of Directors meeting to each director in plenty of time so that they are able to clear their schedules and attend the meeting. Otherwise, some directors might not be able to attend and bad decisions could be taken without their advice.

Example in external communication

It is important that the production manager sends the orders for new stock to the suppliers in plenty of time. If she leaves it until the last minute to order new stock, she may find that the supplier cannot deliver when she wants and so the business will be left without any stock to sell to customers. This will result in the business losing sales and profits.

Principle of Good Communication #4: Listen Carefully

An important principle of good communication is to listen carefully to what the other person is saying. In this way, the receiver will understand the message exactly as intended.

Example in internal communication

It is important that the manager listens very carefully to what the employees' trade union says to her. If she does not listen carefully to the issues they raise, she may end up with a strike on her hands that will lead to lower sales and profits for the business.

Example in external communication

It is important that the marketing manager conducts market research and listens to what customers say. This will make sure that the business doesn't waste money bringing out products nobody wants and it may give it ideas for new products.

Principle of Good Communication #5: Be Honest

An important principle of good communication is to be trustworthy and honest in all your communications. If people cannot trust a business, they will not believe its communications and will not act on them appropriately.

Example in internal communication

It is important that the managers are honest with the employees about the reasons for any changes being brought in. This will help the employees accept the change more readily.

Example in external communication

It is important that the business communicates honestly with its consumers. It should never make false or misleading claims in its advertisements. If consumers cannot trust the business, they will shop elsewhere and the business will lose sales and profits.

Choosing a Method of Communication

When deciding on the correct method of communication to use (i.e., whether you should use a type of written or oral or visual communication and, if so, which type), you should consider the following factors:

Cost	■ Business is about making a profit so businesspeople must use a method that keeps their costs low. ■ A good example of a cheap but effective method is e-mail. ■ It allows the business to send multiple copies of the same message all over the world for the price of one local phone call. If the firm has broadband, it can send as many e-mails as it wants for a flat monthly fee.
Urgency of the Message	■ If the message is urgent and must get to the receiver immediately, the business must use the quickest method possible to get the message across. ■ The telephone is a quick method of communication. ■ The slowest method is a letter.
Need for Confidentiality	■ If the message is private and the contents are top secret, the business must use a confidential method of communication. ■ A highly confidential method is a face-to-face conversation.
Nature of the Message	■ The contents of the message can determine the best method of communication to use. ■ For example, if the message is long, very detailed and complicated, the best method to use is written communication. ■ If proof of the communication is needed, the business must use a method of communication that keeps a record. The best to use is written communication, in this case.

Legal Requirements	■ The law of the country might determine the method of communication that must be used. ■ For example, in Ireland, for an agreement to buy a house to be a legal contract, the communication of the agreement must be in writing.

Meetings

A meeting is when two or more people come together to discuss a predetermined topic.

Purpose/advantages of Meetings

1. **To give/receive information to many people at the same time.**
    All companies must have an Annual General Meeting (AGM) every year. The purpose of this meeting is for the directors to give all the shareholders (owners) information about how the company is doing and for the shareholders to ask questions of the directors. This can all be done at one meeting.

2. **To bring people together to solve problems.**
    Meeting people face to face is a great way to build up a rapport and a relationship with them. The personal nature of the communication makes it easier to reach agreement. A shop steward and a manager would meet each other to solve an industrial dispute in the factory.

3. **To make decisions**
    At a company's AGM, the shareholders meet to decide who is going to run the company, how the profits are to be shared out between them and so on. They come together to vote on each issue that has to be decided.
    eircom held an Extraordinary General Meeting (EGM) to decide whether to take over the mobile phone network, Meteor.

Essential Elements of Meetings

■ The meeting must be **well planned** in advance by the secretary. A suitable venue and all the necessary facilities (such as handouts, seating, refreshments and so on) must be organised.

■ A **notice** of and an **agenda** for the meeting must be sent out to all those concerned in plenty of time.

- A **Chairperson** and a **secretary** are needed.
- Before the meeting can begin, the Chairperson must ensure that a **quorum** is present.
- **Minutes** of the meeting must be kept.

Notice

The notice is like an invitation to people to come to the meeting. It is a written document setting out the date, time and venue of the meeting. The secretary sends out the notice of the meeting.

Agenda

An agenda is a written list of all the topics to be discussed at the meeting. The topics are put in order of importance. The first item is the most important and the last item is the least important.

The agenda always starts with the minutes of the last meeting. This means that the people at the meeting review what took place at the last meeting. It always ends with Any Other Business (AOB).

An agenda is important for the following reasons:

- To let people know what the meeting is about so that those interested will attend.
- To allow people to prepare in advance what they are going to say at the meeting on particular issues contained in the agenda.
- To ensure that all the important work is covered first and that the meeting does not get bogged down with trivial matters.

Notice and Agenda for a Club

Notice and Agenda for Finglas LTC
The Annual General Meeting of the Finglas Lawn Tennis Club will take place in the Clubhouse at 7.00pm on 1st July 2012.
The agenda is as follows:
1. Minutes of the 2011 AGM
2. Matters arising from those minutes
3. Club Chairperson's Report
4. Club Treasurer's Report
5. Club subscriptions for 2013
6. Election of new President
7. AOB
Signed
Paul Flynn
Paul Flynn
Secretary

Notice and Agenda for a Company

Notice and Agenda for Alpha Ltd.
The Annual General Meeting of Alpha Ltd. will take place in the Divan Hotel, Gardiner Street, Limerick at 3.00pm on 1st July 2012.
The agenda is as follows:
1. Minutes of the 2011 AGM
2. Matters arising from those minutes
3. Chairperson's Report
4. Auditor's Report
5. Dividend for 2012
6. Election of new directors
7. AOB
Signed
Angela Duffy
Angela Duffy
Secretary

Quorum

The quorum is the minimum number of people that must be present at the meeting before it can start.

The company or club can choose whatever number it wants for its quorum. If that minimum number of people does not show up at the meeting, the meeting cannot proceed and has to be postponed.

A quorum is important to:
- Stop decisions being taken by a few people who show up but are only a minority of those who could attend.
- Ensure that topics are fully discussed by a range of people.

Chairperson

Every meeting must have a Chairperson to start it, run it, control it and end it. The functions of the chairperson are to:

1. Make sure that a quorum is present before the meeting begins. This means that she must count the number of people who have turned up for the meeting and check that the minimum number necessary (quorum) is present. If not, she must postpone the meeting.

2. Open the meeting. If a quorum is present, the Chairperson starts the meeting and begins with the first item on the agenda and works down through it.

3. Maintain proper order at the meeting. This involves making sure that standing orders are obeyed. (Standing orders are the rules for conducting the meeting, such as raising your hand to speak and imposing a time limit on how long a person can speak for.) The Chairperson also ensures that all discussion is relevant, that everyone gets a chance to speak and that no one person dominates the meeting.

4. Call for a vote on a motion (particular topic of discussion).

5. Use her casting vote in the event that a vote is tied. This means that if the meeting is split 50:50 on a decision, the Chairperson must then vote. Whatever way she votes is obviously the winner.

6. Close the meeting when it is over and the agenda has been worked through.

Characteristics of a Good Chairperson

Impartial	A good Chairperson must be unbiased. No matter what her own views are, she must be fair to all sides and give everyone an equal chance to speak.
Tactful	The Chairperson is in charge of the meeting and must make sure that people do not talk too long. If they do so, she must

	stop them. But she should not be rude to them. She should be pleasant but firm. Unpleasantness to one speaker may make other speakers reluctant to air their views.
Speaks Clearly	The Chairperson is in charge of the meeting. It is important, therefore, that everyone present can hear her and understand her. This helps to ensure that they will obey her instructions and the meeting will run smoothly.
Knows the Rules	A good Chairperson must know all the rules for running the meeting. If any problems arise at the meeting, she will know exactly how to handle them, according to the rules.

Secretary

The secretary is responsible for all the organisation, administration and paperwork associated with the meeting.

The functions of the secretary are to:

1. Organise the venue and all the facilities and equipment needed for the meeting.
2. Send out the notice and agenda to people in plenty of time.
3. Record the minutes of the meeting. This means that he takes a summarised written record of exactly what is said at the meeting and what decisions are made.
4. Deal with all the correspondence (writing and receiving letters and paperwork) arising from the meeting.
5. Advise and assist the Chairperson if she is having any difficulties at the meeting.

Characteristics of a Good Secretary

Good Organiser	A good secretary must get all his jobs done on time. He must be organised to get the venue booked in time so that it is available for the date of the meeting. He must send out the notice and agenda in plenty of time so that people will have time to organise themselves to come to the meeting.
Good Writer	The secretary has a lot of writing to do before (*notice and agenda*), during (*minutes*) and after (*letters*) the meeting. It is important that he can write clearly so that everyone can understand the notice, agenda and minutes properly.

Good Summariser	The secretary must prepare a written summary of each meeting, called the minutes. It is important, therefore, that he is able to take down the most important points raised at the meeting and prepare a summary that is good enough to allow someone who was not actually at the meeting to understand what happened at it.

Minutes

The secretary writes up the minutes of each meeting. Minutes are a summarised written record of what happened at the meeting – who was there, who spoke, what they said, what decisions were made and so on.

They are *not* a word-for-word transcript of every single word that was spoken at the meeting. They are a summary of the meeting. They must be complete and precise enough so that anyone who was not at the meeting could read the minutes and understand exactly what occurred.

Notice and Agenda for a Club

Notice and Agenda for Finglas LTC
The Annual General Meeting of the Finglas Lawn Tennis Club will take place in the Clubhouse at 7.00pm on 1st July 2012.

The agenda is as follows:
1.   Minutes of the 2011 AGM

2.   Matters arising from those minutes
3.   Club Chairperson's Report

4.   Club Treasurer's Report |

Minutes For a Club

Minutes for Finglas LTC
The Annual General Meeting of the Finglas Lawn Tennis Club took place in the Clubhouse at 7.00pm on 1st July 2012.

The minutes are as follows:
1.   The minutes of the 2011 AGM were read and approved.
2.   There were no matters arising from the minutes.
3.   The Chairperson addressed the meeting. She said that it had been a very successful year for the club in terms of new members and trophies won.
4.   The Treasurer addressed the meeting and stated that the club's finances were in a healthy position and the club could now afford to take out a loan for the clubhouse extension. |

109

5. Club subscriptions for 2013	5. The meeting voted by 12 votes to 3 that the annual subscription for 2013 be increased to €400 per annum.
6. Election of new President	6. Marian Cassidy beat Tom Patterson by 10 votes to 5 and was elected Club President for 2013.
7. AOB	7. As there was no AOB, the Chairperson closed the meeting at 8.15pm.
Signed *Paul Flynn* Paul Flynn Secretary	Signed *Paul Flynn* Paul Flynn Secretary

Notice & Agenda for a Company

Minutes for a Company

Notice and Agenda for Alpha Ltd.

The Annual General Meeting of Alpha Ltd. will take place in the Divan Hotel, Gardiner Street, Limerick at 3.00pm on 1st July 2012.

The agenda is as follows:
1.   Minutes of the 2011 AGM
2.   Matters arising from those minutes
3.   Chairperson's Report

4.   Auditor's Report

5.   Dividend for 2012

6.   Election of new directors

Minutes for Alpha Ltd.

The Annual General Meeting of Alpha Ltd. took place in the Divan Hotel, Gardiner Street, Limerick at 3.00pm on 1st July 2012.

The minutes are as follows:
1.   The minutes of the 2011 AGM were read and approved.
2.   There were no matters arising from the minutes.
3.   The Chairperson addressed the meeting stating that profits were lower than last year due to the huge increase in oil prices in the world economy.
4.   The auditor stated that the company kept proper books and that the accounts gave a true and fair view of the company's financial position.
5.   The meeting decided that the dividend for the financial year 2012 would be €0.07 per share.
6.   Kathleen Brady and Michael Foley were elected to the Board of Directors unopposed.

7. AOB	7. As there was no AOB, the Chairperson closed the meeting at 4.15pm
Signed *Angela Duffy* Angela Duffy Secretary	Signed *Angela Duffy* Angela Duffy Secretary

Memos

Memos (short for memorandum) are written documents used for internal communication (from manager to employee, for example). They are small notes.

MEMORANDUM

To: Date:
From: Subject:

_____

_____

Signed

2004 Higher Level – Section 1 (10 marks)

4.   Draft a memorandum (memo) using an appropriate format, to all department managers suggesting two topics for an upcoming management-training day.

MEMORANDUM

To: All Department Managers   **Date:** 12th June 2012
From: Human Resource Manager   **Subject:** Management Training Day

The upcoming management training day will take place at 3.00pm on 4th July 2012 in the Boardroom. The topics to be covered are leading skills and motivating skills.

SIGNED: *Cathal Doyle*
                Cathal Doyle
                Human Resources Manager

Business Letters

Sender's Business Name
and Address

Date

Name,
Title and
Address of receiver

Re: _____

Dear **[Sir/Madam if you don't know their name]**
      [Mr. / Ms. "X" if you do]

Paragraph 1   I am writing to you to…

Paragraph 2   Main body of the letter. Give all the facts.

Paragraph 3   Conclusions. State what you would like to happen now.

Yours faithfully/sincerely

Signature _____

NAME IN CAPITALS
TITLE IN CAPITALS

1999 Higher Level – Section 3 – Question 4

(a) Using a fictitious name and address, draft a letter to the Human Resource Manager of a business, setting out four characteristics of managers to be looked for when interviewing candidates for management positions.   (20 marks)

Alpha Management Consultants Ltd.
88 Leeson Street, Dublin 22

12th June 2012

Human Resource Manager
Finnie Ltd.
Glenageary
Co. Dublin

RE: Characteristics of Managers

Dear Sir/Madam

I am writing to you to set out four characteristics of a manager to be looked for when interviewing candidates for management positions.

These are as follows:

1. **DECISIVENESS**
   Good managers can analyse a situation and quickly come up with an effective solution to deal with it. They can quickly and firmly resolve problems.

2. **INITIATIVE**
   Good managers do not need to be told what to do to. They are able to start things. They can think up new ideas and find solutions to problems themselves.

3. **HARDWORKING**
   Good managers put the effort and time into their job. They are not strictly "9 to 5" people. If a problem has to be dealt with, they stay behind and work until it is solved.

4. **CHARISMATIC**
   Good managers have charisma, the ability to charm people. This makes people respect and like them. Employees are more likely to do what a charismatic manager wants.

I hope this information proves useful to you.

Yours sincerely

Angela Dunne

ANGELA DUNNE
Management Consultant

Reports

A report is a written document in which one person sets out the findings of her investigation into a certain issue. She also makes recommendations to solve the issue.

Objectives of a Report

1.	To give information to people about a specific topic	Your school report tells your parents how you are doing in each of your subjects.
2.	To investigate an incident (i.e., to find out how and why it happened)	Example: The 9/11 Commission Report was established by the US government to investigate how the terrosist attacks of 11 September 2001 happened.
3.	To come up with solutions to a particular problem	Example: The Bacon Report was commissioned by the Irish government to come up with ideas to stop house prices rising so rapidly.
4.	To investigate the impact of decisions	Example: An Environmental Impact Statement assesses the impact on the environment of specific actions.
5.	To convince the reader to take a particular course of action	Example: Publicans had economic reports drawn up to show that their businesses would suffer and jobs would be lost if the smoking ban was introduced in Ireland. They used these reports to try to convince people that the smoking ban was a bad idea.

Layout of a Report

1.	**Title**	The title sets out the objective of the report, together with the name of the person who commissioned the report and the name of the person who wrote the report.
2.	**Table of contents**	This is a list of each section of the report and the page number where it can be found.
3.	**Executive summary**	The summary briefly points out the major findings and conclusions of the report.
4.	**Terms of reference**	The terms of reference set out the issues that the report writer was asked to investigate and the instructions given to her on how to carry out her investigation.
5.	**Findings**	This section sets out the basic facts that were discovered by the report writer.

6. Conclusions and recommendations	The report writer sets out the reasons for the event and what action she thinks should now be taken.
7. Appendices	This contains extra, more detailed information such as statistics that readers can refer to if they wish.
8. Bibliography	This sets out all the sources of information used by the report writer.

2002 Higher Level – Section 3 – Question 4

(a) Draft a report to the Managing Director of a limited company explaining the four main barriers to effective communications in the business.
State relevant assumptions where necessary.   (20 marks)

REPORT

1. **Title**
Four Main Barriers to Communication in Alpha Ltd.

2. **Table of Contents**
Page 1   Report

3. **Executive Summary**
The four main barriers to effective communication in the company are the use of jargon, prejudice, information overload and poor listening skills.

4. **Terms of reference**
To explain the four main barriers to effective communications in the business.

5. **Findings**
The main barriers to effective communication in the business are as follows:

(A) **Jargon.** This is a technical language, specific to certain technical jobs in the business that only such technical people understand. Because the receiver doesn't understand the jargon, she is not able to carry out the instruction and the communication fails. For example, when the accountant asks the factory supervisor for her P&L, she doesn't understand her.

(B) **Prejudice.** Personal feelings about and bias against other people affect how we interpret information. Because we are prejudiced against the person, we don't interpret properly what they are saying to us. For example, the factory supervisor ignored the safety complaints of temporary workers because she knows they'll soon be leaving. Two serious accidents could have been avoided if she hadn't been so prejudiced.

(C) **Information Overload.** Too much information in a communication can turn people off and they actually ignore the communication because they cannot cope with any more information. Therefore, it isn't effectively received and the correct action isn't taken. For example, factory operatives are receiving so many memos from the factory supervisor that they actually bin them, without reading them.

(D) **Poor Listening Skills.** Sometimes, people in the company do not listen properly to the information being communicated to them. They may be bored or distracted or thinking about what they're going to say. If they don't receive the communication, they cannot take the correct action. For example, the factory supervisor is so defensive when listening to complaints that she doesn't actually get to the root of the problem. She is all the time preparing a smart put-down for the employee.

6. **Conclusions and Recommendations**

   Better communication can be achieved by avoiding jargon, prejudice and information overload, and by improving listening skills.

7. **Appendices**

8. **Bibliography**

ICT

Electronic Data Interchange (EDI)

This is a system that electronically links the computers of two different companies. The computers are then programmed to send standard documents (such as orders and invoices) directly from one to the other without the need for any further human involvement.

For example, when Marks and Spencer's stock of shirts falls to a certain level, its computer is programmed to automatically send an order to the shirt manufacturer's computer for more shirts.

Advantages of EDI

1. There is no need for paper documents because all the communication is sent and stored electronically. Thus EDI helps a business to save money on stationery and storage of documents. These savings increase the business's profits.

2. The business no longer needs employees to process stock orders because the computer does all this work. It can make these employees redundant and hence reduce its wages bill. Lower wage bills mean higher profits for the business.

3. Orders are automatically sent by the business's computer. There is no time delay for posting. The supplier receives the order instantly. The supplier can start getting the business's order ready as soon as it is received. Therefore, the business will receive new stock faster, so there is less chance of it running out of stock. In this way, EDI helps a business to manage its stock properly so that it never runs out.

Videoconferencing

This is a meeting held between people who are in different locations. The participants sit in front of a camera. Live pictures and sound of each person are sent via the telephone line – such as an ISDN (integrated services digital network) or broadband line – to screens in all the other locations so that all participants can see and hear each other as if they were in the same room.

Advantages of Videoconferencing

1. Managers do not have to travel to meetings. This saves them a lot of time. They can devote this time to other more important tasks to make the business a success.

2. The business saves money. It does not have to pay for all the expenses associated with managers travelling for meetings. This lowers the business's costs and increases its profits.

Internet – World Wide Web (WWW)

The World Wide Web is a vast collection of information on millions of topics that you can access on your computer once you are connected to the Internet. Many businesses have their own websites on the Web. The website displays information about the business and its products (for example, www.coca-cola.com).

Advantages of the Web

1. It enables businesses to advertise their products on their website, which people all over the world can see. This leads to a better-known brand name and increased sales for the business.

2. Consumers all over the world can order products from the business's website. This saves the business a lot of money because it doesn't have to open shops all over the world or employ sales staff. This is called e-commerce.

3. It helps managers to make decisions. If they need information about a particular problem, they can download the information they need from the Internet in seconds. Quick, easy information about a problem helps them to make a quick and easy decision.

E-mail

E-mail allows you to send a typed message (and other information such as pictures, sounds, movies and so on) directly from your computer to another via the Internet. Each user has a unique e-mail address. If you want to send an e-mail to someone, you type the message on your computer and send it to the receiver's e-mail address where it is stored in a mailbox. They can then open the mail on their computer at any time.

Advantages of E-mail

1. It saves money for a business on postage and stationery. The message is typed on the computer and sent via the computer. The business does not waste money on paper. With broadband, a business can send as many e-mails as it wants for one fee.
2. It is a quick form of communication. Messages can be sent and received instantly at the other end. Therefore, the business can get an instant reply. This saves a lot of time.

Problems with E-mail

1. E-mail can be used only if the other person has a computer.
2. Sending information over the Internet is not always secure. People can hack in to your computer or you may send it to the wrong address.
3. Businesses often receive malicious e-mails containing viruses which, when opened, can destroy the business's computer system.

Data Protection Act 1988

1. This law gives people rights regarding the information held about them on other people's *computers*.
   If someone has information about you on their computer, you are called a **data subject** and you have the right to:

(a) Get a copy of data that is kept about you on a computer

You have the right to be given a copy, clearly explained, of any information kept on computer about you. All you have to do is make a written request. For example, you could ask your doctor, your bank, your employer or the government for a copy of your computer file.

(b) Have errors corrected or deleted

You can write to the person who keeps information about you on computer and tell them to correct any mistakes in your file or delete any information about you that they have no good reason to keep or delete information they obtained about you unfairly.

(c) Complain to the Data Protection Commissioner

If someone refuses to give you a copy of your computer file or refuses to correct or delete information on it, you can complain to the Data Protection Commissioner. He will investigate the matter for you. He has legal powers to force them to correct or delete your information from their computer.

(d) Compensation if you have suffered as a result of incorrect information

If you suffer damage through the mishandling of information about you on computer, then you may be entitled to claim compensation through the courts.

2. People who keep information on computers about others are called data controllers. Data controllers must:

(a) Obtain personal information fairly and openly

When the data controller is asking you for your information, she must identify herself, tell you what she wants the information for and tell you who will get to see your information.

(b) Keep the information safe and secure

The data controller must ensure that only authorised people get to see your information, that the computer system is password protected, that callers to the office cannot see the information on the computer screens and that all printouts are disposed of carefully.

(c) Delete the information once they no longer need it

If there is no good reason for keeping someone's information on the computer, it should be deleted. Information should never be kept "just in case" a use can be found for it in the future.

(d) Give a copy of her personal data to a person who asks for it

The data controller must give the individual a copy of the information requested within 40 days of receiving the request. The information must be clearly presented (for example, any codes must be explained). The data controller can charge the individual a fee, but it can't be more than €6.35.

Data Protection Commissioner

3. This law set up the office of the Data Protection Commissioner whose functions are to:

    (a) Keep a register of data controllers

    Certain organisations must register with the Data Protection Commissioner. These include public bodies, financial institutions, insurance companies, direct marketing businesses, businesses that provide credit references, debt collectors and anyone keeping personal information about race, political opinions, religion, health, sexual life or criminal convictions.

    Anyone can call to see the register at the offices of the Data Protection Commissioner.

    (b) Force data controllers to correct or delete personal data

    The Data Protection Commissioner does this by giving the data controller a written **enforcement notice**. It is an offence not to comply with the enforcement notice.

    (c) Force data controllers to give him any information he needs to carry out his duties

    The Data Protection Commissioner does this by giving the data controller a written **information notice**. It is an offence not to comply with the information notice.

    (d) Investigate complaints made by the public

    The Data Protection Commissioner must investigate any complaints he receives from individuals who feel that personal information about them is not being treated according to the rules of the act. He can force the data controller to give him any information he needs to carry out his investigation by giving the data controller an information notice. His staff can enter the data controller's premises and inspect the computer equipment, force the data controller to help them get any information they want and copy any information. The Data Protection Commissioner considers all the evidence and then makes a decision on the matter and writes to the individual to let her know his decision.

For example, the Data Protection Commissioner received the following complaint:

A mother took part in the Women's Mini Marathon in June 2002 with her 14 year old daughter. Her daughter subsequently received a letter in July 2002 from a UK company offering her photos of herself taken on the day of the marathon.

The mother complained that she had not given permission to the organisers of the mini marathon to supply her daughter's name, address and race number to another company or to take photos of her daughter.

When the Data Protection Commissioner contacted the organisers of the mini marathon, they admitted that they had given the UK company access to their computer records of the runners. The Data Protection Commissioner ruled that the mini marathon organisers had broken the Data Protection Act, 1988 because the entry form did not tell the women that their details would be used for any purpose other than registering for the marathon. The organisers agreed to change their entry form for the 2003 race.

EVALUATION OF THE DATA PROTECTION ACT, 1988

This act does a good job of protecting data subjects because:

1. They are entitled to see all the information held about them on computer and get any errors deleted or corrected. This means that they will not suffer as a result of inaccurate information thereafter.
2. If they do lose out as a result of any inaccurate information, this law entitles them to financial compensation for the loss suffered.
3. There is a government-backed official, the Data Protection Commissioner, who will fight for their rights of access to their files, and get them corrected or deleted. If not, he will take the offender to court.

Management Skills in Different Situations

	Leading	Motivating	Communicating
Home Parents decide to convert attic into a study for you	Democratic parents will involve you in the decisions about the study – ask you what is needed, how you would like it decorated and so on.	Parents will incentivise and energise the builders by offering extra money if the study is ready before you go into 6th Year.	Parents must discuss clearly with the builder exactly what they want. Regular meetings will be held to discuss progress on the construction work.
Community You set up a Tidy Towns Committee to clean up your area	You must delegate work to the volunteers and appoint a leader for each road to oversee the tidy up of that road.	You must energise and incentivise the volunteers by recognising their hard work with praise.	You must explain clearly to each volunteer exactly what she must do so that the whole area is ready for the judges' inspection.
School A teacher sets up a drama class after school	The teacher will delegate different jobs to different students involved with the play, such as lighting, stage design and so on.	The teacher must incentivise the principal into allowing the drama class by satisfying her needs. Extra-curricular activities will make it a better school and satisfy the principal's esteem needs.	The teacher must communicate with each student what he expects them to do so that the play runs smoothly with no hitches.
Public Life The Minister for Finance introduced the Special Savings Incentive Scheme in 2001 to help Ireland's economy	The minister delegated the job of implementing the scheme to his civil servants.	The minister energised and incentivised the public into saving harder by offering a 25% bonus on all money saved.	The minister informed the public of the scheme through advertising to ensure that everyone knew about it.

Business Start Up	The entrepreneur must delegate various jobs to different managers and employees to make sure that everything gets done.	The entrepreneur must incentivise investors to provide the capital needed by promising a good return on investment.	The entrepreneur must inform the public that her product is available for sale by advertising.

Ordinary Level Questions

EXAM SECTION 1 (25%) – SHORT ANSWER QUESTIONS [10 marks each]

1. Distinguish between "internal" and "external" communications.

2. List four methods of internal communication.

3. List four methods of external communication.

4. List four methods of oral communication.

5. List four methods of visual communication.

6. Draw a bar chart using the following information:

Cases dealt with by the Labour Relations Commission					
Year	2005	2006	2007	2008	2009
Number of Cases	2,000	2,500	3,000	4,000	3,500

7. Draw a bar chart using the following information:

Value of Irish Exports					
Country	UK	US	Belgium	China	Others
Value of exports in €'m	18	12	10	4	6

8. Draw a pie chart to illustrate the following information:

Costs of a Business				
Cost	Wages	Electricity	Rent	Advertising
€'000	200	100	50	50

9. Draw a pictogram to illustrate the following information:

New Houses Built in Ireland				
County	Dublin	Meath	Kildare	Wicklow
Number of houses built	45,000	35,000	30,000	15,000

10. Draw a line graph to illustrate the following information:

Inflation in Ireland					
Year	2005	2006	2007	2008	2009
%	5	6	4	2	8

11. Draw a line graph to illustrate the following information:

Number of students sitting the Leaving Certificate					
Year	2005	2006	2007	2008	2008
Number of Students	55,000	50,000	45,000	60,000	65,000

12. Column 1 is a list of business terms. Column 2 is a list of possible explanations for these terms. Match the two lists by placing the letter of the correct explanation under the relevant number below. One explanation has no match.

Column 1	Column 2: Explanations
1. Poor Listening Skills	a) Message does not get through because the receiver cannot believe the sender
2. Prejudice	b) Technical language, only understood by people in a specific profession
3. Jargon	c) Message is made unclear because it is far too long
4. Timing	d) Receiver is biased against the sender and so doesn't take the message in properly
5. Trust	e) Message does not get through because the receiver is not listening
6. Information Overload	f) The law states that the message must be sent in a certain way
	g) Message is sent too late to be effective

1	2	3	4	5	6
E	D	B	G	A	C

13. Indicate whether each of the following (A, B, C, D and E) is true or false.

	Sentence	True or False
A	It is best to use oral communication for a very complicated and difficult message.	False
B	Businesses should use the quickest method of communication possible in all situations.	True
C	The law of Ireland can sometimes dictate how a business must communicate.	True
D	A face-to-face conversation is a confidential method of communication.	True
E	If proof of communication is needed, it is best to use a written method.	True

14. What do the following letters stand for?   AGM   AOB   EGM

15. Define "quorum".

16. With regard to meetings, outline two characteristics of a good chairperson.

17. With regard to meetings, outline two characteristics of a good secretary.

18. Distinguish between "agenda" and "minutes" at meetings.

19. Draft a memorandum (memo) using an appropriate format, from Ciara Doyle, Managing Director, to all directors listing three methods of written communications used in the business. Use today's date.

20. Draft a memorandum (memo) using an appropriate format from Alan Small, Secretary, to all managers listing three barriers to communications found in the company. Use today's date.

21. What do the following letters stand for?   EDI   WWW   ICT

22. Outline two advantages of the Internet for business.

EXAM SECTION 2 (75%) – LONG QUESTIONS

1. Describe three barriers to effective communications.   (15 marks)

2. Outline three factors to be considered when deciding the best method of communication to use.   (15 marks)

3. Draft a notice and agenda for a private limited company.
You may use fictitious dates and names but the agenda must contain
at least five items.   (25 marks)

4. Describe the role of the Chairperson at meetings.   (15 marks)

5. Describe the role of the secretary at meetings.   (15 marks)

6. You are the secretary of the Fareham Tennis Club, which held
its AGM last night. Draft the minutes of the meeting.   (25 marks)

7. Outline three reasons why a business would ask for a report to be drawn up.   (15 marks)

8. Explain the term "e-mail". Give two advantages of e-mail as a method of communication.   (15 marks)

9. Under the Data Protection Act, 1988, explain three rights that people have over information held about them on computer.   (15 marks)

10. Under the Data Protection Act, 1988, explain three functions of the Data Protection Commissioner.   (15 marks)

Higher Level Questions

EXAM SECTION 1 (20%) – SHORT ANSWER QUESTIONS [10 marks each]

1. Define "communications".

2. Illustrate your understanding of the term "external communications".

3. The following table shows three types of communication and four qualities. For each quality, tick (✔) the type of communication that is *most* likely to match that function.

	Written	Oral	Visual
It is personal and good for reaching agreement		✔	
Good for showing body language		✔	
Good for presenting statistical information			✔
Provides a permanent record	✔		

4. Explain two reasons why businesses use meetings as a method of communications.

5. What is a quorum? Explain its use in business.

6. Column 1 is a list of business terms. Column 2 is a list of possible explanations for these terms. Match the two lists by placing the letter of the correct explanation under the relevant number below. One explanation has no match.

Column 1	Column 2: Explanations
1. Agenda	a) Minimum number of people that must be present at a meeting before it can begin *(Quorum)*
2. Minutes	
3. Chairperson	b) Outlines the date, time and venue for an upcoming meeting
4. Secretary	c) Deals with all the correspondence arising from meetings
5. Notice	d) Summary of business transacted at a meeting
	e) Maintains proper order at a meeting
	f) List of topics to be discussed at an upcoming meeting

1	2	3	4	5
F	D	E	C	B

7. Draft a memorandum (memo) using an appropriate format to all department managers listing two advantages of written communications.

8. Draft a memorandum (memo) using an appropriate format to all directors listing two factors to be considered when deciding which method of communication to use.

9. What is a report? Explain its use in business.

10. Complete this sentence: Video-conferencing can help a business to…

11. What do the following letters stand for?   AOB   EGM   ISDN   ICT   EDI

EXAM SECTION 2 (20%) – APPLIED BUSINESS QUESTION – 80 MARKS

ABQ1

Tiny Tots Ltd.

Gayle Jordan set up her crèche business, Tiny Tots Ltd., ten years ago after graduating top of her class from childcare college. She borrowed money from a local bank and got a generous grant from the government, which helped her to buy a crèche and equip it with the very best childcare facilities. Gayle advertised by meeting parents outside supermarkets and schools and talking to them directly. While the reaction was always positive, Gayle was surprised how few follow up phone calls she received.

Gayle keeps all the children's personal details on computer. One day, Gayle found a parent using her computer to print the children's addresses to invite them to a child's party. Gayle has been approached by a children's clothing company asking for personal details of her children for marketing purposes. They have offered to sponsor her crèche in return.

The crèche has become extremely busy in recent years. Employees have been complaining about the stressful conditions, but Gayle ignored them telling them that they didn't know what stress was. Some parents have complained that their children are not getting the individual attention that Gayle promised them. Others complained that they had to take time off work because they did not get enough warning that Gayle was closing the crèche for two weeks holiday.

(A)   Evaluate, from the above information, the effectiveness of Gayle's reliance on oral communications when advertising her business to parents.   (25 marks)

(B)   Outline Gayle's obligations under the Data Protection Act, 1988.   (25 marks)

(C)   Evaluate the importance of good communications for Gayle's business. Support your answer with reference to the above text.   (30 marks)

ABQ2

> **Dalton Ltd.**
>
> Jane Dalton set up her own cake-making business, Dalton Ltd., six years ago. The business has proved a great success and Jane has been rushed off her feet, designing and baking cakes for her customers. Jane has hired a number of other bakers and two office staff to cope with the demand.
>
> However, there have been some customer complaints recently. One lady remarked that Jane's designs were too conventional. Others have complained about mistakes and delays with their orders. Jane blames his supplier for the delays. Others have raised the issue of lengthy queues in the shop.
>
> To address these issues, Jane wrote a seven-page memo to each employee outlining the changes that were needed. In it, she invited the staff to make suggestions to improve the business. She wrote, "it behoves us all to ameliorate our endeavours". A week later, she had not received one suggestion. Some employees fear being victimised by Jane because she does not respond well to criticism.

(A)   Draft a short report outlining the main barriers to communications
         in Dalton Ltd.   (30 marks)

(B)   You are a communications consultant. Write a letter describing
         the benefits to Jane's business of using a meeting as method of internal
         communication. Support your answer with reference to the above text.   (25 marks)

(C)   Analyse the contribution to the business that would result
         from introducing Information and Communications Technology [ICT].   (25 marks)

EXAM SECTION 3 (60%) – LONG QUESTIONS

1. Illustrate the importance of written communications in business.   (10 marks)

2. Describe four barriers to effective communications.
    Analyse how each one may be overcome.   (25 marks)

3. Draft an agenda and minutes for the AGM of a football club.   (25 marks)

4. Draft a report to the managing director of a business,
    explaining four factors to be considered when deciding on
    a method of communication.   (20 marks)

5. Evaluate the benefits of ICT for a business.
    Illustrate your answer with examples.   (25 marks)

6. You are a communications consultant. Draft a letter to client of yours,
    explaining her rights as a data subject under the Data Protection Act, 1988. (20 marks)

7. Evaluate the role of the Data Protection Commissioner.   (20 marks)

8. Illustrate the importance of management skills in the community.   (20 marks)

CHAPTER 8

Management Activities

In the last two chapters, we looked at the skills a manager must have. He must be able to lead, motivate and communicate with his employees.

This chapter looks at what a manager actually *does* every day. Most managers don't actually work "on the factory floor". For example, your school principal probably doesn't teach any classes. So, what does he do all day?

A manager carries out three basic jobs, which are called the management activities: **planning**, **organising** and **controlling**.

Management Activity of Planning

The management activity of planning is where the manager:

- Sets goals (objectives) for the business to achieve in the future.
- Comes up with business strategies to achieve those objectives.

Examples:

OBJECTIVE	STRATEGY
600 points in the Leaving Cert	Study hard
Increase sales by 10% in 2012	Advertise more; Reduce price

Steps Involved in Planning

Step 1 SWOT Analysis

Before the manager actually sets objectives for the business, he must first analyse the situation facing the business by conducting a SWOT analysis.

He must critically examine the business itself and the competitive environment it faces.

	DEFINITION	EXAMPLES
Strengths	Something the business owns or does well that gives it a competitive advantage	■ Excellent staff ■ Up-to-date machines
Weaknesses	Something the business does badly or is lacking altogether that puts it at a competitive disadvantage	■ Not enough money ■ Out-of-date machines
Opportunities	Something in the outside world that the business can avail of to make money or benefit from	■ New countries join EU (chance to sell more)
Threats	Something in the outside world that can prevent the business from succeeding	■ Competition from new countries joining EU

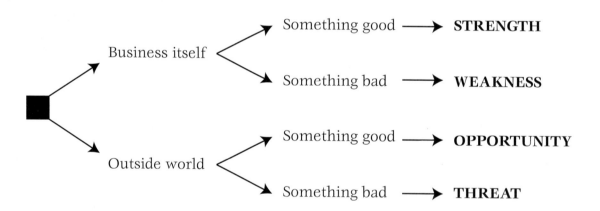

Example

You are the managing director of a company. You analyse the company and identify the following issues:

	S/W/O/T?
1. The company has no money left in its bank account.	X̶ W
2. Most of the equipment in the factory is old and needs to be replaced.	W
3. The business is facing increased competition from South American companies.	T
4. The EU is planning to admit more countries.	O

5. The government provides grants to help businesses to export.	O
6. The company has a famous brand name.	S
7. The company does not have money to spend on research and development.	W
8. The government is planning to reduce the rate of Value Added Tax.	O
9. The company is run by excellent managers.	S
10. The managers and employees of the company have a bad relationship.	W

Step 2 Set Objectives

The business should use the results of the SWOT analysis to help it set its objectives. Objectives are the goals that the business wants to achieve.

For example, when Aer Lingus did its SWOT analysis a few years ago, a major weakness was that its costs were too high and it was losing money. A major threat was competition from Ryanair. Aer Lingus then set itself the objective of cutting costs and becoming a low fares airline.

Step 3 Devise Strategies

Now that the business knows the objectives it is aiming to achieve, the next step is to come up with strategies to achieve these goals.

Aer Lingus came up with the strategy of making 2,000 employees redundant in order to achieve the goal of cutting costs.

There are three basic strategies that any business can use to be successful:

1. **Low Cost Leadership Strategy**

    The business achieves its goal of being successful by keeping its costs as low as possible so that it can sell its products as cheaply as possible. Low prices help the business to attract price-conscious consumers who like a bargain. Thus the business's sales and profits increase.

    Many businesses use this strategy. Among the most famous are Ryanair and Lidl.

2. **Differentiation Strategy**

    The business achieves its goal of being successful by making its products so different that they stand out from the competition. Because customers appreciate this difference, they are willing to pay more for the business's products. Thus the business increases revenue and profits.

A common way to make consumers believe that a business's products are different from the competition is to use a brand name. Many people will pay more for a brand name product. For example, a chain store might sell a jumper for €20 but a Ralph Lauren jumper might cost €200.

3.   **Niche Strategy**

The business achieves its goal of being successful by spotting a group of customers with certain specific needs (a niche market) and making a product that it knows these customers will love. These customers then flock to the business and its sales and profits increase.

Businesses that follow this strategy include many who target the "luxury niche", such as Ferrari. Ferrari does not make small city cars or family cars. It makes very expensive, high speed and high performance cars that only a certain number of people are interested in. But this niche is willing to pay high prices for the ultimate status symbol car.

Step 4 Implement the plan

The manager must now put the plan into action. He must break the plan down into manageable jobs and give each person in the business a job to do. It is important that he communicates the plan to all the employees in the organisation. This lets them know what they must do in order to achieve the business's objectives. It also ensures that the employees back the plan and try to make it work.

Aer Lingus implemented its plans by asking employees to volunteer for redundancy.

Types of Planning

1.   **Manpower Planning**

Manpower planning involves setting the goal of making sure that the business has enough workers with the right skills to do all the jobs needed. A manager must devise an appropriate recruitment or redundancy strategy to achieve this goal. Manpower planning involves three steps:

Step 1   Forecast Future Demand

The Human Resources manager must estimate how many employees and what skills the business will need in the future.

Step 2 **Calculate Existing Supply**

The Human Resources manager must conduct an audit of the existing employees who work in the business (including numbers, age and skills) to see how many workers the business has.

Step 3 If demand exceeds supply (i.e., if the business needs more employees than it has), the strategy is to recruit more employees.

If supply exceeds demand (i.e., the business has too many workers), the strategy is to make some of the existing employees redundant.

Evaluation: This type of planning contributes a lot to the success of a business by ensuring that it avoids the problem of having too few workers. Too few workers might result in products not getting made on time, leading to unhappy customers and lower sales.

2. Cash Flow Forecasting

A cash flow forecast is where the manager plans out the money the business expects to receive and spend in the future. The objective is to make sure that the business will have enough money in the future. If it looks like the business will not have enough, the strategy will be to try to increase the money coming in and/or cut down on spending.

Example of a Cash Flow Forecast

Cash Flow Forecast for Sample Ltd.			
	June 2012	**July 2012**	**August 2012**
Receipts (A)	500	400	800
Payments (B)	450	300	1,000
Net Cash (A – B)	50	100	(200)

Evaluation: This type of planning contributes a lot to the success of a business by ensuring that it can spot in advance the months in the future when there will not be enough money coming in to pay all the bills This allows the business to take corrective action *now* to prevent this (e.g., by making cutbacks or organising a bank overdraft to cover the bad months).

3. Mission

The mission is the overall fundamental objective of the business. It sets out the reasons for the existence of the business. Many businesses draw up a mission statement. This is a written document setting out:

(a) What the business does *now*

(b) What it plans to do in the *future*

(c) The business's values and beliefs.

For example, the mission statement of Boots Chemists states that it **"aims to be the place for health and beauty customers"**.

The mission statement of Tommy Hilfiger states that it **"is dedicated to living the spirit of the American dream"**.

4. Strategic Plan

A strategic plan is a *major* plan for the entire business. It is written by the senior managers in the business. They take the business's mission and break it up into major plans of action (strategic plans) that must be achieved if the business is to realise its mission. While the business will strive to achieve its mission over its lifetime, strategic plans are to be achieved within five years.

Example for Airline

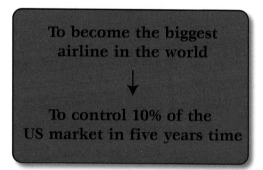

5. Tactical Plan

A tactical plan is a *short-term* plan for one section of the business. It is written by the middle managers in the business. They take the business's strategic plans and break them up into smaller plans of action (tactical plans) that must be achieved if the business is to achieve its strategic plans. Tactical plans are to be achieved usually within one year.

Example for Airline

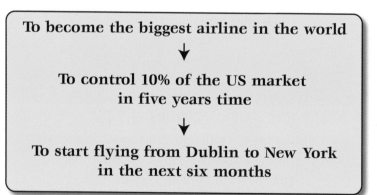

Advantages of Planning

1. Planning forces managers to think about the future

When planning, the manager sits down and tries to anticipate problems that may be facing the business in the future. This enables him to take the necessary steps now to deal with those future problems.

For example, a manager prepares a manpower plan to see how many workers the business will need in the future. If the manager does his manpower plan now for next year and realises that the business won't have enough workers next year, he can take steps to avoid this by starting a recruitment drive now.

2. Planning identifies the business's weaknesses

When the business conducts its SWOT analysis, the second stage is to identify the business's weaknesses. In this way, a business will find out what it does badly or the things that it is lacking in and then can take steps to eliminate these.

For example, when a manager prepares the business's cash flow forecast, he will identify over-spending (e.g., excessive heating bills) and take steps to eliminate it for good (energy conservation programme).

3. A business plan is essential in order to raise capital

When seeking to raise finance, a business must prove that it is capable of paying back the loan.

A business plan (*see Chapter 15*) is used to convince the investor that the business idea is a sound one and is likely to be successful. Good planning persuades investors to provide the business with capital.

4. Plans motivate employees and managers

Plans set out goals for the employees and managers to achieve within a given time period. Everyone in the business has a target to achieve. When they reach this target, they will be rewarded. This motivates them to work hard.

Management Activity of Organising

Once the manager has come up with plans for the business, he must then get the business structured in the best possible way to achieve the goals he set. The structuring of the business is called organising.

In the same way that a Leaving Cert student organises her bedroom to study (tidy room, desk beside the window, lamp on the desk and so on), a business manager must arrange the factory, shop or office in the most logical way to achieve the business's goals.

To cover all the work in time for the exam, a student breaks her Leaving Cert study into subjects to be studied each night (study timetable). In the same way, to get all the work done in a business, the manager will split the business up into different departments and make someone responsible for each department (organisation structure).

In other words, both need to get organised to achieve the goals they set out when planning for their future.

- ■ Organising involves arranging all the resources (employees, machines and money) of the business into the most suitable form to achieve its objectives. This means drawing up an organisation structure.

- ■ An organisation structure involves splitting all the work to be done in the business into departments and appointing people to be in charge of these departments to run them and make sure that each department achieves its objectives. The main organisation structures are functional, product, geographic and matrix.

Functional Organisational Structure

This involves splitting the business up into different jobs or functions. A person is put in charge of each functional department. He is responsible for ensuring that the department achieves its objectives.

ADVANTAGES	DISADVANTAGES
1. **Specialisation** Each department concentrates on the same job and so becomes expert at it.	1. **Isolation** People in each department may know and care little about what goes on in other departments.
2. **Accountability** The director of each department is responsible for everything that goes on in it.	2. **Co-ordination** It can be difficult to get all the departments to pull together in the same direction.
3. **Clarity** Everyone knows who reports to whom and who is responsible for what jobs.	

Line Organisation

Line departments are those that are directly responsible for making and selling the business's products, such as Production, Marketing and so on. Every person in the business is connected to another by a line. The line shows the chain of command in the business. People above you in the chart have authority over you. You have authority over people below you in the chart. You have no authority over people on the same level as you. The line also shows the official channel of communication in the business.

Staff Organisation

This consists of all the employees in the business who provide expert advice to the line departments. Examples of staff departments include the Information Technology department and the Legal department. While they don't directly make and sell the business's products, they help all those departments that do. For example, the Legal department will help the Marketing department if it runs into difficulties with the National Consumer Agency over its advertisements.

Product Organisation Structure

The business is split up into departments based on products made.

Example: *Cadbury*

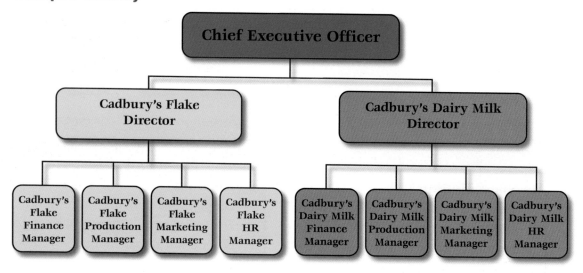

ADVANTAGES	DISADVANTAGES
1. Focus on Customer Each department makes sure that it delivers the best possible product to customers.	**1. Duplication** The business ends up with a number of Marketing departments, Finance departments and so on. This can lead to wasteful higher costs.
2. Competition The healthy competition between departments to be the most successful benefits the business.	**2. Brand Cannibalisation** The Product director may steal customers from other company products in a bid to be the most successful. For example, the company's website might take customers away from its shops.
3. Lower Costs Each product is run almost as a separate business and judged on the profits it makes so there is greater incentive for it to keep costs to a minimum.	

Geographical Organisation Structure

The business is split up into departments based on the geographical areas it operates in.

Example: *Vodafone*

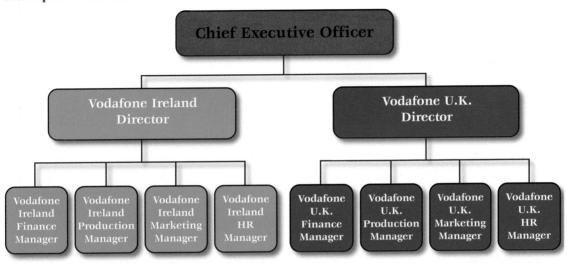

ADVANTAGES	DISADVANTAGES
1. **Serve Local Needs Better** Local directors know local needs and can give locals exactly the products and services that they want.	1. **Duplication** The business ends up with a number of Marketing departments, Finance departments and so on. This can lead to wasteful higher costs.
2. **Competition** The healthy competition between regional departments to be the most successful benefits the business.	2. **Conflict** Conflict can arise between senior company managers and local managers over who knows best for the business.
3. **Lower Costs** Each geographical department is run almost as a separate business and is judged on the profits it makes so there is greater incentive for it to keep costs to a minimum.	

Matrix Organisation Structure

This structure combines two types of organisation structure:

(i) functional organisation structure

(ii) project team structure

It is used when the business is involved in major *temporary* projects that require expertise from all the business's departments (such as the launch of a new product, for example). Employees are temporarily removed from their normal job and invited to work on a project team. They report to the project team leader when they are working on the project. When doing their normal work, they report to their normal functional department manager.

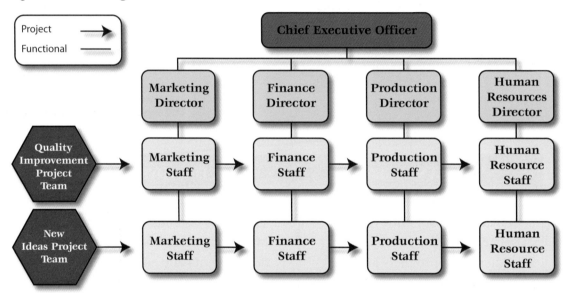

ADVANTAGES	DISADVANTAGES
1. **Motivation** Employees chosen to join the project team feel special. It satisfies their esteem needs and motivates them to work harder in the business.	1. **Two Bosses** Employees on the project team report to two bosses – their functional boss when they are doing their regular job and their project boss. When both give conflicting orders, employees may become stressed.
2. **Better Relationships** The project team is made up of people from each department who interact with each other and develop a better understanding of each other's departments.	2. **Increased Cost** The business must pay to train managers to become project managers. There will be extra secretarial and administrative costs.

Span of Control

The span of control is the number of employees that report directly to a manager. In other words, it is the number of employees that a manager can *effectively* supervise. In the diagram below, the CEO's span of control is four.

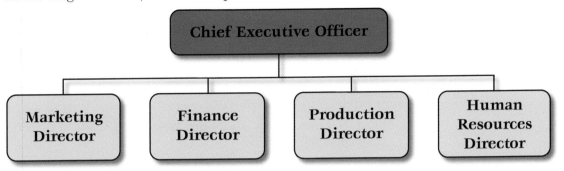

A manager's span of control can be:

(a) **Wide** (this means that he can supervise a lot of employees effectively at the same time)

(b) **Narrow** (this means that he can effectively supervise only a few employees at the same time)

There is no one correct span of control. A manager's span of control depends on the following:

The manager s experience and ability	If the manager is not very experienced, his span of control will be narrow. He will not be able to cope with large numbers at first.
The employees' experience and ability	If the employees are not very experienced and don't really know what they are doing, the manager's span of control will be narrow as he will have to supervise them closely.
The type of work to be done	If the work the employees do is complicated and dangerous, the manager will have to keep a close eye on them and so his span of control will be narrow.
Outside pressure on the manager	If the manager is under a lot of pressure outside work, he will not be able to concentrate as much on his job and so his span of control will be narrow.
Location of employees	If the employees are located in different parts of the factory, it will be hard for the manager to get around to all of them and his span of control will be narrow.

Advantages of Organising

1. **Organising means that everyone in the business knows who to go to with a problem**

    A clear organisation structure shows every person in the business what their job is and to whom they report. This structure helps employees and customers find exactly the right person to go to in order to deal with a certain issue. Therefore, organising ensures that problems are solved quickly

2. **Organising the business makes it more effective**

    In a functional organisation the business is split up into jobs to be done. Instead of doing lots of different types of work, employees specialise in one type of job. This way, they become better and faster at it. Therefore, organising leads to better quality work.

3. **Organising saves the business time**

    Time management helps a manager to better organise his time. He first of all sets out the amount of time he has available to him. Then he sets out the jobs he has to do. He then prioritises these jobs in order of importance and organises his schedule so that he starts with the most important job first and continues to the least important. Therefore, organising ensures that the manager gets all the most important jobs done on time.

4. **Organising gets the work done more quickly**

    It would take one person a long time to do all the work in a business on his own. By sharing the work out between the various departments, the business gets the work done more quickly.

Management Activity of Controlling

The management activity of controlling involves the manager making sure that the business stays **on target** to achieve the objectives that were set during planning. The manager checks up periodically on the business's performance to see whether it is off target or on target to achieve its goals. If the business is off target, the manager can then take corrective action to get it back on target.

Steps in Controlling

	Example 1	Example 2
1. Set targets	A1 in Leaving Cert Business	To increase sales by 36% this year
2. Measure actual performance regularly	Mock Exam: "F"	After first month, sales had increased by 1%
3. Measure any deviations (whether the business is *on target* or *off target*) and investigate them	Off target	Off target
4. Take corrective action to ensure that the business stays on target to achieve its goals	■ Study harder ■ Do homework ■ Pay more attention	■ Advertise more ■ Reduce price

Examples of Controls Used in Business

- Stock Control
- Quality Control
- Credit Control

1. Stock Control

The aim of stock control is to make sure that the business has exactly the right amount of stock in the shop or factory at all times. It is bad for the business if it has too much or too little stock in its storeroom.

Too much stock will result in money wasted by stock not selling, going off (deteriorating) and going out of date (obsolete). Too little stock will mean that the business will run out (stockout) and customers will be unhappy.

To control the amount of stock it keeps, the business has to set stock levels:

	Definition	To Prevent
Maximum stock level	The business should never have more than this amount in stock.	Too much stock
Minimum stock level	The business should never have less than this amount in stock.	Too little stock
Re-order point	When stock falls to this level, it is time to put in a new order.	Too little stock
Re-order quantity	This is the correct amount of stock you should buy each time you make a purchase.	Too much stock

Advantages of stock control

1. Having lower amounts of stock will help a business to lower its insurance costs.
2. Lower amounts of stock will make it easier to spot and eradicate theft by staff, customers and so on.
3. The business will always have the right amount of stock in the shop. Customers will never call to the shop and be unable to find what they want. This helps to improve the business's sales and reputation.
4. If the business keeps the right amount of stock, it will not lose money because of deterioration and obsolescence and excessive storage costs.

Just-in-Time

Another technique to control stock is called **just-in-time**. The aim of this system is to keep the minimum amount of stock possible in the factory while at the same time never running out of stock.

It involves buying from a supplier who delivers *exactly* the right amount of *perfectly made* stock at *exactly* the time when it is going to be used by the business. Materials come into the factory only when they are needed (not before, not after) and are then immediately used to make the product. The finished product goes straight out to the customer.

In this way the business does not have to hold *any* stock.

2. Quality Control

Quality control involves making sure that the quality of a business's products meets the expectations of consumers. There are various ways that a business can control its quality, including:

- ⊙ Physical Inspection
- ⊙ Quality Circles
- ⊙ ISO 9000 Awards

Inspection

To make sure that the business's products meet the quality standard required, a trained inspector physically examines them before they leave the factory. Products that meet the standards are passed and shipped out to the shops. Products that do not meet the quality standards are rejected by the inspector and sent back to the factory to be fixed or scrapped.

An inspector inspects *every* single product for businesses only when perfect quality is needed. In Waterford Crystal, the inspectors examine every single product before it leaves the factory to ensure that Waterford lives up to its image as the best crystal in the world.

Otherwise, the inspector uses a method called **sampling**. This works as follows:

	Example
1. The factory makes a batch of the product.	Mars makes 10,000 Mars bars in a batch.
2. The inspector picks out a small amount (sample) at random and tests them to see whether they meet the quality standard set by the business.	The inspector tastes ten of the bars in the batch to make sure that no more than one out of ten is imperfect.
3. If the sample passes, the inspector passes the whole batch.	If nine or more of these ten are perfect, the inspector approves the whole batch of 10,000 and they are sent out to the shops.
4. If the sample fails, the inspector fails the whole batch.	If six of those ten are defective, the inspector rejects the whole batch of 10,000. They are all sent back to the factory to be scrapped.

Quality Circles

A Quality Circle is a way to control quality in a business. It involves the employees spotting quality problems in the factory and coming up with suggestions to solve these problems. A small group of employees volunteer for the Quality Circle. They meet regularly to discuss quality problems in the factory and to suggest solutions to them. The idea is that employees on the factory floor are best placed to know the business's quality problems and how to solve them.

Quality Circles operate as follows:

1. The employees meet and raise quality problems they have found.
2. They discuss the problem and recommend a solution to the manager. The manager makes the decision whether to accept their recommendation.
3. If the manager decides to go ahead with the solution, the members of the Quality Circle help to implement it.

Advantages of Quality Circles include:

1. The employees eliminate mistakes and quality problems in the factory. So the quality of the business's products improves. This leads to an increase in sales and profits.
2. The Quality Circle tries to ensure that products are perfectly made. This leads to lower costs because the business does not waste money on repairing faulty products or giving refunds.
3. Employees involved in quality circles feel more motivated and committed to the business because they feel valued when their recommendations are accepted.

ISO 9000

To make sure that its products are of the highest quality standards, the business applies for the ISO 9000 award. This is an internationally recognised award that is given only to businesses that can consistently prove to an *independent* team of inspectors that their products meet the highest quality standards.

A business applies for the award as follows:

1. After the business applies to the International Organisation for Standardisation (ISO), it is sent a questionnaire asking very detailed questions about its quality.

2. The business fills in the questionnaire and sends it back to the ISO.

3. The ISO considers the business's answers and sends back a list of changes that the business must make to improve its quality if it wants to have the highest quality standards in the world.

4. When these changes have been made, the ISO sends a team of inspectors to the business. It inspects every aspect of the business's quality to make sure that it meets strict ISO quality standards. If it does, the business is awarded the ISO 9000 mark.

5. After that, the inspectors can call out to the business at any time to carry out a surprise inspection to make sure that the business is still achieving top quality.

3. Credit Control

The aim of credit control is to make sure that all customers (debtors) pay their bills in full and on time. It seeks to eliminate bad debts (customers who go bankrupt and don't pay their bills) and to make late-paying customers pay their bills now. It involves these steps:

Step 1. The business must set an overall limit for the maximum amount of credit it will give all its customers. This ensures that it never loses more than this amount.

Step 2. The business vets each customer carefully to see whether he can be trusted with credit. This can be done by running a credit check on the customer, asking him in for an interview and asking for references from his bank and/or other businesses he has dealt with in the past.

Step 3. When customers use their credit, their bills should be sent out to them immediately. They should be offered discounts if they pay early to encourage them to pay quickly.

Step 4. The business must have a procedure for getting money off customers who won't pay. This can involve ringing them up, calling out to them, adding interest to their bill or taking them to court.

Advantages of Credit Control

1. Credit control ensures that a business receives its money from its customers in plenty of time before it has to pay its bills. This helps to ensure that the business will not go bankrupt.

2. Credit control reduces costs. It avoids losing money on bad debts.

Advantages of Controlling

1. Controlling makes sure that the business achieves its objectives

The purpose of controlling is to periodically check the progress of the business to ensure that it is on target to achieve the goals set out in planning. If the business is off target, steps can be taken to correct this and get the business back on target to achieve its goals.

2. Controlling reduces the business's costs

An effective quality control programme (such as ISO 9000) ensures that the business's products are of excellent quality. If the business's products are perfect, the business will enjoy lower costs, as money is not wasted on repairing faulty goods or giving dissatisfied customers a refund. This leads to lower costs for the business.

3. Controlling the business improves its cash flow

An effective credit control policy (such as offering discounts for speedy payment) ensures that debtors pay their accounts on time. This means that the business receives cash in plenty of time before it has to hand it out to pay its bills. Therefore, controlling improves a business's cash flow and reduces the risk of bankruptcy caused by an inability to pay bills.

4. Controlling increases a business's sales and profits

Quality control ensures that the business's products are of top quality. Stock control ensures that the business always has enough stock on the shelves to meet customers' demands. When customers know that a certain business can always guarantee availability of excellent products, they will shop there. Therefore, controlling leads to higher sales and profits for the business.

Ordinary Level Questions

EXAM SECTION 1 (25%) – SHORT ANSWER QUESTIONS [10 marks each]

1. List the three management activities.

2. Define "planning".

3. Explain what is meant by "objectives" and give one example of an objective in business.

4. Column 1 is a list of business terms. Column 2 is a list of possible explanations for these terms. Match the two lists by placing the letter of the correct explanation under the relevant number below. One explanation has no match.

Column 1	Column 2: Explanations
1. Objectives	a) Things that a business does well
2. Strengths	b) Methods of achieving goals
3. Weaknesses	c) External factors that can prevent a business from succeeding
4. Opportunities	d) Arranging a business's resources in the best way to achieve its goals
5. Threats	e) Goals that a business wants to achieve
6. Strategies	f) External factors that a business can use to succeed
	g) Things that a business does badly

1	2	3	4	5	6
E	A	G	F	C	B

5. Indicate whether each of the following (A, B, C, D and E) is true or false.

	Sentence	True or False
A	A strategic plan is a short-term plan.	False
B	A mission sets out the overall purpose of a business.	True
C	A tactical plan takes more than five years to achieve.	False
D	Manpower planning ensures the business has enough workers.	True
E	Lidl, ALDI and Ryanair follow a low cost leadership strategy.	True

6. Name one organisation structure. Draw a chart of that structure.

7. Explain the tem "span of control".

8. Indicate whether each of the following (A, B, C, D and E) is true or false.

	Sentence	True or False
A	A functional organisation structure divides the business into different geographic locations.	
B	A matrix organisation structure is a combination of a functional structure and project teams.	
C	Staff departments provide advice to the other departments in the business.	
D	The less experienced a manager is, the narrower her span of control will be.	
E	A geographic organisation structure splits the business up into different products.	

9. List three reasons why it is bad for a business to have too much stock.

10. Outline two advantages of quality control for a business.

11. Distinguish between "credit control" and "quality control".

EXAM SECTION 2 (75%) – LONG QUESTIONS

1. Name two types of planning and explain one of them. (20 marks)

2. What is meant by the term "mission statement"? (10 marks)

3. Describe three benefits for a business of planning. (15 marks)

4. Distinguish between "product organisation structure" and "geographic organisation structure". (10 marks)

5. Distinguish between a "line department" and a "staff department" in a business. (10 marks)

6. What is meant by the term "span of control"?
   Outline three factors that affect a manager's span of control. (25 marks)

7. Describe three benefits for a business of organising. (15 marks)

8. Describe three benefits for a business of good stock control. (15 marks)

9. Name three quality control techniques available to a business and explain one of them. (25 marks)

10. Define credit control. (10 marks)

Higher Level Questions

EXAM SECTION 1 (20%) – SHORT ANSWER QUESTIONS [10 marks each]

1. Distinguish between "objectives" and "strategies".

2. Distinguish between "manpower planning" and "cash flow forecasting".

3. The following table shows three types of plans and four statements. For each statement, tick (✔) the type of plan that is *most* likely to match that statement.

	Mission	Strategic Plan	TacticalPlan
To be achieved in under a year			✓
Sets out the fundamental objective of a business	✓		
Major plans to be achieved in the next five years		✓	
Generally applies to one section of the business			✓

4. Define "organising".

5. What is a staff department? Give two examples.

6. Complete this sentence: A product organisation structure involves…

7. Illustrate your understanding of the term "span of control".

8. Explain the term "stock control". Outline its importance for a business.

9. Outline three advantages of quality circles for a business.

10. Complete this sentence: Credit control requires managers to…

EXAM SECTION 2 (20%) – APPLIED BUSINESS QUESTION – 80 MARKS

Ralan Ltd.

Rachel Nolan set up her office furniture making business, Ralan Ltd., in her hometown 12 years ago. The business has done well and enjoys a reputation for quality workmanship. Rachel employs skilled carpenters who take great pride in the fact that they source materials, make the furniture and even come up with the business's marketing campaigns. Rachel has heard that a rival office furniture business is to open in the new industrial estate planned for the town. This has caused Rachel some concern and her business advisor has recommended that she carry out a SWOT analysis to cope with the competition.

Recently, Rachel has noticed a number of problems that were not a feature of the business in the past. Some customers have cancelled orders because they bought better quality furniture at a lower price on the Internet. Others have complained about delays in getting their orders. Employees are grumbling that they find their work repetitive and boring. Some have already left for jobs elsewhere. Profits have dropped in recent years. Rachel's advisor has recommended the introduction of a Quality Circle.

Rachel knows that if she is to compete, she must invest in the latest production technology. She realises that the competition are way ahead of her when it comes to selling over the Internet and she now wishes to set up her own website.

(A) Explain what is meant by the term SWOT analysis.
Conduct a SWOT analysis for Rachel's business.   (30 marks)

(B) Describe how a Quality Circle will operate in Ralan Ltd. and
its potential benefits for the business.   (30 marks)

(C) Explain the benefits of better planning and organising for Rachel's business.   (20 marks)

EXAM SECTION 3 (60%) – LONG QUESTIONS

1. In the case of a business of your choice, illustrate the various stages
   in planning.   (25 marks)

2. Distinguish between low cost leadership, niche and differentiation strategies.
   Illustrate your answer with examples.   (20 marks)

3. Explain two types of planning and analyse their impact on a business.   (20 marks)

4. Describe the factors that affect a manager's span of control.   (20 marks)

5. Explain what is meant by a product organisation structure and
   outline its importance to a business.   (20 marks)

6. Explain what is meant by a matrix organisation structure and
   outline its importance to a business.   (20 marks)

7. Explain the term "stock control" and describe a method of stock control.   (25 marks)

8. Explain the term "quality control" and describe a method of quality control.   (25 marks)

9. Explain the term "credit control" and describe a method of credit control.   (25 marks)

10. Which of the three management activities is the most important?
    Explain your answer with reasons and examples.   (25 marks)

CHAPTER 9

HRM

Human Resource Management

Human Resource Management (HRM) involves managing the employees (human resources) in a business. Its main purpose is to ensure that the business finds, keeps and makes the best possible use of its employees.

The functions of the Human Resources manager are as follows:

- ▶ Manpower Planning
- ▶ Recruitment and Selection
- ▶ Training and Development
- ▶ Performance Appraisal
- ▶ Pay and Rewards
- ▶ Employer/Employee Relationships

Manpower Planning

Manpower planning means making sure that the business has enough workers with the right skills to do all the jobs in the business. There are three steps in manpower planning.

		EXAMPLE
Step 1	**Forecast Future Demand** The Human Resources manager must estimate how many employees and what skills the business will need in the future.	An airline plans to run 100 flights a day from next October. Each flight needs 2 pilots, so the airline needs 200 pilots.

Step 2	**Calculate Existing Supply** The Human Resources manager must conduct an audit of the existing employees who work in the business (including numbers, age and skills) to see how many workers the business has. She must take into account how many are close to retirement age.	At the moment the airline employs 180 pilots.
Step 3	■ If demand exceeds supply (i.e., if the business needs more employees than it has), the strategy is to **recruit** more employees. ■ If supply exceeds demand (i.e., if the business has too many workers), the strategy is to make some of the existing employees **redundant**.	The airline will have to start recruiting 20 pilots *now* to be ready for next October.

Importance of Manpower Planning

▶ Manpower planning ensures that the business always has enough workers to carry out all the jobs needed to make the business a success.

▶ Manpower planning saves the business money by ensuring that there are not too many workers employed. This helps to reduce the business's wages bill.

Recruitment and Selection

Recruitment

1. **Recruitment** means finding suitable people for a job vacancy in the business and persuading them to apply. This involves preparing a job description to establish the work that the vacancy entails and a person specification outlining the type of person needed to do the job.
2. The HR manager must then find this person. There are two methods. Internal recruitment means finding a candidate from among the business's existing workers. External recruitment means finding a candidate from outside the business by advertising the position.

Selection

1. **Selection** means choosing the best applicant for the vacancy from all those who applied. The first thing the Human Resources manager will do is go through all the applications received and screen out those who do not meet the requirements of the job description and/or person specification.

2. The manager can then use a variety of techniques to choose from among the remaining candidates, including tests, interviews and checking references. The job is offered to the best candidate.

Stages in Recruitment and Selection

Step 1 Prepare a Job Description

A job description is a document that describes the duties and responsibilities of the job. Here is a sample job description.

JOB DESCRIPTION

JOB TITLE: Office Manager

SALARY: €35,000 per annum

HOURS: 34 hours per week

DUTIES AND RESPONSIBILITIES:

1. Responsible for organising staff rota
2. Responsible for dealing with customer queries by phone and letter
3. Responsible for ensuring all bills are paid on time

Step 2 Prepare a Person Specification

A person specification is a document that describes the type of person needed to carry out all the work described in the job description. Here is a sample person specification.

PERSON SPECIFICATION

The ideal candidate will have the following:

ACADEMIC QUALIFICATIONS: Leaving Certificate

EXPERIENCE: Previous management experience desirable

CHARACTERISTICS: Confident, motivated person

SKILLS: Good communication and organisation skills
                Ability to work well as part of a team
                IT skills essential

The Human Resources manager may then use the information from the job description and person specification to draft an advertisement for the vacancy. Here is a sample advertisement.

OFFICE MANAGER REQUIRED

Murray's Department Store requires an Office Manager for immediate start.

The job involves managing the office in the store.

The ideal candidate is a confident, motivated person with good communication and organisation skills and with the ability to work well as part of a team. Previous management experience is desirable and IT skills are essential for this position.

Salary: €35,000 per annum

Apply with CV and letter of application to:

Margaret Murphy
Human Resources Manager
Murray's Department Store
Dublin 9

Closing date for applications is 12th June.

The store is an equal opportunities employer.

> An "equal opportunities employer" will not discriminate against candidates in any way based on their gender, age, disability, sexuality, race, religion and so on.

Step 3 Encourage Suitable Candidates to Apply

Now that the HR manager knows the job to be done and the type of person needed to do it, she must find a number of suitable candidates to apply for the job.

There are two main sources of recruitment – **Internal** and **External**.

External Recruitment

Definition   External recruitment means finding someone from outside the business (i.e., who does not already work in the business) to apply for the job.

Sources
1. Media advertisements (newspapers, radio and so on)
2. Recruitment agencies (irishjobs.ie; monster.ie)
3. FÁS (FÁS is the national training and employment authority. It maintains a register of all the people in Ireland looking for a job. If an employer needs to fill a vacancy, she can contact FÁS, who will match the vacancy with a suitable jobseeker from its register.)
4. Headhunting (The business approaches people who work for rival businesses.)

Advantages **1.** A person from outside may bring lots of new, fresh ideas to the business.

2. Hiring an outsider may cause less jealousy and resentment than appointing someone who already works for the business.

3. By opening the vacancy up to outsiders, the business can get the best qualified person for the job.

Internal Recruitment

Definition Internal recruitment means finding someone from among those who already work in the business.

Sources **1.** Promotion (A current employee who has done a good job so far might be able for a more challenging position and could be offered a higher level job.)

2. Demotion (A current employee who is struggling with her job could be asked to move downwards to fill a vacancy at a lower level.)

3. Transfer (A current employee in one branch could be asked to move to another branch and do the same job there.)

Advantages **1.** Existing employees know the business, how it works and everybody in it, so they won't take as long as an outsider to settle into the role.

2. The manager has seen the employee's work first hand and knows exactly how good an employee he is.

3. Internal recruitment provides a career path for employees and motivates them to work harder to get a promotion.

4. It is cheaper and quicker than external recruitment. There is no need for expensive ads in newspapers. A sign on the staff notice board or a memo to all staff is enough.

The HR manager must let applicants know how to apply for the job. The most common methods of application used in Ireland are the curriculum vitae (CV), the application form and the covering letter.

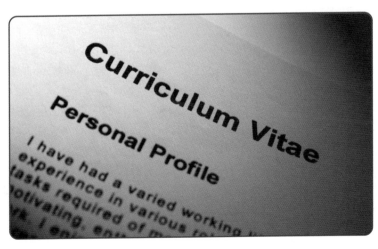

Curriculum Vitae (CV)

A curriculum vitae is a document prepared by an applicant for a job in which she summarises her qualifications and work experience. It is used to obtain an interview when seeking a job. It contains details such as:

- Name
- Address
- Education
- Work Experience
- Hobbies
- References
- Signature and date

Curriculum Vitae

Name: Sandra Manning

Address: 12 Knock Street, Patrickstown, Co. Leitrim

Education

Leaving Certificate 2011 – 3 honours in Spanish, Business and Art

Work Experience

2009-2012   Kathleen's Café, Main Street, Patrickstown

              I work here are a part-time waitress.

Hobbies and Interests

I enjoy swimming, football, reading and music.

I am a member of the Patrickstown Ladies GAA football team.

References

Kathleen Cleary	Mr. Len O'Connor
Owner	Principal
Kathleen's Café	St. Vincent's Secondary School
Main Street	Ardagh Avenue
Patrickstown	Patrickstown

Signed *Sandra Manning*   **Date** 11th June 2012

Application Form

An application form is a document printed by an employer asking a series of personal questions regarding education, experience, hobbies and so on from applicants for a job vacancy in the business. The candidate answers the questions in the spaces provided and sends the form back to the business to apply for the vacancy.

Application Form

Name: _____

Address: _____

Education
Leaving Certificate. Year Taken _____

Subject	Level	Grade

Work Experience

Employer	Dates employed there	Main duties and responsibilities	Reason for leaving

What attracts you to this job? What strengths can you bring to it? _____

_____

Describe a situation when you were in a position of leadership and what you achieved in that position.

_____

How would your colleagues describe you in five words? _____

Give the names and addresses of three people willing to act as referees for you. One of them must be

your current or most recent employer. _____

_____

_____

Signed: _____ Date: _____

Letter of Application/Covering Letter

Regardless of whether the employer asks for a CV or an application form or both, candidates should always submit a covering letter with their application. It is a letter in which the applicant introduces herself, states the job she is applying for and outlines a brief summary of why she wants it and the qualities she can bring to the job.

Address of Applicant

Date

Name
Title and
Address of Company she is applying to

Re: Vacancy for

Dear Sir/Madam or Mr/Ms

I am writing to you to apply for the position of _____ in your company which
I saw advertised in The _____ newspaper. This is an ideal job for me because
_____

As you can see from my CV/application form, I completed my Leaving Certificate in _____ and
obtained good grades in all my subjects, especially _____.
I have _____ years' experience working in _____.
I was responsible for _____.

As a _____ in your company, I would bring _____
to the job.

Thank you for considering my application. I look forward to hearing from you.

Yours faithfully/sincerely

Applicant's Signature _____
APPLICANT'S NAME IN CAPITAL LETTERS

Step 4 Screening

The selection process now begins. The Human Resources manager examines all the applications (CVs, application forms and letters of application) received. She must then reject those applicants who do not meet the requirements of the job description and person specification. Those who have not been screened out in this way are "shortlisted" for the next stage of the selection procedure.

Step 5 Selection Tests

The shortlisted applicants undergo a series of tests to assess their abilities and suitability for the vacancy.

- ■ Intelligence tests measure a candidate's general level of intelligence.
- ■ Aptitude tests measure a candidate's skills in a particular area (such as maths skills, language skills and so on).
- ■ Personality tests measure a candidate's characteristics.

Step 6 Interview

Those candidates who performed best in the selection tests are then called for an interview. An interview is a face-to-face conversation between the candidate and the business. The purpose of the interview is to find out more about the applicant – to see if she can do the job and to see if she will fit in with the business and its culture.

The interview is the most common selection technique used in Ireland but it has many potential flaws, including interviewer bias and the fact that interview performance is no guarantee of actual job performance.

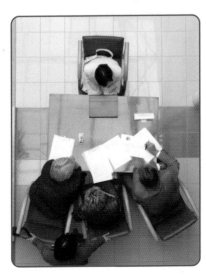

To overcome the problem of interviewer bias, many businesses use a panel interview. This is where the applicant is interviewed by a number of interviewers who each have a vote. This ensures that *one* interviewer's prejudice does not exclude a suitable candidate.

To overcome the problem that a good interview does not guarantee a good worker, the business can use a stress interview. This is where the interviewer deliberately puts the candidate under stress to see how she reacts and copes in a pressurised situation.

Step 7 Check References

The Human Resources manager checks the references of those who did best at the interview to confirm the information already obtained about the candidates and to hear first-hand what they were really like in their previous jobs.

Step 8 Offer the Job

The Human Resources manager offers the job in writing to the best candidate. If she declines the offer, it is then made to the next applicant in order of merit. When an applicant accepts the job, a contract of employment is drawn up. It sets out the duties and behaviour expected from the new employee. The employer and the new employee sign it. The Human Resources department keeps a record of it and the employee is given a copy of it.

Importance of Recruitment

▶ Drawing up a job description and a person specification in advance helps the business to find exactly the right person to do the work needed.

▶ Good recruitment discourages unsuitable people from applying. This saves the business time and money by not having to process lots of totally unsuitable applications.

Importance of Selection

▶ Choosing a candidate who the business knows shares its beliefs will lead to less industrial action in the future.

▶ Choosing the right person is essential to make sure that the job is done well. This helps the business to succeed.

Training and Development

The Human Resources manager must teach the new worker the knowledge, skills and attitude needed to perform the duties of the job properly. There are two ways to train workers.

On-the-job training means that the worker is trained while she is at work. She is shown how to do the job by a more experienced worker. She learns the job through practice. **Off-the-job training** means that the worker is taught how to do the job by attending courses.

ON-THE-JOB Training

This is teaching the employee the knowledge, skills and attitude needed to do the job well, while she is in the normal working situation. The employee learns through practical experience gained from working with and observing experienced employees. She learns by having a go and practicing the tasks involved in the job.

Techniques used include job rotation, where the employee is trained in gradually by moving her from one department to another in the business. In this way, she learns about each part of the business.

For example, the Human Resources manager in a hospital might train a nurse as follows:
1. Six months in Emergency Department
2. Six months in Operating Theatre
3. Six months in hospital wards

OFF-THE-JOB Training

This is teaching the employee the knowledge, skills and attitude needed to do the job well, away from the normal working situation. The employee learns by attending courses away from her place of work.

Techniques used include attending evening classes, conferences and so on. For instance, before a nurse is allowed to work in a hospital, she must obtain a degree in nursing from a university.

Development

This is giving employees the life-long skills and knowledge that will help them to grow as individuals and tackle any future work challenges.

It is more than training. Training teaches employees the skills needed for *one* particular job. Development teaches them skills that they can use in *any* job they have in the future. Development enables employees to seek promotion and more challenging work.

Showing employees how to use the company e-mail system is an example of training. Sending employees on communications skills courses is an example of development.

Importance of Training and Developement

- ◉ Good training and development gives the workers the skills needed to do a good job and make excellent quality products. Better quality leads to higher sales and profits for the business.

- ◉ Good training and development gives workers a variety of skills and makes them more flexible. They are better able to cope with changes in the business.

- ◉ Good training and development means that workers are excellent at their job and therefore will need less supervision. This frees managers up to concentrate on more important issues in the business.

- ◉ Good training and development means that workers do their jobs well. This leads to less conflict between managers and employees over unsatisfactory work. It improves industrial relations.

Performance Appraisal

Performance appraisal involves the Human Resources manager assessing how well/badly each worker is doing her job. Workers are set goals and tasks to achieve. When the task is done, the manager will grade the worker on how well she has performed the task.

Workers who score highly may be rewarded with promotions, bonuses or pay rises. Workers who score badly will be given more training.

The steps involved in performance appraisal are as follows:

Step 1   The employee and the manager meet to set targets for the employee to
          achieve during the next period.

Step 2   The manager regularly evaluates the employee's progress in reaching her
          target.

Step 3   The manager fills in a formal performance appraisal form about the
          employee and the two meet to discuss the results.

Example of a Performance Appraisal Form:

	Excellent	Good	Average	Unsatisfactory
Punctuality				
Teamwork				
Speed of work				
Accuracy				
Personal apperance				

Importance of Performance Appraisal

○ It identifies employees who need training.
   Employees who score badly on their performance appraisal are the ones who
   need to be helped to improve with more training. After the training, their
   performance should be evaluated again to see if they have improved. If not, the
   manager may have to consider sacking them.

○ It identifies employees who are suitable for promotion.
   Employees who get an excellent performance appraisal are the ones who are
   suitable candidates for internal promotion. They have proved their ability at their
   current job and show potential for more responsibility.

○ It helps decide future pay rises and bounses.
   The results of the performance appraisal can be used to determine an employee's
   pay rise or bonus. Employees who score well get a higher pay rise or bonus than
   those who score badly. Thus, performance appraisal motivates employees.

○ It improves communications between managers and employees.
   Because performance appraisal involves regular meetings between the manager
   and the employee, the relationship between them should improve. These
   meetings give both a chance to talk to each other and sort out any problems that
   may exist. Thus, performance appraisal can lead to improved industrial relations.

Pay and Rewards

Pay and rewards consist of the incentives offered to employees for work done. They can be **financial** or **non-financial**.

Financial Rewards

Financial rewards are when the employer gives the employee money as payment for work or some other "gift" that has a money value.

Basic Wage

The employee is paid a fixed amount each week or month. Teachers are paid this way, for example.

Advantage: It is easy for the employer to operate.

Disadvantage: It does not give the employee any incentive to work harder.

Hourly Rate

The employee is paid a fixed hourly rate for a certain number of hours (for example, €10 per hour for 37 hours). Hours worked in excess of this are paid at a higher rate. This is called overtime. Example: "Double time" would be €20 per hour.

Advantage: It is easy for the employer to operate.

Disadvantage: It may cause employees to "drag out" the work to make it last longer so that they earn more money.

Piece Rate

The employee is paid a fixed amount for each item she makes.
Example: €1 per item made.

Advantage: It encourages employees to work harder and be more productive.

Disadvantage: Employees may rush their work to get as many products finished as possible and hence make mistakes.

Commission

The employee receives a percentage of the sales they make.

Advantage: The commission is an incentive for employees to work harder.

Disadvantage: Commission may cause some salespeople to be too pushy with customers. In the long-run, this will turn customers off the business.

Bonus

This is an additional lump-sum payment given to an employee when she reaches her target. It is usually paid at the end of the year.

Advantage: It encourages employees to work towards their target.

Benefits-in-kind

BIKs are a non-cash payment made to the employee. The employer gives the employee things that are worth money, rather than actual cash itself. They are also called perks of the job or fringe benefits.

Examples include company car, subsidised meals and so on.

BIKs are used to raise the status of the job and to improve employee morale.

Share Ownership

Employees are given free or cheap shares in the business as a form of bonus. In this way, the employees become part owners in the business. It provides a big incentive to work hard because the better the business does, the greater the dividends the employees will receive and the more their shares will be worth.

Profit Sharing

This is a form of bonus. Employees are paid a percentage of the profit made by the business as a reward.

Advantages: 1. Employees are motivated to work hard for the business because the more profits it makes, the more they get.

2. It helps the business to recruit the best staff because they are attracted by the profit sharing.

3. Employees feel part of the business and this leads to better industrial relations.

Non-Financial Rewards

Non-financial rewards are when the employer gives the employee inducements other than money or some "gift" that has a money value, as payment for work.

Job Enlargement

Employees are given extra duties to do in order to relieve the boredom of work. The extra duties do not carry any extra responsibility, though.

Job Enrichment

Employees are given greater responsibility in the business. They are given tasks intended to develop them and to get them to use their full abilities and skills.

Improved Working Conditions

The employer may be flexible about what time the employees start and finish work. This is called **flexitime**. This is a very important reward, especially for commuters or people with young children. Longer holidays are also a way to reward employees.

Importance of Pay and Rewards

● Good pay and rewards motivate employees to work harder and produce better quality products. This leads to greater sales and profits for the business.

● Good pay and rewards help the business to attract the very best employees (recruitment and selection).

Employer/Employee Relationships

Another function of the Human Resources manager is to ensure good industrial relations in the business. The term "industrial relations" means the relationship between employers and employees. It refers to how they communicate with each other, work together and generally get along with each other. Industrial relations can be good or bad.

Importance of Good Employer/Employee Relationships

▶ If there are good industrial relations in a business, the employees are happier in their work and therefore employee morale increases. If the employees are happy with their employer, their willingness to do their best for the business increases. Thus, employee motivation is increased.

▶ If the employees have a good relationship with their employer, they will put in extra effort at their job, do more and work harder for her. Thus employee productivity is increased.

▶ If there are good industrial relations in a business, the employees will stay in the job because they are happy there. Thus labour turnover (the rate at which employees leave the business) and absenteeism (employees taking days off) will decrease. This saves the business money recruiting, selecting and training replacement employees.

▶ If there are good industrial relations in a business, the employer will delegate work to the employees because she trusts them and has faith in them. She will also give them power to make decisions for the good of the business. (This is called employee empowerment.) This means that the employees make a useful contribution to the success of the business.

▶ If there are good industrial relations in a business, there will be less chance of industrial action and strikes. Strikes are bad for the business (loss of reputation, loss of sales) and for the employees (no wages).

Improving Industrial Relations

There are a number of things that the Human Resources manager can do to improve industrial relations in a business. These include the following:

1. Regular Open Communications

The Human Resources manager should hold regular face-to-face meetings with the employees to keep them informed about the current state of the business. The business should not hide things from the employees. It should be honest and open with them. This helps to build trust between the two and to reduce gossip and misinformation that can lead to unnecessary disputes.

2. Grievance Procedures

The Human Resources manager and the employees should agree in advance on procedures for dealing with conflict situations, such as promotions, redundancies and grievances. This means that whenever conflict does arise, there is an agreed way to solve it. Grievance procedures minimise the risk of industrial action.

For example, a grievance procedure may be drawn up to deal with any redundancies that may arise in the business. The Human Resources manager and the employees might agree to use the "Last In First Out" method.

3. Train Managers

Managers should be given training in how to deal with employee problems in a sensitive and understanding way. They should be taught how to handle conflict so that issues do not turn into serious industrial relations problems.

4. Careful Selection

To avoid industrial relations problems arising in the first place, the Human Resources manager should select employees who will fit in and share the business's beliefs. This will minimise the likelihood of conflict.

5. Train Employees

Employees should be given adequate training so that they can perform the duties expected of them. This will reduce conflict between managers and employees over the employee's work.

Teamwork

In many businesses, employees do not work on their own in isolation, but in teams. A team is a group of employees working together to achieve a certain objective.

Stages In Forming Teams

In 1965, Bruce Tuckman developed a theory on the stages of forming teams. He identified four stages:

1. **Forming**
   - Members of the team meet for the very first time.
   - They are very polite to each other.
   - They discuss the job that they have to do together.
   - However, they do not reveal too much about themselves.
   - They are "sussing each other out".

2. **Storming**
   - As team members get to know each other a bit better, conflict occurs.
   - Arguments arise as strong personalities emerge within the team.
   - Rows happen when team members vie for position within the team, such as team leader.

3. **Norming**
   - Team members resolve their conflicts, reach a consensus and start working together.
   - They agree on who the leader is, who has the power and each other's roles.
   - Team members start to trust each other.
   - They set "norms", which are standards of behaviour and work that all team members must obey.

4. **Performing**
   - Team members pull together as one and focus on getting the job done.
   - They co-operate with each other and work together as a unit.
   - There is a strong sense of unity in the team.

Advantages of Teams for the Business

1. **Teams make better decisions**

   The members in a team can brainstorm with each other and come up with creative solutions to problems that individuals wouldn't think of on their own. Each team member brings different ideas, experiences and perspectives to the team's discussions. Therefore, teamwork can lead to better solutions for the business.

2. **Teamwork increases employee motivation**

   Employees are happier working in a team. In work teams, they are mixing with other people. This satisfies their social needs, according to Maslow's Hierarchy of Needs. Satisfying the employees' social needs motivates them to work harder and stay with the business.

3. **Teams make better quality products**

   The members of the team develop a team spirit and do their best to make their team a success. Team members do their jobs to the best of their ability because they don't want to let the others down.

   Furthermore, the business can use rivalry between teams in the business to its benefit. Each team will try and beat the others. This means that all the teams in the business are doing their best to make the best products.

4. **Teamwork improves relationships and communications in the business**

   The team members may come from different departments in the business (such as Finance, Marketing, Production and Human Resources). In this way, employees from the different parts of the business mix with each other on a daily basis. This leads to better relationships in the business. People are working with each other and respect each other and therefore fewer disputes occur between employees within the business.

Advantages of Teams for the Employees

1. **Allows the employee to make contributions**

   The members in a team can brainstorm with each other and come up with creative solutions to problems that individuals wouldn't think of on their own. Making contributions to the team in this way can satisfy the employee's esteem needs. She can get respect and praise from her team members for her ideas. This will make her more motivated and happier at work.

2. **Teamwork satisfies the employee's social needs**

   Employees are happier working in a team. In work teams, they are mixing with other people. Being a member of a team gives the employee a sense of belonging. She enjoys her work more when she has friends who understand the job and with whom she can discuss any issues or problems she has with work.

3. **Team Spirit**

   The members of the team develop a team spirit and do their best to make their team a success. No team member wants to let her team mates down. Team spirit means that employees in the team support and help each other through difficult times.

4. **Teamwork Improves Relationships**

   The team members may come from different departments in the business (such as Finance, Marketing, Production and Human Resources). In this way, employees from the different parts of the business mix with each other on a daily basis. This leads to better relationships in the business, a happier working environment for the employees and increased morale in the business.

Ordinary Level Questions

EXAM SECTION 1 (25%) – SHORT ANSWER QUESTIONS [10 marks each]

1. Name three functions of a Human Resources manager.

2. Explain the purpose of manpower planning.

3. Distinguish between a "job description" and a "person specification".

4. Explain the term "external recruitment" and give one source of external recruitment.

5. Column 1 is a list of business terms. Column 2 is a list of possible explanations for these terms. Match the two lists by placing the letter of the correct explanation under the relevant number below. One explanation has no match.

Column 1	
1. CV	4. Internal Recruitment
2. Application Form	5. Selection
3. Letter of Application	6. Headhunting

Column 2: Explanations
a) List of questions prepared by the employer and answered by candidates for a job vacancy
b) Finding someone from outside the business to fill a job vacancy
c) Finding someone from among the existing workforce to fill a job vacancy
d) Offering workers in rival companies a job in your business

e)	Curriculum Vitae
f)	Letter written by applicants for a job to introduce themselves to the employer
g)	Choosing the best applicant for the job

1	2	3	4	5	6
E					

6. Distinguish between "on-the-job training" and "off-the-job training".

7. Explain the term "performance appraisal".

8. Indicate whether each of the following (A, B, C, D and E) is true or false.

	Sentence	True or False
A	Employees who receive a bad appraisal from their manager will get a promotion.	
B	Development involves teaching workers skills that they will use throughout their entire career.	
C	Good recruitment minimises the number of unsuitable applications received.	
D	Panel interviews are when an applicant is interviewed by a number of interviewers.	
E	Aptitude tests measure a candidate's skills in a particular area.	

9. Column 1 is a list of business terms. Column 2 is a list of possible explanations for these terms. Match the two lists by placing the letter of the correct explanation under the relevant number below. One explanation has no match.

Column 1	
1.　BIK	4.　Commission
2.　Bonus	5.　Basic Wage
3.　Piece Rate	6.　Profit Sharing

Column 2: Explanations
a)　Additional payment received when an employee reaches her target
b)　Employee is paid a fixed amount every month
c)　Employee receives a percentage of the value of everything he sells
d)　Employee receives a percentage of the profits made by the business
e)　Benefit-in-kind
f)　Employee receives free or cheap shares in the business
g)　Employee receives a fixed amount for every product she makes

1	2	3	4	5	6
E					

10. The four stages in team formation include: Performing, Forming, Norming and Storming. Put these stages in the correct order and explain any one of the stages.

EXAM SECTION 2 (75%) – LONG QUESTIONS

1. Draft a job description for a Business Teacher.   (10 marks)

2. Draft a person specification for a Business Teacher.   (20 marks)

3. Use your answers from Q1 and Q2 to draft an advertisement for a school looking for a new Business Teacher.   (20 marks)

4. Identify and explain two sources of external recruitment.   (10 marks)

5. Outline three advantages of external recruitment.   (15 marks)

6. John McLaughlin lives at 10 Marsh Street, Tralee. He passed his Leaving Certificate in 2007 and got honours in Art and Agricultural Science. He plays senior hurling for St. Enda's Club, Tralee and coaches the junior team as well.

    Draft a suitable CV for John.   (20 marks)

7. Outline the importance of recruitment and selection to a business.   (20 marks)

8. Outline the importance of training and development to a business.   (20 marks)

9. Explain three different types of rewards that employers can offer employees.   (15 marks)

10. Outline three advantages of teamwork for a business.   (15 marks)

Higher Level Questions

EXAM SECTION 1 (20%) – SHORT ANSWER QUESTIONS [10 marks each]

1. Complete this sentence: Manpower planning involves…

2. Illustrate the difference between a "job description" and a "person specification".

3. Distinguish between "internal" and "external" recruitment.

4. What do the letters CV stand for? Explain its use in business.

5. Name three selection tests used by a human resources manager and explain any one of them.

6. Illustrate your understanding of the term "training and development".

7. Which function of a human resources manager do you feel is the most important? Explain your choice.

8. What is a "non-financial reward"? Name two non-financial rewards.

9. Column 1 is a list of business terms. Column 2 is a list of possible explanations for these terms. Match the two lists by placing the letter of the correct explanation under the relevant number below. One explanation has no match.

Column 1	Column 2: Explanations
1. On-the-job Training	a) Employees are taught life-long skills
	b) Candidates without the basic qualifications are rejected
2. Development	c) Employees are taught through practical experience at work
3. Interview	
4. Screening	d) Involves testing candidates' intelligence and aptitudes
5. Off-the-job Training	e) Face-to-face conversation with candidate to find out more about him
	f) Employees are taught by attending courses outside work

1	2	3	4	5

10. The following table shows four stages in team formation and four behaviours. For each behaviour, tick (✔) the stage in team formation that is *most* likely to match that behaviour.

	Forming	Storming	Norming	Performing
Team members work together as a unit				
Team members meet for the first time				
Team members resolve their conflict and reach a consensus				
Team members set standards of behaviour and work				

EXAM SECTION 2 (20%) – APPLIED BUSINESS QUESTION – 80 MARKS

Fish-Are-Friends Ltd.

Diarmuid Furlong established his tropical fish business, Fish–Are–Friends Ltd., five years ago. The business has experienced massive growth because of increased interest in fish-keeping. As the business grew, Diarmuid had to take on extra staff. Some employees found it hard to settle in and left soon after joining. Diarmuid pays his workers a basic wage and a bonus based on a review of their work over the year. He holds regular staff meetings and generally gets on well with his employees.

The rapid expansion has not come without problems, though. Diarmuid has found it increasingly difficult to find knowledgeable staff. Some customers have complained that they weren't warned that the fish they bought would eat the other fish in their tank. Diarmuid was furious with the new employees he had recruited for causing this error. The new employees blamed existing staff who saw what happened and ignored it. In a bid to keep customers, Diarmuid assured them of his personal service at all times. He now finds himself under constant stress dealing with staff, customers and suppliers.

Diarmuid knows that changes are needed in the business. The business needs to import new stock but Diarmuid hasn't had the time to research what to buy. Employees are complaining about being watched all the time and having no say. A friend recommended he introduce training and work teams but Diarmuid is unsure.

(A)   Evaluate Diarmuid's effectiveness as a Human Resources manager.   (25 marks)

(B)   Illustrate, using the above text, how introducing work teams
can benefit Diarmuid's business.   (25 marks)

(C)   Evaluate how the business might do better if Diarmuid introduced
Training and Development in his business.
Support your answer with reference to the above text.   (30 marks)

EXAM SECTION 3 (60%) – LONG QUESTIONS

1.   Explain the term "manpower planning".   (10 marks)

2.   Differentiate between recruitment and selection.   (20 marks)

3.   Describe, using examples, three types of training available
to a Human Resources manager.   (30 marks)

4.   Explain the term "performance appraisal" and its importance to a business.   (25 marks)

5.   Discuss the importance of good employer/employee relationships
in business.   (25 marks)

6.   "The Human Resources manager has a central role to play in a business."
Do you agree with this statement? Support your answer with four reasons.   (20 marks)

CHAPTER 10

Change

Changing Role of A Manager

If you ask your grandparents, parents or teachers what Ireland was like when they were your age, they will tell you that it was a very different place back then. Irish people did not enjoy the same freedoms that they have today. In school, students could be physically punished for misbehaviour. (And many were!) So, not surprisingly, children behaved in school. Irish people looked up to political and religious leaders and, for the most part, went along with what they said, without question. Ireland was a more authoritarian country back then.

The Ireland you are growing up in, however, is a different country altogether. Irish people are better educated, better travelled and more aware of other cultures and practices and as a result are less willing to be told what to do. The old authoritarian ways don't work anymore.

These changes in Irish society have also affected Irish business. Because their employees will no longer put up with being ordered about, Irish managers have had to change the way they deal with workers. They have changed from the old style controller manager to the more modern facilitator manager.

Change from Controller to Faciliator

▶ Previously, the controller manager was "the boss" who told employees exactly what to do and expected them to do it without question. He assumed he knew everything and did not ask employees for their opinions about the business. He made all the decisions.

Nowadays, the facilitator manager is more like a coach who trains and develops the employees to give them the skills they need so that they can make decisions and solve problems in the business *themselves*. This enables them to make a much more useful contribution to the business.

▶ Previously, the controller manager's job was to catch employees when they made a mistake, tell them where they went wrong and show them how not to make the same mistake again.

Nowadays, the facilitator manager's job is to *help* employees when they make mistakes or have a problem at work. He gives the employees everything they need to do their job better, such as training, advice, equipment, new technology and so on.

▶ Previously, the controller manager kept a close eye on employees to make sure they obeyed all the rules. He threatened and punished employees who broke the rules.

Nowadays, the facilitator manager *encourages* employees to do better and *rewards* them for work well done. He rewards employees with more responsibilities and makes sure they have everything they need to carry them out.

Employee Empowerment

Because employees today are no longer willing to be told what to do, but expect a say in how they do their jobs, managers have had to change. They now use employee empowerment.

Employee empowerment means giving employees power to make decisions on their own without having to ask the manager's permission. Employees are given freedom to decide what to do and when to do it. Employees use their skills and knowledge as they see fit in the best interests of the business.

Example

Michelle works in a fast food restaurant. A customer asks her for sweet and sour sauce with his chips. Michelle says she cannot give him the sauce. Her employee rulebook states that sweet and sour sauce is given out only with chicken nuggets. She tells him she can give him ketchup instead. The customer complains bitterly and calls for the manager. Michelle calls the already over-worked manager over and asks her whether she can give the customer sweet and sour sauce.

■ What impression does this incident give the customer about the restaurant?

■ How do you think the manager felt about being called over to deal with the situation?

■ How do you think Michelle felt having to call over the manager to deal with the situation?

■ What should the manager do to make sure this incident never arises again?

Benefits of Employee Empowerment

▶ The business gives better service to its customers. If a customer has any query or complaint, the employee she is dealing with has the power to solve her problem. Customers are impressed that the first person they speak to in the business can help them. There is no waiting for managers.

▶ Employees' morale and motivation increase because they are given more responsible jobs to do (*Theory Y – Chapter 6*). It satisfies their esteem needs (*Maslow – Chapter 6*). They are happier in their jobs and work harder.

▶ The business makes the most of its employees' skills and talents. Employees are not just used for simple mindless tasks. Instead, the business uses their analytical and decision-making skills to sort out problems in the business.

▶ Because employees are given the power to make decisions related to their jobs, they have to consult with their managers less. Managers can thus spend less time supervising employees, allowing them to concentrate on other important matters.

Employee Participation

Employee participation means involving employees to a greater extent in decision-making and in the running of the business. It is sometimes called industrial democracy, as it means giving the employees, and not just the managers, a say in the running of the business.

Employee participation may be achieved in a number of ways:

1. Works Councils

Works councils are groups of employees, elected by their fellow employees, who are allowed to have a say in the business's plans and strategy and to make some decisions. Every business with more than 1,000 employees must have a works council.

2. Worker Directors

The business allows employees to have seats on the company's Board of Directors. Worker directors are elected by their fellow employees. This gives the employees an input into decision-making at the highest level in the business.

3. Share Options

Employees are allowed to buy shares in the business at a reduced price. This allows them to become owners in the business and have a vote at the company's annual general meeting.

Benefits of Employee Participation

▶ Employee motivation increases as employees' esteem needs (*Maslow – Chapter 6*) are satisfied because they feel important when they are involved in the business.

▶ The business benefits from the input of employees. They may offer useful solutions to the business's problems and/or suggestions to make the business better. This is called intrapreneurship (*see Chapter 4*).

▶ There is more communication between employees and managers through works councils and worker directors. This leads to better industrial relations in the business, which reduces the risk of industrial action and strikes.

Total Quality Management (TQM)

Irish consumers have changed in recent years. Previously, they may have put up with inferior products. But increased wealth means that they can afford to buy the best, and foreign travel has exposed them to superior products abroad. As a result, Irish consumers now expect the very best quality from the products and services they buy.

This means that businesses have had to change their approach to quality and must now aim to deliver top quality products to customers. One technique that they can use to achieve this is called Total Quality Management (TQM).

TQM is a management strategy designed to ensure 100% perfection and 100% customer satisfaction. It says that every person in the business is responsible for delivering quality to the customer. If a business follows the principles of TQM, the business will have perfect quality products. There are four main principles of TQM:

1. Focus on the Customer

The customer is the most important person in the business. The definition of perfection is *whatever the customer wants*. The business conducts market research to find out what customers want and then makes exactly that product for them.

2. Employee Empowerment

Employees are given real power, responsibility and authority to decide what to do in order to make perfect products. Employees use their skills and knowledge as they see fit to produce perfect products. They are allowed make whatever purchases or changes they think are needed to improve the quality of the product to make it perfect.

3. Teamwork

Employees are put into teams. This motivates them to work to make perfect products so as not to let their team mates down.

The business and its suppliers also work together as a team. The business promises to deal exclusively with the supplier if he promises to deliver perfect materials. Perfect materials lead to perfect products.

4. Continuous Improvement

The aim of TQM is to make perfect products. The business must strive for "zero defects" in its products. While the aim of making 100% perfect products 100% of the time might be unrealistic, the business tries each time to do better than the last. This is called continuous improvement.

Benefits of Total Quality Management

▶ Employees, managers and suppliers all work together to make perfect products. So, the quality of the business's products improves. This leads to an increase in sales and profits.

▶ Products are now made perfectly. This leads to lower costs because the business does not waste money on repairing or giving refunds on faulty products.

▶ Employees are more motivated and committed to the business because they feel valued by the business when their recommendations are accepted. Empowerment satisfies their esteem needs. Teamwork satisfies their social needs.

Example of TQM in Guinness

■ Guinness's vision is to have the perfect pint, everywhere, every time
   This requires TQM at every stage in the production (making) and distribution (selling) chain.

■ Raw materials
   Guinness deals only with quality suppliers of barley. Guinness researches new types of barley, checks that its suppliers are growing the right type of barley and checks the quality of each barley harvest.

- Manufacturing process

  Guinness makes sure that its brewing process is the best quality by using trained "testers" and modern technology. Every day at St. James's Gate, trained testers undertake tests on dozens of samples of stout at regular stages in the brewing process to ensure that it is in peak condition for the customer. The tasters score the stout for its aroma, flavour and head quality, and they detect any hint of deviation from the normal.

  In addition to tasting, Guinness uses leading-edge technology to continuously monitor the brewing process. The company employs 80 Quality Assurance Laboratory employees who take samples of the stout at every stage in the brewing process and check them micro-biologically.

- In pubs

  To ensure a perfect pint, Guinness has invested heavily in sales quality. It spent over €1 million developing the current Guinness tap. It is easy to operate and ensures that every pint is perfectly presented.

  The Guinness Quality Team regularly visits all the pubs in Ireland to check the quality of the pint and to advise the bar staff about delivering the perfect pint.

  More than 15,000 bar staff have attended Guinness training courses, which cover all aspects of product knowledge, beer cooling, cleaning beer lines, cleaning glasses and hygiene.

How Technology Changes the Role of Managers

We have so far looked at changes in Irish employees (who now expect to be treated better by their managers and given a say in running the business) and changes in Irish consumers (who now expect top quality products). The next big change that has taken place in Ireland and worldwide is new technology – the explosion in communication methods, such as powerful computers, the Internet and mobile phones.

New technology has had a big impact on the job of a manager in a number of ways.

1. Marketing

Managers can now use the Internet to advertise their products to consumers throughout the world. This can reduce the business's printing and stationery costs because customers can download brochures from the business's website. Furthermore, the business's website can be used to sell products to consumers all over the world. This enables managers to run an international business without the expense and hassle of foreign travel, buying foreign shops, employing staff in other countries and so on.

2. Decision-making

Managers can use Information and Communications Technology (ICT) to help them make better and faster decisions. They can download information in seconds from the Internet about any topic and use this to help them make a decision. For example, if a manager has to decide which computer to buy, he can download prices from different suppliers' websites and choose the best deal for the business.

3. Production

Managers can use Computer Aided Design (CAD). This is computer software that is used to design new products for the business. Instead of drawing up designs by hand and manually building prototypes to test them, the computer can design and test the new product. This means that products can be designed and made much more quickly and cheaply.

Managers can use Computer Aided Manufacture (CAM). This is computer software that controls the machines in the factory. It switches them on and off and tells them exactly what to make. This means that the machines can run 24 hours a day without making mistakes. This enables the business to mass-produce enough products to sell all over the world.

4. Redundancies

New technology can replace the employees in the business. This reduces a manager's span of control, as there are fewer employees to supervise. This frees the manager up to spend time on other aspects of the business. Ryanair and Aer Lingus have replaced their reservations staff with Internet reservations.

5. Employee Retention and Motivation

Managers can use modern technology to motivate and keep employees. The Internet enables teleworking, which means that employees can work from home. Their work is sent to their home computer and they complete it at home and e-mail it back to the office. This reduces the time and money employees spend commuting and also may suit employees with children. Therefore, it can be a very effective way to retain employees.

Impact of Technology on Personnel

New technology has not just affected the managers in a business. It has had a major impact on employees as well. Changes for employees include the following:

1. Changing Nature of Jobs

New technology makes some jobs easier for employees. For example, robots take the danger out of car manufacturing. However, some employees may have to retrain for their jobs. For example, secretaries who used to type letters on a typewriter had to retrain to learn how to use computers.

2. New Types of Jobs

New technology creates opportunities for employees to work in new areas, such as computer programming and website design.

3. Redundancies

Some new technologies have replaced a business's need for employees. This leads to redundancies. Online reservations (for example, www.aerlingus.com and www.jurys.com) mean that businesses don't need reservation clerks anymore.

4. Teleworking

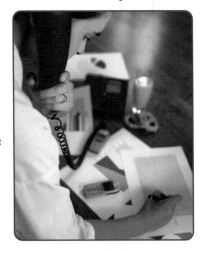

Information and communications technology (ICT) enables certain employees to work from home. The employee's home computer is linked to the office computer. The office e-mails work for the employee to do. He completes it in his own home and e-mails it back to the office. In this way, the costs and hassle of commuting are eliminated or reduced.

Teleworking may also suit employees with families.

Impact of Technology on Business Costs

New technology has also impacted on the costs incurred by businesses. Some aspects of technology have led to lower costs for a business while others have caused increased costs.

Increased Costs

1. New technology can increase a business's costs. It costs a lot of money to buy the new technology – the hardware (equipment) and the software (programs to run on the hardware). It also costs money to maintain the hardware.

2. Employees have to be trained to operate the new technology. This training costs money.

Reduced Costs

1. New technology can reduce a business's costs. Techniques such as Computer Aided Manufacture (CAM) and robots can produce perfect quality products. CAM uses computers to monitor the tools and machines used in the factory and to make any adjustments needed to ensure perfect products are made. This reduces the money the business spends on giving refunds and repairing faulty products.

2. Fewer workers are needed because machines and technology now do the jobs that employees once did. This leads to a reduced wage bill.

Impact of Technology on Business Opportunities

New technology offers the business a number of opportunities.

1. Design

Modern technology can be used to design, test and manufacture new products more quickly and cheaply than before. For example, businesses can design and test a new car using Computer Aided Design (CAD), without the expense or hassle of drawing up plans by hand, building prototypes, building wind tunnels to test the car and so on.

2. Increases Sales

The Internet enables businesses to sell their products anywhere without setting up shops all over the world. The business advertises its products on its website and any customer in any part of the world can view the website and order products from it, paying by credit card. In this way, a business can use new technology to develop into an international business.

3. Direct Marketing

Businesses can use computer databases to store information about their customers. They can then use this information to send marketing literature to those customers who they know will be interested in it. This means that they don't waste money targeting customers who have no interest in their product.

For example, loyalty schemes such as the Tesco Clubcard, the Superquinn Reward Card and the Dunnes Value Club card all do this.

4. New Products

New technology gives entrepreneurs the opportunity to develop brand new products. For example, mobile phone ringtones are now bigger business than CD single sales.

Another example of new technology leading to a new product is Ticketmaster's online ticket sales service. Other "new" businesses developed from technology include Google and eBay.

Change

All businesses must change. For example, the government banned smoking in pubs in 2004, so pubs *had* to change to cope with this. Many now have outdoor, seated and heated areas for their smoking customers.

Aer Lingus had to change to compete with Ryanair. It too became a low cost airline.

Resistance to Change

Although businesses must change to survive, some people do not like change. They prefer things to stay the way they are. Can you remember feeling nervous when you went into First Year? Maybe you wished you could have stayed in Sixth Class, where you knew everyone and how everything operated. Employees feel exactly the same. They may fight change for a number of reasons.

Fear of losing their jobs

Employees might resist the introduction of new computers if they thought it would lead to job losses.

Fear of losing power

Gardaí resisted the introduction of the Garda Reserve. They didn't want unqualified people doing a job that was always the preserve of trained, qualified gardaí.

Fear of failure

Employees might fear that they will not be able to cope with the change. Rather than face up to their fear of change, they resist the change.

Laziness

Employees might resist the change because they don't want the hassle involved. They simply can't be bothered changing.

Strategies for Managing Change

A business *has* to change if it is to survive. The employees will often fight the change. The job of the manager is to overcome this resistance. There are four main strategies for managing change.

1. Managers must lead by example

If a manager wants employees to accept a new change, he must set them a good example. He must show them that he is

willing to put in the extra effort to cope with the change and then they will follow his lead and accept it too. He must show them that the change is extremely important to the business and that he is totally committed to it. If the employees see that the manager is resisting the new idea, they will resist it too and the change will fail.

Example:

You work in an accountancy firm. You start work every morning at 9.00am.
Your manager then announces that the starting time is being changed to 8.00am.
You turn up every day at 8.00am for the first three weeks.
Your manager continues to come in at any time between 9.00 and 9.15.
What time do you come in on Monday of Week 4? _____

2. Managers must communicate with employees

Managers must discuss the change – what it is and the reasons for it – with the employees in order to win their acceptance of it. Imposing the change without communication will not work.

Managers must be open and honest with employees and negotiate the change with them. This will reduce gossip and rumours. It will also increase employee acceptance of the change.

3. Managers must train employees

A major reason why employees resist change is that they fear that they will not be able to do the new work required of them. They fear that they don't have the necessary skills. To overcome this, employees should be trained in all the skills needed to adapt to the change. This will help overcome their resistance.

4. Managers must allow employees to participate in the change

Employees must be allowed to have an input into the change. They should be asked to give suggestions on how to improve it, implement it and so on.

Giving employees a say will help to generate new ideas to make the change more successful. And by having a say in the change, employees are more likely to accept it.

Ordinary Level Questions

EXAM SECTION 1 (25%) – SHORT ANSWER QUESTIONS [10 marks each]

1. Name three characteristics of a "controller" manager.

2. Explain the purpose of employee empowerment.

3. Name three ways to increase employee participation in a business and explain any one of them.

4. Explain how Information and Communications Technology can help marketing managers.

5. Explain how Information and Communications Technology can help production managers.

6. What do the following letters stand for?   TQM   CAM   IT

7. What is Computer Aided Design?

8. Outline two ways in which technology can reduce a business's costs.

9. Name three well-known products or services that have come about thanks to information technology.

10. Column 1 is a list of business terms. Column 2 is a list of possible explanations for these terms. Match the two lists by placing the letter of the correct explanation under the relevant number below. One explanation has no match.

Column 1	Column 2: Explanations
1. TQM	a) Computer software that operates the machines in the factory
2. Facilitator Manager	
3. Employee Empowerment	b) Giving employees power to make decisions on their own without having to ask the manager's permission
4. Controller Manager	c) Manager makes all the decisions without consulting employees
5. CAD	d) Giving employees more of a say in the running of the business
6. CAM	
	e) Total Quality Management
	f) Manager helps employees to do their very best
	g) Computer software used for designing new products

1	2	3	4	5	6
E					

EXAM SECTION 2 (75%) – LONG QUESTIONS

1. Explain the changing role of a manager from "controller" to "facilitator".   (25 marks)

2. Outline three benefits of employee empowerment for a business.   (15 marks)

3. Explain the term "employee participation".   (10 marks)

4. Explain the term "TQM". Describe three advantages of TQM for a business.   (20 marks)

5. Identify and explain three ways that technology affects the role of management.   (15 marks)

6. Using examples, describe three ways in which technology has impacted on personnel.   (20 marks)

7. Using examples, describe three ways in which technology has affected business opportunities.   (20 marks)

Higher Level Questions

EXAM SECTION 1 (20%) – SHORT ANSWER QUESTIONS [10 marks each]

1. Define the term "facilitator manager".

2. Explain the term "controller manager".

3. Distinguish between "employee empowerment" and "employee participation".

4. Complete this sentence: Employee participation helps a business to…

5. Illustrate your understanding of TQM.

6. Column 1 is a list of business terms. Column 2 is a list of possible explanations for these terms. Match the two lists by placing the letter of the correct explanation under the relevant number below. One explanation has no match.

Column 1	Column 2: Explanations
1. Teleworking	a) Employees are given the power to make decisions without their managers' permission
2. Redundancies	
3. Worker Directors	b) Employees are elected by their peers to represent them on the company's Board of Directors
4. Works Councils	
5. Share Options	c) Employees can buy shares in the business at a reduced price
	d) Enables employees to work from home
	e) Employees are dismissed because they are replaced by technology
	f) A group, consisting of employees elected by their peers, who have a say in the running of a business

1	2	3	4	5

7. What do the letters CAD stand for? Explain its use in business.

8. Differentiate between CAD and CAM.

9. Describe two ways that technology has changed the role of the marketing manager.

10. Outline two reasons why employees will resist change.

EXAM SECTION 2 (20%) – APPLIED BUSINESS QUESTION – 80 MARKS

> ### Whales Ltd.
>
> Laura Evans owns and manages her own business, Whales Ltd., which makes soft toys. Laura is tough on her employees. She likes to be in control and make all the decisions. Everything has to go through her.
>
> A large number of toys have been returned as faulty in the last year. Laura has been rushed off her feet dealing with this and many customers were annoyed at how long they had to wait to see her. When not dealing with complaints, Laura spends most of her time checking employees' work. She has recently started docking employees' wages for every mistake they make because repairing all these faults has caused delays in production and the cancellation of some big orders. Sales in the business have declined but costs have increased and, for the first time in years, Laura's business is making a loss.
>
> Laura's employees are not happy. Many are bored with their jobs, assembling soft toys. They frequently make suggestions to Laura, but she hasn't the time to listen. Laura held a meeting with them recently at which she told them she was introducing new technology as a matter of urgency. Employees were extremely worried when they came out of the meeting.

(A) Do you think that Laura is a controller or facilitator manager? Support your answer with reference to the above text. (15 marks)

(B) Illustrate, using the above text, how introducing employee empowerment will benefit Laura's business. (25 marks)

(C) Evaluate how the business might do better if Laura introduces new technology in her business. (40 marks)

EXAM SECTION 3 (60%) – LONG QUESTIONS

1. "Most employees would prefer to work for a facilitator manager rather than a controller manager." Discuss this statement with appropriate reasons. (20 marks)

2. Outline, using an example, the role of employee empowerment in a business. (20 marks)

3. Describe the importance of employee participation in a business. (20 marks)

4. Explain the term "Total Quality Management" and its importance in business. (25 marks)

5. Discuss, using examples, how technology changes the role of management. (25 marks)

6. Evaluate the effect on a firm's personnel and costs of the introduction of new technology into the business. (25 marks)

7. Describe four strategies for managing change in a business. (20 marks)

Accounting

A major reason why an entrepreneur sets up her business is to make money. To find out how much money she is making, the entrepreneur will draw up a set of accounts, called financial statements. The two main financial statements are called the Profit and Loss Account and the Balance Sheet. These financial statements tell the entrepreneur how much profit she is making every year and how much her business is actually worth.

Profit And Loss Account (P&L)

The Profit and Loss Account (P&L) calculates the profit that the business makes in a year. The Profit and Loss Account has two parts. The first part is the Trading Account. It works out the business's gross profit by subtracting the cost of making or buying the products from the money made from selling them. The next section is called the Profit and Loss Account. It works out the business's net profit by subtracting the costs of running the business (such as wages, electricity, telephone bills and so on) from the gross profit. The net profit is the money made by the business after all the expenses have been paid.

- ◗ **Sales** shows how much money the business sold its products for.
- ◗ **Cost of sales** shows how much the business bought or made its products for.
- ◗ **Gross Profit** shows the profit the business makes from selling its products before any expenses are paid.

Profit and Loss Account of X Ltd. For the Year Ended 31st December 20--	
	€
Sales	80,000
Less: Cost of sales	30,000
Gross Profit	**50,000**
Less: Expenses	40,000
Net Profit	**10,000**

- **Expenses** shows the bills (such as wages, electricity rent, interest on loans and so on) that the business has to pay.
- **Net Profit** shows the actual profit made by the business after all the bills have been paid. It tells you how much is left over to pay dividends to the shareholders and to reinvest in the business.

Importance of the P&L

The P&L Account is an important document for managers because:

- A low gross profit tells the managers that their prices are too low and that they should consider raising them to cover costs.

- A low gross profit tells the managers that the price they pay for their materials is too high and that they should consider looking for a cheaper supplier.

- A low net profit tells the managers that the business's expenses are too high. The managers can then examine the expenses carefully and make cutbacks to reduce expenses and increase profits.

- The size of the net profit tells managers how much they can afford to pay out as dividends to the shareholders and how much money they have left to reinvest in the business.

Balance Sheet

The purpose of the Balance Sheet is to show the business's financial position (its wealth). It shows everything the business owns (called assets) and all the money it owes (called liabilities).

- **Fixed Assets** includes valuable items the business owns that it will keep for more than one year, such as buildings, cars, computers, equipment and so on.
- **Current Assets** includes valuable items the business owns that it will keep for less than one year, such as stock, debtors, cash and so on.
- **Current Liabilities** includes loans the business owes that have to be repaid within one year, such as bank overdrafts, creditors and so on.

Balance Sheet of X Ltd.
As on ~~For the Year~~ Ended 31st December 20--

	€	€
Fixed Assets		70,000
Current Assets	30,000	
Current Liabilities	(5,000)	
Working Capital		25,000
Total Net Assets		95,000
Financed By		
Ordinary/(Equity) Shares		50,000
Retained Earnings/Reserves		15,000
Preference Shares		10,000
Long Term Loans		20,000
CAPITAL EMPLOYED		95,000

- **Working Capital** shows the cash left over in the business to pay bills that come in. It is Current Assets – Current Liabilities.
- **Financed By** shows the amount of money invested in the business by the investors. It includes shares and loans.
- **Retained Earnings** shows the total amount of profits previously made by the business that have been reinvested in the business.

Importance of the Balance Sheet

The Balance Sheet is an important document for managers because:

- The value of the business's fixed assets tells managers whether the business has enough security to offer a bank when applying for a loan.

- The working capital figure tells the managers whether the business has enough cash available to pay any bills that may arise in the near future.

- The "Financed By" section of the Balance Sheet tells managers whether the business will be able to take out any more loans. If there are already lots of loans in "Financed By", managers know it may be harder to borrow more money because banks may be unwilling to lend to a business that already has lots of unpaid loans.

Ratio Analysis

In the same way that a doctor examines a patient to find out what is wrong with him, an entrepreneur must examine her business to make sure that it is in a healthy position. Just like a doctor examines basic things such as blood pressure, temperature and so on, the entrepreneur must examine her business under three basic headings:

- **Profitability**
- **Liquidity**
- **Gearing**

Profitability Ratios

Profitability ratios examine whether the profit made by the business is good or bad for the size of the business. The answers can be compared to previous years, other businesses and the industry average to see how the business is performing.

There are three ways to measure a business's profitability.

Profitability Ratios

Gross Profit Percentage or Gross Margin

Formula

> **[Gross Profit ÷ Sales] x 100**

For example, a 40% gross profit percentage tells the manager that 40% of the money the business takes in from customers is the business's profit. However, the business's expenses still have to be paid out of this.

Importance
- A decreasing ratio from one year to the next means that the selling price is falling or cost price is increasing.
- This can be corrected by increasing the selling price or buying from a cheaper supplier.

Net Profit Percentage or Net Margin

Formula

> **[Net Profit ÷ Sales] x 100**

For example, a 30% net profit percentage tells the manager that even after the business has paid all its expenses, 30% of the money the business takes in from customers is the business's profit to keep.

Importance
- A decreasing ratio from one year to the next means that expenses are increasing.
- This can be corrected by making cutbacks, such as banning overtime.

Return on Investment Or Return on Capital Employed

Formula

> **[Net Profit ÷ Capital Employed] x 100**

For example, a 10% return on investment (ROI) tells the manager that for every €1 invested in the business, the business made a 10 cent profit. Is this good or bad? The Irish government will give you 5% if you invest with it (government bonds) and there is no risk of losing your money. So the business's ROI should be much higher than this, given the risk involved. Therefore, a 10% return is a good one.

Importance
- A decreasing ratio from one year to the next means that managers are not as good at turning business resources into profits.
- Correct this by making cutbacks and by hiring more efficient managers.

Note:

Capital Employed = Equity (Ordinary) Share Capital + Retained Earnings (Reserves) + Long Term Loans + Preference Shares if any.

Example

The accountant in Alpha Ltd. has prepared the following figures for the business:

	2009	2010
	€	€
Sales	400,000	500,000
Gross Profit	100,000	120,000
Net Profit	60,000	70,000
Capital Employed	600,000	750,000

You are required to:
- (a) Calculate the gross profit percentage, the net profit percentage and the return on investment for both years.
- (b) Analyse the trend in profitability in the business.

Gross Profit Percentage	[Gross Profit ÷ Sales] x 100	
2009	[100,000 ÷ 400,000] x 100 =	**25%**
2010	[120,000 ÷ 500,000] x 100 =	**24%**

Trend in Profitability

The gross profit percentage has decreased from 25% in 2009 to 24% in 2010. This is a bad trend because it means that the business is less profitable than last year. The reason for this is perhaps that the selling price the business gets for its products has decreased and/or the cost price it pays for them has increased. The business should shop around for a cheaper supplier so that the gross profit margin will increase next year.

Net Profit Percentage	[Net Profit ÷ Sales] x 100	
2009	[60,000 ÷ 400,000] x 100 =	**15%**
2010	[70,000 ÷ 500,000] x 100 =	**14%**

Trend in Profitability

The net profit percentage has decreased from 15% in 2009 to 14% in 2010. This is a bad trend because it means that the business is less profitable than last year. The reason for this is that the business's expenses have increased. The business should try to reduce its expenses by cutting back on staff overtime, and changing electricity and telephone suppliers to cheaper ones.

ROI	[Net Profit ÷ Capital Employed] x 100	
2009	[60,000 ÷ 600,000] x 100 =	**10%**
2010	[70,000 ÷ 750,000] x 100 =	**9·33%**

Trend in Profitability

The return on investment has decreased from 10% in 2009 to 9.33% in 2010. This is a bad trend because the business is making a lower return for the shareholders. The business should try to reduce its expenses and use its resources more efficiently in order to improve.

However, the return on investment in both years is much higher than the risk-free return available on government investments.

Liquidity Ratios

Liquidity examines whether the business has enough cash available to pay its *short-term bills*. There are two liquidity ratios:

1. Working Capital Ratio

> **Current Assets ÷ Current Liabilities**

- The working capital ratio tells a business how much money it has (current assets) for very €1 it owes (current liabilities).
- The answer is shown as *x*:1.
- The ideal ratio for a business to have is 2:1.
- The working capital ratio is important because it tells a business the following:
  1. If the ratio is less than 2:1, the business does not have enough cash to pay its bills as they come in. This means that the business will lose out on cash discounts given by suppliers for early payment. This can be corrected by selling investments to raise the cash needed.
  2. If the ratio is much higher than 2:1, the business has too much spare cash lying around. It should invest this excess cash to make a profit from it.

2. Acid Test Ratio

> **{Current Assets – Closing Stock} ÷ Current Liabilities**

- The acid test ratio tells a business how much real cash it has, when the stock in the shop or factory is ignored (CA – closing stock), for every €1 it owes (current liabilities).

■ The answer is shown as *x*:1. The ideal ratio for a business to have is 1:1.
■ The acid test ratio is important because it tells a business the following:
   1. It lets a business know its liquidity position in an emergency situation. If creditors want to be paid *immediately*, stock is no use because creditors want cash. Therefore, this ratio takes stock out of the equation to see how the business can cope. If the ratio is less than 1:1, the business is **illiquid**. It does not have enough cash to pay its bills. This means that the business may lose its credit rating and find it hard to get supplies on credit.
   2. If the business is illiquid, it may have to sell investments or sell stock at a massive discount to try to raise the cash needed to pay bills.

Example

Calculate the liquidity ratios of Beta Ltd. for both years from the following figures and analyse the trend in the firm's liquidity.

	2009	2010
Current Liabilities	€100,000	€140,000
Closing Stock	€100,000	€100,000
Current Assets	€200,000	€230,000

Working Capital Ratio	Current Assets ÷ Current Liabilities	
2009	200,000 ÷ 100,000 =	**2:1**
2010	230,000 ÷ 140,000 =	**1·64:1**

Trend in Liquidity

The working capital ratio has decreased from 2:1 in 2009 to 1·64:1 in 2010. This is a bad trend because the business has less cash available to pay its bills. The ratio in 2009 was the ideal of 2:1 but in 2010 it was less than the ideal 2:1. The business could sell some of its investments to raise cash to improve its liquidity.

Acid Test Ratio	[Current Assets – Closing Stock] ÷ Current Liabilities	
2009	[200,000 – 100,000] = 100,000 ÷ 100,000	**1:1**
2010	[230,000 – 100,000] = 130,000 ÷ 140,000	**0·93:1**

The acid test ratio has decreased from 1:1 in 2009 to 0·93:1 in 2010. This is a bad trend because the business has less cash available to pay its bills. The ratio in 2009 was the ideal 1:1 but in 2010 it was less than the ideal of 1:1.

Stock levels have increased a lot over the year. The business should have a sale to get rid of some of this stock to raise cash to bring the ratio back to 1:1.

Debt/Equity Ratio

The formula for the debt/equity ratio is:

Debt Capital	÷	**Equity Capital**
Long Tem Debt (Loans) **+ Preference Shares**	÷	**Equity (Ordinary) Shares** **+ Retained Earnings (Reserves)**

The answer is expressed as x:1.

There is no *ideal* ratio.

The debt/equity ratio examines how the business is financed. It tells a business where the money came from to establish and run it – how much money has been borrowed from banks in long-term loans (debt capital) compared with how much the owners of the business have invested (equity capital) in it.

Debt capital consists of all the long-term loans the business has taken out, such as debentures and preference shares. Debentures are long-term loans that a company takes out; they have to be repaid in one lump-sum at some point in the future. Until they are repaid, the business pays a fixed rate of interest every year on the amount borrowed. Preference shares are really the same thing as debentures. Even though they are called "shares", they are just another type of long-term loan.

Equity capital is the total amount of money invested by the owners of the business. It consists of the original amount of money the owners put into the business (called ordinary share capital or equity share capital) and all the profits that the owners reinvested in the business (called retained earnings or reserves).

The debt/equity ratio is important because it tells a business the following:

1. The debt/equity ratio lets the manager know how much the business has borrowed relative to how much the owners have invested. She can work out if the business is high geared, low geared or neutral geared.

    ■ **Low Gearing**   Debt < Equity   **[Formula answer < 1:1]**
      This means that the business has borrowed less money than the shareholders have invested.

- **Neutral Gearing   Debt = Equity   [Formula answer = 1:1]**
  This means that the business has borrowed exactly the same amount as the shareholders have invested.

- **High Gearing   Debt > Equity   [Formula answer > 1:1]**
  This means that the business has borrowed more money than the shareholders have invested.

2. The debt/equity ratio lets a manager know how much interest she can expect the business to have to pay back. A business that has borrowed a lot of money and is high geared will have a lot of interest to pay back. This may reduce the business's profits.

3. The debt/equity ratio lets a manager know whether the business is in danger of going bankrupt. A business that has borrowed a lot of money and is high geared will have a lot of loans and interest to pay back. If the business cannot afford to pay back all its loans and the interest on them, the lenders will take it to court and get a judge to close it down and sell it off to repay the lenders. Thus high gearing increases the risk of the business going bankrupt.

4. The debt/equity ratio lets a manager know whether the business is able to take out more loans. A business that has borrowed a lot of money and is high geared has a lot of loans and interest to pay back. The business will find it difficult to get a new loan until the old ones are repaid. This is because the bank considers businesses with lots of loans a high risk.

Example

Calculate the debt/equity ratio for both years and comment on the trend:

	2009	**2010**
Equity Share Capital	€12,000	€15,000
Long-term Debt	€4,000	€45,000
Retained Earnings (Reserves)	€3,000	€7,500

Debt/Equity Ratio	**[Long-term Debt + Preference Shares] ÷ [Equity Shares + Retained Earnings]**		
2009	[4,000 + 0] ÷ [12,000 + 3,000] 4,000 ÷ 15,000		**0·27:1**
2010	[45,000 + 0] ÷ [15,000 + 7,500] 45,000 ÷ 22,500		**2:1**

Trend in Debt/Equity Ratio

The debt/equity ratio has increased from 0·27:1 in 2009 to 2:1 in 2010. This is a bad trend because it means that the business has borrowed relatively more. Increased levels of borrowing mean more interest to repay and a higher chance of bankruptcy. To reduce the debt/equity ratio, the business could reinvest more of its profits, sell more shares or sell investments to repay long-term loans.

Users of Ratio Information

USERS	INTERESTED IN:
Shareholders	■ Net profit percentage – to see whether they will get a decent dividend ■ Return on investment – to see whether it exceeds the ROI available risk free from the government
Suppliers	■ Working capital ratio – to see whether the business is liquid and can repay its short-term loans ■ Acid test ratio – to see whether the business can pay the suppliers immediately
Employees	■ Profitability ratios – to see whether the business can afford to give them a pay rise ■ Debt/equity ratio – to see whether the business is in danger of bankruptcy and hence how safe their jobs are
Lenders	■ Liquidity ratios – to see whether the business can repay the interest on the loan ■ Debt/equity ratio – to see whether the business is worthy of another loan

Ordinary Level Questions

EXAM SECTION 1 (25%) – SHORT ANSWER QUESTIONS [10 marks each]

1. Column 1 is a list of business terms. Column 2 is a list of possible explanations for these terms. Match the two lists by placing the letter of the correct explanation under the relevant number below. One explanation has no match.

Column 1	Column 2: Explanations
1. P&L	a) Bills that have to be paid by a business, such as wages, rent, interest on loans and so on
2. Balance Sheet	b) Assets owned by a business that it will have for more than one year
3. Fixed Assets	c) Debts owed by a business that must be repaid within one year
4. Current Assets	d) Financial statement showing assets and liabilities of a business
5. Current Liabilities	e) Profit and Loss (Account)
6. Expenses	f) Assets owned by a business that it will keep for less than one year
	g) Debts owed by a business that take longer than one year to be repaid

1	2	3	4	5	6
E					

2. The following information is taken from the final accounts of Gamma Ltd.

    Sales   €100,000
    Cost of Sales   € 40,000

    Calculate (i) the gross profit and (ii) the gross profit percentage.

3. The following information is taken from the final accounts of Lambda Ltd.

    Sales   €40,000
    Gross Profit   €10,000
    Net Profit   €8,000

    Calculate (i) the gross profit percentage and (ii) the net profit percentage.

4. The following information is taken from the final accounts of Delta Ltd.

    Sales   €500,000
    Gross Profit   €300,000
    Net Profit   €200,000

    Calculate (i) the gross margin and (ii) the net margin.

5. The following information is taken from the final accounts of Epsilon Ltd.

   Sales   €300,000
   Gross Profit   €150,000
   Expenses   €120,000

   Calculate (i) the net profit and (ii) the net profit percentage.

6. The following information is taken from the final accounts of Zeta Ltd.

   Current Assets   €60,000
   Current Liabilities   €42,000

   Calculate (i) the working capital and (ii) the working capital ratio.

7. The following information is taken from the final accounts of Theta Ltd.

   Current Assets   €900,000
   Current Liabilities   €540,000

   Calculate (i) the working capital and (ii) the working capital ratio.

8. The following information is taken from the final accounts of Iota Ltd.

   Current Assets   €800,000
   Current Liabilities   €480,000
   Closing Stock   €320,000

   Calculate (i) the working capital ratio and (ii) the acid test ratio.

9. The following information is taken from the final accounts of Kappa Ltd.

   Current Assets   €50,000
   Current Liabilities   €22,000
   Closing Stock   €26,000

   Calculate (i) the working capital ratio and (ii) the acid test ratio.

10. The following information is taken from the final accounts of Mu Ltd.

    Equity Capital   €750,000
    Long-term Debt   €500,000
    Retained Earnings   €250,000

    Calculate the debt/equity ratio.

11. The following information is taken from the final accounts of Nu Ltd.

    Equity Capital   €18,000
    Long-term Debt   €36,000
    Retained Earnings   €2,000

    Calculate the debt/equity ratio.

12. The following information is taken from the final accounts of XI Ltd.

    Equity Capital   €120,000
    Long-term Debt   €360,000
    Retained Earnings   €480,000

    Calculate the debt/equity ratio.

EXAM SECTION 2 (75%) – LONG QUESTIONS

1. The following figures are available for Omicron Ltd.

		2010	2011
Sales	€	100,000	120,000
Gross Profit	€	60,000	66,000
Net Profit	€	40,000	32,000

   (A) Calculate the gross profit percentage for 2010 and 2011 (showing the formulae and all your workings) and comment on the trend.   (30 marks)

   (B) Calculate the net profit percentage for 2010 and 2011 (showing the formulae and all your workings) and comment on the trend.   (30 marks)

2. The following figures are available for Pi Ltd.

		2010	2011
Net Profit	€	800	1,250
Sales	€	20,000	25,000
Gross Profit	€	1,600	2,500

   (A) Calculate the gross profit percentage for 2010 and 2011 (showing the formulae and all your workings) and comment on the trend.   (30 marks)

   (B) Calculate the net profit percentage for 2010 and 2011 (showing the formulae and all your workings) and comment on the trend.   (30 marks)

3. The following figures are available for Rho Ltd.

		2010	2011
Sales	€	400,00	600,000
Capital Employed	€	800,000	950,000
Net Profit	€	200,000	150,000

   (A) Calculate the net profit percentage for 2010 and 2011 (showing the formulae and all your workings) and comment on the trend.   (30 marks)

   (B) Calculate the return on capital employed for 2010 and 2011 (showing the formulae and all your workings) and comment on the trend.   (30 marks)

4. The following figures are available for Sigma Ltd.

		2010	2011
Capital Employed	€	400,00	600,000
Net Profit	€	800,000	950,000
Sales	€	200,000	150,000

   (A) Calculate the net profit percentage for 2010 and 2011 (showing the formulae and all your workings) and comment on the trend.   (30 marks)

   (B) Calculate the return on investment for 2010 and 2011 (showing the formulae and all your workings) and comment on the trend.   (30 marks)

5. The following figures are available for Tau Ltd.

		2010	2011
Net Profit	€	450	1,000
Sales	€	1,800	4,000
Capital Employed	€	10,000	12,000

(A) Calculate the net profit percentage for 2010 and 2011 (showing the formulae and all your workings) and comment on the trend.   (30 marks)

(B) Calculate the return on investment for 2010 and 2011 (showing the formulae and all your workings) and comment on the trend.   (30 marks)

6. The following figures are available for Upsilon Ltd.

		2010	2011
Current Assets	€	200,000	300,000
Current Liabilities	€	100,000	180,000
Closing Stock	€	100,000	160,000

(A) Calculate the working capital ratio for 2010 and 2011 (showing the formulae and all your workings) and comment on the trend.   (30 marks)

(B) Calculate the acid test ratio for 2010 and 2011 (showing the formulae and all your workings) and comment on the trend.   (30 marks)

7. The following figures are available for Phi Ltd.

		2010	2011
Current Liabilities	€	42,000	64,000
Current Assets	€	84,000	96,000
Closing Stock	€	40,000	48,000

(A) Calculate the working capital ratio for 2010 and 2011 (showing the formulae and all your workings) and comment on the trend.   (30 marks)

(B) Calculate the acid test ratio for 2010 and 2011 (showing the formulae and all your workings) and comment on the trend.   (30 marks)

8. The following figures are available for Chi Ltd.

		2010	2011
Current Assets	€	600,000	800,000
Closing Stock	€	200,000	320,000
Current Liabilities	€	500,000	400,000

(A) Calculate the working capital ratio for 2010 and 2011 (showing the formulae and all your workings) and comment on the trend.   (30 marks)

(B) Calculate the acid test ratio for 2010 and 2011 (showing the formulae and all your workings) and comment on the trend.   (30 marks)

9. The following figures are available for Psi Ltd.

	2010	2011
Equity Capital €	20,000	30,000
Long-term Debt €	10,000	60,000
Retained Earnings €	5,000	6,000

Calculate the debt/equity ratio for 2010 and 2011 (showing the formulae and all your workings) and comment on the trend.   (30 marks)

10. The following figures are available for Omega Ltd.

	2010	2011
Retained Earnings €	100,000	120,000
Long-term Debt €	900,000	450,000
Equity Capital €	500,000	500,000

Calculate the debt/equity ratio for 2010 and 2011 (showing the formulae and all your workings) and comment on the trend.   (30 marks)

11. The following figures are available for Sho Ltd.

	2010	2011
Equity Capital €	300,000	320,000
Long-term Debt €	600,000	10,000
Retained Earnings €	60,000	80,000

Calculate the debt/equity ratio for 2010 and 2011
(showing the formulae and all your workings) and comment on the trend.   (30 marks)

Higher Level Questions

EXAM SECTION 1 (20%) – SHORT ANSWER QUESTIONS [10 marks each]

1. Distinguish between "Profit and Loss Account" and "Balance Sheet".

2. Distinguish between "Cost of Sales" and "Expenses" of a business.

3. What is a fixed asset? Give two examples.

4. What is a current liability? Give two examples.

5. The following information is taken from the final accounts of A Ltd.

   Sales   €100,000
   Cost of Sales €40,000
   Expenses   €25,000

   Calculate (i) the gross profit percentage and (ii) the net profit percentage.

6. The following information is taken from the final accounts of B Ltd.

Expenses   €6,000

Cost of Sales   €50,000

Gross Profit   €10,000

Calculate (i) the gross margin and (ii) the net margin.

7. The following figures relate to C Ltd.

		2010	2011
Fixed Assets	€	1,500,000	2,000,000
Current Assets	€	600,000	550,000
Current Liabilities	€	400,000	350,000
Closing Stock	€	130,000	180,000

Calculate the working capital ratio for both years. State whether the trend is improving or not and give one possible reason for this.

8. The following figures relate to D Ltd.

		2010	2011
Ordinary Share Capital	€	50,000	60,000
Closing Stock	€	32,000	56,000
Current Assets	€	80,000	85,000
Closing Liabilities	€	48,000	51,000

Calculate the acid test ratio for both years. State whether the trend is improving or not and give one possible reason for this.

9. The following figures relate to E Ltd.

		2009	2010
Closing Stock	€	6,000	12,000
Current Liabilities	€	4,000	9,000
Current Assets	€	10,000	15,000

Calculate the acid test ratio for both years. Suggest two things the business can do to improve the trend.

10. The following figures relate to F Ltd.

		2009	2010
Ordinary Share Capital	€	700,000	750,000
Long-term Debt	€	250,000	150,000
Creditors	€	160,000	80,000
Retained Earnings	€	50,000	75,000

Calculate the debt/equity ratio for both years. State whether the trend is improving or not and give one possible reason for this.

11.   The following figures relate to G Ltd.

		2010	2011
Reserves	€	10,000	22,000
Equity Share Capital	€	40,000	48,000
Bank Overdraft	€	20,000	11,000
Long-term loans	€	100,000	10,000

Calculate the debt/equity ratio for both years. State whether the trend is improving or not and give one possible reason for this.

12.   The following figures relate to H Ltd.

		2010	2011
Reserves	€	25,000	35,000
Ordinary Share Capital	€	175,000	255,000
Fixed Assets	€	600,000	750,000
Long-term loans	€	40,000	500,000

Calculate the debt/equity ratio for both years. State whether the trend is improving or not and give one possible reason for this.

EXAM SECTION 2 (20%) – APPLIED BUSINESS QUESTION – 80 MARKS

Thodun Ltd.

Thomas Dunphy set up his engineering business, Thodun Ltd., two years ago. His mother and father invested their life savings in the business in return for a 40% share of the company. They hope that the investment will pay off and supplement their pension. Thomas used his own savings to fund the remainder of the capital he needed. His accountant prepares a Profit and Loss Account and Balance Sheet each year. Thomas was delighted that at the end of this year, the business had lots of money in its bank account because last year, it had none and suppliers were breathing down Thomas's neck looking to get paid.

However, he was disappointed to see that his net profit had fallen since last year. He thinks that the problem is the fact that he hasn't raised prices in line with inflation. His employees are excellent and Thomas pays them well above the going rate for the job. There is a relaxed atmosphere in the business and employees can use company facilities at will.

To expand the business, Thomas needs to invest in technology. He is considering taking out a ten-year loan to finance the purchase of the equipment needed. Because technology is changing so rapidly, he knows that more equipment and more long-term loans will be a feature of his business in the future.

(A) Referring to two ratios, advise Thomas on the benefits of
preparing liquidity ratios. (25 marks)

(B) If Thomas takes out the loan, his business's debt/equity ratio will increase.
Evaluate the impact of this on Thomas's business and its shareholders. (20 marks)

(C) Evaluate the importance of the Profit and Loss Account and Balance Sheet
for the good financial management of Thodun Ltd. (35 marks)

EXAM SECTION 3 (60%) – LONG QUESTIONS

1. The accountant in Eye Ltd. has prepared the following figures for the business:

	2011	2010
	€	€
Capital Employed	400,000	500,000
Sales	100,000	120,000
Net Profit	35,000	38,000
Cost of sales	40,000	24,000

You are required to:

(a) Calculate the gross profit percentage, the net profit percentage and
the return on investment for both years.

(b) Analyse the trend in profitability in the business. (40 marks)

2. The accountant in Jay Ltd. has prepared the following figures for the business:

	2011	2010
	€	€
Gross Profit	3,000	4,000
Capital Employed	20,000	25,000
Expenses	2,000	1,500
Sales	6,000	7,000

You are required to:

(a) Calculate the gross margin, the net margin and the return
on capital employed for both years.

(b) Analyse the trend in profitability in the business. (40 marks)

3. Compute the liquidity ratios of Kay Ltd. for both years from
the following figures and analyse the trend in the firm's liquidity. (20 marks)

		2010	2011
Current Assets	€	15,000	18,000
Current Liabilities	€	11,000	8,500
Closing Stock	€	8,000	8,700

4. Compute the liquidity ratios of Elle Ltd. for both years from the following figures. Analyse the trend and discuss how the firm's creditors might use this knowledge in making decisions.   (30 marks)

		2010	2011
Current Assets	€	700,000	450,000
Working Capital	€	200,000	210,000
Closing Stock	€	380,000	205,000

5. Using two ratios in each case, analyse the profitability and liquidity trends in Emm Ltd. from the following figures for 2011 and 2010. Suggest how the trends might be improved.   (40 marks)

	2011 €	2010 €
Current Assets	150,000	130,000
Current Liabilities	100,000	65,000
Closing Stock	70,000	65,000
Sales	900,000	810,000
Gross Profit	400,000	540,000
Net Profit	100,000	180,000

6. From the figures given below, calculate the debt/equity ratio for both years and analyse any trends you notice from your calculations.   (40 marks)

	2011 €	2010 €
Equity Share Capital	20,000	25,000
Long-term Debt	60,000	5,000
Retained Earnings (Reserves)	10,000	5,000

7. Compute the debt/equity ratio of Enn Ltd. for both years from the following figures. Analyse the trend and discuss how a potential lender might use this knowledge in deciding whether to lend the business more money.   (30 marks)

		2011	2010
Long-term Loans	€	3,000,000	300,000
Equity Share Capital	€	900,000	900,000
Retained Earnings	€	100,000	90,000

8. Compute the debt/equity ratio of Oh Ltd. for both years from the following figures.
    Analyse the trend and discuss how it can be improved.   (30 marks)

		2011	2010
Equity Share Capital	€	2,000,000	2,200,000
Retained Earnings	€	400,000	350,000
Long-term Loans	€	4,000,000	150,000

Insurance and Tax

Insurance

In life we all face certain risks. Someone could steal our car. A fire could burn down our garage. Most sensible people take steps to prevent these risks happening (this is called risk management). To minimise these risks, we can buy a car alarm and install a sprinkler system in the garage.

However, despite risk management, these risks may still occur. And when they do, we will be out of pocket – we'll have to buy a replacement car and pay to get a new garage built. To minimise these financial losses, we can take out insurance.

Insurance offers financial protection from risks. Businesses and households pay a relatively small premium to an insurance company every year for protection. If anything happens to them or their assets, the insurance company pays them money as compensation for the value of what they have lost. In this way, they do not lose any money.

You may be wondering how the insurance company makes a profit if it charges each business and household only a small premium every year and may have to pay out a fortune to them when they make a claim. The insurance company makes money by insuring a *large* number of businesses and households. It therefore takes in a lot of money. Bad things such as theft and fires are thankfully rare, so only a small number of households and businesses make a claim each year. This means that the insurance company pays out less than it takes in and thus makes a profit.

Principles of Insurance

To protect themselves from being ripped off by people making false claims, insurance companies have certain rules. These are called the principles of insurance.

Principle of Insurance #1: Utmost Good Faith

This principle states that when the business/household is applying to the insurance company for insurance cover and is filling in the **proposal form**, it must answer every question asked of it *truthfully*.

Furthermore, it must *volunteer* any **material information**, even if it is not asked for it. Material information is defined as any information that would affect the insurance company's decision whether to insure the business/household and, if so, what premium to charge it. For example, a person seeking life assurance must tell the insurance company that he takes part in dangerous adventure sports whether it asks this or not.

If the insurance company later finds out that he lied or withheld material information, he will receive no compensation because he broke the rule.

In Latin, this rule is called *uberrimae fidei*.

Note:

- An insurance proposal form is an application form that a person fills in when he wants to get something insured. It asks a lot of questions that must be answered truthfully. The insurance company uses the answers to decide what risk the person is and then whether to insure that person and, if so, what premium to charge him.
- An insurance policy is a document you get from the insurance company. It is your legal contract with it. It sets out what risks you are covered for and what you are not covered for. It tells you how much your annual premium is.

Principle of Insurance #2: Insurable Interest

This principle states that *you* can only insure something that you own. It must be something valuable to you. You must derive some benefit from it and you would lose money if anything happened to it. In insurance law, we say that the person must have a **legal relationship** with the item he is insuring.

So you can insure your house, your car and so on. But you cannot insure David Beckham's legs against injury or the Empire State Building, because if anything happened to them, you would not lose any money.

Principle of Insurance #3: Indemnity

This principle states that you cannot make a profit from an insurance claim. The compensation you receive is exactly equal to the value of the item you lost. So you are no better and no worse off, after making the claim.

For example, Angela bought a new car in 2000 for €10,000. Its value yesterday was €2,400. This morning, it was totally written off in a crash. A similar brand new car would cost €18,000. Angela submits a **claim form** to her insurance company as a result of the accident. How much compensation will she receive?

Answer: €2,400. Under the indemnity rule, she receives the value of what she lost. The car was worth €2,400, so she lost €2,400. The insurance company pays her €2,400. She is no better and no worse off after the claim.

Note:

An insurance claim form is a form filled in by the insured person when seeking compensation. In it, he sets out details of the asset, the damage to it, how the damage happened, the amount of compensation sought and so on. The insurance company uses the claim form to decide how much compensation, if any, to pay out.

The indemnity rule means that there is no point in **over-insuring** an asset. Over-insurance is when you insure an item for *more* than it is actually worth. For example, a business insures a factory for €10,000,000 even though it is only worth €50,000. If this factory is totally destroyed in a fire today, how much compensation will the business receive?

The indemnity rule states that the business will receive €50,000 because this is the value of what it lost (even though it paid premiums for €10,000,000). So it makes no sense to over-insure an asset. Some people think that over-insuring an item is a handy way to make money, but the principle of indemnity prevents this.

The indemnity rule also affects businesses and households who **under-insure** an asset. This means that you insure an item for *less* than it is actually worth. For example, your factory is worth €200,000 but you only insure it for €100,000. This is very dangerous.

In the case of under-insurance, the insurance company uses a rule called the **average clause** to calculate the amount of compensation to pay out. It states that because you are only insured for a fraction of what the item is worth, you only receive that *same fraction* of any compensation. It is computed as follows:

Claim x	**Amount Insured for with this Insurance Company**
	How much the item is worth

EXAMPLE

Thomas has his factory insured for €300,000. It is currently worth €500,000.
Yesterday there was a fire in the factory, causing damage of €6,000.
Thomas puts in a claim for €6,000.
How much compensation will Thomas receive? Explain your answer.

ANSWER

Claim x	**Amount Insured for with this Insurance Company**
	How much the item is worth

$$= €6,000 \quad \times \quad \frac{€300,000}{€500,000}$$

Average Clause = $\frac{Insured}{value}$ x Loss

$$= \textbf{€3,600}.$$

Thomas will receive only €3,600 compensation from the insurance company.

Because the factory is underinsured, the average clause applies. It states that because the factory is insured only for a fraction of its value (3/5ths in this case), the business will receive only that fraction (3/5ths) of any claim made.

Principle of Insurance #4: Contribution

This principle states that if you insure an asset with a number of insurance companies (say 5), you will *not* receive 5 times the compensation. Instead, each will pay you a fraction of the compensation in the ratio of the amount you were insured with each as follows:

Claim x	**Amount Insured for with this Insurance Company**
	Total amount Insured for with all the Companies

EXAMPLE

X Ltd. insured its lorry with two insurance companies as follows:

	Company A	Company B
Value insured with each	€14,000	€16,000

Vandals caused €12,000 of damage to the lorry. How much compensation will X Ltd. receive from each company?
Explain your answer.

ANSWER
From Company A, X Ltd. will receive:

Claim	x	Amount Insured for with this Insurance Company
		Total amount Insured for with all the Companies

$$= €12,000 \times \frac{€14,000}{€14,000 + €16,000}$$

$$= €12,000 \times \frac{€14,000}{€30,000}$$

$$= \mathbf{€5,600}$$

From Company B, X Ltd. will receive:

Claim	x	Amount Insured for with this Insurance Company
		Total amount Insured for with all the Companies

$$= €12,000 \times \frac{€16,000}{€14,000 + €16,000}$$

$$= €12,000 \times \frac{€16,000}{€30,000}$$

$$= \mathbf{€6,400}$$

X Ltd. will receive €5,600 compensation from Company A and €6,400 from Company B.

Explain your answer
Because X Ltd. insured its lorry with two insurance companies, the insurance principle of contribution applies.
It states that each insurance company will pay X Ltd. a proportion of the compensation in the ratio of the amount X Ltd. was insured with each.

DIFFICULT EXAMPLE

Tina insured her house with two insurance companies as follows:

	Company C	Company D
Value insured with each	€140,000	€70,000

A storm caused damage of €9,000. The house is worth €280,000
How much compensation will Tina receive from each company?

ANSWER

■ This question has two problems – she is insured with two companies
   (contribution principle) and she is underinsured with each company
   (indemnity principle – average clause).

■ The solution to this problem is to use the contribution and average clause
   formulae together as follows:

From C she receives:

$$\text{Claim} \times \frac{\text{Amount Insured with this Company}}{\text{Total Insured with all Companies}} \times \frac{\text{Insured with this Company}}{\text{Value of the Item}}$$

(Contribution) (Average Clause)

$$= €9,000 \times \frac{€140,000}{€140,000 + €70,000} \times \frac{€140,000}{€280,000}$$

$$= \mathbf{€3,000}$$

From D she receives:

$$\text{Claim} \times \frac{\text{Amount Insured with this Company}}{\text{Total Insured with all Companies}} \times \frac{\text{Insured with this Company}}{\text{Value of the Item}}$$

$$= €9,000 \times \frac{€70,000}{€140,000 + €70,000} \times \frac{€70,000}{€280,000}$$

$$= \mathbf{€750}$$

Tina will receive €3,000 compensation from Company C and €750 from Company D.

Principle of Insurance #5: Subrogation

This principle states that once the insurance company has given you full compensation for an item, that is *all* you can get. You give up all your rights to further claims on the item to the insurance company. The insurance company now owns the item and it "owns" the right to claim compensation from the person who caused the damage.

For example, if your bicycle worth €800 is destroyed in an accident and the insurance company pays you €800 in compensation, you cannot:

(a) Sell the wreck of the bicycle. The subrogation rule states that it now belongs to the insurance company. If you could sell it for say €20, you would be making a profit, which breaks the indemnity rule.

(b) Sue the person who caused the accident for the value of the bicycle. The subrogation rule takes this right away from you and gives it to the insurance company. They can try to reclaim the money from the person who caused the accident. If you could sue the person who crashed into you for another €800, you would be making a profit, which again breaks the indemnity rule.

Insurance Premium

The premium is the amount of money that the business/household pays to the insurance company every year for its insurance cover. The amount of premium a business/household has to pay depends on the following factors:

Risk

■ The greater the risk of a claim the higher the premium you will be charged.

■ The insurance company sometimes adds a **loading** for higher risk people and businesses. A loading is an extra charge added to the basic premium to cover such higher risks.

■ Inexperienced drivers pay higher car insurance premiums than those who have been driving a long time, because inexperienced drivers are more likely to have an accident and claim from the insurance company.

■ Smokers pay higher life assurance premiums than non-smokers because they are a higher risk of dying and claiming sooner.

■ People who live in Dublin pay higher house insurance premiums than people who live outside Dublin because they are a higher risk of claiming for theft and damage.

Value of the Item

■ The more valuable the asset, the higher the insurance premium

■ Rita and Anna are twin sisters living in the same part of Kilkenny. Recently, each sister received a necklace from her husband for her birthday. Rita's necklace is worth €100. Anna's is worth €35,000. They both decide to insure their necklaces. Clearly, the insurance company will charge Anna a higher premium than Rita, because they will have to pay her a lot more money if her necklace is stolen.

Claims

■ The more the insurance company pays out in compensation claims, the higher the premiums they will charge to cover their costs.

■ For example, if insurance compensation payouts increase by 10%, the insurance company will have to increase premiums by 10% to cover this increased payout.

Profit

■ The insurance company charges a premium that gives it a decent profit. The premiums collected must exceed the amount paid out in claims.

Government Tax

■ The government adds tax (currently 2% stamp duty) to the premium charged by the insurance company, thus increasing the cost for the consumer.

EXAMPLE

Deirdre wishes to insure her house for €300,000 and its contents for €40,000. The insurance company tells her that the annual premiums are as follows:

Buildings: €2 for every €1,000 of cover

Contents: €3 for every €1,000 of cover

1. **What premium will Deirdre have to pay for her house and contents insurance?**

2. **Why does the insurance company charge a higher premium to insure the contents of the house rather than the house itself?**

ANSWER

$$\text{Buildings premium} = \text{Premium} \times \frac{\text{Insured for}}{€1,000}$$

$$= €2 \times \frac{€300,000}{€1,000}$$

$$= €2 \times 300$$

$$= €600 \text{ premium for the year}$$

$$\text{Contents premium} = \text{Premium} \times \frac{\text{Insured for}}{€1,000}$$

$$= €3 \times \frac{€40,000}{€1,000}$$

$$= €3 \times 400$$

$$= €120 \text{ premium for the year}$$

Answer:

1. Deirdre will pay a total premium of €720 to the insurance company every year.

2. The insurance company charges a higher premium for the contents (€3 for contents but only €2 for the buildings) because there is a *higher risk* of something happening (theft, for example) to the contents than there is to the building.

EXAMPLE

Ross wishes to insure his new car for €22,000. He is 19 and has been driving for only six months, has a provisional license and lives in Dublin. He has no penalty points and has never been involved in an accident.

The insurance company tells him that the annual premium is €15 for every €1,000 of cover.

But it adds a **loading** as follows:

Driving less than one year	700%	Had a serious accident	2,000%
Provisional license	400%	2 or more penalty points	150%
Male driver	60%	Dublin driver 40%	

What premium will Ross have to pay?

ANSWER

$$\text{Basic premium} = \text{Premium} \times \frac{\text{Insured for}}{€1,000}$$

$$= €15 \times \frac{€22,000}{€1,000}$$

$$= €15 \times 22$$

$$= €330 \text{ would be the premium for the year.}$$

But the insurance company adds a loading onto Ross's basic premium as follows:

Basic Premium		€330
Add: Loading for Ross		
Driving less than one year	700%	
Provisional license	400%	
Male driver	60%	
Dublin driver	40%	
Total loading	1200%	
Loading = €330 Basic Premium ×	1200%	€3,960
Premium that Ross has to pay		**€4,290**

Insurance a Business Should Have

1. Theft Insurance

The insurance company pays the business compensation for the value of any stock or other items that are stolen from the business.

2. Public Liability Insurance

This insurance protects the business if any member of the public makes a claim against it as a result of an injury that happened to him in the business's premises. The insurance company will pay the compensation to the member of the public.

3. Product Liability Insurance

This insurance protects the business if a customer makes a claim against it as a result of an injury that happened to him from using the business's products. The insurance company will pay the compensation to the customer.

For example, in 1992, Stella Liebeck sued McDonald's when she spilled the coffee she had bought in McDonald's and it burned her legs. She was awarded millions of dollars.

4. Employer's Liability Insurance

This insurance protects the business if an employee makes a claim against it as a result of an injury that happened to him while at work. The insurance company will pay the compensation to the employee.

5. Plate Glass Insurance

If the business's windows are damaged, the insurance company pays compensation to the business to get them fixed or replaced.

6. Motor Insurance

If the business has cars, lorries or vans, it *must* get them insured. There are three types of motor insurance:

- Third Party – The insurance company pays only for any damage caused to another person by the business's vehicles. It will not pay any compensation for damage to the car or the person driving it.
- Third Party, Fire and Theft – The insurance company pays compensation for any damage caused to a third party and also if the car is stolen or burned out. It will not pay any compensation for any other damage to the car or the person driving it.

- Comprehensive – The insurance company pays compensation for any damage caused to the car and to the person driving it and to any third party.

Importance of Insurance for a Business

⊙ Business Survival

Having insurance means that the business will not be wiped out by some catastrophe (if the factory burned down, for example). The insurance company will pay for the loss, so the business can keep operating.

⊙ Risk Management

Insurance helps a business to lower its risks. When taking out insurance the business must examine all the risks facing it (such as theft, fire, vandalism and so on). To lower the premium it has to pay, the business might take steps to reduce the chance of these risks occurring. For example, to reduce the risk of customers claiming for injuries from falls in the shop on a rainy day, the business puts down mats and signs warning customers of the danger.

⊙ Improved Cash Flow

Paying a relatively small premium every year is better for the business's cash flow than facing a large cash outlay all in one go to pay for some unexpected crisis (such as replacing stolen stock).

Insurance a Household Should Have

1. Health Insurance

If any member of the family gets sick, the insurance company will pay for the medical bills (such as bills for doctors, hospitals, medicines and so on). There are a number of health insurance companies operating in Ireland, including VHI, Quinn Healthcare and AVIVAS.

2. Life Assurance

The insurance company pays compensation to the other members of the family when the insured person dies. There are two main types of life assurance:

- Whole Life Policies: The insurance company pays out only when the insured person dies.
- Endowment Policies: The insurance company pays out at the *earlier* of two events – the death of the person or when they reach a certain age.

3. House and Contents Insurance

The family takes out this kind of insurance to protect their home and all its contents. If anything happens to either, the insurance company pays them compensation for any loss suffered.

4. Motor Insurance

Motor insurance is statutory. This means that if the family has a car, it must get it insured. The three types of car insurance are:

- Third Party
- Third Party, Fire and Theft
- Comprehensive

For more information about the types of car insurance, see the section earlier about insurances a business should take out.

5. Mortgage Protection Insurance

If the family has a mortgage loan on their house, they should take out this insurance. If they cannot pay their monthly mortgage repayment due to ill health, redundancy or death, the insurance company will pay it for them until they can afford to pay it themselves again.

Household and Business Insurance

SIMILARITIES	DIFFERENCES
■ By law, both businesses and households must pay motor insurance if they have vehicles, and PRSI if they have/are employees.	■ Businesses face more risks than households and therefore have to take out many more insurance policies that households don't need (such as product liability insurance).
■ Both must obey the principles of insurance.	■ Businesses tend to be worth more than households and therefore face much higher insurance premiums.
■ Both fill in proposal forms when applying for insurance.	
■ Both make claims from the insurance company and both must fill in claim forms to do so.	

Taxation

Taxation is the money that all businesses and households must pay to the government. The government uses this money to run the country's schools, hospitals and so on. The Minister for Finance decides the amount of taxes we pay and uses a government organisation called Revenue (short for Revenue commissioners) to make sure that we all pay the correct amount of tax on time.

Reasons for Taxation

Governments impose taxes for a number of reasons:

1. To raise money

A major reason why the government collects taxes from businesses and households is to raise money to pay for government services such as building roads, running schools and maintaining hospitals.

2. To redistribute wealth

The government can use taxation to take money from well-off people and give this to the less well off. For example, in Ireland, the government takes a high percentage of income tax from people on high wages. It uses this money to pay social welfare to people in need.

3. To discourage consumption

The government can impose high taxes on products that are bad for us such as cigarettes and alcohol, to make them more expensive so that we buy less of them.

Taxes Paid by Households

- Pay As You Earn (PAYE) Income Tax
- Employees' Pay Related Social Insurance (PRSI)
- Value Added Tax (VAT)
- Motor Tax
- Capital Gains Tax (CGT)
- Capital Acquisitions Tax (CAT)
- Deposit Interest Retention Tax (DIRT)

1. PAYE – Pay As You Earn

Employees pay income tax on their wages under the Pay As You Earn system.

Under this system, their employer calculates the PAYE tax payable by the employee. He then deducts the PAYE tax from the employee's gross wages and pays it over to Revenue for her. The employer must deduct the PAYE tax every time the employee is paid her wages. The employee then receives the net wage.

The employer calculates the PAYE tax due by multiplying the gross wages by the rate of tax and then deducting the employee's tax credits.

Tax credits are amounts that all taxpayers, including employees, can deduct from their gross tax bill. Different people qualify for different tax credits. For example, there are different tax credits for single and married people. Employees get an extra employee tax credit, which the self-employed don't get. Employees who are members of a trade union get an extra tax credit that non-union employees don't get. People with disabled children, people who are blind, people who pay rent on their home and people who take care of their sick relatives all get additional tax credits to further reduce the amount of tax they have to pay.

EXAMPLE

Mary's annual salary is €50,000. PAYE tax is paid as follows:

■ First €40,000 @ 20%
■ Balance @ 40%

Mary's tax credits for the year are €3,000.

(a) **Compute Mary's PAYE tax for the year.**
(b) **Compute Mary's net pay for the year.**

ANSWER

PAYE Tax = (Gross Pay × Rate of Tax) – Tax Credits

€50,000	→	€40,000	×	20%	=	€8,000
		€10,000	×	40%	=	€4,000
Gross Tax						€12,000
Minus Tax Credits						(€3,000)
PAYE Tax						€9,000

Net Pay = Gross Pay – PAYE Tax

= €50,000 – €9,000
= **€41,000**

Forms Used In PAYE Tax

■ **P45.** This is a form the employer gives to an employee when he leaves his job. It contains details of the pay earned and the PAYE and Pay Related Social Insurance (PRSI) paid by the employee from the start of the year up to the date he left the job. The employee uses it to sign on the dole or to give to a new employer to make sure his tax is worked out correctly by the new employer.

■ **P60.** This is a form the employer gives to an employee at the end of every tax year. It contains details of the pay earned and the PAYE and PRSI paid by the employee in that tax year. The employee uses it to claim tax refunds and social welfare benefits.

■ **P21.** This is a form that Revenue gives an employee at the end of the tax year showing him the difference between how much tax he paid that year and how much he actually owes for the year. If he overpaid tax, he will get a refund. If he underpaid, he will have to send Revenue a cheque for the amount owing. The P21 is called a Balancing Statement for this reason.

■ **Form 12A.** This is a form that all employees must fill in when they start working for the very first time. They send it to Revenue so that Revenue can work out their tax credits and the rate of tax they should be paying. If you don't fill in this form when you start working, you will have to pay emergency tax. Emergency tax operates by taking more and more tax from your wages until you fill in this form.

2. PRSI– Pay Related Social Insurance

This is another tax taken out of an employee's wages by his employer and paid to Revenue on his behalf. The amount taken out is a percentage of the employee's gross wages.

Employees pay PRSI so that they can qualify for welfare benefits in the future, such as dental, optical and medical benefits, unemployment benefit and contributory old age pension.

EXAMPLE

From the following information, calculate the net annual take-home pay of Stephen Connolly.

■ Stephen earns a gross annual salary of €100,000.
■ He is allowed the following tax credits: Single Person credit of €2,000 and Employee credit of €1,500.
■ The income tax rates are: 20% on the first €40,000 and 38% on the balance.
■ The employee PRSI rate is: 6% on the first €80,000 and 2% on the balance.

PRSI	Gross Income × PRSI %				

€100,000	–	€80,000	×	6%	=	€4,800
	–	€20,000	×	2%	=	€400
Total PRSI to be deducted from gross wages					=	€5,200

PAYE	[Gross Income × PAYE %] – Tax Credits				

€100,000	–	€40,000	×	20%	=	€8,000
	–	€60,000	×	38%	=	€22,800
					=	€30,800
Less Tax Credits [Single €2,000 + Employee €1,500]					=	(€3,500)
Total PAYE to be deducted from gross wages					=	€27,300

NET	Gross Income – PAYE – PRSI				

€100,000	–	€27,300	–	€5,200	=	**€67,500**

Answer:
Stephen's net annual take-home pay is €67,500.

3. VAT– Value Added Tax

This is a tax that households pay when they buy products and services from a business. The tax is a percentage of the value of the goods. The tax is included in the price they pay in the shops because the government makes all businesses add Value Added Tax (VAT) to the prices of the goods and services they sell to consumers. Therefore, VAT increases the prices households have to pay for goods and services.

EXAMPLE

An electrical shop decides to charge €1,000 for a TV	€1,000
By law, it *must* add VAT to this price (say 21%)	€210
And so the household ends up paying	€1,210

VAT is not charged on all products. Education, funerals, medicines and children's clothing are not liable to VAT. This makes these essential products more affordable for all.

4. Motor Tax

Every household that has a car must pay this tax to their local council every year. The amount payable depends on the car's emissions level. The more polluting the car is, the more car tax has to be paid.

5. CGT – Capital Gains Tax

This is a tax that households have to pay when they sell an asset (such as shares, holiday homes, investment properties, antiques and so on) and make a profit on the sale.

The Capital Gains Tax (CGT) payable is equal to a percentage of the profit. Unlike PAYE and PRSI, which are calculated by the household's employer, households *themselves* have to work out how much CGT they owe Revenue and they have to pay this amount to Revenue themselves.

A small amount of the profits made in a year is tax free. This is called the annual exemption. In addition, a household does not have to pay any tax on any profit made from the sale of their home.

EXAMPLE

Margaret bought shares in Z PLC for €5,000. She sold them for €11,000 five months later.
Calculate the CGT payable by Margaret if the rate of CGT is 20% and the first €1,500 of gains each year is exempt from CGT.

She sells the shares for €11,000. She bought them for €5,000. Margaret made a profit of €6,000 (€11,000 – €5,000).

Profit	€6,000
Deduct annual exemption	(€1,500)
Taxable profit	€4,500
CGT payable = €4,500 × 20%	**€900**

The first €1,500 is exempt from tax, so the remaining €4,500 is to be taxed at 20%. Margaret will pay CGT of €900.

6. CAT – Capital Acquisitions Tax

Capital Acquisitions Tax is the tax you pay if you receive a gift or an inheritance. The amount of tax you pay depends on who gave you the gift or inheritance and how much it is worth. However, you can receive a certain amount of gifts and inheritances tax free.

You yourself must work out the CAT that you owe and you must pay it to Revenue.

Married couples do not pay any CAT on gifts and inheritances they receive from each other.

7. DIRT – Deposit Interest Retention Tax

Deposit Interest Retention Tax is the tax that a household pays on the interest it earns on its savings in a bank, building society or credit union deposit account.

The financial institution automatically deducts the DIRT from the household's interest and pays it straight to Revenue for them.

EXAMPLE

Thomas earns €100 interest on his deposit account.	€100
Before he receives this, the bank deducts DIRT (say 20%)	(€20)
So Thomas only gets the net interest of	€80

Taxes Paid by Businesses

- ◉ Self-assessment Income Tax
- ◉ Corporation Tax
- ◉ Value Added Tax (VAT)
- ◉ Commercial Rates
- ◉ Employers' Pay Related Social Insurance (PRSI)
- ◉ Customs Duties
- ◉ Pay As You Earn (PAYE)

1. Self-assessment Income Tax

This is the income tax that self-employed entrepreneurs (sole traders and partners in a partnership) pay on their business profits. Self-employed people have to work out the amount of self assessment tax they owe. They are responsible for calculating their own tax bill. That is why it is called "*self*-assessment".

They must pay their income tax for the year by 31st October of that year. They must also send in an annual tax return detailing all their income and tax credits for the year by 31st October of the following year.

To stop self-employed people evading* tax, they are subject to revenue audits, whereby Revenue tax inspectors call out to check their accounts and their tax returns to make sure that they paid the right amount of tax. If they find any fraud, the entrepreneur can be fined and/or imprisoned.

> ## Note:
>
> ■ **Tax evasion*** is when taxpayers deliberately fail to pay the correct amount of tax they owe by not declaring the full amount of their income or by claiming tax deductions they are not entitled to. Tax evasion is illegal and the government imposes very heavy penalties on those found guilty.
>
> ■ **Tax avoidance** is when taxpayers take advantage of the tax system to reduce the amount of tax they owe. For example, high-income earners can reduce their tax bill by investing in certain Irish films and businesses. This is perfectly legal.

2. Corporation Tax

This is the tax that *companies* pay on their annual profits. Companies themselves work out the amount of tax they owe. They are responsible for calculating their own tax bill and for sending the tax into Revenue. They must also send in an annual tax return, detailing all their income and tax deductions.

To stop companies cheating, they are subject to revenue audits whereby Revenue tax inspectors call out to check their accounts and their tax returns to make sure that they are correct. If they find any fraud, the company can be fined and the directors can be fined and/or imprisoned.

3. Value Added Tax

This is the tax businesses *must* add on to the price of goods and services they sell to consumers. They collect this tax from the consumer when he pays for his products.

For example, a shop wants to sell a pair of jeans for €100. It must add VAT (say at 21%) of €21 to the price. Therefore, the price displayed is €121. When the shop takes the €121 from the customer, it has to pay the €21 VAT to Revenue.

Furthermore, when a business buys goods, it has to pay VAT (like a consumer) to the supplier. For example, when a shop buys its cash registers, its display stands, its stock and so on, it pays VAT to the shop it bought them from.

Unlike consumers, however, businesses get a refund of the VAT they pay. Revenue gives businesses back any VAT they have paid.

4. Commercial Rates

This is a tax that businesses must pay to their local council every year. The amount paid is based on the value of the business's premises. The money raised helps finance the local council's activities (such as roads, lighting and so on).

5. Employers' PRSI

A business pays this tax to Revenue if it has employees. The amount payable is equal to a certain percentage of the employee's gross wages. But this money is *not* taken from the employee's wages. The entrepreneur has to pay it out of his own profits.

Therefore, Employers' PRSI increases an entrepreneur's costs and hence reduces his profits.

> #### EXAMPLE
>
> David owns a restaurant. He employs one waiter who earns €1,800 gross per month.
> If the rate of Employer's PRSI is 10%, how much Employer's PRSI must David pay to the Revenue each month?
>
> **Answer:**
> €1,800 × 10% = €180.

6. Customs Duties

When a business imports goods from a non-EU country, it must pay a tax on the value of those imports to Revenue. This import tax is called customs duties. The amount of tax payable is a percentage of the value of the goods. The goods will not be released from customs until the business pays the tax.

7. Pay As You Earn

Businesses must deduct PAYE tax from all their employees' wages and pay it to Revenue on behalf of the employees. In this way, businesses act as unpaid tax collectors.

Effects of Taxation on Business

1. Lower Profits

Taxes taken from a business's profits (Self-Assessment tax or Corporation Tax) reduce the profits left for the business to spend on expanding the business.

2. Lower Sales

Value Added Tax is added to the price of many of the products and services a business sells, making them more expensive. The higher price causes consumers to buy fewer products, resulting in lower sales for the business.

3. Higher Costs

Businesses have to work out lots of taxes and pay them to Revenue. Because taxation can be complicated, many businesspeople will hire an accountant to do this for them. The accountant's fees increase the business's costs. Also, Employer's PRSI is an added cost as it is money taken directly from the business.

4. Less Overtime

High taxes taken from employees' wages act as a disincentive for employees to do overtime. Because the government takes up to half their gross wages in tax, some employees feel it is not worth their while doing overtime. This can leave the business short of workers in busy times.

Household and Business Taxation

SIMILARITIES	DIFFERENCES
■ Both businesses and households must register with Revenue for tax purposes. They must fill in a form detailing name, address, sources of income and claims for tax credits or deductions.	■ Businesses get more tax deductions than households. For example, businesses can claim a tax deduction for the cost of buying fixed assets such as cars or furniture. This reduces the tax they owe. Households get no tax deduction whatsoever for the cost of buying fixed assets.
■ Both must pay the correct amount of tax on time. If they don't, both businesses and households can be fined by Revenue.	■ Businesses get a refund of any VAT they have paid on their business purchases. Households do not.
■ Both must keep proper tax records. If they are claiming tax credits or deductions, they must have proof that they are eligible.	■ Businesses collect taxes from others (such as PAYE and Employees' PRSI from their employees' wages and VAT from customers) on behalf of Revenue. Households do not.

■ Both will try to avoid tax by taking advantage of government tax incentives. A householder may put money into his pension scheme to claim a tax deduction. A businessperson may set up a company because the rate of corporation tax is lower than the rate of self-assessment income tax.	■ Businesses pay more taxes than households.

Ordinary Level Questions

EXAM SECTION 1 (25%) – SHORT ANSWER QUESTIONS [10 marks each]

1. Define "insurance".

2. List three principles of insurance.

3. Outline three insurances that a business might pay.

4. Name two insurances that a household *must* pay by law and outline any one of them.

5. Thomas has his factory insured for €250,000. It is currently worth €500,000.
   Yesterday there was a fire in the factory, causing damage of €6,000.
   Thomas puts in a claim for €6,000.
   How much compensation will Thomas receive? Show your workings.

6. Paula has her house insured for €120,000. It is currently worth €200,000.
   Yesterday there was a storm which resulted in damage of €4,000 to her roof.
   How much compensation will Paula receive? Show your workings.

7. Indicate whether each of the following (A, B, C, D and E) is true or false.

	Sentence	True or False
A	The more valuable the item you wish to insure, the lower your insurance premium will be.	
B	The greater the risk you are, the more your insurance premium will be.	
C	The more claims that an insurance company has to pay, the more each person's premium will be.	
D	All households must take out health insurance by law.	
E	A loading is a reduction on the basic premium because the person is a lower risk of claiming.	

8. Column 1 is a list of business terms. Column 2 is a list of possible explanations for these terms. Match the two lists by placing the letter of the correct explanation under the relevant number below. One explanation has no match.

Column 1	Column 2: Explanations
1. Utmost Good Faith	a) Filled in when seeking compensation following a loss
2. Average Clause	b) Applies when a person insures the same asset with more than one insurance company
3. Claim Form	c) Filled in when applying for insurance cover
4. Contribution	d) You cannot make a profit from insurance
5. Loading	e) When applying for insurance, you must answer every question truthfully and volunteer material information
6. Indemnity	f) Extra charge added to the basic premium because the person is a higher than average risk
	g) The insurance company only pays out a fraction of the compensation because the business or household is only insured for a fraction of the item's value

1	2	3	4	5	6
E					

9. Write out what the following letters stand for: VAT   DIRT   PAYE

10. Write out what the following letters stand for: PRSI   CGT   CAT

11. Yvonne and Paul are married. Their combined annual salary is €150,000. PAYE tax is paid as follows:
First €80,000 @ 20%
Balance @ 40%
PRSI is 6% on the first €100,000 and 2% on the balance. Their tax credits for the year are as follows: Married persons' credit of €5,000, Employee credit of €2,000, Child credit of €3,000 and Age credit of €2,000
Compute their net pay for the year.

12. Arthur's annual salary is €68,000. PAYE tax is paid as follows:
First €30,000 @ 24%
Balance @ 46%
PRSI is 5% on the first €50,000 and 1.5% on the balance. Arthur's tax credits for the year are €4,000 in total.
Compute Arthur's take-home pay for the year.

13. List four taxes paid by a business.

14. Outline the purpose of the following forms used in taxation: P45   P60

15. Column 1 is a list of business terms. Column 2 is a list of possible explanations for these terms. Match the two lists by placing the letter of the correct explanation under the relevant number below. One explanation has no match.

Column 1	Column 2: Explanations
1. DIRT	a) Tax deducted from an employee's wages
2. Corporation Tax	b) Tax paid on gifts and inheritances
3. PAYE	c) Tax paid on a company's profits
4. Commercial Rates	d) Tax paid by sole traders on their business profits
5. Customs Duties	e) Tax deducted from interest on savings
6. Self Assessment Tax	f) Tax paid by businesses to their local council
	g) Tax paid on goods imported into Ireland from outside the European Union

1	2	3	4	5	6
E		a		G	D

EXAM SECTION 2 (75%) – LONG QUESTIONS

1. State and explain three principles of insurance.   (20 marks)

2. Describe three types of insurance you would expect a *restaurant* to have.   (15 marks)

3. Describe two factors that would affect the premium a person has to pay for car insurance. Give an example of each.   (15 marks)

4. Distinguish between "insurable interest" and "indemnity".   (20 marks)

5. Outline the reasons why a person would take out life assurance.   (10 marks)

6. Mark insured his van with two insurance companies as follows:

	Company E	Company F
Value insured with each	€14,000	€6,000

   Vandals caused €3,000 of damage to the van.
   Calculate the compensation to be paid to Mark.
   Name the principle of insurance that applies in this case.   (15 marks)

7. Pauline insured her house with two insurance companies as follows:

	Company G	Company H
Value insured with each	€400,000	€500,000

   A fire in the kitchen caused damage of €18,000.
   Calculate the compensation to be paid to Pauline.
   Name the principle of insurance that applies in this case.   (15 marks)

8. Outline three types of insurance that you would expect a household to have.   (15 marks)

9. Describe three taxes that you would expect a *supermarket* to pay.   (15 marks)

10. John works for Stamp Ltd as a welder. He puts €50 every week into his bank deposit account and spends the rest of his wages on clothes and his car. Outline four taxes that you would expect John to pay.   (20 marks)

11. Distinguish between "commercial rates" and "corporation tax".   (10 marks)

12. Outline three effects of taxation on a business.   (15 marks)

13. Outline two similarities and two differences in managing business taxation and managing household taxation.   (20 marks)

Higher Level Questions

EXAM SECTION 1 (20%) - SHORT ANSWER QUESTIONS [10 marks each]

1. Distinguish between the insurance principles of "contribution" and "subrogation".

2. Complete this sentence: Utmost good faith requires…

3. Illustrate what is meant by the term "average clause".

4. Complete this sentence: In insurance, a loading involves…

5. Martin insured his factory with four insurance companies as follows:

   | Insured with each | A €400,000 | B €200,000 | C €300,000 | D €100,000 |

   A storm caused damage of €16,000.
   How much compensation will Martin receive from each company? Explain your answer.

6. Michael has his office building insured for €400,000. It is currently worth €1,000,000. Yesterday there was a fire in the office, causing damage of €20,000.
   How much compensation will Michael receive? Explain your answer.

7. Explain the insurance term "premium".

8. Column 1 is a list of business terms. Column 2 is a list of possible explanations for these terms. Match the two lists by placing the letter of the correct explanation under the relevant number below. One explanation has no match.

Column 1	Column 2: Explanations
1. Material Information	a) All questions on a proposal form must be answered honestly
	b) Addition to basic premium for increased risk
2. Endowment Policy	c) Pays compensation on the earlier of death or reaching a certain age
3. PRSI	d) Insurance pays a fraction of compensation because you are only insured for a fraction of asset's value
4. Loading	
5. Average Clause	e) Details that would affect an insurance company's decision to insure a person
	f) Compulsory insurance payable to the government to provide an employee with future government benefits such as pension

1	2	3	4	5

9. What is a "tax credit"?

10. What do the following letters stand for?   PAYE   PRSI   VAT   DIRT   CGT

11. Arthur's annual salary is €105,000. PAYE tax is paid as follows:
    First €45,000 @ 24%
    Balance @ 42%
    PRSI is 6.75% on the first €100,000 and 2.5% on the balance.
    Arthur's tax credits for the year comprised the following:
    Single Person €2,000; Employee €1,500; Union Member €50.
    Compute Arthur's take-home pay for the year.

12. List four contrasting activities in managing business taxation and managing household taxation.

13. Distinguish between "gross pay" and "net pay".

14. Illustrate the importance of a P21.

15. Complete this sentence: Self assessment tax requires….

EXAM SECTION 2 (20%) – APPLIED BUSINESS QUESTION – 80 MARKS

Cocinar.

Ita Hayden had long thought about setting up her own business. She had worked successfully as a chef in an up-market Athlone restaurant for many years. She made the decision to set up her business in nearby Moate, as a sole trader – a Spanish restaurant that she called "Cocinar".

Ita found it very expensive to set up the restaurant. She had to buy kitchen equipment, tables and chairs. Recently she bought a van to deliver take-away food around the town. The restaurant has done well thanks to Ita's ambition, hard work and fresh ideas and Ita now employs two other chefs and five waiting staff.

Ita's restaurant is busy most nights but especially at weekends when customers who don't book in advance find it almost impossible to get a table. Customers from all over the midlands come to the restaurant as Ita uses only the freshest ingredients, including fish caught in the local River Shannon. The restaurant got an excellent review in the newspaper from the food critic who especially praised Ita's wine list which included Chilean, Australian and South African wines. Ita has often had to ask the staff to work overtime but they are becoming increasingly unwilling to do so.

(A) Describe four taxes that you would expect Ita to pay. Give reasons for your answer. Support your answer with reference to the above text.

(25 marks)

(B)   Describe four insurances that you would expect Ita to pay.
Give reasons for your answer. Support your answer with reference
to the above text.   (25 marks)

(C)   Evaluate the impact of taxation on Ita's business. Support your answer
with reference to the above text.   (30 marks)

EXAM SECTION 3 (60%) – LONG QUESTIONS

1. Explain four principles of insurance.   (20 marks)

2. Nuala insured her house with two insurance companies as follows:

	C	D
Value insured with each	€250,000	€300,000

    A storm caused damage of €10,000. The house is worth €750,000
How much compensation will Nuala receive from each company?
Explain your answer.   (15 marks)

3. Describe the various insurances that you would expect a household to pay. (20 marks)

4. Explain the purpose of the principle of contribution.   (10 marks)

5. Evaluate the importance of insurance to a business.   (20 marks)

6. Discuss the factors that determine the premiums charged by
insurance companies.   (20 marks)

7. Miriam inherited €2,000,000 from her late aunt. Having sought advice from
a friend, she decided to save €400,000 in a bank deposit account and
invest €1,500,000 in shares in the Irish stock exchange. She spent the rest on
a new car and new clothes. At the end of the year, she sold her shares and
made a large profit.
Describe the taxes that Miriam would be liable for.
Give reasons for your choice.   (20 marks)

8. Distinguish between a proposal form and a claim form in insurance.   (10 marks)

9. Compare and contrast business and household taxation.   (20 marks)

10. Using examples, discuss the effect of taxation on a business.   (20 marks)

Finance

This chapter examines the important issue of money. Both businesses and households must manage their money properly so that they can afford to pay for the things they need. Households need money to pay for food, a car, a house and so on. Businesses need money to buy stock, equipment and premises. To help them manage their finances, both must budget carefully and take out suitable loans when needed.

Budgeting

A business and a household must manage their money properly. If a business does not have the cash ready to pay its bills, its creditors may take it to court and have it liquidated (closed down and sold off). Similarly, if a family does not have the cash available to pay its mortgage, their house may be repossessed.

To prevent this, households and businesses need to prepare a household budget or a cash flow forecast.

Business Budgeting – Cash Flow Forecast

A cash flow forecast is used to predict how much money a business will have in the future. It does this by subtracting expected future payments from expected future receipts. It is an example of planning.

Cash Flow Forecast for Sample Ltd			
	July	August	September
(A) Receipts	€55,000	€80,000	€90,000
(B) Payments	€57,500	€63,000	€77,000
(C) Net Cash (A) – (B)	(€2,500)	€17,000	€13,000
(D) Opening Cash	€1,500	(€1,000)	€16,000
Closing Cash (C) + (D)	(€1,000)	€16,000	€29,000

Cash Receipts for a Business	Cash Payments for a Business
■ Cash received from selling goods to customers	■ Cash paid to buy stock for the business
■ Cash received from credit customers when they pay their bills (The business sells goods to customers on credit and they pay later. Such customers are called debtors.)	■ Cash paid to pay bills owing to suppliers for stock the business bought from them on credit (These suppliers the business owes are called creditors.)
■ Income received from investments such as interest on a bank deposit account	■ Cash paid to buy fixed assets, such as cars, buildings, equipment, machinery, computers, vans and so on.
■ Rent received from tenants	■ Cash paid out in dividends to shareholders
	■ Cash paid out to pay expenses such as wages, insurance, electricity, phone and so on
	■ Cash paid to Revenue for taxes owing, such as VAT, PAYE, PRSI and so on

Dealing with an Expected Future Deficit

If a business's payments are expected to be more than its receipts (there is more going out than coming in), the business must take action, such as:

Increase Cash Receipts

1. Use better credit control methods to make debtors pay up more quickly (such as offering discounts for early payment or charging interest on late payers' accounts).

2. Sell investments to raise cash.

3. Have a sale to increase the amount of money taken in from customers.

Reduce Cash Payments

1. Instead of paying a large amount of cash out in one go to pay for expensive fixed assets (such as a new van), the business can spread the payments out over a longer period by using methods such as hire purchase or leasing. Although this will be more expensive in the long-run, it avoids having a large amount of cash leave the business all at once.

2. Reduce payments for expenses by making cutbacks. To lower the wages bill, overtime can be banned. Telephone bills can be reduced by switching to a cheaper telephone company and banning all non-business calls.

3. Reduce cash paid out to shareholders as dividends by offering them free shares in the business instead.

Why Does a Business Prepare a Cash Flow Forecast?

▶ It lets the business know in advance when it is going to run short of money (deficit). Therefore, it gives the business plenty of time to arrange a bank overdraft to deal with this deficit. This ensures that the company can pay its bills on time and does not go bankrupt.

▶ It lets the business know in advance when it is going to have money left over (surplus). The business can then make plans to invest this money. The business can earn extra interest by not leaving an unexpected surplus lying around.

▶ The cash flow *forecast* can eventually be compared to the *actual* receipts and payments of the business later on to see whether the business is on target or off target with its cash flow forecast. This helps the business control its cash flow.

▶ A cash flow forecast can be used to show a bank manager that the business's finances are properly managed. This is especially important when the business is applying for a loan.

Example

The cash flow forecast of Irish Beachwear Ltd. for next summer is set out below:

	July	August	September	Total
Receipts	€32,000	€31,500	€29,700	€93,200
Payments	€56,000	€26,000	€49,000	€131,000
Net Cash	(€24,000)	€5,500	(€19,300)	(€37,800)
Opening Cash	€17,000	(€7,000)	(€1,500)	€17,000
Closing Cash	(€7,000)	(€1,500)	(€20,800)	(€20,800)

Analyse the cash flow forecast. Explain, and offer solutions to, any two problems you think the business may have.

The business will have a negative net cash figure in July and September. Furthermore, it will have a negative closing cash balance in each one of the three months in question. Overall, the business's cash will decrease from €17,000 at the start of July to minus €20,800 at the end of September. The business will overspend by €37,800 over the three-month period.

PROBLEM	SOLUTION
1. The business's forecasted receipts are expected to fall each month as the summer progresses. This would be expected for a beachwear business, which is a seasonal business.	The business should have a sale in August and September to encourage more customers to buy from it. This will help to boost receipts in these months.
2. The business's forecast payments vary widely each month. They are expected to be especially high in July and September. Perhaps the reason for this is that the business plans to buy expensive fixed assets (such as delivery vans) in these months.	The business should avoid paying for these fixed assets in one lump sum. It should instead spread the payments over a longer period of time, using hire purchase. This will prevent a lot of cash leaving the business all in one go.

Household Budgeting

Just like businesses, households have to keep an eye on their finances to make sure that they can pay their bills. Many families prepare a household budget. In it, they list the money they expect to make (income) and the money they plan to spend (expenditure).

Household expenditure can fall into one of three categories:

- ● Fixed – bills that must be paid every month and the amount stays the same.

- ● Irregular – bills that must be paid but the amount changes from month to month.

- ● Discretionary – money that the family does not have to spend. It is optional.

Cregan Household Budget			
	July	**August**	**September**
Income			
Wages	€4,000	€4,000	€4,000
Child Benefit	€400	€400	€400
(A) Total income	€4,400	€4,400	€4,400
Expenditure			
Fixed			
Mortgage	€1,200	€1,200	€1,200
Insurance	€100	€100	€100
Irregular			
Groceries	€800	€1,000	€1,200
Car running costs	€400	€600	€500
Light and Heat	€100	€200	€200
Discretionary			
Holiday			€3,400
Entertainment	€300	€500	€400
Birthday presents	€100	€400	
(B) Total Expenditure	€3,000	€4,000	€7,000
(C) Net Cash (A) –(B)	€1,400	€400	(€2,600)
(D) Opening Cash	€100	€1,500	€1,900
Closing Cash (C) + (D)	€1,500	€1,900	(€700)

Cash Receipts for a Household	Cash Payments for a Household
■ Cash received from wages if they have a job or unemployment benefit if they don't	■ Cash paid for household expenses such as groceries, mortgage or rent, insurance, school expenses and so on
■ Cash received from Child Benefit if the family has children	■ Cash paid to buy fixed assets such as cars, televisions, fridges and so on
■ Interest received from the credit union or bank on the family's savings	■ Cash paid to local authority for bin charges, motor tax and so on

Dealing with an Expected Future Deficit

If a household's payments are predicted to be more than its receipts (in other words, it is spending more than is coming in), the household must take action to stop this.

Increase Receipts

1. Do overtime at work or take on an extra job to increase the amount of wages coming into the household.

2. Rent a spare room in the house to a student. The extra cash received in this way is tax-free.

Reduce Payments

1. Instead of paying a large amount of cash out in one go to pay for expensive fixed assets, the household can spread the payments out over a longer time by using hire purchase. This will be more expensive in the long-run, but it avoids having a large amount of cash leave the household all at once.

2. Reduce payments for expenses by making cutbacks. To reduce grocery payments, the family can buy non-branded products. They can also cut back on telephone bills by switching to a cheaper telephone company.

Why Does a Household Prepare a Budget?

▶ It lets the family know in advance when it is going to run short of money (deficit). Therefore, it gives the family plenty of time to arrange a bank overdraft to deal with this deficit. It ensures that the family can pay its bills on time.

▶ It lets the family know in advance when it is going to have money left over (surplus). The family can then make plans to invest this money, such as putting more money into their savings account. This means that the family can earn extra interest by not leaving an unexpected surplus lying around.

▶ It shows the family exactly where its money is going and highlights particular areas of overspending that can be cut back.

▶ It shows a bank manager that the household's finances are properly managed. This is especially important when the family is applying for a loan.

Spreadsheet

Many businesses and households use a spreadsheet to draft their cash flow forecasts.

A spreadsheet is computer software that is used for basic accounting (such as cash flow forecasts, Profit and Loss Accounts and Balance Sheets).

The spreadsheet itself consists of cells (boxes). Numbers and words can be entered into each cell. The spreadsheet can do maths calculations when the user types in a maths formula (+ − × ÷). Once a formula is typed in, it can be copied into other cells. When you change the numbers, the formula automatically recalculates the new answer for you.

B3–B4

	A	B	C	D
1		July	August	September
2		€	€	€
3	Receipts	10,000	12,000	18,000
4	Payments	6,000	14,000	19,000
5	Net Cash	4,000	(2,000)	(1,000)

Advantages of a Spreadsheet

1. It performs basic mathematical calculations accurately and quickly. This enables a business and a household to prepare its accounts and cash flow forecasts quickly, saving time and money.

2. It allows for "what if" analysis, i.e., what will be the answer if the numbers change? Once the business/household has prepared its accounts or cash flow forecast on the spreadsheet, it can then change any of the numbers and the spreadsheet will instantly calculate the new answer. This will let the business/household know how vulnerable it is to changes in the original forecast. (For example, what will net cash be if receipts in August increase to €22,000? What will the net cash be if payments increase each month by 20%?)

Sources of Finance

Most businesses and households do not have enough cash on hand to pay for all the things they need. For example, very few families have the cash to buy a €550,000 house, a €25,000 car, or even a €2,000 fridge. But they can buy these things if they borrow.

The different ways for a household and business to raise the money it needs are called sources of finance. There are three types – short term, medium term and long term.

	Household	Business
Short Term (Finance that will take up to one year to repay)	■ Bank overdraft ■ Accrued expenses ■ Credit card	■ Bank overdraft ■ Accrued expenses ■ Trade credit ■ Factoring
Medium Term (Finance that will take up to five years to repay)	■ Hire purchase ■ Leasing ■ Personal loan	■ Hire purchase ■ Leasing ■ Term loan
Long Term (Finance that will take more than five years to repay)	■ Mortgage ■ Savings	■ Debentures ■ Retained earnings ■ Grants ■ Equity capital

Short-term Sources of Finance

Bank Overdraft   [Household and Business]

A bank overdraft is a source of finance whereby the bank allows the household/business to pay for things by writing cheques for the amount (*up to an agreed limit*), even though they don't have enough money in their current account to cover these cheques.

When the shop/supplier cashes the cheque it doesn't bounce. The bank pays the shop/supplier the amount written on the cheque. The household/business pays the bank back later with interest.

Bank overdrafts are used to get a small value item or an item that will be used up within a year, such as stock for a business or groceries for a household.

Advantages
1. Interest is paid only on the amount that the business/household is actually overdrawn, not on the full overdraft limit.
2. No security is needed to get an overdraft. This means that the household's house and the business's premises are not at risk if they can't pay the overdraft back.

Disadvantages

1. The rate of interest on an overdraft is expensive.
2. The household/business must be overdraft free for at least 30 days in the year.
3. The bank can ask the household/business to pay back the overdraft immediately.
4. The bank imposes extra charges if the household/business goes over its overdraft limit.

Accrued Expenses   [Household and Business]

The household/business gets services now and pays for them later, when the bill comes in. It is used to finance electricity, gas and phone services.

For example, the phone company allows the household/business to make calls now. It sends out a bill at the end of the month telling the household/business how much it owes and when it has to pay.

Advantages

1. No interest is charged so it is a free form of finance.
2. No security is needed to get this finance. This means that the household's house and the business's premises are not at risk if they can't pay the service provider back.

Disadvantages

1. If the household/business takes too long to pay its bill, it will be cut off. This will mean no service for a time and the household/business may have to pay a reconnection fee.
2. Accrued expenses are only suitable financing for certain purchases such as utility services.

Credit Card   [Household only]

A household pays for goods and services in a shop with a credit card. The shop scans the card and the purchase is recorded on the household's credit card bill. The credit card company pays the shop. The household pays the credit card company back when it can.

Credit cards are used to get a small value item or an item that will be used up within a year, such as groceries.

Advantages

1. No interest is charged if the household pays its bill in full and on time.
2. It is safer than carrying cash around because a stolen credit card can be cancelled and therefore the household won't lose any money.

Disadvantages

1. If the household doesn't pay its credit card bill in full or on time, it must pay interest at a very high rate.
2. The household must pay a government tax for every credit card it has.

Factoring   [Business only]

The business raises money by selling its debtors to a bank for cash. Rather than waiting for the debtors to pay, the business gets money up front right now from the bank.

There are two types. **Factoring with recourse** means that the business must reimburse the bank if any debtors don't pay up. **Factoring without recourse** means the business doesn't have to reimburse the bank if debtors don't pay the bank.

The bank usually pays about 80% of the value of the debtors immediately and the balance at the end of the normal collection period (30 days, for example).

Advantages

1. The business can get much-needed cash immediately.
2. No security is needed to use factoring. This means that the business's buildings are not at risk if the debtor doesn't pay the bank.
3. The owners' control over the business is not affected – the business does not have to give the bank shares to use factoring.

Disadvantages

1. It is an expensive form of finance because the bank charges a high fee for the service.
2. Factoring can only be used by businesses that sell a lot of goods on credit (have lots of debtors).

Trade Credit   [Business only]

This allows a business to buy stock now and pay for it later. The supplier delivers the stock and gives the business a bill called an invoice. The invoice shows the amount the business owes and states the date when payment is due.

Example

Maria is a newsagent. On 1st April, she buys 300 magazines on credit from Magazine Importers Ltd.

She then receives an invoice from Magazine Importers Ltd., telling her that the bill for the magazines is €800 and must be paid by 8th April.

Maria sells all the magazines to her customers within the week and therefore has the money to pay Magazine Importers Ltd. in full and on time.

Advantages

1. It is a free source of finance for the business if it pays its bill on time. No interest is charged.

2. No security is needed to use trade credit. This means that the business's buildings are not at risk if the business doesn't pay the supplier.

3. The owners' control over the business is not affected – the business does not have to give the supplier shares to use trade credit.

Disadvantages

1. If the business pays its bills late, it loses out on any cash discounts available for early payment.

2. If a business deliberately keeps its suppliers waiting for their money all the time, this is called leaning on the trade and will result in the business losing its credit rating (reputation).

Medium-term Sources of Finance

Hire Purchase (HP)   **[Household and Business]**

Hire Purchase involves buying an asset and taking delivery of it now but paying for it in instalments. When the household/business pays the last instalment, it then legally owns the asset.

Once the household/business has paid one-third or more of the HP price, the HP company can repossess the item but only with the permission of a judge.

A household/business can end an HP agreement provided that it has paid the HP company one-half of the HP price.

Hire purchase is used to buy relatively expensive items that will be used up within five years, such as cars, furniture and TVs for a household and equipment and machinery for a business.

Advantages

1. The household/business gets the asset immediately without handing all the money over in one go.
2. The household/business does not have to provide any collateral because the HP company owns the asset until the household/business has paid back the last instalment. So the family's house or the business's premises are not at risk.
3. Businesses (but not households) can claim a tax deduction for the HP interest they pay. This helps to reduce their annual tax bill.

Disadvantages

1. It is an expensive form of finance. The interest charged is normally high, which usually makes hire purchase the most expensive medium-term finance.
2. If the household/business cannot pay back the instalments, the asset will be repossessed.
3. The household/business pays interest on the initial sum borrowed. There is no reduction for instalments repaid.

Leasing   [Household and Business]

This involves renting an asset from a finance company. The finance company buys the asset and rents it to the household/business for a fixed period in return for regular payments. The household/business never owns the asset. At the end of the lease period, it hands back the asset to the finance company.

Leasing is used to get relatively expensive items that will be used up within five years, such as cars, furniture and TVs for a household and equipment and machinery for a business.

Advantages

1. The household/business gets the asset immediately without handing all the money over in one go.
2. The household/business does not have to provide any collateral because the finance company owns the asset. So the family's house or the business's premises are not at risk.
3. The household/business can always have up-to-date equipment. It simply hands the asset back at end of lease agreement and gets a brand new one.
4. Businesses (but not households) can claim a tax deduction for the lease payments they make. This helps to lower their annual tax bill.

Disadvantages

1. If the household/business cannot pay back the instalments, the asset will be repossessed.
2. If the household/business rents for a long time, it may have spent so much money renting the item that it would have been cheaper to buy it.

Personal Loan   [Household only]

The household borrows money from a bank, building society or credit union and pays it back in regular instalments over five years. The instalments pay back the loan itself (the capital) and the interest.

The household can get a **fixed rate** personal loan. This means that the interest rate on the loan does not change and so the loan repayments stay the same every month. Alternatively, the household can get a **variable rate** personal loan. This means that the monthly repayments go up and down as the European Central Bank increases and decreases interest rates.

Personal loans are used to get relatively expensive items that will be used up within five years, such as cars, furniture and TVs.

Advantages

1. The rate of interest charged is cheaper than on hire purchase.
2. No security is needed. So the family's house is not at risk.

Disadvantages

1. The household pays interest on the initial sum borrowed. There is no reduction for instalments repaid.

Term Loan   [Business only]

The business borrows money from a bank and pays it back in regular instalments over five years. The instalments pay back the loan and interest. The business can get a fixed rate term loan or a variable rate term loan.

Term loans are used to get relatively expensive items that will be used up within five years, such as cars, machines and equipment.

Advantages

1. The rate of interest charged is cheaper than on hire purchase.
2. The interest the business pays is a tax-deductible expense. This means it reduces the business's annual tax bill.

3. The owners' control over the business is not affected – the business does not have to give the bank shares to get a loan.

Disadvantages

1. Security is normally required and therefore the bank will take some of the business's assets if the business cannot repay the loan.
2. If the European Central Bank increases interest rates and the business's loan is variable, monthly repayments will increase.

Long-term Sources of Finance

Mortgage   [Household only]

A mortgage is a long-term (usually 20 to 35 years) loan used by a household to buy their home. The loan is secured on the house. If the family can't repay their mortgage, the bank will repossess their house.

The household makes monthly repayments to pay back the mortgage. The government makes a contribution towards these repayments (called tax relief at source), which means the family has to pay less each month to the bank.

The household can get a fixed or variable rate mortgage.

Mortgages are used to buy a house or to do major home improvements such as extensions.

Advantages

1. The government makes a contribution towards the family's monthly repayments, which makes it easier for them to afford a mortgage.
2. The interest rate on a mortgage loan is the cheapest rate on any loan.

Disadvantages

1. If the family cannot afford their monthly repayments, they will lose their home

Savings   [Household only]

Savings are the amount of income the family hasn't spent but has set aside to use in the future. Savings are used to buy relatively expensive items that will that will last for more than five years.

Advantages

1. Because the household hasn't borrowed, there is no interest to repay.

2. Because the household hasn't borrowed, no security is needed so there is no risk of losing their home.

Disadvantages

1. It may take the household many years to build up its savings so that they are large enough to buy something.

Retained Earnings   [Business only]

Retained earnings (also called reserves) are the profits that the business has saved up over the years, which it reinvests in the business.

They are used to get major, expensive items that will last for more than five years, such as premises or business expansion. When Ryanair tried to buy Aer Lingus, it did not borrow. It intended to use its retained earnings of over €2 billion to do so.

Advantages

1. Because the business hasn't borrowed, there is no interest to repay.
2. Because the business hasn't borrowed, there is no security needed. So the business's buildings are not at risk.
3. Because the business hasn't borrowed, there is no worry over bankruptcy.

Disadvantages

1. Retained earnings are not available to new businesses and it may take many years to build up decent retained earnings.
2. Businesses that save a lot of their profits and pay low dividends may have a bad relationship with shareholders.

Grants   [Business only]

A grant is a sum of money the government gives a business to help it pay for the things it needs, such as buildings, machinery and so on. The government gives grants to help entrepreneurs set up and run businesses in Ireland because businesses create jobs and wealth in the economy.

A grant is a permanent source of finance because it does not have to be repaid to the government, provided that the business obeys all the conditions of the grant.

Grants are used to get major, expensive items that will last for more than five years, such as premises or business expansion.

Advantages

1. Because the business hasn't borrowed, there is no interest to repay.

2. Because the business hasn't borrowed, there is no security needed. So the business's buildings are not at risk.

3. Grants are free money that does not have to be repaid.

Disadvantages

1. The business will only get a grant subject to strict conditions. If the business breaks these, it will have to pay the money back to the government.

2. The government gives the business only a percentage of the money it needs.

Debentures [Business only]

A debenture is a long-term for a company. The loan is secured on the company's assets. If the company can't repay the debenture, the bank will repossess its buildings or other valuable assets.

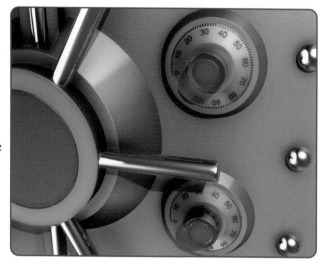

The company pays the interest on the loan every year but pays back the loan itself in one lump sum in the future. The rate of interest is fixed, which means that the company pays the same rate of interest every year.

Debentures are used to get major, expensive items that will last for more than five years, such as premises or business expansion.

Advantages

1. The interest the company pays is a tax-deductible expense. This means it reduces the company's tax bill.

2. The owners' control over the business is not affected – the business does not have to give the bank shares to get the debenture

Disadvantages

1. Security is required so the bank will take the company's buildings if the company can't repay the loan.

2. Debentures increase the company's debt/equity ratio. This increases the company's interest payments and its chances of going bankrupt and makes it harder for it to get any more loans.

Equity Capital [Business only]

The owners of the business sell some of their shares in it to investors in return for money. The investors who buy these shares now own part of the business and have a say in how it is run. (For every share they buy, they get one vote.)

Because they own part of the business, the investors get part of the profits every year. This is called a **dividend**. The directors of the business decide how much the dividend will be (if any).

Equity capital is used to get major, expensive items that will last for more than five years.

Advantages

1. Because the business hasn't borrowed, there is no interest to repay and dividends need only be paid at the directors' discretion.
2. No security is needed when selling shares so the business's buildings are not put at risk.
3. The money raised from investors (equity capital) is a permanent source of finance. It does not have to be repaid until the business closes down.
4. Because the business hasn't borrowed, there is no worry over bankruptcy.

Disadvantages

1. The existing owners must give away some of their shares in the business. This reduces their control over the business.
2. Any dividends paid are not tax-deductible. So selling shares does not help the business to reduce its tax bill.
3. Organising the sale of shares is expensive. The business must pay for brochures to be printed, advertisements, stockbrokers and lawyers.

Qualifying for a Loan

When a business or a household applies for a loan, the lender (the bank, for example) will judge them on the following criteria:

Character

- Is the household/business honest, reliable and reputable?
- The bank will ask the family questions such as how long they have lived at their present address and how long they have been in their current job.
- The bank will ask the business how long it has been established and for details of the directors and the managers.

Capacity

- Will the household/business have enough income/profits left after paying all its other expenses to repay the loan and the interest?
- The bank will ask the household for its P60, a statement of earnings from the employer and so on.
- The bank will ask a business for a copy of its Profit and Loss Account to see whether its profits are sufficient to repay the loan.

Collateral

- Does the household/business have any assets (preferably a building or a house) that it can use as security for the loan? If it can't pay back the loan, the bank will take the asset instead.

■ The bank will ask the family for details regarding the house they live in and any other properties they may own.

■ The bank will ask a business for its Balance Sheet so that it can examine the business's fixed assets to see whether it has good security for the loan.

Credit rating

■ Has the household/business a history of paying back loans in full and on time?

■ The bank will ask the household/business whether it has ever gone bankrupt before or ever defaulted on any loans.

Choosing a Source of Finance

We have seen that there are lots of different sources of finance for a business and a household to choose from. The next question therefore is: How do you decide which one to go for? Both a business and a household should consider the following factors:

1. Cost

Households and businesses should *shop around* for the cheapest source of finance. The repayments on a source of finance include paying back the original amount borrowed and paying back the interest. Different banks and lenders charge different interest rates. Many of them also charge fees, such as documentation fees, valuation fees and so on.

Households and businesses should therefore compare the APRs (annual percentage rates) of different lenders to get the best-value loan.

The APR shows the total cost of borrowing expressed as a percentage of the amount borrowed. It includes the interest charged by the lender *and* any other charges it imposes (such as documentation fees).

By law, all lenders must show their APRs. This makes it easier for consumers to compare different lenders.

2. Purpose

The household/business should match the source of finance to the item it is buying. The life of the loan should never be longer than the life of the asset bought with it. You do not want to be still paying for something that you no longer use.

For example, say you buy a designer dress/suit for your debs for €100,000 and use a 25 year mortgage to pay it back. You will be still paying €600 a month for that dress/suit when you are in your 40s! It really does not make sense.

- Short-term sources of finance are loans that have to be repaid within one year. Therefore, they should *only* be used to pay for items that last up to one year, such as an annual holiday or stock.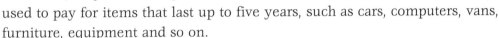

- Medium-term sources of finance are loans that have to be repaid within five years. Therefore, they should *only* be used to pay for items that last up to five years, such as cars, computers, vans, furniture, equipment and so on.

- Long-term sources of finance are loans that take longer than five years to repay. Therefore, they should *only* be used to pay for items that will last longer than five years, such as houses, factories, shops and so on.

3. Security

Households and businesses must take into account whether they have to put up some of their assets as security (collateral) for the loan. If they cannot repay the loan, they stand to lose the assets pledged as security. Lenders will only take assets that hold their value or go up in value as collateral for a loan. For most households, this means their house. For most businesses, this means their business premises. Therefore, the household/business must weigh up the advantages of a particular source of finance with the risk of losing their home/business, if security is required.

4. Tax Implications

Households and businesses must look at the source of finance to see if they will get a tax deduction for the interest they pay on it. If so, this will reduce their repayments. In the case of a business, debenture interest is tax deductible and will lower the business's tax bill, but dividends paid on equity shares will not. In the case of a household, the government effectively pays some of the family's mortgage by giving tax relief at source. If the family use their savings to buy the house, they do not get any tax relief.

5. Control (For Businesses Only)

The business must look at the source of finance to see whether it involves the owners giving away some of their shares in the business. If so, this will reduce their control over their business. For example, debentures do not involve giving away shares but equity capital does. The business owners must balance their desire for money with their control over their company.

Bank Current Accounts

A current account is a bank account that businesses and households can use for handling money that comes in and goes out all the time. A current account provides the following services:

Cheque

- A cheque is a form that the current account holder fills in. It tells the bank to take a sum of money out of her account and give it to the person named on the cheque. It is a handy way of paying for things without using cash.

Standing Order *(fixed intervals)*

- The current account holder tells the bank to deduct a fixed sum of money from her account at *regular* intervals and pay it into another person's account.

- Standing orders are used to pay regular bills, such as insurance premiums and debenture interest.

Direct Debit

- The current account holder instructs the bank to *regularly* take an amount of money out of her account and pay it into another person's account.

- It is similar to a standing order except that the amount *changes* each time.

- It is used to pay bills such as telephone or electricity where the amount changes all the time.

Paypath *(current account holders)*

- This is a system whereby an employee's salary is paid directly into her bank account. Her wages are transferred electronically from her employer's account into hers.

- It is safer than cash for both the employer and the employee. It is also more convenient than receiving a cheque.

ATM Cards

- ATM stands for Automated Teller Machine.

- This is a facility that allows the current account holder to withdraw sums of money from her account using a machine in the wall of the bank. Withdrawals can be made 24 hours a day.

- The account holder needs a PIN (Personal Identification Number) to access her account.

Laser Cards

- These are debit cards. They allow the account holder to pay for things without the inconvenience or cost of writing a cheque.

■ To pay for an item, you hand the laser card to the shop assistant who scans it. The bank then automatically takes the money from your account and deposits it in the shop's account within a few days.

Bank Statements

■ This is a document sent by the bank to the account holder, usually every month.

■ It sets out all the withdrawals and lodgements that took place in the account that month. It also shows how much money is left in the account (balance).

Bank Statement

Bank of Glasnevin

Name:	Colin Dunne		Date:	30th March 2012
Account No.:	12345678		Branch Sort Code	80-08-90

Date	Details	Debit - OUT	Credit - IN	Balance
		€	€	€
1st Mar	Balance			100
2nd Mar	Paypath 12345		1200	1300
4th Mar	ESB DD	150		1150
6th Mar	ATM 20154	20		1130
19th Mar	AA Insurance SO	30		1100
27th Mar	Bank charges	10		1090

This bank statement is explained as follows:

Date	Explanation
1st March	Colin Dunne had €100 in his current account, left over from February.
2nd March	Colin's employer paid his wages of €1,200 directly into his bank account. This brought his balance up to €1,300.
4th March	Colin's bank paid his ESB bill of €150 by direct debit. This reduced his balance to €1,150.
6th March	Colin withdrew €20 from his account using his ATM card. This reduced his balance to €1,130.
19th March	Colin's bank paid his regular insurance premium of €30 per month to the AA. This reduced his balance to €1,100.
27th March	Colin's bank charged him €10 for providing him with a current account. His balance drops to €1,090.

Cheque

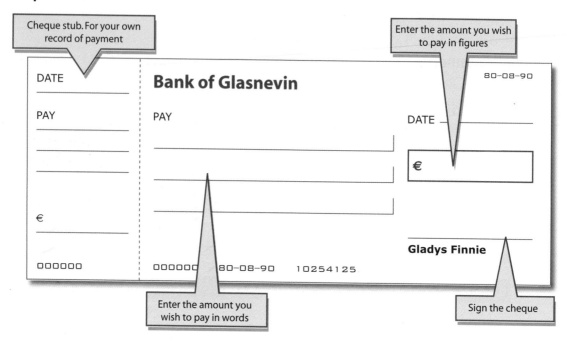

Cheque stub. For your own record of payment

Enter the amount you wish to pay in figures

Bank of Glasnevin

80–08–90

DATE

PAY

PAY

DATE

€

€

Gladys Finnie

000000

000000 80–08–90 10254125

Enter the amount you wish to pay in words

Sign the cheque

Household and Business Management

Common Activities

1. Both a business and a household engage in cash flow forecasting. This is the management activity of planning. Both the manager of the business and the head of the household plan all the money they will receive and all the money they will spend, in the future. This determines whether they will have money left over (surplus) or if they will run short of money (deficit). Each can then take appropriate steps to deal with the deficit

   or surplus by arranging an overdraft or an investment opportunity respectively.

2. Both a business and a household engage in the management activity of controlling. Businesses use stock control to make sure that they don't run out of products to sell to their customers. Similarly, a family uses stock control to make sure that it doesn't run out of food to eat.

3. Both a business and a household use internal and external communications. The manager of the business uses internal communications to give instructions to employees. Similarly, the head of the household communicates instructions to

children. Both use external communications with banks to arrange loans, and with the government to pay taxes.

4. Both a business and a household raise finance. Both fill in forms to apply for loans. Both must make decisions on the most suitable type of finance to be used.

Different Activities

1. Business managers have to work out the taxes the business owes. They must compute the amount of Self-Assessment Income Tax or Corporation Tax and Value Added Tax the business owes and pay this amount over to the Revenue. In total contrast, households do not have to calculate their PAYE income tax or their VAT. Their employer and shops do this for them. Therefore, business managers engage in the activity of tax calculation. Households do not.

2. Businesses engage in manpower planning to make sure that they have the right number of employees to do all the jobs needed. If they have too few employees, they recruit more. If they have too many, they make redundancies. Households do not engage in manpower planning.

3. Businesses tend to be much larger than households. Businesses are usually run by professional managers, hired by the owners. Households tend to manage themselves.

4. A business manager will be responsible for producing and marketing a product that the business will sell. The manager has to persuade the public to buy the business's products by advertising them. In total contrast, a household does not make any products and does not advertise to the public.

Ordinary Level Questions

EXAM SECTION 1 (25%) – SHORT ANSWER QUESTIONS [10 marks each]

1. List three items that could be included in the Receipts section of a business's cash flow forecast.

2. List three items that could be included in the Payments section of a business's cash flow forecast.

3. List three items that could be included in the Income section of a household budget.

4. List three items that could be included in the Expenditure section of a household budget.

5. Explain the term "spreadsheet".

6. List three sources of finance that a business and a household can use.

7. Distinguish between "credit card" and "trade credit".

8. Column 1 is a list of business terms. Column 2 is a list of possible explanations for these terms. Match the two lists by placing the letter of the correct explanation under the relevant number below. One explanation has no match.

Column 1	Column 2: Explanations
1. Bank Overdraft	a) Business raises cash by selling its debtors to a bank
2. Accrued Expenses	b) Business raises cash by selling shares to investors
	c) Renting an asset
3. Factoring	d) Business/household uses services now (such as the telephone or electricity), and pays for them later
4. Hire Purchase	
5. Leasing	e) Short-term loan from a bank
6. Term Loan	f) Pay for an item in instalments and own it when last instalment is paid
	g) Medium-term business loan from a bank.

1	2	3	4	5	6
E	D	A	F	C	G

9. Indicate whether each of the following (A, B, C, D and E) is true or false.

	Sentence	True or False
A	No interest is charged on a bank overdraft.	True
B	Phone, gas and electricity are often financed by accrued expenses.	True
C	Hire purchase interest paid by a business is tax deductible.	False
D	Leasing reduces the owners' control over their business.	True
E	When the European Central Bank increases interest rates, the repayments on a variable rate loan also increase.	True

10. Explain the term "mortgage".

11. Outline two advantages of retained earnings as a source of finance for a business.

12. Column 1 is a list of business terms. Column 2 is a list of possible explanations for these terms. Match the two lists by placing the letter of the correct explanation under the relevant number below. One explanation has no match.

Column 1	Column 2: Explanations
1. ATM	a) Document showing lodgements to, withdrawals from and balance on a current account
2. Standing Order	b) Employee's wages are paid directly into her current account
3. Paypath	c) Bank takes fixed amount from current account at regular intervals to pay bills
4. Laser Card	d) Form instructing bank to take money from a person's current account and pay it to another
5. PIN	e) Automated Teller Machine
6. Bank Statement	f) Debit card used to pay bills
	g) Personal Identification Number

1	2	3	4	5	6
E		B	F	G	A

13. What do the following letters stand for?   APR   ATM   ECB

EXAM SECTION 2 (75%) – LONG QUESTIONS

1. Outline three reasons why a business would prepare a cash flow forecast.   (15 marks)

2. Discuss two things that a business facing a deficit in its cash flow forecast can do to solve this problem.   (10 marks)

3. Name three sources of short-term finance available to a household and explain one of them.   (25 marks)

4. Name three sources of medium-term finance available to a business and explain one of them.   (25 marks)

5. Name three sources of long-term finance available to a business and explain one of them.   (25 marks)

6. Explain two appropriate sources of finance suitable for the purchase of a new car by the Dunne household.   (20 marks)

7. Explain two appropriate sources of finance suitable for the purchase of a new factory by Hyland Ltd.   (20 marks)

8. List two pieces of information that a bank would look for from a household applying for a mortgage.   (10 marks)

9. Describe two similarities between managing a business and managing a household.   (10 marks)

10. Describe two differences between managing a business and managing a household.   (10 marks)

Higher Level Questions

EXAM SECTION 1 (20%) – SHORT ANSWER QUESTIONS [10 marks each]

1. Complete this sentence: A cash flow forecast is…

2. What is a spreadsheet? Explain its use in a household.

3. List four sources of finance that both a business and a household can use.

4. Define medium-tem finance. Outline two medium-term finance options available for a newly established business.

5. The following table shows three sources of finance and four characteristics. For each characteristic, tick (✔) the source of finance that is *most* likely to match that characteristic.

	Debenture	Leasing	Trade Credit
Increases the business's debt/equity ratio			
Used to purchase stock			
Short-term source of finance			
Discounts available for early repayment			

6. Distinguish between fixed rate loans and variable rate loans.

7. Define long-tem finance. Outline two long-term finance options available for a household.

8. Outline two advantages of grants as a source of finance for a business.

9. Define "retained earnings".

10. Outline two factors that a bank will take into account when considering whether to give a loan to a business.

11. In the context of banking, describe two features of a current account.

EXAM SECTION 2 (20%) – APPLIED BUSINESS QUESTION – 80 MARKS

Décor Ltd.

Philippa Hudson used her redundancy package from her previous job to set up her own interior design business, Décor Ltd., one year ago. The business has prospered and Philippa now employs three painter/decorators and another designer.

Philippa is finding it difficult to manage her business. She never knows from one month to the next if she'll have enough cash to pay her bills or have a massive surplus. She recently received a hefty tax demand from Revenue and has no idea how she is going to pay it. She tried putting €50 a month away to pay her insurance premium but found herself dipping into this to pay the phone bill when she was threatened with disconnection. A friend advised her that tighter controls were needed in the business.

Philippa's employees have asked not to be paid in cash because one of them was mugged last Friday and all of his pay was taken. This has made Philippa nervous when carrying large amounts of cash around. The employees have also asked for a pay rise. She knows they work hard and deserve one but she is unsure if the business can afford it, especially as she needs to make some purchases in the future. Her stock of paint is running low and her second-hand van is giving her lots of hassle that she can do without. It needs replacing. Work keeps flooding in and she is thinking of buying a second premises in a nearby town to expand the business.

(A) Outline how preparing a cash flow forecast will help Philippa's business.   (20 marks)

(B) Discuss how the features of a current account would benefit Philippa's business.   (30 marks)

(C) Recommend a source of finance for each of the three purchases Philippa wishes to make.   (30 marks)

EXAM SECTION 3 (60%) – LONG QUESTIONS

1. The household budget of the Furlong family for next summer is set out below:

		July	August	September	Total
Income	€	12,000	14,000	8,000	34,000
Expenditure	€	9,000	13,900	11,500	34,400
Net Cash	€	3,000	100	(3,500)	(400)
Opening Cash	€	200	3,200	3,300	200
Closing Cash	€	3,200	3,300	(200)	(200)

(i) Why would this budget be prepared by the Furlong household?

(ii) How might the Furlongs deal with the financial issue highlighted in this budget?

2. The cash flow forecast of Shropshire Hotel Ltd. for next summer is set out below:

		July	August	September	Total
Receipts	€	240,000	360,000	100,000	700,000
Payments	€	220,000	400,000	180,000	800,000
Net Cash	€	20,000	(40,000)	(80,000)	(100,000)
Opening Cash	€	30,000	50,000	10,000	30,000
Closing Cash	€	50,000	10,000	(70,000)	(70,000)

(i) Explain why a business would prepare a cash flow forecast.

(ii) In which month(s) has the above business got a problem?
Outline possible reasons why. Suggest two things that the business
can do to help solve the problems.   (20 marks)

3. The Cleary family wish to go on their annual holiday to Mayo.
Recommend, with reasons, a suitable source of finance to fund their holiday.   (20 marks)

4. Discuss whether leasing is a suitable source of finance for the acquisition
of a van by a business.   (20marks)

5. Manning Ltd. needs to purchase a new computer system and
a new factory in Galway. Outline, with reasons, a suitable source of finance
to fund each purchase.   (20 marks)

6. "Equity capital is the most appropriate long-term source of finance for a business."
Discuss with reasons why a manager might deem this statement to be true.   (20 marks)

7. Describe four criteria that banks use when considering loan applications.   (20 marks)

8. In the context of banking, explain five different features of a current account.   (15 marks)

9. Using today's date, draft the cheque that Fiona Murphy wrote to pay
Electrics Ltd. for a washing machine that cost her €800.   (20 marks)

10. Contrast managing a business with managing a household.   (20 marks)

11. Compare managing a business with managing a household.   (20 marks)

CHAPTER 14

Business Ideas

If you are thinking about setting up your own business, the first thing you need is a good idea – one that will make you lots of money. You need to get your thinking cap on and think of a promising idea. You don't necessarily need to be an inventor. You just need to get **inspiration** from somewhere.

In 1990, Ireland played Holland in the World Cup. Irish fans in England couldn't watch the match because British TV was showing an England game instead. This inspired Michael O'Rourke and Leonard Ryan to rent a club in London, organise a satellite feed of the match and charge Irish fans £10 to watch it in the club. More than 800 Irish fans turned up. This success inspired O'Rourke and Ryan to set up Setanta Sports to broadcast Gaelic football and hurling into the UK and US.

These entrepreneurs became wealthy because they had an inspired idea for a business. So, the question is: Where do *you* get a good idea for a business? There are two main sources:

- ● **Internal sources –**   you get ideas from your own strengths and weaknesses.
- ● **External sources –**   you get ideas from opportunities and threats in the outside market.

Internal Sources of Business Ideas

1. Skills and Hobbies

A would-be entrepreneur may have special aptitudes or talents that he could turn into a profitable business. He may have been born with these aptitudes or may have learned and developed them over time.

If he is good at art, he could set up a business decorating shop windows for Christmas. If he can drive a car, he could set up a business giving driving lessons to his friends and family.

2. Experiences

A person wishing to set up his own business may have seen or learnt or experienced something that could give him the idea for a profitable business.

Richard Branson set up Virgin Atlantic Airways because he was not happy with the service he got on other airlines. *"The reason I moved into the airline business was that I flew a lot of other airlines and I hated the experience. I felt we could create an airline that people wanted to fly, and that turned into Virgin Atlantic Airways."*

3. Research and Development [R&D]

An entrepreneur can set up an R&D department within her business, consisting of creative and innovative employees whose job is to invent new products.

Nokia has an R&D department to constantly develop new ideas for its phones to ensure sales remain high.

4. Customer Feedback

Customer complaints can be a source of a new idea. Salespeople meeting with customers develop new ideas based on their experience of dealing with these customers.

Examples of businesses that got ideas from their customers include the following:

- Pizza Hut observed customers in its restaurants. It noticed that although most families shared a pizza, each person usually wanted a different topping. This gave Pizza Hut the idea to launch its "4 for All" pizza (one pizza divided in four with four separate toppings) and sales went through the roof.

- McDonald's realised that fewer young women were eating in its restaurants. The company asked women why and found out that women perceived its food as unhealthy and fattening. This gave McDonald's the idea to launch "Salads Plus" and sell fruit and salads in its restaurants.

5. Employee Suggestions [Intrapreneurship]

A business can get good ideas for new products and services from its employees. To encourage intrapreneurship, the business can set up a formal employee suggestion scheme offering rewards for good ideas. It is important that the managers are approachable and open to ideas from workers.

For example, Art Fry, a worker at 3M, heard about of a special glue invented by a 3M scientist. Art thought about uses for the glue and came up with the idea for the Post-it. Post-its are now one of the most popular office products.

External Sources of Business Ideas

1. Family and Friends

A would-be entrepreneur may get an idea for a business after hearing his family and friends complain about not being able to get a product or service they need.

For instance, hearing others complain about the lack of good affordable childcare might give an entrepreneur the idea to set up his own childcare business.

Jack Odell thought of the idea for Matchbox toys when his daughter told him that she was allowed to bring toys into school only if they were small enough to fit into a matchbox.

2. State Agencies

Irish government agencies provide ideas for new products and new markets. For example, Enterprise Ireland produces market research reports about business opportunities around the world.

3. Media

A person wishing to set up her own business may get an idea by reading something in a magazine or newspaper, or hearing something on the radio or TV. These media give an indication of trends taking place that an entrepreneur can make money from.

A few years ago, newspaper and TV reports about the booming Irish economy and Irish employees working harder and longer gave many entrepreneurs the idea for their business.

- Tara Dalrymple set up a business called Busy Lizzie Lifestyle Management, offering to do people's basic chores, such as shopping, gardening, cleaning and so on.

- Grace McDonnell set up her own dog walking business, Animal Adventures.

4. Competition

Businesses can get an idea by copying and adapting successful ideas developed by their rivals.

- Coca Cola brought out Deep River Rock water when it saw the success of other bottled waters. The Bewley's group got the idea for a chain of budget hotels when it saw the success of similar chains such as Jurys Inns.

- After witnessing the worldwide success of the Sony Playstation, Microsoft developed its own games console, the Xbox.

5. Import Substitution

Entrepreneurs can get an idea for a business by examining products that are currently imported with a view to making similar products here in Ireland.

- Irish entrepreneur Richard Brierley got the idea for Fiacla toothpaste when he saw that there was no Irish-made toothpaste on sale in supermarkets.

- Joe Murphy spotted that most of the crisps sold in Ireland were made in the UK. This inspired him to set up an Irish crisp business in 1954, which he called Tayto.

Brainstorming

Brainstorming is a technique that can be used by individuals and businesses to generate ideas. A group of creative people is brought together and asked for suggestions for business ideas. Everyone calls out as many ideas as they can think of. Hearing others' ideas encourages people to add to these ideas and think up their own.

The group leader records all the ideas. No one is put down for making "stupid" suggestions. The aim is to encourage creativity and imagination.

When the group has come up with all the ideas it can, then each idea is examined (using a SWOT analysis of its strengths, weaknesses, opportunities and threats) to assess its potential. Only worthwhile ideas go forward to the next stage.

Development Process of a New Product/Service

Getting your idea may be considered the easy stage! The next thing you have to do is turn your idea into an actual product or service and make it available for sale to consumers. This is a complicated process involving a number of stages.

1. Idea Generation

The first step in bringing out a new product or service is to generate new ideas. In business, it is said that for every 60 ideas a person might have, on average, only one will be a success. The business can find good ideas from internal and external sources. A good technique for generating a long list of ideas is brainstorming.

Example: Cadbury's Fuse bar

Cadbury's market research identified the growth of snacking and found a definite gap in the market for a more "chocolatey" snack. Cadbury's R&D team was asked to combine various ingredients to develop a number of new product ideas. They thought up over 250 ingredients including cereal, wafer, biscuits, peanuts, fruit and chocolate in various combinations.

2. Product/Service Screening

The next step is to go through all the ideas and pick the ones that have the greatest potential for development. The purpose of screening is to spot good ideas and to drop bad ones as soon as possible. This is done by conducting a SWOT analysis on each idea and by asking the following questions: Is the idea good enough to be a success in the market? Could it beat off any competition?

Example: Cadbury's Fuse bar

Cadbury's R&D team thought up over 250 ingredients in various combinations. It rejected recipes that did not have the right balance of chocolate, food elements and texture until it had narrowed the recipe ideas down to the most promising.

3. Concept Development

This involves writing a detailed essay about the product idea, setting out the answers to the following questions: What exactly will the product do? What will the product look like? What is its USP (unique selling point)?

A USP is some feature of a product that makes it different from the competition's product and that difference is valued by customers. For example, the USP of Volvo cars is quality. The USP of Superquinn is customer service.

Example: Cadbury's Fuse bar

Cadbury developed the following concept for the Fuse bar: Whereas other confectionery snacking products focus primarily upon ingredients, with chocolate used only to coat the bar, the product developers decided to use Cadbury chocolate to "fuse" together a number of popular snacking ingredients such as raisins, peanuts, crisp cereal and fudge pieces.

4. Feasibility Study

A feasibility study is an investigation into the new product idea to see whether it is actually possible to make the product and, if it is, to see whether it can be made at a reasonable cost and whether it will sell enough to make a profit.

The business might use a **cash flow forecast** (*see Chapter 13*) to predict the receipts and payments expected from the venture to see whether the idea is viable. It may also draw a **breakeven chart** (*see Chapter 16*) to work out how many products it will have to sell to ensure that all the expenses of the venture can be paid. Selling less than this breakeven amount will result in a loss for the business.

Feasibility studies are used to find out whether the idea is commercially viable. State agencies provide grants for businesses to carry out feasibility studies into new product ideas.

Example: Cadbury's Fuse bar

Because approximately 85% of all new products launched into the grocery sector fail in their first year, extensive research helps to reduce the risk of launching a new product into an already competitive market. Fuse went through two extensive tests. The results of these tests helped Cadbury estimate how many Fuse bars it would sell and the figures were high enough to suggest the venture would be profitable and so Cadbury continued with the project.

5. Prototype Development

A prototype is the first working model of a new product. It is a sample product made as an experiment to see whether the product idea actually works in practice and whether it would appeal to consumers.

The prototype is tested and refined to eliminate any "bugs". This process is repeated until the business is satisfied that it has the "perfect" product.

Example: Cadbury's Fuse bar

Cadbury tried out many different recipes for the new bar using different ingredients in various combinations until it finalised the recipe for the Fuse bar. It also tried out different brand names and different packaging.

6. Test Marketing

Test marketing involves launching the product on a small segment of the market and evaluating consumers' response to it. Consumers in the test market are surveyed for their opinion on the product. Their reactions are used to refine the product, its price and the way it is advertised and distributed. This helps to further reduce the risk of the launch failing.

Example: Cadbury's Fuse bar

Consumers were asked to test market the new Fuse bar. In research, Fuse scored higher in the "interesting eat" category and for texture and combination of ingredients than its competitors. It achieved the highest rating ever for a new Cadbury product: 82% of consumers rated Fuse as excellent or very good and 83% said they would buy it regularly.

7. Product Launch

Full-scale production of the product now begins and it is made available for sale in the entire market. The company must undertake a marketing campaign to get the product known.

Example: Cadbury's Fuse bar

When launching the product, Cadbury held one-to-one briefings with over 70 of the biggest retailers in the UK to inform them about Fuse and to get them to support its launch in their shops. Cadbury advertised the launch of Fuse with a catchy "hook": it would become available for the first time ever on "Fuseday", Tuesday 24th September. Public relations (PR) stories were given to the press, telling the story of Fuse, explaining that it had taken five years to develop, involved an investment of £10 million and resulted in the development of a new factory near Bristol, England. The launch was a big success – Fuse sold over 70 million bars in its first three months.

Ordinary Level Questions

EXAM SECTION 1 (25%) – SHORT ANSWER QUESTIONS [10 marks each]

1. List three internal sources of business ideas.

2. Identify two external sources of business ideas and outline any one of them.

3. Indicate whether each of the following (A, B, C, D and E) is true or false.

	Sentence	True or False
A	Brainstorming is a technique for generating ideas.	
B	Employee suggestions are an internal source of business ideas.	
C	State agencies provide entrepreneurs with business ideas.	
D	A business can get an idea for a business by copying its rivals.	
E	Internal sources of business ideas come from one's own strengths and weaknesses.	

4. Write out what the following letters stand for: R&D   USP

5. Column 1 is a list of business terms. Column 2 is a list of possible explanations for these terms. Match the two lists by placing the letter of the correct explanation under the relevant number below. One explanation has no match.

Column 1	Column 2: Explanations
1. Idea Generation	a) Making the first working model of a product
2. Brainstorming	b) Carried out to see whether the product will be profitable
3. Prototype Development	c) Launching the product on a small segment of the market
4. Concept Development	d) Eliminating ideas that have no chance of success
5. Product Screening	e) The first stage in new product/service development process
6. Feasibility Study	f) Writing a detailed analysis of exactly what a product will do
	g) A group of creative people generates lists of ideas

1	2	3	4	5	6
E					

6. What does "Product/Service Screening" mean?

7. In the context of new product/service development, what does "test marketing" mean?

8. Put the following stages in new product/service development in the correct order: Concept Development, Idea Generation, Test Marketing, Feasibility Study, Product Launch, Prototype Development, Product/Service Screening.

EXAM SECTION 2 (75%) – LONG QUESTIONS

1. Outline three internal sources of business ideas.   (15 marks)

2. Using examples, describe three external sources of business ideas.   (30 marks)

3. Explain the term "brainstorming".   (10 marks)

4. The stages in new product/service development include: Idea Generation,
    Product/Service Screening and Concept Development.
    Explain what each of these stages means.   (30 marks)

5. The stages in new product/service development include:
    Feasibility Study, Prototype Development and Test Marketing.
    Explain what each of these stages means.   (30 marks)

Higher Level Questions

EXAM SECTION 1 (20%) – SHORT ANSWER QUESTIONS [10 marks each]

1. Distinguish between "internal" and "external" sources of business ideas.

2. Illustrate your understanding of the term "import substitution".

3. Complete this sentence: The role of brainstorming in a business is to…

4. Complete this sentence: Idea generation requires…

5. What do the letters R&D stand for? Explain the use of R&D in business.

6. Explain why a business would conduct a feasibility study.

7. What is a USP? Give two examples.

8. Define "prototype".

9. Complete this sentence: Test marketing helps a business to…

10. Column 1 is a list of business terms. Column 2 is a list of possible explanations for these
    terms. Match the two lists by placing the letter of the correct explanation under the
    relevant number below. One explanation has no match.

Column 1	Column 2: Explanations
1. Intrapreneurship	a) Establishes whether an idea is commercially viable
2. Media	b) Internal source of new business ideas
3. Concept Development	c) Examining ideas and dropping those with least potential
4. Product/Service Screening	d) Launching the product on a small segment of the market to see the reaction to it
5. Feasibility Study	e) Turns an idea into a detailed statement of what the product will do
	f) External source of new business ideas

1	2	3	4	5

EXAM SECTION 2 (20%) – APPLIED BUSINESS QUESTION – 80 MARKS

Violet Ltd.

Margaret Doyle is a very successful and well-known Irish entrepreneur. Her company, Violet Ltd., has interests in a number of business sectors including newspapers, airlines, cosmetics and fashion. Her budget airline business "Violair" was set up when she saw the success of other Irish budget airlines. She attributes her accomplishments to listening to other people. A conversation with her brother in which he complained about the lack of good quality childcare for his two daughters inspired Margaret to set up a successful nationwide chain of crèches. An employee's suggestion that she should set up a men's cosmetic range turned into a very profitable business.

Although she was not especially academic at school, she loved metalwork and her first business venture involved selling metal key rings in school. Recent TV reports on immigration inspired her to set up a Polish daily newspaper, which is now on sale throughout Ireland.

When she couldn't find fashionable clothes to fit her, she set up her own ladies' clothes shop specialising in larger sizes. Overhearing customers in the shop one day wishing that a similar shop was available for their husbands motivated her to set up a men's clothing store. Margaret's latest business venture is car manufacturing. She jumped on the idea as soon as she realised that no one else made cars in Ireland.

(A) Illustrate, from the above information, the internal sources of product ideas used by Margaret. (20 marks)

(B) Outline the external sources of product ideas employed by Margaret in the above situation. (20 marks)

EXAM SECTION 3 (60%) – LONG QUESTIONS

1. Illustrate three internal sources of new business ideas. (20 marks)

2. Illustrate three external sources of new business ideas. (20 marks)

3. In the context of new product/service development, distinguish between concept development and prototype development.
   Illustrate your answer with reference to a product/service of your choice. (20 marks)

4. Evaluate the importance of feasibility studies and test marketing in the new product/service development process. (20 marks)

5. Outline the stages in the development of a new product/service. (30 marks)

CHAPTER 15

Business Startup

The first step in becoming an entrepreneur is to think of a good idea for a product or service. The next step is to set up a business to make money from that idea. This chapter examines the process of setting up a business. It looks at the three big choices the entrepreneur must make – **organisational options**, **production options** and **financial options**.

Organisational Options

The first choice facing an entrepreneur is deciding which type of business structure is best to ensure the business runs effectively. There are three options: **sole trader**, **partnership** and **private limited company**.

Sole Trader

A sole trader is a person who sets up, owns and runs a business on her own. It suits people setting up a small business who want to keep it small and own and control it themselves. Examples of sole traders include farmers, local pubs, chemists, hairdressers and newsagents.

The advantages of a sole tradership for any entrepreneur are as follows:

1. A sole trader is an easy business to set up. There are few legal registration requirements to satisfy before setting up. No government permission is required to set up in business as a sole trader.

2. The sole trader keeps all the profits. This provides a great motivation to work hard in the business. She is directly rewarded for all her effort.

3. It is a confidential type of business. The business's financial accounts do not have to be published (made public). Therefore, no one else can get access to the sole trader's business secrets.

4. The sole trader is in full control of her business. She can make all the decisions quickly because no time is wasted having discussions with others.

The disadvantages of a sole tradership for any entrepreneur are as follows:

1. The sole trader has **unlimited liability**.

    This means that if the business goes bankrupt and owes a lot of money, the sole trader herself is totally personally responsible for paying back *all* the business's loans. If after selling the business to repay the loans, debts are still owed, she will have to sell off her own personal assets, such as her house, to pay back these loans.

    In other words, setting up as a sole trader involves a huge risk. She risks losing everything she owns if the business fails – her business, her home and anything else she owns.

2. It is difficult to run a business alone. The sole trader has to rely on one person – herself – to know everything that is needed to run a business. There is no one to help her.

3. It is hard to raise the money on your own to set up and run a business. You cannot sell shares to raise money and you cannot bring partners on board. It is difficult to get loans from banks because sole traders are the business organisation most likely to go bankrupt.

4. Running a business alone can result in putting in long hours and lots of stress.

Partnership

To overcome the disadvantages of being in business alone, the entrepreneur could consider setting up in business with other people in a partnership.

A partnership is a business owned and managed by between 2 and 20 owners called partners. They set up the business together to pool their resources and talents to make a profit. Examples of partnerships include many professions such as solicitors, doctors and accountants such as KPMG and PricewaterhouseCoopers.

The advantages of setting up in business as a partnership for an entrepreneur are as follows:

1. A partnership is a simple business to set up. There are few legal registration requirements to satisfy before setting up. No government permission is required to set up in business as a partnership.

    However, it is advisable for partners to draw up a contract before setting up the business.

Such a contract is called a **deed of partnership**. It is used in the event of any disagreements between the partners. It sets out in advance issues such as how the profits are to be shared, what each partner is expected to do in the running of the business, what happens if the business closes down, what salaries each partner is to be paid for working in the business and whether partners can take money from the business and, if so, how much. Then, if there are any disputes between the partners, they can refer to the rules they wrote down in their deed of partnership to sort them out.

2. Because more people are setting up the business, more capital is available to the business. Each partner contributes some capital, so the business can raise more money to set up than a sole trader.

3. Each of the partners may bring different areas of expertise, making it easier to run the business. Also, because there are more people to consult with and discuss problems with, the partnership should make better decisions than someone on their own.

4. It is a confidential type of business. The business's financial accounts do not have to be published (made public). Therefore, no one else can get access to the partnership's business secrets.

The disadvantages of setting up in business as a partnership for an entrepreneur are as follows:

1. The partners have unlimited liability. This means that if the business goes bankrupt and owes a lot of money, the partners are *jointly and severally liable* for paying back *all* the business's loans.
    If, after selling the business to repay the loans, debts are still owed, the partners will have to sell off their own personal assets, such as their houses, to pay back their share of the loans. If one partner cannot pay back her share of the loans, the other partners have to pay it for her.

2. Profits have to be shared between the partners.

3. The partners may be incompatible, resulting in disputes that could harm the business's success.

4. Decision-making is slower because all the partners have to be consulted. This may make the business less flexible and less responsive to change. The partners may spend so much time debating new opportunities that by the time they agree, someone else may have exploited the opportunity.

Private Limited Company (Ltd.)

We have seen that a major disadvantage for an entrepreneur of setting up in business as a sole trader or partnership is unlimited liability. To overcome this difficulty many entrepreneurs establish their businesses as private limited companies.

A private limited company is a business set up by 1 to 50 people called shareholders. Although a private limited company can be owned by one person, it must have at least two directors to run it. Directors are voted in by the shareholders to run the business on their behalf. The company is totally separate from the owners. The company can make contracts, the company can be sued and the company can sue others.

Examples of private limited companies include Eason and Son Ltd. and Jurys Doyle Hotel Group Ltd.

The advantages of setting up in business as a private limited company for an entrepreneur are as follows:

1.   The shareholders in the company have **limited liability**.
     This means that if the business goes bankrupt and owes a lot of money, the shareholders are *not personally liable* for paying back the business's debts. If, after selling the business to repay the loans, debts are still owed, the shareholders do not have to sell their own personal assets, such as their houses, to pay back their share of the loans. All they lose is the capital they put into the business.

2.   Because more people (up to 50) are putting money into the business, it is easier to raise capital for the business. Each shareholder invests some money in the business. The business can raise more money to set up than a sole trader could.

3.   A private limited company is a good choice when setting up a new business venture because there can be up to 50 owners. Each owner can bring her knowledge, skills and experience to bear when making important decisions. The owners can brainstorm ideas for the new business venture and this inventive, creative process will yield better decisions and ideas than a person operating on her own.

4.   Companies pay less tax on their business profits than either sole traders or partnerships. The rate of tax that companies pay on their profits (called Corporation Tax – *see Chapter 12*) is much

less that that paid by sole traders and partnerships on their profits (called Self-Assessment Income Tax – *see Chapter 12*).

5. A private limited company has continuity of existence. This means that, if the owners of the company die, it does not cease to exist. Once the company is legally established, it can continue to operate forever provided that it does not go bankrupt.

The disadvantages of setting up in business as a private limited company for an entrepreneur are as follows:

1. It is complicated to set up a private limited company. The shareholders must first apply for permission from the Registrar of Companies. This involves submitting detailed lists of the business's rules, called the memorandum of association and articles of association. The business cannot begin trading until the shareholders receive a **Certificate of Incorporation** from the Registrar. Furthermore, they must also pay a fee for this service.

2. The company must publish its financial accounts each year, for all to see. This means that a private limited company is not a very confidential type of business. Customers, competitors, employees and anyone else who is interested can see the company's financial position and may use this information to their advantage.

3. Profits have to be shared between the shareholders.

4. There are a lot of legal requirements to obey. Every year the company must send an annual return to the Companies Registration Office. Every year, the company must get its financial accounts audited.

In conclusion, every entrepreneur faces the same choice when setting up a business – which type of business to go for. Each has its pros and cons, so it is up to each entrepreneur to pick the one with the most advantages for her.

Production Options

The entrepreneur has to decide how to make the products that she intends selling. Again, there are three basic options.

She could decide to make one-off products to suit each individual customer. This is called **job production**. For example, an optician makes a different set of lenses for every patient because every patient has a different eye problem. In O'Briens Sandwich Bars, they

will make any sandwich a customer asks for right there in front of the customer.

Alternatively, the business can make a lot of products, all at the same time. This is called **batch production**. *The Irish Times* prints a batch of identical newspapers every morning. Obviously, it wouldn't make sense to make a different newspaper for every single customer. It would cost far too much.

The final production option is called **mass production**. This means making the product continuously 24 hours a day, 7 days a week. This is an option only if there is massive demand for the entrepreneur's product.

Job Production

Job production involves making the products one at a time. Each product is *individual and unique*. A customer comes in and sets out exactly what she is looking for. Then the business makes that product to the exact specifications of the customer.

Examples of products made by job production include a tailor making a hand-made (bespoke) suit. The tailor must measure the customer and make a suit that fits him exactly. The customer then chooses a fabric for the suit and a lining and the tailor will make *exactly* what the customer orders.

Generally, job production uses highly skilled workers to make the products. Making a suit by hand to fit a customer perfectly is a very skilful job.

Job production usually uses machines that are flexible and capable of doing many jobs. This is because each customer will ask for something different and the machines must be capable of doing any job needed.

Because job production uses highly skilled labour and each product has to be made individually for the customer, products made this way tend to be expensive.

Batch Production

Batch production involves making a large amount of the product all in one go (**production run**). The product is the *same* for all customers.

Examples of products made by batch production include newspapers, CDs, books and so on. A bakery uses batch production. The baker makes her cakes in batches of however many will fit in her oven at a time. When that batch is made, the baker will start the process again with a new batch of cakes.

Because it is the same product for all customers, it is made in advance and ready for the customer when she comes into the shop looking for it.

Generally, batch production uses workers who are not as highly skilled as those involved in job production. In batch production, the workers are not creating one-off unique products from scratch.

Batch production usually uses machines that are flexible and capable of doing many jobs. A printing business may be printing an order of large colour atlases in the morning, pocket-size notebooks in the afternoon and Leaving Cert exam papers in the evening. Therefore, the printer needs a machine that can do all three jobs.

Because the business makes a lot of products at the same time, it costs less than job production, so a product that is batch produced tends to be cheaper than one made by job production. A tailor earning €1,000 a week might make only two hand-made suits every week, whereas a baker earning €1,000 a week could easily make 1,000 cakes in a week.

	A. Cost of her weekly wages	B. Number of products made in a week	Cost per product [(A) ÷ (B)]
Tailor	€1,000	2 suits	€500 per suit
Baker	€1,000	1,000 cakes	€1 per cake

You can see that the more products that are made, the lower the cost of producing each product. This is known in business as **economies of scale**.

Mass Production

Mass production involves making the product continuously, 24 hours a day, 7 days a week, 365 days a year. Therefore, mass production is suitable only for products that are in continuous demand by consumers.

Examples of mass-produced products include toilet paper and KitKats. Once you use a mass-produced product, you will probably want or need to replace it. So, you keep buying it time and time again. This is not true for CDs. Once you have bought a certain CD, you do not keep buying that same CD for the rest of your life. This is why CDs are batch produced.

The product is the same for all customers. Because of this, it is made in advance and is ready for the customer when she comes into the shop looking for it.

Mass production mainly uses machines, rather than workers, in the factory. These machines are very specialised. This means that they normally do just one job. In the example of Nestlé, it makes sense for it to have a machine that makes only KitKats because it is used every single day.

Generally, mass production uses unskilled workers in an assembly line to make the products.

Because of huge economies of scale (because so many products are made), mass production tends to have the lowest cost of all the three production options and therefore the price is lower under mass production than either job or batch production.

Finance Options

The entrepreneur has to decide where she will get the money from (called **sources of finance**) to set up and run the business. Sources of finance fall into three major categories.

Short-term sources of finance *(see Chapter 13)* are monies given to the entrepreneur that she has to pay back within a year. Therefore, they are only suitable to buy things that will be used up within a year, such as the business's stock. The main short-term sources of finance available to an entrepreneur starting up in business include a bank overdraft, accrued expenses and trade credit.

Medium-term sources of finance *(see Chapter 13)* are monies given to the entrepreneur that she has to pay back within five years. Therefore, they are only suitable to buy things that will be used up within five years, such as the cars, vans and equipment. The main medium-term sources of finance available to an entrepreneur starting up in business include hire purchase, leasing and a term loan.

Long-term sources of finance *(see Chapter 13)* are monies given to the entrepreneur that she has longer than five years to repay. Therefore, they are only suitable to buy things that will be used in the business for more than five years, such as buildings. The main long-term sources of finance available to an entrepreneur starting up in business include debentures, grants and equity capital.

Short Term	Medium Term	Long Term
(finance that will take up to one year to repay)	(finance that will take up to five years to repay)	(finance that will take more than five years to repay)
■ Accrued expenses ■ Bank overdraft ■ Trade credit	■ Hire purchase ■ Leasing ■ Term loan	■ Grants ■ Debentures ■ Equity capital

When choosing a source of finance, the entrepreneur must consider the following factors:

Cost   How much interest has to be paid on the loan? Are there any other charges to be paid?

Risk   What will happen to the business if it cannot repay the source of finance?

Security   Does the business have to put up its buildings and other valuable assets as collateral to get the finance?

Control   Does the entrepreneur have to give away part of her business (shares) to the person giving her the finance?

Short-term Finance: ACCRUED EXPENSES   *See Chapter 13*

Cost   It is a free source of finance. No interest is charged.

Risk   Failure to repay will damage the business's credit rating and will result in the business being "cut off".

Security   No security is needed. The business's assets are not at risk.

Control   The owner keeps full control. She does not have to give the service provider shares in her business to use accrued expenses.

Short-term Finance: BANK OVERDRAFT   *See Chapter 13*

Cost   A high rate of interest and surcharges are payable.

Risk   The bank can demand full repayment at any time. Failure to repay will damage the business's credit rating.

Security   No security is needed. The business's assets are not at risk.

Control   The owner keeps full control. She does not have to give the bank shares in her business to get the overdraft.

Short-term Finance: TRADE CREDIT   *See Chapter 13*

Cost   Generally it is a free source of finance. But the supplier can charge interest if the business doesn't pay on time.

Risk   Failure to repay will damage the business's credit rating and make it very difficult to get any more goods on credit.

Security   No security is needed. The business's assets are not at risk.

Control   The owner keeps full control. She does not have to give the suppliers shares in her business to use trade credit.

Medium-term Finance: HIRE PURCHASE (HP)   *See Chapter 13*

Cost   An expensive rate of interest must be paid.

Risk   Failure to repay will damage the business's credit rating and result in the asset being repossessed.

Security   No security is needed. The business's assets are not at risk.

Control   The owner keeps full control. She does not have to give the HP company shares in her business to use HP.

Medium-term Finance: LEASING   *See Chapter 13*

Cost   The rent paid may end up being much dearer than the cost of buying the asset.

Risk   Failure to pay rent will damage the business's credit rating and result in the asset being repossessed.

Security   No security is needed. The business's assets are not at risk.

Control   The owner keeps full control. She does not have to give the leasing company shares in her business to use leasing.

Medium-term Finance: TERM LOAN   *See Chapter 13*

Cost   The interest payable tends to be cheaper than hire purchase and leasing.

Risk   Failure to repay will damage the business's credit rating and result in the security provided being taken from the business and sold to repay the loan.

Security   Security is needed. The business's assets are at risk.

Control   The owner keeps full control. She does not have to give the bank shares in her business to get a term loan.

Long-term Finance: GRANTS   *See Chapter 13*

Cost   Grants are free and do not have to be repaid.

Risk   The government will ask for the money back if the business breaks the conditions of the grant.

Security No security is needed. The business's assets are not at risk.

Control The owner keeps full control. She does not have to give the government shares in her business to get a grant.

Long-term Finance: DEBENTURES   *See Chapter 13*

Cost A fixed rate of interest is payable.

Risk Failure to repay will damage the business's credit rating and result in the security provided being taken from the business and sold to repay the loan.

Security Security is needed. The business's assets are at risk.

Control The owner keeps full control. She does not have to give the lender shares in her business to get a debenture loan.

Long-term Finance: EQUITY CAPITAL   *See Chapter 13*

Cost Dividends are paid to investors usually every year but the company directors can decide how much to pay.

Risk If the business goes bankrupt, the directors are banned from getting involved in another company for five years.

Security No security is needed. The business's assets are not at risk.

Control The owner loses some of her control. She must give the investors some shares (and votes) in the business to get the money from them.

Business Plan

When a person applies for a job, she sends a CV to impress the potential employer with her qualifications and experience in the hope of getting the job. Similarly, an entrepreneur draws up a **business plan** in the hope of impressing investors with her product and ideas for the business so that they will provide the finance needed to get the business up and running.

A business plan is a document that sets out the *objectives* of the business and the *strategies* by which these will be achieved. It is like a map for the entrepreneur telling her what she has to achieve to make her business a success and what steps she must take to get there.

It sets out details about the entrepreneur setting up the business, her business idea and especially her unique selling point (USP). It also details how the entrepreneur is going to make and sell the product and how she intends to finance the business.

A typical business plan contains the following details:

BUSINESS PLAN for _____

1. **Description of Business**

   The entrepreneur describes the people starting the business, its products and its long-term objectives.

2. **Market Analysis**

   The entrepreneur must show that there is a viable market for her product. She must also show how she intends to beat the competition to win customers. The entrepreneur describes her target market, market trends, the competition and her competitive advantage over them.

3. **Marketing Plan**

   The entrepreneur describes her marketing strategy, i.e., how she intends to arouse customers' interest in the product and convince them to buy it.

4. **Production Plan**

   The entrepreneur describes how she will make the product. She describes the manufacturing process (job, batch or mass), the equipment that will be used and how she will make sure that the products are made to the best quality.

5. **Finance Plan**

   The entrepreneur describes how much it will cost to finance the business, how much money she has and how much she still needs. She sets out any collateral she has for the loan. She also sets out a projected Profit and Loss Account and Balance Sheet and Cash Flow Forecast for the next few years.

Here is an example of a business plan. The question is taken from a past Leaving Cert Higher Level paper.

2006 Higher Level – Section 3 – Question 6

Paula and Thomas have recently returned to Ireland having worked with transnational companies for ten years. They wish to set up in business together in Ireland manufacturing a range of new organic breakfast cereals. Paula has particular expertise in production and finance, and Thomas in marketing and human resources.

(A) Draft a Business Plan for the proposed new business under five main headings, outlining the contents under each heading.   (40 marks)

Business Plan for Paula and Thomas

1. **Description of Business**
    We are Paula and Thomas. We have a lot of international experience in business, having worked abroad for ten years for transnational companies. Paula has particular expertise in production and finance, while Thomas's areas of expertise are marketing and human resources.
    We are setting up a business that will make a range of new organic breakfast cereals. Our aim is to become the biggest organic cereal producer in Ireland and to export abroad.

2. **Market Analysis**
    We have conducted market research that shows that the market for breakfast cereals in Ireland is very large and growing. A big market trend in the entire food industry is the increasing interest in organic products. We therefore believe that our target market of health-conscious consumers is large enough for our business to be very profitable. Our unique selling point is that unlike most cereal manufacturers, our cereals will be made from entirely organic ingredients.

3. **Marketing Plan**
    To arouse consumers' interest in our range of organic cereals, we will advertise on TV during sports and health programmes which our target market is likely to watch. We will use a price penetration strategy – we will charge a low price for our cereals to win as many customers away from the competition as possible. We will negotiate with all the leading supermarkets and health stores to stock our range of cereals, so that they will be readily available for consumers throughout Ireland.

4. **Production Plan**
    Our range of cereals will be manufactured in our factory in Ireland from organic ingredients sourced in Ireland. We will use batch production to make a variety of flavours to meet consumer demand. We will use Computer Aided Manufacture (CAM) to run the machines to make enough cereals for consumers. We will apply for ISO 9000 certification to make sure that the quality of our production process and our cereals is of the highest standard.

5. **Finance Plan**
    The costs of setting up the business are as follows:

Factory and Equipment	€1,000,000
Stock	€100,000
	€1,100,000

We plan to finance €200,000 of our needs from our personal savings and are seeking a loan for the remaining €900,000. The factory will be the collateral for the loan. Our projected profits are as follows:

	2010	2011	2012
Sales	€200,000	€200,000	€400,000
Expenses	€180,000	€250,000	€310,000
Net Profit	€20,000	(€50,000)	€90,000

Importance of a Business Plan

A business plan is essential for all entrepreneurs. The main reasons why every entrepreneur should draft a business plan are listed below:

1. It forces the entrepreneur to **focus on the future**. It sets out the objectives of the business and the strategies by which they will be achieved. Thus, it is like a "map" for the entrepreneur to guide her towards success.

2. It helps the entrepreneur to **anticipate problems** and prepare solutions to them in advance, including how she is going to make the product, sell the product and finance the entire business venture. Solving problems in advance will help the entrepreneur to avoid business failure.

3. It is used to **impress investors** when seeking finance for the business. Investors will consider the business plan like an employer considers a CV. They use it to judge whether the idea and the business are sound. If the plan impresses them, they will give the entrepreneur the much-needed finance to start, run and expand the business.

4. It is used to **control the business**. It sets out targets to be achieved. After a while, the business's actual performance can be measured against these targets to see whether the business is on target for success. If not, corrective action can be taken to keep the business on target for success.

Ordinary Level Questions

EXAM SECTION 1 (25%) – SHORT ANSWER QUESTIONS [10 marks each]

1. Explain the term "sole trader" and give two examples.

2. Explain the term "unlimited liability".

3. As a type of business organisation, explain three features of a partnership.

4. Outline two benefits of a private limited company as a type of business organisation.

5. Explain the term "limited liability".

6. Explain the term "job production" and illustrate your answer with an example of a product produced using job production.

7. What does "batch production" mean?

8. Complete the sentence: Mass production means… (Give an example of a product produced using mass production.)

9. Indicate whether each of the following (A, B, C, D and E) is true or false.

	Sentence	True or False
A	Job production is usually used to make inexpensive products.	
B	The assembly line is often a feature of mass production.	
C	Newspapers are mass-produced.	
D	Highly skilled craftsmanship is a feature of mass production.	
E	Mass production is best suited to products that have little consumer demand.	

10. Indicate whether each of the following (A, B, C, D and E) is true or false.

	Sentence	True or False
A	A bank can demand repayment of an overdraft at any time.	
B	Accrued expenses result in a loss of control for the entrepreneur.	
C	Hire purchase is usually more expensive than a term loan.	
D	Using equity finance reduces control over one's business.	
E	Trade credit is always free.	

11. Column 1 is a list of business terms. Column 2 is a list of possible explanations for these terms. Match the two lists by placing the letter of the correct explanation under the relevant number below. One explanation has no match.

Column 1	Column 2: Explanations
1. ECB	a) Long-term loan for a business
2. Debentures	b) Paying for an item in instalments (You own it when you pay the last instalment)
3. Trade credit	
4. Hire Purchase	c) Selling shares in the business
5. Leasing	d) Money given to a business by the government to help it buy things it needs
6. Grant	e) European Central Bank
	f) Business gets stock now and pays for it later
	g) Renting an asset

1	2	3	4	5	6
E					

12. List four headings in a business plan.

EXAM SECTION 2 (75%) – LONG QUESTIONS

1. Eileen wishes to set up her own business. Outline two risks and two rewards for Eileen if she sets up as a sole trader.   (20 marks)

2. Peter and Amy are thinking of setting up a business together as a partnership. Outline three disadvantages of a partnership.   (15 marks)

3. Outline two similarities between a sole trader and a partnership.   (10 marks)

4. Outline three features of a private limited company.   (15 marks)

5. Explain three disadvantages of a private limited company as a type of business organisation.   (15 marks)

6. Outline three features of job production.   (15 marks)

7. Distinguish between "batch production" and "mass production".   (20 marks)

8. Describe two sources of finance suitable for a new business that wishes to acquire a lorry.   (20 marks)

9. Describe two sources of finance suitable for a new business that wishes to acquire stock.   (20 marks)

10. Describe two sources of finance suitable for a new business that wishes to acquire a new factory.   (20 marks)

11. Describe three benefits for an entrepreneur of preparing a business plan.   (15 marks)

12. Eileen Redmond opened her first gym, Fit Fighters, on Pearse Street,

Monasterevin, five years ago after graduating from college with a degree in fitness and nutrition. The gym offers an extensive range of fitness classes for all levels and is kitted out with the latest fitness equipment. She often has promotions offering off-peak membership at reduced prices.

She now wants to expand her business and buy a new premises in nearby Kildare town. She has savings of €50,000 and she needs a long-term loan of €300,000. She is preparing a business plan to accompany her loan application to the bank.

Draft a business plan for Eileen to help her loan application to the bank under the following three headings:

- ■ Ownership
- ■ Finance
- ■ Marketing   (30 marks)

13. Maurice Fahy set up his own crèche business four years ago after graduating from college with a certificate in childcare. The crèche is situated in a large town in the west of Ireland and has been very busy since Maurice first opened it. There is currently a waiting list for parents who wish to enrol their children for next year. Because of the high level of demand, Maurice wishes to expand the crèche by building an extension to his existing premises. He has savings of €10,000, reserves of €40,000 and needs a long-term loan of €400,000. He is preparing a business plan to accompany his loan application to the bank.

Draft a business plan for Maurice to help his loan application to the bank under the following three headings:

- ■ Ownership
- ■ Finance
- ■ Marketing   (30 marks)

Higher Level Questions

EXAM SECTION 1 (20%) – SHORT ANSWER QUESTIONS [10 marks each]

1. Distinguish between "sole trader" and "partnership".

2. What is a private limited company? Give two examples.

3. Illustrate your understanding of the term "unlimited liability".

4. Explain the term "limited liability". Outline its impact on the development of the Irish economy.

5. The following table shows three types of production and four qualities. For each quality, tick (✔) the type of production which is *most* likely to match that quality.

	Job	Batch	Mass
Uses specialised machinery			
Continuous production of identical products			
Enjoys massive economies of scale			
Product is never in stock when the customer first asks for it			

6. Column 1 is a list of business terms. Column 2 is a list of possible explanations for these terms. Match the two lists by placing the letter of the correct explanation under the relevant number below. One explanation has no match.

Column 1	Column 2: Explanations
1. Grants	a) Medium-term source of finance
2. Equity Capital	b) Collateral that must be pledged to get a loan
3. Debentures	c) Money obtained from the government
4. Security	d) Short-term source of finance
5. Bank Overdraft	e) Money invested in a business by the owners of that business
	f) Long-term loan carrying fixed rate of interest

1	2	3	4	5

7. Define "business plan".

8. Outline two headings contained in a business plan.

9. Explain why an entrepreneur would prepare a business plan.

EXAM SECTION 2 (20%) – APPLIED BUSINESS QUESTION – 80 MARKS

> **Kaona**
>
> Andrew Cullen worked for a leading firm of architects in Galway after graduating from college with an honours degree in architecture four years ago. He left the firm of architects recently to set up his own bathroom design business, Kaona, as a sole trader. He operates the business from the garage of his house. Andrew is finding the challenges of setting up a new business very daunting. He is concerned about the risk

he is taking. A friend, experienced in business, advised him to draw up a business plan and to keep costs to a minimum.

Andrew also needs to find a more permanent premises to operate the business from but was surprised by the costs involved in purchasing a building in Galway. His friend advised him to change the business structure to a private limited company but Andrew is reluctant to give away shares in his business.

Andrew is finding the world of bathroom design extremely competitive. He finds himself under huge pressure from more established competitors who some customers tell him have better designs and charge a lower price. Andrew now wishes to purchase computer equipment to help him improve the quality of his designs.

(A) Evaluate one medium-term and one long-term source of finance available to Andrew. (20 marks)

(B) Evaluate the benefits to Andrew from changing his business to a private limited company. (20 marks)

(C) Draft a business plan for Andrew under five headings. (40 marks)

EXAM SECTION 3 (60%) – LONG QUESTIONS

1. A friend of yours has come to you looking for advice. She is setting up her own business but is unsure about the different options – sole trader, partnership and private limited company. Recommend one type of business organisation to her. Support your answer with well-explained reasons. (20 marks)

2. Contrast a partnership and a private limited company as suitable forms of business organisation for a business start-up. (20 marks)

3. Peter is setting up a new business. He will need to purchase a factory, stock and a delivery van. Recommend, with reasons, one suitable source of finance for Peter for each purchase. (30 marks)

4. Maureen Lambert has recently graduated from catering college with a higher diploma in cookery. Prior to this she worked in a restaurant in various positions for ten years. She now wishes to set up her own restaurant specialising in healthy menus.

   Draft a business plan for the proposed new business under five main headings, outlining the contents under each heading. (40 marks)

5. Evaluate the usefulness of a business plan when starting a business. (20 marks)

CHAPTER 16

Marketing #1

Marketing is very important because it helps a business to make a lot of money. It does this by enabling the business to make a product that consumers really want and by convincing consumers to purchase that product.

Definition of Marketing

Marketing is the management process of finding out what customers want and then making a product that will satisfy their needs and persuading them to buy that product.

The first step in marketing is to conduct market research to find out exactly what customers want from a product. Armed with this knowledge, the business can then start making such a product. The business must then let customers know about its product and convince them to buy it, using four tools called the marketing mix.

Market Research

Market research involves collecting, analysing and reporting information about marketing issues to enable managers to make effective marketing decisions.

There are two ways to carry out market research. Field research means collecting original information. Desk research means using existing research that someone else has already collected.

Field Research

This is research that has never been done before. The researcher goes out into the market (the "field") and collects new information directly from consumers, specifically for the project in hand. It is the most expensive and time-consuming type of research.

The following techniques can be used to obtain field research:

1. Observation

Researchers watch and learn from how customers behave and react in certain situations. Usually, the researchers do not tell customers that they are watching them because the customers might behave differently if they knew they were being observed.

Centra and Supervalu use observation. Skilled market researchers watch customers as they shop in the store to find out what prompts them to buy the products they do. Watching how customers shop has helped Centra and Supervalu to improve the layout of their stores and to maximise sales.

SuperValu
Real Food, Real People

2. Consumer Panel (also called a Focus Group)

These are groups of consumers who are regularly monitored to find out about their purchases and/or reactions to products. They may be asked to fill in diaries or meet to discuss a product. They give very useful insights into consumers' perceptions and attitudes.

Superquinn holds weekly consumer panels at which it listens to groups of volunteer Superquinn shoppers who tell Superquinn how they think it could serve them better.

3. Survey

Surveys involve researchers interviewing consumers directly. Consumers can be contacted by phone, mail, the Internet (online survey) or in person.

Consumers complete a questionnaire. The aim is to find out what people think and how many share the same opinion. Surveys produce qualitative data (people's opinions) and quantitative data (statistical facts and figures).

As it would be very difficult and expensive to survey *everyone* in Ireland, a survey uses a *representative* sample of the population.

Desk Research

Desk research uses information that someone else has found. The information already exists, so there is no need to go out and collect it yourself. It is therefore relatively inexpensive. But sometimes the information the business needs may not exist or may be out of date.

Desk research can be obtained from the following sources:

1. Internal Reports

A business can obtain information from its own sales reports and financial reports into matters such as what its most popular products are, which of its shops is the most successful and so on.

2. Government Publications

The Irish government publishes a whole range of information that businesspeople can buy or obtain free of charge. Examples include the census, the Household Budget Survey and various other statistical reports from the Central Statistics Office.

Central Statistics Office
An Phríomh-Oifig Staidrimh

Enterprise Ireland, a state-owned company, has a computer database containing a huge amount of export trade information. It contains market statistics and market research on foreign markets which can help an Irish business to identify opportunities to export its products.

3. Internet

A business can obtain information from the Web on any topic it wants. The Web is estimated to have over 2 billion pages of freely available information.

If a business needs market research information on any topic, it can type that topic into its Internet search engine (Yahoo, Google and so on) and it will produce the information for the business. Sometimes this information is free.

For market researchers, the Internet has two important sources of information:

- Websites that businesses, organisations and individuals have created to promote their products and views.
- User groups (news groups and discussion groups) that comprise people who have an interest in a particular subject. Researchers can read the discussions to find out what users think.

Importance of Market Research

1. **Market research can save the business money in the long run.**

   By finding out in advance what consumers like and don't like, the business can avoid wasting money making products that consumers don't like. Product ideas that get an unfavourable reaction in consumers' surveys are not developed further.

   In the 1980s, Coca-Cola was facing huge competition from Pepsi. Coca-Cola decided to launch a new soft drink called "New Coke" to beat Pepsi. The president of Coca-Cola called it "the surest move ever made". Sales were disastrous and the product was withdrawn within months. The company had not bothered to do market research to see what consumers would think of New Coke replacing the existing Coke soft drink.

2. **It reduces the risk of failure for the product and the business.**

    By asking consumers what they want, the business can then make such products. Because they are made to meet consumers' demands, the business's products are more likely to sell well.

    Before it was launched in Dublin, the radio station Spin 1038 conducted research into what its target market of young people liked most and least about radio. Most young people disliked advertisements and DJs talking too much. Spin 1038 used this information and introduced "Ten Spin hits, in a row" whereby it plays ten songs in a row, with no interruptions. It is now the most popular radio station in Dublin among younger listeners.

    In 2006 the National Lottery conducted market research to see why Lotto ticket sales were falling. The research revealed that Irish people thought the prizes on offer were too small. The Lotto used this information to increase the number of balls in the drum to 45 to make it harder to win, thus ensuring bigger rollovers. Bigger rollovers led to higher sales.

3. **It helps a business to improve its advertising.**

    Market research can be used to ask customers what they think of the business's advertising campaign. Have they seen the ad? Did they like the ad? Did it make them interested in the product? Would they buy the product?

    If the answer to any of these questions is No, the business can change its advertising in the future to make sure that it does appeal to consumers and is therefore more effective.

4. **It helps managers decide the best price, packaging and design to use.**

    It is very important that the business chooses the right price in order to maximise sales revenue. Too low a price may mean a loss and too high a price may discourage consumers from buying the product. Asking consumers what they think of various prices for the product can solve this problem.

    Similarly, packaging and design are important to consumers. Alternatives must be tested on consumers so that the business picks the most attractive packaging and design. This will help the product to sell well.

Market Segmentation

There are very few products that every single person likes. We all have different tastes when it comes to food, clothes, cars, music and so on. Therefore, most businesses do not try to create one single product that appeals to everyone. Instead, they choose a *particular group* of people with similar tastes and aim at that group. For example, Brown Thomas does not sell clothes for everyone. It sells high-end designer clothes that only certain people will buy. *The Irish Times* newspaper aims at business and professional people. Jurys Inns aim at budget travellers. Most businesses target certain customers in this way.

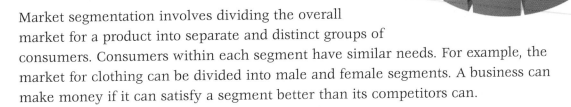

So, how does a business choose which customers to go for? The first thing the business must do is split the overall market up into the different groups that exist within it. This is called market segmentation. The business can then choose a segment to target that it thinks it will be able to satisfy.

Market segmentation involves dividing the overall market for a product into separate and distinct groups of consumers. Consumers within each segment have similar needs. For example, the market for clothing can be divided into male and female segments. A business can make money if it can satisfy a segment better than its competitors can.

The main ways to segment a market include:

1. **Geographic segmentation**
    The market is divided into different geographical areas. A business makes money by satisfying local needs. For example, the Irish radio market is segmented geographically with each county having its own radio station (Tipp FM, Radio Kerry and so on).

2. **Demographic segmentation**
    The market is divided on the basis of different characteristics of the population such as gender and age. For example, NIVEA segments the market for moisturisers on a gender basis. It produces a 'NIVEA FOR MEN' range as well as its traditional NIVEA range for women.

Advantages of Market Segmentation

Most businesses use market segmentation because it has lots of benefits for them. The main benefits of market segmentation are as follows:

1. It helps a business to **establish a presence** in a market. It is very difficult to set

up a new business in an established industry, for example a national radio station. It is easier to segment that overall market and launch yourself in a small part of it. For example, Newstalk started off in the Dublin segment of the radio market. When it became successful in this segment, it then launched nationwide.

2. It helps a business to **increase sales**. When a business segments a market and offers a marketing mix to a previously neglected segment, it can make massive sales in this segment. For example, NIVEA's sales rocketed when it launched its range for men.

3. It helps a business to lower its marketing costs. Instead of wasting money marketing to all consumers who may or may not be interested in the product, the business develops a marketing campaign that it knows will appeal to each particular market segment. For example, instead of producing a bulky catalogue featuring men's and women's clothes, many catalogue retailers produce smaller separate men's and women's catalogues and send only the appropriate one to each customer.

Target Market

After a business segments a market, it then chooses a particular segment to aim its product at. It picks a segment that it believes will like its product and that it can satisfy better than the competition can. The particular segment the business chooses is called its **target market**.

The target market is the specific segment within the overall market for a product that a business sets its sights on.

The target market for Penneys is budget-conscious consumers who like a bargain. The target market for Lucozade Sport is people who are interested in sport – those who play it and those who watch it.

Niche Market

Almost all businesses target a particular segment of the market. *The Irish Times* assumes that its target market of professional and business people is interested in world events and stock markets and politics. This is most likely true, but what about those professional and business people who also like to read celebrity gossip? They are a small subset within the target market segment for *The Irish Times*. In business, we call such people a **niche market**.

A niche market is a narrowly defined group of potential customers within a market for a product or service. These customers are not satisfied with the mainstream product in the market because they have different needs to the rest of the market. Generally, these customers are willing to pay a high price to the business that can satisfy their needs.

One geographical segment of the radio market in Ireland is radio for people who live in Dublin. A niche market within this Dublin segment consists of those who like country music. This niche is served by Dublin's Country Mix 106.8.

A major segment in the overall market for clothes is women's clothes. A niche within this segment is *haute couture* garments. These are custom-made clothes of the highest quality designed to fit the customer exactly, made by highly skilled craftspeople. Apparently, there are only 3,000 women in the world who can afford *haute couture* and only 1,000 buy it regularly. Designers such as Christian Dior and Chanel serve this niche.

Once the business has thoroughly *researched* the market and knows consumers' *wants and needs*, it then makes products that will *satisfy* those needs. The final step is to get consumers to *buy* their products. This is done by adopting the marketing concept and having an effective marketing plan and marketing mix.

Marketing Concept

The marketing concept states that the customer is the most important person to the business. Keeping the customer happy is the way to make money. The business must find out and understand what customers need and then make products that satisfy customers' needs better than competitors can. When customers are happy with a business, they will buy lots from it.

When customers are treated well by the business and get good quality products and service:

1. They are happy and so they buy more of the business's products and hence the business's sales increase. This leads to **increased profits** for the business.
2. They tell their friends about the business and word of mouth spreads about how good the business is to its customers. This leads to a **better reputation** and enhanced goodwill for the business. This acts as a form of free advertising for the business.
3. They will not have any reason to complain to the business afterwards. Thus, there are **fewer returns and repairs**. This reduces the business's costs, as money is not wasted on these. This in turn leads to increased profits for the business.

Example: Superquinn (downloaded from www.superquinn.ie)

"A customer at Superquinn is offered a range of services that is unrivalled not only in Ireland but virtually anywhere in the world. These include free playhouses for customers' small children, an umbrella service on wet days, carry-out service to the customer's car and many others."

Superquinn's prices tend to be higher than other supermarkets, but customers are willing to pay more because of the superior level of service.

Marketing Plan/Strategy

The marketing strategy is a written plan that sets out the business's marketing objectives and the means by which it will achieve these.

It involves the following steps:

STEP 1   Investigate the market to develop business opportunities

The business must conduct a detailed SWOT (Strengths, Weaknesses, Opportunities and Threats – *see Chapter 8*) analysis of the market to try to spot a gap that it can fill to make money. It must examine its own strengths and weaknesses and the opportunities and threats that exist in the market. The aim is to spot an opportunity that the business can take advantage of to make money.

Before Meteor set up, it conducted desk research into the mobile phone market in Ireland and found out that it was experiencing massive growth. For example, 100,000 phones were sold at Christmas. So the company decided to enter the mobile phone market.

STEP 2   Select a Target Market

The business must split the market into different segments and target one or more of these segments.

Meteor initially decided to go for the youth market because its SWOT analysis revealed that a huge percentage of young people had or wanted a mobile phone. Its research also revealed that young people wanted a cheap phone service because they didn't have a lot of money.

STEP 3   Developing a Marketing Mix

The business must use the research about its target market to develop four strategies (called the marketing mix) to persuade its target market to buy its product. The business must have a good product at the right price on sale in all the places where its target market shops. It must promote it in a way that appeals to them.

Meteor's marketing campaign was designed to appeal to young people. Meteor used the marketing tactic of emphasising that it provides great value calls and texts. It also uses a lot of humour in its ads. And it sponsors the Ireland Music Awards to "reach" young people.

Benefits of a Marketing Plan

1. It sets out the steps (strategies) that the business must take in order to attract and keep customers. Thus it acts like a road map guiding the business towards increased sales and profits.

2. It helps the business to control its progress. After a while, the business can measure its actual performance with the goals set out in the marketing plan. If it is off target, the business can take steps to get back on target. Thus, it helps the business to identify the strategies that are working and eradicate those that are not.

3. A good marketing plan shows potential investors that the business knows its market well and has good marketing strategies to help it be successful. Thus, it will persuade them to provide the business with the capital it needs to develop and expand.

Marketing Mix

The marketing mix consists of four tools that a business can use to persuade customers to buy its products. The four tools are known as the 4Ps: Product, Price, Promotion and Place.

Marketing Mix (4Ps) – Product

A product is defined as anything that can be offered to satisfy a need or want. To help its product sell in greater quantities, the business must give a lot of consideration to the packaging and brand name it uses.

Product Brand Name

A brand name is when a business gives its product a name (such as Lacoste) and/or a symbol (such as the Lacoste crocodile) to make it easily identifiable and to make it stand out from its competitors' products.

The top brands in the world include Coca-Cola, Sony, Pepsi, McDonald's and Toyota.

A product is given a name for practical business reasons:
1. Businesses can charge a **higher price** for their products and hence increase

profits. Many consumers think that branded goods are better quality and so are willing to pay more for them.

2. Branding helps a business to **increase sales**. A well-known brand name makes it easier for consumers to buy the product. They recognise the name in the shop and buy it straight away. They do not have to think about the purchase. The business does not have to rely on shop assistants to push the product.

2. Branding makes consumers "**brand loyal**". They stick with the product even if the price goes up. This acts as a defence for the company against price wars with competitors.

4. It is easier for the business to bring out **new products** once it has a famous name. People already know the name and are more willing to try its new products.

5. Branding can be used as a **bargaining tool** against retailers (shops). Businesses can get a good price from retailers for their goods because they know that shops must stock their products because customers expect branded products.

Product Packaging

Packaging involves designing and making the container or wrapper for the product. Packaging is very important for the following reasons:

1. It protects the product
Tetra Pak packaging makes sure that liquids do not spill from juice and milk cartons.

2. It gives an image to the product
The packaging on men's deodorants and shaving gels are usually coloured black, silver and grey whereas women's are usually coloured white, pink, yellow and so on.
Rolex watches and Waterford Crystal come in luxurious boxes to emphasise the luxurious image.

3. It is used to make the product a convenient size for consumers
Most soft drink manufacturers produce a 2 litre bottle for home and 500 ml bottles for carrying around with you.

4. It gives information about the product
Kellogg's cereals' packets give information about the contents, the vitamins, the sell-by date and whom to contact with problems or questions.

Product Life Cycle

Sales of a product change over time. Like humans, products have a life cycle: they are "born", "grow up", "mature" and eventually "die". The product life cycle charts the five stages of a product's sales over time. Businesses can use their knowledge of the product life cycle to develop the best strategy for that stage.

The diagram below charts the stages in the sales history of a product:

Product Life Cycle

Sales | Introduction | Growth | Maturity | Saturation | Decline | **Time**

Introduction

The product is first launched on the market. Sales usually grow very slowly at first because few people have heard about the product and those who have may be afraid to try it until they hear good reports about it from people they know.

The business must spend a lot of money to promote the product to make it known. It usually does not make a profit at this stage because it is selling very little but spending a lot on advertising.

The business may use a **price skimming strategy** and charge a very high price for the product, so that it can recoup the money it spent developing it.

Growth

Sales begin to increase rapidly. The product has proved successful among the initial customers who bought it and, as word spreads, more people begin to buy it. Profits start to increase rapidly. This causes new competitors to enter the market with their version of the product.

Maturity

The rate of sales *growth* slows down and sales of the product reach their highest level. The product has been accepted and bought by most consumers. The business is making large profits on the product. There is intense competition in the market.

Saturation

Sales *growth* stops and sales remain at their peak for some time. Everyone who wants the product now has bought it. There is very little opportunity to increase sales any further. The market is now full of similar products.

To maintain sales in the face of this stiff competition, businesses will cut prices and/or bring out "new and improved" versions. They may also spend a lot of money on marketing to fight back against the intense competition.

Decline

Sales of the product fall off rapidly. This can be due to advances in technology (DVDs replaced videos and now Blu-Ray is replacing DVDs), changes in consumers' tastes and/or increased competition. The product is withdrawn from the market.

Marketing Mix (4Ps) – Price

The **price** is the amount of money the business charges consumers for its product. It is important that the business charges the right price for its product. If it is too high, consumers will not buy it. If it is too low, the business might make a loss and consumers might think it is inferior. Therefore, what is the *right* price that a business should charge for its products?

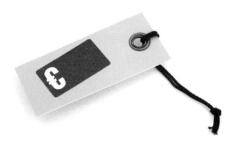

Factors that determine the price a business sets for its products

When setting the price for its products, the business should consider the following factors:

1. **Cost of the Product**

   The business must charge a price that is at least equal to the total cost of making and selling the product. This is called the breakeven price. This is the absolute minimum the business can charge for the product. If it charges less than this, it will make a loss.

2. **Competitors' Prices**

   The price the business can charge for its product is determined by what its competitors charge.

   ◗ If the competitors' product is better, the business must charge a lower price. This is why Dunnes trainers are cheaper that Nike trainers.

- If the competitors' product is inferior, the business can charge a higher price. This is why freshly squeezed orange juice is dearer than concentrated orange juice.

- If the competitors' product is similar, the business must charge a similar price. This is why Coca-Cola and Pepsi are the same price.

3. Consumers' Perceptions of Prices

The business must be aware of what price consumers are willing to pay for the product (i.e., what their price range is). The business must also note that pricing has a psychological impact on consumers. If consumers are not familiar with a product, they associate high prices with high quality and low prices with low quality.

4. Legal Regulations

The government can set the maximum or minimum price that a business is allowed to charge for its product. For example, it was illegal in Ireland to sell basic foodstuffs (such as bread and milk) below their cost price until March 2006. In the past, the Irish government also set the maximum price that newsagents could charge for UK magazines.

Strategies for setting the price

Another useful guide to help a business when it is picking the price for its products is to look at some common pricing strategies. These can help the business to choose the right price for the situation that it is facing. The main pricing strategies are set out below:

Price Skimming Strategy

- The business charges a high price for its product when it first comes out so that it can recoup all the money it spent developing the product, as soon as possible. The price then drops later on (as competition enters the market and to help the business to maintain sales).

- New mobile phones and new games consoles tend to be very expensive when they are first launched.

Penetration Pricing Strategy

- The business deliberately charges a low price for its product so that it is cheaper than its competitors. The aim is to get as many of the competition's customers to switch over to it as soon as possible. This helps the business to increase its market share.

- When the *Daily Mail* newspaper was launched in Ireland, the company charged only 30c a copy to attract as many readers as possible.

Price Discrimination Strategy

- The business charges different customers different prices for the same product.

- Most newspapers have a special discounted rate for students. By selling cheaply to students when they have little money, the papers hope to make them customers for life.

Loss Leader

- The business sells one product below cost price. The aim is to attract customers who like a bargain into the store where they will hopefully buy more products.

- A lot of the major supermarkets in Ireland sell bottled beers below cost to attract customers to their shop.

Psychological Pricing

- Businesses can manipulate the price to get consumers to respond on an emotional rather than a rational basis.

- Businesses know that consumers associate high prices with high quality and low prices with low quality. To give itself a quality image, the business charges a high price for its product.

- To appeal to more customers, many businesses will charge €299.99 for a product rather than €300 because many consumers see the product as being in the €200+ range rather than the €300+ range.

Price – Breakeven Charts

The minimum price a business must charge for its product is one that is equal to the total costs of making that product. In business, we call this the **breakeven price**. The money earned from selling the product is exactly equal to the costs of making it. So, the business makes neither a profit nor a loss. It just breaks even.

For example, you organise the school debs at a cost of €1,000 and you sell only €1,000 worth of tickets. You've broken even.

A business's costs can be classified as either:

- **fixed** – the cost never changes no matter how many products the business makes and sells. Factory rent is an example of a fixed cost. The cost of the rent is not dependent on how many products the business sells. Even if it sells nothing, the rent must still be paid in full.

▶ **variable** – the cost increases or decreases as the number of products made and sold increases or decreases. The cost of ingredients is an example of a variable cost. The more products the business sells, the more ingredients it needs, so the cost increases,

These are the formulae for working out a business's breakeven point in units and in euro:

Breakeven Point in units	Fixed Costs ÷ (Price – Variable Cost)

Price – Variable cost is known as the **contribution per unit**.

Breakeven Point in €	BEP in units × Price

Example

Angela is considering setting up a business selling flags from a stall in Croke Park. She has to pay the GAA €100 to rent the stall for each match. (Fixed costs = €100)
The flags wills sell for €6 each. (Selling price = €6)
Each flag costs €4 to make. (Variable cost = €4)

  (a)   How many flags will Angela have to sell at each match to break even?
  (b)   How much in € will she have to sell to break even?

Breakeven Point in units	Fixed Costs ÷ (Price – Variable Cost)

$$= €100 ÷ (€6 – €4)$$
$$= €100 ÷ €2$$
$$= \textbf{50 units}$$

Angela must sell 50 flags to break even. If she sells more then this, she will make a profit. If she sells fewer than 50 flags, she will make a loss.

We have seen that Angela must sell 50 flags to break even. We can express this figure another way. We can work out the amount of money she must take in to break even. This is called the **breakeven point in euro** and is worked out as follows:

Breakeven Point in €	BEP in units × Price

$$= 50 \text{ units} × €6 \text{ selling price}$$
$$= €300$$

Angela must sell €300 worth of flags to break even. If she takes in more than this, she will make a profit. If she takes in less than €300, she will make a loss.

We can work out the profit (or loss) that Angela will make for any level of sales as follows:

- A business's profit is defined as Total revenue − Total costs.

- Total revenue is the money the business makes from selling its products. It is calculated by multiplying the number of products sold by the selling price (Units × Selling price).

- Total costs are all the money the business spends making the product. It is the total of the business's fixed costs + its variable costs (units × variable cost per unit).

- Profit at full capacity (also known as profit at forecast sales) is the profit that a business expects to make if it sells all the products that it is expecting (forecasting) to sell.

Let's assume that Angela expects to sell 100 flags at each match. How much profit will she make if she sells 100 flags?

Net Profit from Selling 'X' units €

Total revenue	=	X units	×	Selling price per unit	
	=	100 flags	×	€6	600
Subtract Total costs					
Fixed costs					(100)
Variable costs	=	X units	×	Variable cost per unit	(400)
	=	100 flags	×	€4	
Net Profit					100

Angela now knows that she will make €100 profit if she sells 100 flags. But remember she only *expects* to sell 100 flags. This is just her estimate. What if she has a bad day? By how much can sales drop from what she expects before she is in trouble?

We can work this out. It is called the margin of safety.

Margin of Safety

The margin of safety is the difference between a business's forecast sales and its breakeven point. It shows the business by how much its sales can fall before it will start making a loss.

Margin of Safety	Forecast Sales in units – BEP in units

What is Angela's margin of safety?

Margin of Safety	Forecast Sales in units – BEP in units

$$100 \text{ flags} \quad - \quad 50 \text{ flags}$$
$$= 50 \text{ flags}$$

Even if Angela sells 50 fewer flags than she expects, she will still break even on the day.

Breakeven Chart

How much profit will Angela make if she sells 40 flags? 63 flags? 81 flags? 218 flags? Rather than working out the sums for every single sales number, many businesses will draw a **breakeven chart**. The business can then read the profit or loss figure straight from the chart for any given level of sales.

STEPS IN DRAWING A BREAKEVEN CHART

Work out the breakeven point, profit and margin of safety *first*.

- A business's profit is defined as Total revenue – Total costs.
- Breakeven is when the business's total revenue and total costs are exactly equal. The business is making zero profit and zero loss.
- So, to draw the breakeven point on a chart, you must draw the Total revenue and Total costs lines.

STEP 1 Draw a horizontal axis (units) and a vertical axis (€).

- To draw the units axis:
  Go as high as forecast sales in units (given in the question).
  Go up in gaps that can fit in the breakeven point as well.

> Angela forecasts that she will sell 100 flags, so we must go as far as 100 on the Units line. Her breakeven point is 50 flags. So, to fit this in as well, we can go up in jumps of 50.

◗ To draw the € axis:

Go as high as total revenue at forecast sales
(i.e. Forecast sales × Selling price).

Go up in gaps that can fit in the fixed costs and the breakeven point
in euro as well.

> Angela forecasts that she will sell 100 flags. Multiply by the selling price to
> get this in €. 100 flags × €6 = €600. We must go as high as €600.
> Her fixed costs are €100. Her breakeven point in euro is €300. So to fit this
> in as well, we should go up in jumps of €100.

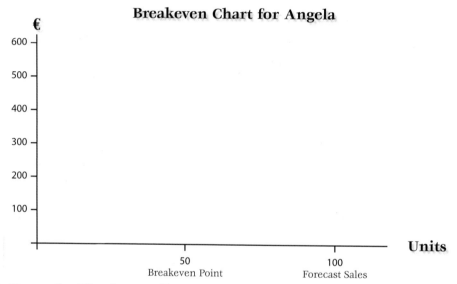

STEP 2 Draw the Fixed costs line.

◗ It is a straight line coming out of the number for fixed costs, parallel to the
horizontal axis.

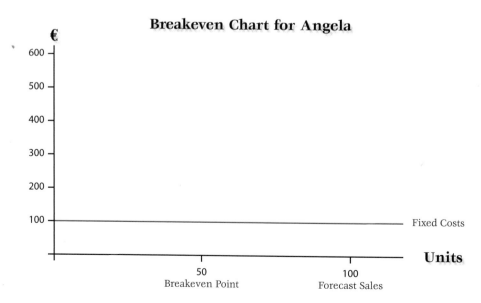

STEP 3 Draw the Total revenue line by plotting the three points you work out in the table below:

TOTAL REVENUE LINE		
NUMBER OF UNITS	× SELLING PRICE	= TOTAL REVENUE
0		
Breakeven point in units		
Forecast sales		

In Angela's case this becomes:

TOTAL REVENUE LINE		
NUMBER OF UNITS	× SELLING PRICE	= TOTAL REVENUE
0	0 units × €6	€0
Breakeven point in units	50 units × €6	€300
Forecast sales	100 units × €6	€600

Plot these three points (0 units, €0), (50 units, €300) and (100 units, €600) on the breakeven chart and join the points to form a straight line, called Total revenue.

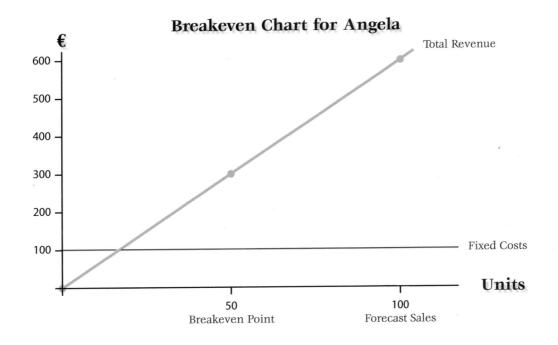

STEP 4 Draw the Total costs line by plotting the three points you work out in the table below:

TOTAL COSTS LINE				
NUMBER OF UNITS	× VARIABLE COST PER UNIT	= TOTAL VARIABLE COSTS	+ FIXED COSTS	= TOTAL COSTS
0				
Breakeven point in units				
Forecast sales				

In Angela's case this becomes:

TOTAL COSTS LINE				
NUMBER OF UNITS	× VARIABLE COST PER UNIT	= TOTAL VARIABLE COSTS	+ FIXED COSTS	= TOTAL COSTS
0	0 units × €4	€0	+ €100	= €100
Breakeven point in units	50 units × €4	€200	+ €100	= €300
Forecast sales	100 units × €4	€400	+ €100	= €500

Plot these three points (0 units, €100), (50 units, €300) and (100 units, €500) on the breakeven chart and join the points to form a straight line, called Total costs.

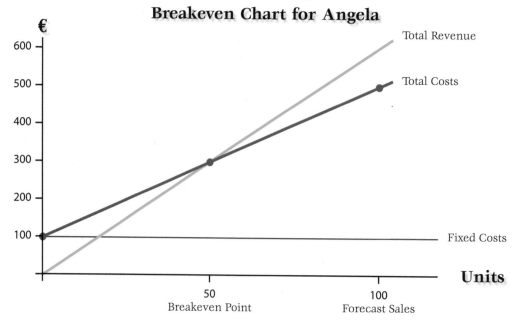

Breakeven Chart for Angela

(1) The breakeven point is the point where the Total revenue and Total costs lines cross.

(2) Profit at forecast sales is the difference between total revenue and total costs at forecast sales.

(3) Margin of safety is the difference between forecast sales and breakeven point.

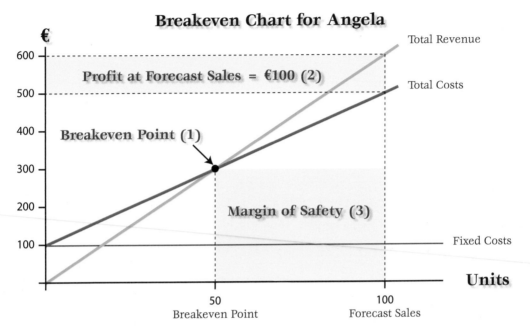

Breakeven Chart for Angela

Uses of Breakeven Charts

(a) Breakeven charts are used to work out how many products a business must sell just to break even. This tells the business the minimum level of sales it must achieve just to survive.

(b) Breakeven charts are used to work out the profit or loss that the business will make at any given level of sales.

(c) Breakeven charts are used to work out the amount by which a business's sales can drop before it starts to lose money (margin of safety).

(d) Breakeven charts are used to show the effect that a change in the price that the business sells its product for will have on its profits.

(e) Breakeven charts are used to show the effect that a change in the business's costs will have on its profits.

(f) Breakeven charts are used to work out how many products a business must sell to achieve a particular profit.

Ordinary Level Questions

EXAM SECTION 1 (25%) – SHORT ANSWER QUESTIONS [10 marks each]

1. Define "marketing".

2. Explain the term "field research" and give one example of field research.

3. Give three examples of desk research for a business.

4. Outline two benefits of conducting market research.

5. Explain the term "marketing concept".

6. Outline two benefits of a marketing plan for a business.

7. Explain the term "market segmentation".

8. Name any three products and outline the target market for each one.

9. Explain the term "brand name" and give two examples.

10. Outline two benefits of a brand name for a business.

11. The stages in the product life cycle include: Growth, Saturation, Decline, Maturity and Introduction. Write these stages out in the correct order.

12. Indicate by means of a tick (✔) the stage of the product life cycle to which each sentence refers:

	Product Life Cycle Stage			
	Maturity	**Introduction**	**Decline**	**Growth**
The product is first launched on the market.				
Sales of the product decrease.				
Sales of the product increase rapidly.				
Sales of the product reach their peak.				

13. Column 1 is a list of business terms. Column 2 is a list of possible explanations for these terms. Match the two lists by placing the letter of the correct explanation under the relevant number below. One explanation has no match.

Column 1
1. Packaging
2. Target Market
3. Breakeven Point
4. Survey
5. Marketing Plan
6. Marketing Mix

Column 2: Explanations
a) The consumers that the business aims its product at
(b) Product, Price, Promotion, Place
(c) A document setting out a business's marketing goals and the strategies it intends to use to achieve them
(d) Splitting the market for a product into different groups of consumers
(e) The wrapper or container for a product
(f) The minimum number of products a business must sell to survive
(g) A questionnaire used in market research

1	2	3	4	5	6
E					

14. Jean has her own business. She tells you that her fixed costs are €4,000, her variable costs are €25 per unit and the selling price of her product is €45. Compute Jean's breakeven point in units. Show all workings.

15. Michael runs a business selling cakes. He sells each cake for €18. The variable cost of making each cake is €11. His fixed costs are €14,000. How many cakes must Michael sell to break even? Show all workings.

EXAM SECTION 2 (75%) – LONG QUESTIONS

1. Distinguish between "desk research" and "field research".
   Give an example of each to illustrate your answer.   (20 marks)

2. Explain the term "market research" and outline three benefits to
   a business of market research.   (20 marks)

3. What is a marketing plan?   (10 marks)

4. Explain the term "market segmentation" and use an example to illustrate
   your answer.   (10 marks)

5. Describe what a brand name is and outline the benefits of a brand name
   to a business.   (25 marks)

6. Draw a diagram of the product life cycle. Indicate clearly the stages
   in the product life cycle on the diagram.   (20 marks)

7. List the stages in a product's life cycle and explain any two of them. (25 marks)

8. Outline the factors that a business would take into account
   when deciding on the price to charge for its products.   (20 marks)

9. Explain what is meant by a "loss leader".   (10 marks)

10. Outline three benefits to a business of preparing a breakeven chart. (15 marks)

Higher Level Questions

EXAM SECTION 1 (20%) – SHORT ANSWER QUESTIONS [10 marks each]

1. Illustrate your understanding of the term "market research".

2. Distinguish between "desk research" and "field research".

3. Explain the term "marketing concept". Illustrate its impact on a business.

4. Define market segmentation. Outline two methods of market segmentation.

5. Explain why a business would engage in market segmentation.

6. Distinguish between "market segment" and "niche market".

7. What is a brand name? Give two examples.

8. Complete this sentence: Product packaging is used to….

9. Column 1 is a list of business terms. Column 2 is a list of possible explanations for these terms. Match the two lists by placing the letter of the correct explanation under the relevant number below. One explanation has no match.

Column 1	Column 2: Explanations
1. Price Skimming	(a) The business sells a product below cost in the hope of attracting customers.
2. Penetration Pricing	(b) The business charges a high price for a product when it is first launched, to recoup its development costs as quickly as possible.
3. Price Discrimination	(c) The business charges a low price to attract as many customers away from the competition as possible.
4. Loss Leader	(d) The business charges a price exactly equal to the cost of making the product.
5. Psychological Pricing	(e) The business charges different customers different prices for the same product.
	(f) The business manipulates the price to convince consumers that the product is good value by charging €99.99 instead of €100.

1	2	3	4	5

10. Complete this sentence: Breakeven charts can help a business to…

EXAM SECTION 2 (20%) – APPLIED BUSINESS QUESTION – 80 MARKS

Cronin Creations Ltd.

Pauline Cronin is an internationally famous and successful designer of ladies' clothes. She caters to a niche market of wealthy women who want cutting-edge designs with superior tailoring. Her refusal to use animal fur or leather in her clothes has attracted many ethically minded women to her brand. She exports her clothes throughout Europe. Despite critical acclaim, Pauline realises that her niche market is too small to be highly profitable.

A friend who studied marketing in college advised her to cash in on her famous name and launch brand extensions such as a perfume. Pauline carried out market research, which has convinced her that a market exists for a perfume bearing her name. She has spent a lot of time and money trying to develop a perfume made from entirely natural ingredients.

While Pauline believes that her perfume will be unique in that it will not contain chemicals, she knows that as soon as it is successful, the other major perfume manufacturers that she is in competition with will bring out copycat perfumes. However, her friend is more optimistic and told her that the success of the perfume could eventually lead to the launch of a complete cosmetics range. Pauline has approached the top department stores in Europe to see whether they will stock her new perfume. The response so far has been lukewarm.

(A) Evaluate, from the above information, the significance of packaging in the launch of Pauline's new perfume.   (25 marks)

(B) Evaluate the importance of a brand name for Pauline's business. Support your answer with reference to the above text.   (25 marks)

(C) Describe three pricing strategies that Pauline can use when launching the new perfume.   (30 marks)

EXAM SECTION 3 (60%) – LONG QUESTIONS

1. Illustrate the use of field research in a business of your choice.   (20 marks)

2. Outline, using an example, the role of the Internet in market research.   (15 marks)

3. Discuss the importance of market research for Irish business.   (25 marks)

4. Distinguish between the marketing concept and market segmentation. Use examples, where appropriate, to illustrate your answer.   (20 marks)

5. Differentiate between demographic and geographic market segmentation. Illustrate your answer.   (20 marks)

6. Evaluate the importance of a marketing plan to the success of a business.   (20 marks)

7. What is a brand name? Evaluate the benefits of a brand name to a business.   (20 marks)

8. Discuss the importance of the product life cycle for a business.   (25 marks)

9. Describe the factors to be considered when setting the price for a product.   (20 marks)

10. Using one example in each case, distinguish between a price skimming strategy and a penetration pricing strategy.   (20 marks)

11. C Ltd. manufactures lamps.

    The business supplies you with the following figures about the company's activities:
    Fixed costs   €6,000
    Variable costs per unit   €3
    Forecast sales (output)   2,000 units
    Selling price   €7
    Illustrate by means of a breakeven chart:
    (a) Breakeven point   **(b)** Profit at full capacity   **(c)** Margin of safety

    Outline the effect on the breakeven point if the selling price increased to €9 per unit. Illustrate your answer on the breakeven chart.

12. E Ltd. manufactures bicycles.

    The business supplies you with the following figures about the company's activities:
    Selling price   €400
    Variable costs per unit   €100
    Fixed costs   €30,000
    Forecast sales (output)   150 units
    Illustrate by means of a breakeven chart:
    (a) Breakeven point   **(b)** Profit at full capacity   **(c)** Margin of safety

    Outline the effect on the breakeven point if fixed costs decreased to €15,000. Illustrate your answer on the breakeven chart.

13. F Ltd. manufactures cakes.

    The business supplies you with the following figures about the company's activities:
    Fixed costs   €360
    Selling price   €30
    Variable costs per unit   €18
    Forecast sales (output)   50 units
    Illustrate by means of a breakeven chart:
    (a) Breakeven point   **(b)** Profit at full capacity   **(c)** Margin of safety

    Outline the effect on the breakeven point if the selling price decreased to €27 per unit. Illustrate your answer on the breakeven chart.

14. M Ltd. manufactures chairs.

The business supplies you with the following figures about the company's activities:

Forecast sales (output)   90 units
Selling price   €50
Fixed costs   €800
Variable costs per unit   €30

Illustrate by means of a breakeven chart:

(a) Breakeven point   (b) Profit at full capacity   (c) Margin of safety

Outline the effect on the breakeven point if the fixed costs increased to €1,000. Illustrate your answer on the breakeven chart.

15. P Ltd. manufactures tables.

The business supplies you with the following figures about the company's activities:

Fixed costs   €200,000
Variable costs per unit   €55
Forecast sales (output)   10,000 units
Selling price   €80

Illustrate by means of a breakeven chart:

(a) Breakeven point   (b) Profit at full capacity   (c) Margin of safety

Outline the effect on the breakeven point if the fixed costs decreased to €180,000 and the selling price decreased to €75. Illustrate your answer on the breakeven chart.

16. W Ltd. manufactures computer games.

The business supplies you with the following figures about the company's activities:

Variable costs per unit   €36
Fixed costs   €80,000
Selling price   €44
Forecast sales (output)   14,000 units

Illustrate by means of a breakeven chart:

(a) Breakeven point   (b) Profit at full capacity   (c) Margin of safety

Outline the effect on the breakeven point if the variable costs per unit increased to €40 and the fixed costs increased to €100,000. Illustrate your answer on the breakeven chart.

CHAPTER 17

Marketing #2

In chapter 16, we looked at two elements of the marketing mix (4Ps) – product and price. This chapter examines the remaining two – **promotion** and **place**.

Marketing Mix (4Ps) – Promotion

If consumers don't know that a business's product exists, they cannot buy it. It doesn't matter how good the product is or how attractive the price is. It will not sell unless people know about it.

There is little point in turning your house into a Bed and Breakfast (B&B) business, spending a fortune doing up the rooms, charging a reasonable price and then waiting for customers to arrive. They won't. How would they know that your house is a B&B?

This is where **promotion** comes in. The business has to let the public know that its product is on sale. It has to get them interested in the product and motivated to buy it.

Promotion involves communicating with customers to let them know about the product and to persuade them to buy it. There are four main ways to promote a product:

1. Advertising
2. Sales promotions
3. Public relations
4. Personal selling

Advertising

Advertising is the paid, non-personal (in other words, it does not involve the business and the customer meeting face to face) communication of information about a product or service through various media.

The main functions of advertising are to remind consumers about a familiar brand, to inform them about the features of a product and to persuade them to buy the business's product.

Types of Advertising

If you think of all the ads you have seen on TV and in newspapers, magazines and so on, you will notice they are all different. This is because businesses advertise for many different reasons and use many different types of advertising.

The main types of advertising are:

1. Reminder Advertising

This lets consumers know that a well-known brand is *still* around and helps to keep the product's name in the consumer's mind. It tends to be used in the maturity and decline stage of the product's life cycle. Coca-Cola regularly uses reminder advertising.

2. Informative Advertising

These ads give factual information to consumers about the product. They let them know about the product and what it does. For example, "Sale starts at 10.00am".

3. Persuasive Advertising

This aims to convince consumers that they must have the product, that it is essential to their life and their happiness. Most ads for toiletries are persuasive ads.

4. Generic Advertising

This advertises the product of an entire industry rather than one firm's product. Examples of generic advertising are the "Drink Milk" or "Buy Irish" campaigns.

5. Comparative Advertising

This is where a business advertises its product by showing how well it compares to the competition. It aims to show that its product is much better than its competitors'. Many supermarkets use comparative advertising. They show how much cheaper products are in their store compared to their competitors.

Functions of Advertising

1. To provide information about the product
2. To remind consumers that the product is still available for sale
3. To persuade consumers to buy the product
4. To offset competitors' advertising (known as defensive advertising)
5. To increase the business's sales and profits

Advertising Media

It is important that a business advertises where its target market will see the ad. The different places where a business can place an ad are called the advertising media. The main advertising media include the following:

Television

TV is a good advertising medium because:

1. Consumers can see the business's product working (for example, ads for washing powders and household cleaners).
2. It is watched by a lot of people all over the country.
3. The business can reach its target market by advertising during programmes that it knows its target market is interested in.
4. The business can use pictures, sound and movement to appeal to consumers' senses (for example, ads for fabric conditioners and scented candles).

The problems with TV advertising are:

1. It costs a lot of money to advertise on TV.
2. Many people no longer watch TV ads – they use their remote control to switch channels as soon as the ads come on.

Radio

Radio is a good advertising medium because:

1. It costs a lot less than TV advertising.
2. The business can reach local people by advertising on local radio stations.
3. The business can reach its target market by advertising on radio stations that it knows its target market is interested in. For example, Spin 1038 is the top radio station in Dublin among 15 – 24 year olds.

The problem with radio advertising is:

1. The business has to rely solely on one thing – sound – to get its message across.

Newspapers

Newspapers are a good advertising medium because:

1. They are good for providing detailed information to consumers about the business's product. The business can include a lot of written information that consumers can read and re-read.
2. They cost a lot less than TV advertising.
3. The business can reach its target market by advertising in newspapers that it knows its target market is interested in. For example, *The Irish Times* has the highest daily readership among professional and business people.
4. The business can reach local people by advertising in local newspapers.

The problems with newspaper advertising are:

1. The quality of pictures displayed in newspapers ads is not as good as TV.
2. The ad will be seen for only one day, if the paper is a daily one.

Magazines

Magazines are a good advertising medium because:

1. They are good for providing detailed information to consumers about the business's product. The business can include a lot of written information that consumers can read and re-read.
2. Pictures of the business's products can be displayed in colour and in much better quality than a newspaper ad. For example, many make-up companies use glossy full-page colour ads in women's magazines such as *Vogue* and *Cosmopolitan* to show how well their make-up looks on women.
3. They have a longer life than newspapers because they are passed around among friends and are usually on sale for a whole week. This means that they can be seen by a lot of people for a long time.
4. They cost a lot less than TV advertising.
5. The business can reach its target market by advertising in magazines that it knows its target market is interested in. For example, a business selling tropical fish can advertise in *Practical Fishkeeping*.

Billboards

A billboard is a large poster displaying an advertisement. Billboards are normally situated on busy roads in an eye-catching position where lots of people will see them. They are a good advertising medium because:

1. They cost a lot less than TV advertising.
2. They have a longer life than most other media. The business's advertisement is generally left on display for a lot longer than any of the other media, so a lot more people see it.
3. The business can reach its target market by placing different posters in different parts of the country. For example, Lucozade Sport uses local sporting heroes in its billboards throughout the country.
4. Unlike most other media, each billboard usually contains only one ad. Therefore, with billboards, the business is not competing with other businesses for the attention of the consumer.

The problems with billboard advertising are:

1. The business cannot give detailed information in the ad.
2. Apart from geographical segments, it is hard for a business to reach its target market precisely because it is impossible to predict who will see the ad.

Direct Mail

Direct mail involves posting advertising material directly to consumers' homes. Direct mail is a good advertising medium because:

1. The business can personalise the ad using each consumer's name and address, making them more likely to pay attention to it.

2. The business can reach its target market effectively by sending letters only to those who it knows are interested in its products. Tesco has a "Baby and Toddler Club" for parents. Members receive extra Clubcard points and offers. Tesco can then send these members the adverts for new Tesco baby products because it *knows* they will be interested in them.

3. Unlike most other media, direct mail contains only one ad. Therefore, with direct mail, the business is not competing with other businesses for the attention of the consumer.

The problems with direct mail advertising are:

1. Direct mail is an expensive way to advertise (printing and postage costs).

2. Many consumers ignore direct mail adverts which they consider to be "junk mail".

Selecting an Advertising Medium

The business must choose the correct advertising medium for its product and target market. When deciding which medium to use, a business will consider the following factors:

Media Habits Of The Target Audience

■ A business should advertise using media that are most likely to be seen by its target audience. In this way, its ads will reach the largest amount of potential customers.

■ For example, Pampers advertises its nappies on TV when parents are likely to be watching.

■ Toy manufacturers advertise on TV during children's programmes, when children are most likely to be watching.

Nature of the Product

■ The type of product the business is selling determines which advertising medium is most suitable. If the product needs to be seen working, the business must use a visual method, such as TV advertising.

■ For example, most washing powders and cleaning products are advertised on TV.

The Message

■ The message that the business wants to get across to consumers can also determine the best medium to use. If the business wishes to convey technical information about a product, it is best to use a written medium so that people can read and re-read the ad in order to understand it.

■ Although many car companies advertise on TV, they also advertise in newspapers. The newspaper ads contain all the technical details about the car such as miles per gallon, brake horse power (bhp) and so on.

The Cost

■ The business's choice of advertising is determined by how much money it has to spend. Different media cost different amounts. It is very expensive to advertise on TV, so this is out for many businesses.

■ Advertising on local media (local papers or local radio) tends to be cheaper than advertising on national media. Therefore a business that operates only locally (such as a hairdresser, butcher or newsagent) should advertise on local media.

■ The business should use the most effective advertising media that it can afford.

Advertising Standards Authority for Ireland

An organisation called the Advertising Standards Authority for Ireland (ASAI) keeps an eye on the advertising industry to ensure that consumers are protected.

The ASAI is an organisation set up by people who work in the advertising industry. Its job is to regulate the advertising industry in Ireland. This means that it tries to protect consumers from false, misleading and offensive advertisements.

It is a voluntary organisation. It has no legal powers. It cannot force any advertiser to do anything. However, because media are members of the ASAI, they ensure that advertisements in breach of the code do not run again.

Its code of advertising standards states that all ads should:
- Be legal, decent, honest and truthful.
- Be prepared with a sense of responsibility to both consumers and society.
- Obey the rules of fair competition.

Any member of the public can complain to the ASAI in writing. It will investigate the complaint and, if it agrees with it, it will *ask* the advertiser to take it down or change it. Generally, all advertisers obey the ASAI.

Example of Offensive Ad

HB ran an ad for its Carte D'Or ice cream. One scene featured an elderly grandmother at mealtime telling her grandson, "He's not your father. We never knew who your father was." The second scene depicts the grandmother being led from the room.

The ASAI received many complaints from people saying they found the portrayal of the elderly grandmother insensitive and offensive to the elderly, especially those suffering from senile dementia.

Example of Misleading Ad

L'Oreal ran an ad for its telescopic mascara featuring Penelope Cruz. The message claimed that L'Oreal's mascara would make eyelashes look "up to 60% longer". However, it later came out that Penelope Cruz was wearing some false eyelashes in the ad.

Sales Promotions

Sales promotions are **incentives** that a business offers consumers to encourage them to buy more of its product and to buy it sooner than they normally might. A number of different techniques can be used.

Free Samples

The business offers customers a free trial of the product. This encourages them to try it and hopefully they like it so much that they are motivated to buy it. Many food companies give out free samples at stands in supermarkets. Many cosmetic companies give free samples of their perfumes. This is a very effective but expensive way to launch a new product.

Money-off Vouchers

The business gives consumers a coupon entitling them to a certain discount (for example, 50c off their next purchase) when they buy the business's product. The voucher may be attached to the product, included in newspapers ads or mailed to the consumers. Money-off vouchers encourage price-conscious consumers who like a bargain to try the product. They can also encourage existing customers who regularly buy the product to buy even more of it. Tesco and Dunnes send money-off vouchers to their customers.

Free Gifts

The business offers customers a gift with every purchase. The gift must be an attractive one that consumers will want. Sometimes the gift is free, as in the free toy with every Happy Meal in McDonald's.

Competitions

The business offers consumers the chance to win money, a holiday or a car, for example, if they buy the product. Customers have to send their entry where it will be judged and the best entry will win a large prize. (For example, "€5,000 to be won. See inside for details.") The prize on offer is so attractive that is creates a lot of attention for the product and motivates many people to purchase it.

Loyalty Cards

The business offers customers points or tokens with every purchase. When the customer has enough points, she can trade them in for a money-off voucher to use in that store. The idea is that consumers will spend more so that they will get more points and more money-off vouchers. Examples include Dunnes Value Club card, Superquinn Reward Card and Tesco Clubcard.

Merchandising

Merchandising means that the business displays its products and lays out its store in an attractive and eye-catching way. It aims to attract customers' attention and get them to buy products they hadn't intended buying (impulse buying). For example, many shops put basics such as bread and milk at the back of the shop. Customers who want them have to walk through the shop, past lots of other tempting products, which they may pick up on their way to the bread and milk.

Public Relations

Public Relations (PR) involves presenting a good image of the business and building a good relationship with consumers by obtaining favourable publicity. A good image is vital for a business because consumers are unlikely to buy from businesses that have a bad reputation or that have suffered negative publicity.

This is such an important area that many businesses employ a Public Relations Officer (PRO) to handle their PR.

Functions of Public Relations

The business (through its PRO) uses Public Relations for a number of reasons:

1.   Attract publicity when launching new products

The business organises a PR "stunt" to get some publicity with the aim of getting the stunt into the newspapers and on TV. Many customers will see the stunt and thus become aware of the product.

When Virgin Brides launched its shop in London, Richard Branson shaved his beard and wore a wedding dress in a bid to get publicity for the new venture.

2. Target certain customers

Businesses can sponsor events and causes that they know will appeal to their target market. For example, Meteor sponsors the Irish Music Awards in order to reach its target market of young people.

3. Build an image that reflects well on the company

Businesses may engage in public service activities so that consumers will admire their efforts and buy more products from them. McDonald's has set up the Ronald McDonald Children's Charities. It donates money to Our Lady's Hospital for Sick Children in Crumlin.

4. Defending products that have encountered bad publicity

The business uses PR to defend itself from bad publicity by putting its side of the story across to the public.

Techniques Used in PR

1. Events

The business can hold events to attract PR. Examples include roadshows, exhibitions and open days.

2. News Conferences and Press Releases

These are used when the business is announcing the creation of new jobs or the launch of a new product range. The business gets its name into the newspapers and onto the TV news for free. Businesses also use news conferences and press releases to respond to negative publicity.

McDonald's suffered a lot of bad publicity following the release of the movie *Super Size Me*, in which film-maker Morgan Spurlock ate nothing but McDonald's food for 30 days and put on a lot of weight as a result. The company fought back by issuing a press release putting its side of the story.

The press release stated, "And contrary to what you might think from watching the film, we don't just offer soft drinks and shakes. We offer a wide range that includes Evian natural mineral water and pure orange juice." It also pointed out that McDonald's is one of the biggest retailers of prepared fruit packs and that its Chicken McNuggets now have less salt. The press release then added, "We would like to think that in five to ten years we may be as famous for our salads, our fruit and our organic food as we are for our hamburgers."

3. Public Service Activities

Tesco's "Computers for Schools" promotion helps local schools obtain free computers and other information and communication technology (ICT) equipment.

During a ten-week promotional period, customers were given one voucher for every €10 spent in a Tesco store. Schools could then collect these tokens and redeem them for computers and ICT-related equipment from a catalogue of equipment.

While the local schools benefited, so too did Tesco. It enjoyed the following advantages:

● Sales increased as local people shopped in Tesco to get the tokens for the local school.

● Tesco's goodwill improved because local people thought better of the company because it was seen to be helping their area.

4. Sponsorship

The business donates money to an event or team. Generally, it will do so only in return for prominent exposure of its name or brands. Think of examples of different sporting teams. Who sponsors them? If you know the answer, you have just proved that sponsorship works in getting the name of the business out there.

Personal Selling

Personal selling is where a salesperson meets with customers face to face to give them information about a product and to persuade them to buy it.

The business relies on the salesperson's knowledge and expertise to convince the consumer to purchase the product. Most computer stores rely on personal selling to make sales because people are not so knowledgeable about the product. It is also used a lot in cosmetic counters in department stores.

Let's now look at some real-life examples of promotion.

Evaluation of Meteor's Promotional Methods

Public Relations [PR]

As part of its PR strategy, Meteor sponsors the annual Ireland Music Awards. This is an event held once a year to recognise the best Irish and international musicians and singers.

Evaluation

This is an excellent PR strategy. Young people are interested in music and singers and are highly motivated to watch the awards on TV and read about them in magazines and newspapers. When they do so, they will see the name Meteor all the time. It gives Meteor a "cool" image to be associated with these awards and singers, which makes Meteor more attractive to young people.

Advertising

Meteor advertises a lot on TV and on billboards around the country. The ads are amusing and feature young people. They emphasise the low prices the company charges for texts and calls and the savings to be made if customers switch to Meteor.

Evaluation

Meteor ads work well. The company is trying to reach the youth market. Having humorous ads that feature young people attracts this target market. Constantly emphasising low prices appeals to the youth market because young people use their phones a lot and may have a limited amount of money.

Personal Selling

Meteor has stores all over Ireland. Its sales people are trained in all the latest mobile phone technology and are able to give customers advice on which phone to go for and which tariff to choose.

Evaluation

Meteor's personal selling is an excellent method of promotion. Many people who are not very knowledgeable about technology rely on experts to advise them. Consumers are more likely to buy a phone if the salesperson explains its features to them and offers her personal recommendation. By using personal selling, Meteor sells more phones.

Evaluation of McDonald's Promotional Methods

Public Relations

McDonald's sponsors children's charities to attract positive PR. It set up the Ronald McDonald Children's Charities of Ireland, which raises money for organisations such as Our Lady's Hospital for Sick Children, Crumlin.

Evaluation

This is a very effective promotional tool. A major target market for McDonald's is children and their parents. When parents see how good McDonald's is to children's charities, they are likely to bring their children to McDonald's rather than to the competition. This promotion technique has an emotional appeal to them as parents.

Advertising

McDonald's advertising campaign features the slogan "I'm lovin' it" and uses a Justin Timberlake song. This is designed to attract the teenage market back to McDonald's and to show that McDonald's is trendy.

Evaluation

This advertising campaign is very effective. By associating itself with the biggest stars in the world, McDonalds ensures that its advertisements will be watched and listened to by its target market. Using pop stars in this way helps it connect with young people.

Sales promotions

McDonald's gives gifts to children when they buy a "Happy Meal". The meal comes in a special carrier box and the gift is contained inside. The gift is usually a toy character from a recent film or TV programme.

Evaluation

This is a very effective promotional method. McDonald's target market is mainly children. Children would be highly motivated to go to McDonald's rather than any other fast-food restaurants just to get that gift.

Marketing Mix (4Ps) – Place

The final "P" in the marketing mix is **place**. If a business wants its product to be a success, it must be available in the right place for customers to buy it. For example, Coca-Cola's aim is to put its product "within an arm's reach of desire". A business can distribute its products in various ways to reach its consumers. These are called the **channels of distribution**.

Traditional Channel of Distribution

- This is called the traditional channel of distribution. The manufacturer makes the products and sells them to a wholesaler in large quantities. The wholesaler sells the products in smaller quantities to the retailer (shop). The retailer sells individual products to the consumer.

- An example of this would be where Mars sells 1,000,000 bars to Musgraves for 50c each.

- Musgraves sells a box of 100 to a sweet shop for 65c each.

- The sweet shop sells one bar to the consumer for 80c.

Alternative Channel of Distribution

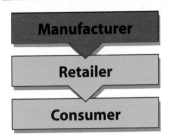

- In this case, the manufacturer sells directly to the retailer. Manufacturers will normally only do so to large retailers who place a big order.

- An example of this would be where Mars sells 1,000,000 bars directly to Dunnes Stores for 50c each.

- Dunnes sells one bar to the consumer for 65c.

Direct Channel of Distribution

- This is called the direct channel of distribution. The manufacturer sells straight from the factory to the consumer.

- Dell sells computers this way.

- Many furniture factories in Navan sell directly to the public.

Note:

The more stages there are in the channel of distribution, the more expensive the product becomes at every stage because each business adds a profit to the price.

Wholesaler and Retailer

- A wholesaler is a business that buys products directly from the manufacturer in huge quantities and then sells them on to the retailer in smaller quantities. This is called **breaking bulk**.
- A retailer is a shop that sells products to the consumers.

Evaluation of a Business's Marketing Mix

Product

Ribena pouch pack

In March 2000, Ribena launched a new product – the Ribena pouch pack. The Ribena pouch pack was developed for older children who like the taste of Ribena but want it in a more grown up and trendy pack. The target market is 8–14 year olds, who might consider other Ribena packs not "cool" enough for them.

Evaluation

This is an excellent product. The pouch pack is cool and streetwise and therefore appeals to its target market. It has the added benefit of a re-sealable cap so it is perfect for "on-the-move" consumption. Since its launch in March 2000, sales have been very good, with more and more consumers buying into this new trendy pack.

Price

The Ribena pouch pack is more expensive than many soft drinks, such as Coca-Cola.

Evaluation

This is an excellent pricing strategy. Ribena's target market is 8–14 year olds. Children of this age have a relatively high amount of money to spend and can easily afford the higher price. Furthermore, it appeals to their parents who think that the higher price is worth paying because they believe Ribena is better for their children than fizzy drinks.

Promotion

Ribena advertises extensively on TV. Its ads feature the Ribenaberry cartoon characters.

Evaluation

This is an excellent advertising strategy. The target market for the Ribena pouch pack watches a lot of TV and is therefore very likely to see the ads. Furthermore, the Ribenaberry cartoon characters are an excellent advertising tool because they convey the essence of the drink – the fact that it is made from blackcurrants – and they also add an element of fun, which appeals to children. This encourages children to buy the product.

Place

Another important concept in marketing a brand is distribution. The product has to be available where and when people need and want it.

Evaluation

The Ribena pouch pack is very well distributed throughout Ireland so that it is available for its target market. It is sold in supermarkets, newsagents and garage forecourts around the country. It is available everywhere children might look for it. If they are shopping with their parents in the supermarket, it is there. If their parents pull in to get petrol, the Ribena pouch pack is there also.

Ordinary Level Questions

EXAM SECTION 1 (25%) – SHORT ANSWER QUESTIONS [10 marks each]

1. List four methods of promotion.

2. Distinguish between "reminder advertising" and "persuasive advertising". Illustrate with an example of each.

3. List three reasons why a business advertises.

4. Column 1 is a list of business terms. Column 2 is a list of possible explanations for these terms. Match the two lists by placing the letter of the correct explanation under the relevant number below. One explanation has no match.

Column 1	Column 2: Explanations
1. Informative Advertising	a) Large posters displaying advertisements
	b) Reminds consumers about a well-known product so that they do not forget it
2. Generic Advertising	
3. Advertising Media	c) Advertising material posted to a person's home
	d) Channels of communication that a business can use to get its message across to consumers
4. Comparative Advertising	
	e) Gives consumers factual information about a product
5. Direct Mail	f) Advertises an entire industry rather than an individual brand
6. Billboards	
	g) One business compares itself against another in its ads, to show that it is better

1	2	3	4	5	6
E					

5. Indicate whether each of the following (A, B, C, D and E) is true or false.

	Sentence	True or False
A	Radio advertising costs less than television advertising.	
B	Advertising in a local paper is cheaper than advertising in a national paper.	
C	Billboard advertisements are good for giving consumers lots of detailed information about a product.	
D	Direct mail allows a business to personalise an advertisement for each consumer.	
E	A magazine advertisement is seen by people for a longer period than a newspaper advertisement.	

6. State two methods of sales promotion and briefly explain one of them.

7. Explain the term "merchandising".

8. Explain the term "Public Relations". Use an example to illustrate your answer.

9. Outline two reasons why businesses use Public Relations.

10. In the context of marketing, explain what is meant by "sponsorship" and illustrate your answer with an example.

11. Draft the traditional channel of distribution for a product.

12. Outline two functions of a wholesaler.

13. List three types of retailer.

EXAM SECTION 2 (75%) – LONG QUESTIONS

1. Peter owns a barbershop in a busy town in Donegal.
   Outline three methods of advertising that Peter could use to increase sales. (15 marks)

2. Many businesses advertise on television. Explain the advantages of television advertising for businesses. (15 marks)

3. Television is one advertising medium in Ireland. Describe three other advertising media. Use an example of each to illustrate your answer. (30 marks)

4. Pauline runs her own hairdressing business in a small town in Waterford.
   Describe three sales promotions that Pauline could use to increase sales. (15 marks)

5. Define the term "personal selling". (10 marks)

6. What does the term "channel of distribution" mean? (10 marks)

Higher Level Questions

EXAM SECTION 1 (20%) – SHORT ANSWER QUESTIONS [10 marks each]

1. Complete this sentence: Advertising means…

2. Illustrate your understanding of term "advertising media".

3. Outline two problems of television as an appropriate advertising medium for a business.

4. What do the letters ASAI stand for? Explain the role of the ASAI in business.

5. Distinguish between the marketing terms (i) promotion and (ii) sales promotion.

6. Define "sales promotion". Outline two types of sales promotion a business could use to promote its products.

7. What do the letters PR stand for? Explain the role of PR in business.

8. Complete this sentence: Personal selling involves…

9. Advertising is a type of promotion. List three other promotions and explain any one of them.

10. Column 1 is a list of business terms. Column 2 is a list of possible explanations for these terms. Match the two lists by placing the letter of the correct explanation under the relevant number below. One explanation has no match.

Column 1	Column 2: Explanations
1. Reminder Advertising	a) Dividing the market for a product into groups of buyers with similar tastes
2. Merchandising	b) Buys from the wholesaler and sells to the consumer
3. Wholesaler	c) Four tools that a business can use to increase sales
4. Retailer	d) Keeps a famous brand name prominent in the minds of consumers
5. Marketing mix	e) Buys from the manufacturer and sells to stores in smaller quantities
	f) Attractive shop displays designed to stimulate impulse buying

1	2	3	4	5

11. Distinguish between the role of wholesalers and retailers in a channel of distribution.

EXAM SECTION 2 (20%) – APPLIED BUSINESS QUESTION – 80 MARKS

Treacy's Tasty Food Ltd.

Sam Treacy owns a fast-food restaurant in the centre of a large town in the north-east, just off the motorway between Dublin and Belfast. When setting up the business, he carried out market research that revealed that a lot of people in the area were interested in eating healthier but, because of their busy lifestyles, they found it hard to find the time to prepare healthy food. Sam uses only the finest healthy ingredients in his burgers and fries.

He is so passionate about healthy food that he allows people a free taste to convince them that healthy food can taste good. The business has done well and the name "Treacy's Tasty Food" is now synonymous with healthy eating. His target market comprises health-conscious young people and parents with small children. Although his menus are more expensive than the competition, many consumers feel that this is a price worth paying for healthy food.

Sales have rocketed since Sam started the TT Club. Customers are given a card that is stamped every time they buy a burger. They can claim a free burger once they have collected ten stamps. All completed cards are entered into a draw for a holiday. Children who order a Treacy's "Tots meal" get a free toy. Sam has recently expanded the business to include healthy pizza. He now sells pizza in the restaurant and offers a home-delivery service. He knows though that extensive advertising is required to promote the pizza venture.

(A) Outline, from the above information, four sales promotions used by Sam. (20 marks)

(B) Recommend, with reasons, four different advertising media appropriate to Sam's new pizza venture. (40 marks)

(C) Evaluate Sam's marketing mix. (20 marks)

EXAM SECTION 3 (60%) – LONG QUESTIONS

1. Describe the main functions of advertising. (15 marks)

2. Discuss the factors that a marketing manager must consider when choosing an appropriate advertising medium for the business. Illustrate your answer with relevant examples. (20 marks)

3. Outline the role of the Advertising Standards Authority for Ireland (ASAI). (15 marks)

4. Describe the various sales promotions that a business can use to promote its products. (20 marks)

5. Evaluate the importance of public relations for a business. (25 marks)

CHAPTER 18

Business Expansion

One of the main objectives of a business is to expand and increase profits.

- ▶ Dunnes Stores' profits are greater today with over 150 stores than when it started with just one store, back in 1944.

- ▶ McDonald's started with one restaurant in 1955. Today, there are over 13,000 McDonald's restaurants worldwide.

Both of these businesses started off small and grew to become large, successful and highly profitable businesses. They expanded in different ways, though. This chapter looks at all the different ways to expand a business. It then examines the reasons why an entrepreneur wants to expand, where he gets the money from to expand and the effects of such expansion.

Strategies for Business Expansion

The two main methods of expanding a business are called **organic growth** and **inorganic growth**.

Organic Growth

Organic growth is the natural, slow expansion of a business. Profits made from one shop are used to buy another shop. This cycle is repeated so that over time, the business expands and owns lots of shops.

A business can use the following organic strategies to help it expand:

1. Increase Sales

The business can grow by selling more products and thus making more profits. It can sell more in Ireland through better marketing and improving its product.

Meteor grew this way. It was the third mobile phone company to enter the Irish market. It grew by using a penetration pricing strategy (*see Chapter 16*) and using ads that emphasised how low its prices were. This was designed to win over customers from Vodafone and O2.

Nintendo traditionally appealed to a young male market. To grow, it needed to attract new and different customers to its brand. The launch of the Nintendo DS game *More Brain Training* succeeded in attracting more and more women and older people to Nintendo. The company achieved this by showing the actress Nicole Kidman using the product in its ads.

Alternatively the business can grow by selling its products in different countries. This is called exporting. Baileys grew by exporting all over the world. Baileys was first launched in Ireland in 1974. Today it is sold in over 130 countries worldwide and is the top-selling liqueur in the world.

2. Franchising

The business can grow by franchising. The original owner (franchiser) grants permission to other entrepreneurs (franchisees) to copy his idea exactly and set up an identical business to his, in return for a fee.

The franchiser trains and advises the franchisees in all aspects of running the business. He also lays down very strict rules for running the business that all franchisees must obey.

For example, O'Briens Irish Sandwich Bars have expanded throughout the world through franchising. Domino's Pizza has grown throughout Ireland in the same way.

Inorganic Growth

Inorganic growth is the quick expansion of a business achieved by merging with, taking over or forming a strategic alliance with another business.

A business can use the following inorganic strategies to help it expand:

1. Strategic Alliance

A strategic alliance is where two businesses agree to co-operate with each other on a single business project. It is sometimes called a joint venture. The businesses remain separate from each other.

This co-operation has benefits for both businesses. The businesses benefit from sharing the costs of the venture between them and sharing their expertise and skills to come up with the best ideas possible (brainstorming).

An example of a strategic alliance is the one between the watch company Swatch and the car manufacturer Mercedes who worked together to make the "smart" car. (SMART stands for Swatch Mercedes Art.)

Both companies co-operated on a joint venture to make the car. By working together, they could share ideas. They combined the styling and design ideas of Swatch with the technological knowledge of Mercedes to produce a radically different car. By working together, they could split the costs of designing and producing the car.

Another example of a strategic alliance is Postbank, a joint venture between An Post and the major international bank Fortis.

By co-operating on this joint venture, Fortis has expanded its business throughout Ireland without the cost of setting up branches nationwide. It simply operates from An Post's existing post offices. An Post benefits from having more customers using its post offices to do their banking.

2. Merger

A merger (also called an amalgamation) is where two separate businesses voluntarily agree to join together permanently to form one larger business.

For example, Irish Life, an insurance company, and Irish Permanent, a building society, merged in 1999 to form Irish Life and Permanent plc. It is now one of the biggest financial services companies in Ireland.

3. Takeover

A takeover (also called an acquisition) is when one business takes control of another by buying it outright, with or without its consent.

In 2005, eircom took over Meteor. It bought Meteor for €420 million. It raised the money needed for the purchase by selling more shares in eircom (equity finance).

Malcolm Glazer took over Manchester United plc in 2005 for over €1.2 billion. He borrowed 2/3rds (debt finance) of the money he needed to buy the company. He put up Manchester United FC assets including the Old Trafford stadium as security for the loan.

Reasons for Business Expansion

The obvious reason why an entrepreneur wants to expand his business is to make more profits. There are plenty of other reasons though, which can be grouped into three categories: psychological reasons, defensive reasons and offensive reasons.

Psyological Reasons

1.   Ambition
Many business-people want to build their business into "the biggest". Such

entrepreneurs are often called "empire builders". They want the fame and sense of achievement that comes from growing the biggest business in the world.

Examples of empire builders include the entrepreneurs Donald Trump and Rupert Murdoch.

2. Challenge

Many businesspeople enjoy the challenge of growing their business. They get a thrill from starting a new business from scratch again to see whether they can make it a success.

Sir Richard Branson of Virgin enjoys the challenge of setting up different businesses. Once they are established, he puts professional managers in to run them, while he concentrates on setting up another new business. For example, his new venture is tourist holidays into space.

Defensive Reasons

A major reason why businesses grow bigger is that bigger businesses are stronger, richer and better able to fight back against competition and other problems.

The main defensive reasons for business expansion include:

1. Economies of scale

The business may want to grow bigger in order to reduce its costs. The bigger a business becomes, the lower its unit costs become. This is called **economies of scale**. Because its costs are lower, it can lower its prices and thus fight back (defend) against competition.

Big businesses such as Dunnes Stores get big discounts from suppliers (such as Mars, Brennans Bread and so on) because they buy so much from them. This helps Dunnes to keep its prices low so that it can successfully fight back against competition from ALDI and Lidl.

2. To protect supplies

A business may grow bigger to defend itself against a lack of good quality, reasonably priced raw materials (ingredients). It might merge with or take over the company it buys its materials or products from. This will guarantee that it will get all the supplies it needs in the future and at cost price.

For example, say an ice cream manufacturer buys milk from ABC Dairies, the best dairy in Ireland. Last year the dairy increased the price of milk by 15% and it has just told the ice cream company that it intends to raise prices a further 25% this month. The ice cream company might decide to make an offer for the dairy and take it over. When it expands and buys the dairy, it gets all the milk it needs and at cost price.

This is called **backward vertical integration**.

3.   To protect distribution

A business may grow bigger to defend itself against its competitors. To ensure that its products are on sale in key markets, the business might merge with or take over the company that sells its products on to consumers. In this way, it guarantees a market for its products.

If Coca-Cola took over Burger King, it could guarantee increased sales, as it would only allow Coca-Cola to be sold in all Burger King restaurants.

A brewery might take over a pub. This guarantees a market for its products. It also increases its profits because all the profits (from making and selling the beer) now go to the brewery.

This is called **forward vertical integration**.

4.   Diversification

A business may grow bigger so that it can defend itself against a downturn in its market. The business expands by taking over or merging with a business in a *totally unrelated* area. If one of its companies goes through a bad patch and makes a loss, profits from the other companies can keep the business going.

In the 1980s, the cigarette manufacturer Carrolls was worried that sales of cigarettes might decline in the near future because of government warnings about the danger of smoking and increased consumer interest in health and fitness. To defend itself against this predicted loss of sales, Carrolls took over a trout farm. It hoped that if cigarette sales fell in the future, profits from the trout farm business would keep the company going.

Gillette diversified when it bought Parker Pens. As the two brands service different markets, Gillette is spreading the risk of doing business across different sectors.

Offensive Reasons

A business may expand so that it becomes the biggest and best in the industry with the highest level of profits. The main offensive reasons for business expansion include:

1.   Eliminate Competition

A business might become bigger by taking over

one of its competitors. It does this in order to get rid of the competitor and thus keep control over the market.

Irish Distillers tried to take over a new company, Cooley Distillery, because it wanted to remain in control of the Irish whiskey market.

Ryanair tried to take over Aer Lingus in 2006. Had it succeeded, it would have become the only major Irish international airline and controlled a huge share of the Irish market.

2. Asset Stripping

A business might take over a company because it sees an opportunity to make money either by using the company's assets better or by selling them off to make a profit. It has no intention of running the company.

For example, a property developer might take over a city centre hotel chain, not to run it, but for the land the hotels sit on. As soon as the developer acquires the hotel business, he knocks down the hotels and builds apartments on the sites and makes a large profit.

3. To Acquire New Products

An entrepreneur may take over another business to get his hands on that business's ideas, products, machines, staff, markets and so on. Once he owns the business, he then owns all its products.

In 2006, Adidas took over Reebok for €3.1 billion. It did this to get a stronger presence in the US market. The US is the biggest market in the world for sports clothing and equipment. Adidas is not very well known in the US. But, by buying Reebok, it now controls 20% of the US market.

4. To Increase Profits

The more shops a business has, the more money it can make. Dunnes Stores makes more profit than a local sole trader shop.

Finance for Business Expansion

We have seen that eircom grew bigger by taking over Meteor and that Malcolm Glazer expanded his business by taking over Manchester United PLC. We now examine where eircom got the €420 million to buy out Meteor and where Malcolm Glazer got the €1.2 billion he needed to buy Manchester United.

Because expansion is the long-term growth of a business, entrepreneurs use *long-term* finance to pay for expansion.

In Chapters 13 and 15, we saw that main sources of long-term finance for a business. You should revise these carefully again for this chapter.

The main sources of long-term finance that a business can use for expansion are equity capital, retained earnings, debentures and grants. Each one has its advantages and disadvantages.

Equity Capital

The entrepreneur raises money to pay for the expansion by selling shares in her company to investors. In return for the money they provide, she gives them part ownership in her business. For every share they buy, they get a vote and a share of the company's profit, called a dividend. This is how eircom raised the money to pay for its takeover of Meteor.

Retained Earnings

Retained earnings are the profits that the business has saved up over the years. It can use these profits to pay for expansion. Because the business hasn't borrowed, there is no interest to repay and no worry about going bankrupt. For example, Ryanair used some of its retained earnings to buy a large number of shares in Aer Lingus.

Debt Capital

The entrepreneur raises money to pay for the expansion by borrowing from investors such as a bank. One long-term loan available to companies is called a debenture. The company must pay interest on the loan every year and it must repay the loan in full at an agreed date in the future. It does not give the investors part of the business. It puts up its assets as security for the loan, though. If it cannot repay the loan, the investors can take the business's assets. This is how Malcolm Glazer raised the money to pay for his takeover of Manchester United plc.

Contrast Debt and Equity Capital

Debt capital involves borrowing, whereas equity capital is the money invested by the owners of the business.

1. A business that is mainly financed by equity has very few loans. Therefore, it has very few repayments to make and, if the business goes through a bad patch, it should still be able to afford the low repayments. So, there is less chance of going bankrupt.

    In *contrast*, a business that is mainly financed by debt has lots of loans. If it goes through a bad patch and can't pay back any of these loans, the lenders will get a judge to close the business down and sell it off so that they can get their money back. Thus there is a higher chance of going bankrupt.

2. Equity is a permanent source of finance. The business does not have to repay this capital to the shareholders until the business is closed down.

    In *contrast*, with loan capital, the business must repay the loan in full on a particular date in the future.

3. With equity finance, the business does not have to pay any dividends to shareholders if it doesn't make a profit, because it is up to the directors of the business to decide how much dividends are paid out.

    In *contrast*, with loan capital, the business must pay interest on the loan every year, whether it makes a profit or not.

4. With equity finance, the business does not have to provide security in order to get the finance. So the business does not risk losing its assets with equity finance.

    In *contrast*, security is needed to get obtain loan capital. So, the business risks losing its assets if it cannot repay the loan.

5. With equity finance, any dividends the business pays to the investors are not tax deductible. The business cannot subtract the dividends from its taxable profits. So the business does not save tax with equity finance.

    In *contrast*, interest paid on loan capital is tax deductible. The business can subtract the interest it pays from its taxable profits. So the business pays less tax with debt finance.

6. Selling equity shares reduces control over the business. The existing owners must give some of their shares and hence control to the new investors, in order to obtain the equity finance.

    In *contrast*, taking out loan capital does not affect control over the business. The existing owners do not have to give any of their shares to the lender.

Choosing Finance for Expansion

When choosing *which* source of long-term finance to use for business expansion, the manager of the business will have to consider the following factors:

1. Cost

The manager should shop around for the cheapest source of finance. This will help to lower the business's costs and thus increase profits. For example, if the manager chooses to finance the expansion by selling shares in the business (equity finance), the business must pay the investors dividends every year. But the directors decide how much to pay. If profits are low, they can pay low or even no dividends. If, however, the manager decides to use loan capital, the business must repay interest on the loan. The interest is fixed and the business must pay it whether profits are high or low or even if it makes a loss.

2. Security

The manager must take into account the fact that if the source of finance requires collateral, the business is risking its assets. For example, if the manager uses equity finance, no security is required and therefore the business's assets are not at risk. However, if the manager uses loan capital, collateral is needed and the business risks losing its assets if it can't repay the loan.

3. Tax Implications

The manager must look at the source of finance to see whether the business will get a tax deduction for the repayments it makes on it. If so, this will reduce the cost of the finance. For example, interest on loan capital is tax deductible and will lower the business's tax bill but dividends paid on equity shares will not.

4. Control

The manager must look at the source of finance to see whether it involves the owners giving away some of their shares in the business. If so, this will reduce their control over their business. For example, loan capital does not involve giving away shares but equity capital does. The business owners must balance their desire for money with their control over their company.

Implications of Business Expansion

FOR:	SHORT-TERM IMPLICATIONS	LONG-TERM IMPLICATIONS
Share Price	When a business expands, its share price should increase because investors want shares in big successful companies and will pay more to get them.	Bigger businesses make bigger profits and therefore the share price should increase because investors will pay more to buy shares in more profitable businesses.

Products	Bigger businesses have a bigger range of products for the customer. For example, eircom took over Meteor. It now offers its customers landline *and* mobile phones.	A bigger business has more money to spend on market research and product development. This should lead to a wider range of products.
Management	The business may need a new organisation structure. For example, when Irish Permanent and Irish Life merged, the new business needed only one CEO.	The bigger the business grows, the harder it becomes for one person to manage and so the greater the amount of delegation (sharing out responsibilities) needed.
Finances	The business will have to raise finance to pay for the expansion. This will involve selling shares or borrowing.	As the business grows and succeeds, it will be easier to raise more debt and equity capital in the future.
Supplies	Bigger businesses get quantity discounts from suppliers because they buy in bulk. They also get quicker delivery and better service because they buy so much from the supplier.	Bigger businesses get quantity discounts from suppliers because they buy in bulk. They also get quicker delivery and better service because they buy so much from the supplier.
Profits	The costs involved in expansion (paying for the new business, redundancy packages and so on) may lead to a decrease in profits.	Economies of scale should lead to increased profits.
Employees	Employees may be worried about their jobs because mergers and takeovers normally mean job cuts. This may reduce employee morale and motivation.	Big successful businesses provide better pay, job security and increased promotion prospects for employees.
Customers	Customers will enjoy a bigger range of products in a bigger business and at lower prices (because of economies of scale).	Although customers enjoy more products and lower prices, they may be turned off by the impersonal nature of big businesses.

Importance of Business Expansion

Importance of Irish Business Expanding in Ireland

It is really important for the Irish economy that Irish businesses grow bigger here in Ireland (domestic market).

1. Bigger businesses in Ireland make bigger profits because of factors such as economies of scale. Bigger business profits result in more taxes for the Irish government to spend improving the country's infrastructure, offering more grants to entrepreneurs and so on.

2. When a business expands in Ireland, it needs to hire more employees to do the extra jobs. Therefore, business expansion leads to lower unemployment in Ireland and a higher standard of living for all. Dunnes Stores has over 100 stores in Ireland employing more than 10,000 people.

3. As a business expands in Ireland and sells more products, it will need to buy more raw materials and ingredients from Irish suppliers, which in turn helps them to expand. Thus, one Irish business's expansion has a spin-off effect on other Irish businesses.

4. As a business expands in Ireland, its unit costs decrease because of economies of scale. Therefore, the business can charge a lower price for its products. This helps to lower the cost of living (inflation) in Ireland.

Importance of Irish Business Expanding Abroad

It is also vital for Ireland that Irish businesses expand abroad in foreign markets. Expansion abroad brings the following benefits:

1. Increased sales abroad can lead to the creation of more jobs here in Ireland. Therefore, business expansion leads to lower unemployment in Ireland and a higher standard of living for all.

2. Exporting improves Ireland's balance of payments. This means that it brings a lot of money into the country and makes Ireland richer.

3. Exporting brings foreign currency into Ireland, which we can use to pay for the goods and services we import.

4. Exporting improves our international relations. We become friendlier with countries that we export to.

Ordinary Level Questions

EXAM SECTION 1 (25%) – SHORT ANSWER QUESTIONS [10 marks each]

1. Explain the term "organic growth" and give two examples.

2. Name three ways that a business can expand inorganically.

3. Explain the term "franchise" and give two examples.

4. Distinguish between a merger and a takeover.

5. Outline two benefits of a strategic alliance for businesses.

6. Define "economies of scale".

7. Column 1 is a list of business terms. Column 2 is a list of possible explanations for these terms. Match the two lists by placing the letter of the correct explanation under the relevant number below. One explanation has no match.

Column 1	Column 2: Explanations
1. Expansion	a) Business sets up a totally different business, to spread its risk
2. Diversification	
3. Asset Stripping	b) Irish businesses sell their products abroad
4. Strategic Alliance	c) Two businesses work together on a joint venture
5. Inorganic Growth	d) Two businesses join together permanently to form one large business
6. Exporting	
	e) Business increases in size
	f) One business buys another, not to run it, but to get its valuable assets
	g) Business grows quickly by buying out another business, for example

1	2	3	4	5	6
E					

8. Indicate whether each of the following (A, B, C, D and E) is true or false.

	Sentence	True or False
A	When a business expands, its share price always falls.	
B	Bigger businesses get big discounts from suppliers for bulk buying.	
C	Bigger businesses offer customers a wider range of products.	
D	In the long run, bigger businesses usually make very low profits.	
E	Bigger businesses find it easier to borrow from banks than smaller businesses do.	

9. Outline two advantages of business expansion for Ireland.

EXAM SECTION 2 (75%) – LONG QUESTIONS

1. Distinguish between organic growth and inorganic growth.   (10 marks)

2. Explain each of the following terms
    (i) Strategic alliance (ii) Merger (iii) Takeover.   (15 marks)

3. Outline three defensive reasons for business expansion.   (15 marks)

4. Describe three offensive reasons for business expansion.   (15 marks)

5. Eimear runs her own hairdressing business and is thinking of opening
    a second shop. Name three sources of finance that she could use
    to expand and explain any one of them.   (20 marks)

6. Explain the implications of business expansion on a business's
    (i) products (ii) management and (iii) finances.   (15 marks)

7. State three advantages for Ireland of Irish firms expanding abroad.   (15 marks)

Higher Level Questions

EXAM SECTION 1 (20%) – SHORT ANSWER QUESTIONS [10 marks each]

1. Illustrate your understanding of term "business expansion".

2. Complete this sentence: Organic growth involves…

3. Define "strategic alliance".

4. Explain the concept of "franchising".

5. Illustrate the difference between a strategic alliance and a merger.

6. What is a takeover?

7. Column 1 is a list of business terms. Column 2 is a list of possible explanations for these
    terms. Match the two lists by placing the letter of the correct explanation under the
    relevant number below. One explanation has no match.

Column 1	Column 2: Explanations
1. Backward Vertical Integration	a) The larger a business becomes, the lower its unit costs become
2. Forward Vertical Integration	b) A business merges with or takes over its supplier
	c) Finance provided by the government to help the business buy things
3. Equity Capital	
4. Diversification	d) Finance provided by the owners of the business
5. Economies of Scale	e) A business merges with or takes over its distributor
	f) Refers to a business's effort to spread its risk

1	2	3	4	5

8. Complete this sentence: Business expansion helps a business to…

9. List four differences between debt capital and equity capital.

10. Name an Irish business that has expanded abroad. Explain two reasons why this expansion is important to the Irish economy.

EXAM SECTION 2 (20%) – APPLIED BUSINESS QUESTION – 80 MARKS

CC's Fast Food.

Ciara Collins graduated from catering college fifteen years ago and immediately set up her own fast-food restaurant, CC's, in her home town, a seaside resort popular with sailing and surfing enthusiasts. The business has done well since then, especially during the busy tourist summer season. Over the years, Ciara has reinvested most of her profits and used them to pay for the building her restaurant is situated in. She enjoys running her own business and making all the decisions.

Recently, however, Ciara has begun to notice an increasing number of problems in the business. Profits have fallen since a new fast-food restaurant opened close by offering cheaper menus. The growing trend towards healthy eating has also impacted negatively on her business. Ciara is finding it harder to find and keep good staff. Employees complain that they are given menial tasks to do, despite the fact that many are catering college graduates just like Ciara.

Ciara's business advisor told her that she needs to expand the business if she is to survive long term. Ciara has doubts about this strategy. She is concerned about her lack of knowledge of suitable locations to expand into and the amount of money needed to pay for the new premises and equipment required. Her advisor recommended that she seek a suitable source of finance. Ciara is wary about borrowing because of difficulties she had getting a loan when she first set up the business and fears about crippling interest rates putting her out of business.

(A) Describe one organic and one inorganic method of expansion suitable for Ciara's business.   (30 marks)

(B) Evaluate the long-term effects of expansion on Ciara's business.   (20 marks)

(C) Contrast debt and equity capital as suitable sources of finance for Ciara's business.   (30 marks)

EXAM SECTION 3 (60%) – LONG QUESTIONS

1. Explain four methods of expansion available to a business.   (20 marks)

2. Distinguish between offensive and defensive reasons for business expansion. (20 marks)

3. Outline and illustrate the term "economies of scale".   (10 marks)

4. Describe three sources of finance suitable for business expansion.   (30 marks)

5. Explain the factors that a manager must consider when choosing a source of finance for business expansion.   (20 marks)

6. Define "business expansion". Outline the implications of expansion for a business.   (20 marks)

7. Analyse the importance of Irish business expansion in the domestic and foreign markets.   (30 marks)

CHAPTER 19

Business Organisations

Many different types of business operate in Ireland today. Irish entrepreneurs own most of them. Some though are owned by the Irish government, whereas others are foreign businesses that have set up here.

Different entrepreneurs choose different types of business, depending on various factors including their attitude to risk, their desire to keep control of their business, the amount of capital they require and their wish to keep their accounts private and confidential.

In this chapter, we look at the main types of business operating in Ireland:

1. Sole trader
2. Partnership
3. Private limited company
4. Public limited company
5. Co-operative
6. State-owned enterprise
7. Franchise
8. Alliance
9. Transnational company
10. Indigenous firms

Sole Trader

A sole trader is a business set up, owned and run by an entrepreneur on her own.

This type of business organisation is often used by entrepreneurs when setting up their first business, mainly because it is very easy to set up. It is also used by entrepreneurs who want to be in full control of their business.

Examples include farmers, local chemists, hairdressers, newsagents and so on.

Advantages of Sole Trader

1. It is easy to become a sole trader. There are few legal registration requirements to satisfy and no government permission is needed to set up.

    The entrepreneur must register the name of the business with the Registrar of Business Names if it is different to her own name. For example, if Mag Collins calls her supermarket "Mag Collins Stores", she doesn't need to register. However, if she called it "Col-mart", she would have to register the name.

    The business must also register with Revenue for taxes such as VAT and Self Assessment Tax and PAYE.

2. Because the entrepreneur owns the business alone, all the profits go to her. This provides a great motivation to work hard in the business. The entrepreneur is directly rewarded for all her effort.

3. It is a confidential type of business. The business's financial accounts do not have to be published (made public). Therefore, no one else can get access to the sole trader's business secrets.

4. The sole trader is in full control over her business. She makes all the decisions. She can take advantage of any business opportunities instantly because there is no time wasted consulting others.

Disadvantages of Sole Trader

1. The sole trader has **unlimited liability**.
    This means that if the business goes bankrupt and owes a lot of money, the sole trader herself is personally responsible for paying back *all* the business's loans.

    If, after selling off the business to repay the loans, debts are still owed, the sole trader has to sell off her own personal assets, such as her house, to pay back these loans.

    In other words, setting up as a sole trader involves a huge risk. The entrepreneur risks losing everything she owns if the business goes bankrupt and has unpaid debts – her business, her home and anything else she owns.

2. It is difficult for a sole trader alone to raise all the money needed to set up and run the business. Sole traders may find it difficult to get loans from banks because sole traders are the business organisation most likely to go bankrupt.

Usually, sole traders provide the capital needed themselves from their savings or they may borrow from family and friends and possibly a bank. They may also apply for a government grant.

3. It is difficult to run a business alone. The sole trader has to rely on one person – herself – to know everything that is needed to run a business. There is no one to help her with major business problems and decisions.

4. Running a business alone requires a lot of effort. The stress that comes from this pressure may cause the sole trader to burn out.

    To overcome these disadvantages of running a business alone, an entrepreneur may set up in business with others – maybe as a partnership, a company or a co-operative.

Partnership

A partnership is a business set up, owned and managed by between 2 and 20 owners, called **partners**. They set up a business together and combine their resources and talents to make a profit.

Examples of partnerships include many professionals such as solicitors, doctors and accountants such as KPMG and PricewaterhouseCoopers.

Having a number of owners brings its own problems, however. Say you open a coffee shop with your friend as your equal partner. Everything is going well. You both come to the shop early and work hard to make it a success. After a while though, your friend starts coming in later and later each day. Some days, he doesn't come in at all. Then he starts taking money from the till. When you question him about this, he tells you that he owns half the business and can do what he likes. What can you do? You can't sack your friend because he's right – he does own half the business and has as much say as you do. You could try buying his share in the business from him but where will you get the money from?

To avoid problems like this, people setting up a partnership together should draw up a contract *before* they set up the business. Such a contract is called a **deed of partnership**. It is used in the event of any disagreements between the partners. It sets out *in advance* issues such as how the profits are to be shared, what each partner is expected to do in the running of the business, what happens if the business closes down, what salaries each partner is to be paid for working in the business, whether partners can take money from the business (and, if so, how much) and so on.

Then, if one partner breaks the terms of the deed of partnership, the others can sue him for breach of contract.

Advantages of Partnerships

1. A partnership is a simple business to set up. There are few legal registration requirements to satisfy before setting up. Government permission is not required. The partners must register the name of the business with the Registrar of Business Names if it is different to the names of the partners. The business must also register with Revenue for the relevant taxes.

2. Because there are more people setting up the business, more capital is available to the business. The business can raise more money to set up than a sole trader can.

3. Each of the partners may bring different areas of expertise and this will make it easier to run the business. Also, because there are more people to consult and discuss problems with, the partnership should make better decisions than someone on their own.

4. It is a confidential type of business. The business's financial accounts do not have to be published (made public). Therefore, no one else can get access to the partnership's business secrets.

Disadvantages of Partnerships

1. The partners have **unlimited liability**.
   This means that if the business goes bankrupt and owes a lot of money, the partners are *jointly and severally liable* for paying back all the business's loans.

   If, after selling the business to repay the loans, debts are still owed, the partners will have to sell their own personal assets, such as their houses, to pay back their share of the loans. If one partner cannot pay back her share of the loans, the other partners have to pay it for her.

2. Profits have to be shared between the partners in their agreed profit-sharing ratio and not necessarily in the ratio of how much effort they put in.

3. The partners may be incompatible and disputes may arise. Such problems can harm the success of the business.

4. Decision-making is slower because all the partners have to be consulted. This may make the business less flexible and less responsive to change. Partners may spend so much time debating new opportunities that, by the time they agree, someone else will have exploited the opportunity.

Private Limited Company

A private limited company is a business owned by between 1 and 50 owners, called **shareholders**. If there is only one owner (shareholder), there must be at least two directors to run the company.

The shareholders have **limited liability**. This means that, if the company fails, all they lose is the money they invested in it. The name of the company must have Ltd (short for limited) or Teo in Irish (short for teoranta) as the last word to show people that it is a private limited company and that the owners have limited liability.

The company cannot sell its shares to the public. The company is totally separate from the owners. It can make contracts, be sued in its own right and it can sue others. Eason Ltd is an example of a private limited company.

Advantages of Private Limited Companies

1. The shareholders (owners) have limited liability.
   This means that if the company goes bankrupt and owes a lot of money, the shareholders are *not personally liable* for paying back the company's loans. If, after selling the business to repay the loans, debts are still owed, the shareholders do not have to sell their own personal assets, such as their houses, to pay back their share of the loans. All they lose is the capital they put into the company.

2. Because there are more people putting money into the company, it will be easier to raise capital for the company.

3. A private limited company is a good choice when setting up a business because a number of people, called directors, are involved in running it. The workload can be split between the various directors, each of whom may have different skills and experience. The directors can brainstorm ideas for the business. This inventive, creative process will yield better decisions and ideas than a person operating on her own.

4. Private limited companies pay less tax on their profits than either sole traders or partnerships. The rate of Corporation Tax that companies pay on their annual business profits is much less than the rate of Self Assessment Income Tax that sole traders and partnerships have to pay.

Disdvantages of Private Limited Companies

1. It is complicated to set up a private limited company. The shareholders must first apply for permission to set up the company from the Registrar of Companies. They cannot begin trading until they receive a certificate of incorporation from the Registrar. Furthermore, they must also pay a fee for this service.

2. The company must publish its financial accounts each year, for all to see. This means that a private limited company is not a very confidential type of business. Customers, competitors, employees and anyone else who is interested can see the company's financial position and may use this information to their advantage.

3. Profits have to be shared between the shareholders in the ratio of how much money each invested in the business and not necessarily in proportion to how much effort each puts in.

4. There are a lot of legal requirements to obey. Every year, the company must send an annual return to the Companies Registration Office. The company must also get its financial accounts audited (verified by an accountant) every year.

Setting up a Private Limited Company

We saw that one of the disadvantages of setting up a private limited company is that it is complicated to set up such a business. The business has to apply for permission and obey certain rules. The rules for setting up a private limited company are contained in the Companies Act, 1990.

The steps in setting up a private limited company are set out below:

Step 1

The people setting up the company (called the **founders**) must prepare the following documents:

   (a) A memorandum of association
   (b) The articles of association
   (c) Form A1

Step 2

The founders must then send these documents (together with the appropriate fee) to the Registrar of Companies at the Companies Registration Office.

Step 3

The Companies Registration Office examines the documents to make sure that they are in order. If they are, it gives the founders a certificate of incorporation. This is the "birth cert" of the private limited company.

Step 4

The company must hold its very first meeting, called its **statutory meeting**. At this meeting, the memorandum and articles of association are explained to each shareholder and each shareholder receives his share certificate, showing how much of the business he owns. The shareholders then vote in the first Board of Directors to run the business on their behalf.

The company can now begin trading. The company is a **corporate body**, totally separate and distinct from its owners, in law. If the company does something wrong, it is the *company* that is sued and not the individual owners. The company can enter into contracts, sue and be sued in its own name.

We must now look at each of the documents needed to set up a company in detail.

Memorandum of Association

- This document is like a constitution for the company. It sets out the limits to the company's powers (i.e. what it can and cannot do).
- It is available for public inspection.
- It contains the following details:
  - (a) Name of the company with Ltd or Teo as the last word.
  - (b) The address of the company's registered office.
  - (c) The objectives of the company (i.e. what the company is going to trade in)
  - (d) A statement saying that the shareholders have limited liability.
  - (e) Details of the company's authorised share capital (the maximum number of shares the company will sell).
  - (f) A list of all the founding shareholders' names, addresses, shares and signatures.

Note

A company is *not allowed* to do anything that is not written in its objectives in the memorandum of association. To do so is illegal and is known in law as acting *ultra vires*, which means acting outside the powers of the company.

MEMORANDUM OF ASSOCIATION

1. The name of this company is Finnie Ltd.
2. The registered office is at 125 Glasgow Street, Enniscorthy, Co. Wexford.
3. The objectives of this company are to buy and sell computer parts and to repair personal computers.
4. The shareholders in this company have limited liability
5. The authorised share capital of this company consists of 500,000 ordinary shares of €1 each.
6. We agree to set up this company and to take the following number of shares:

NAME	ADDRESS	SHARES	SIGNATURE
Tessie Finnie	10 Black Street, Gorey	200,000	*Tessie Finnie*
Joe Finnie	45 Green Street, New Ross	100,000	*Joe Finnie*

Articles of Assocation

◐ This document sets out the internal rules and regulations for running the company.

◐ It contains the following details:
   (a) Details of the company's authorised share capital.
   (b) Procedures for organising and arranging company meetings.
   (c) Procedures for voting at meetings.
   (d) Procedures for appointing and removing directors.
   (e) Powers and duties of directors.
   (f) Rules for the sale of more shares.
   (g) How the company is to be closed down.

ARTICLES OF ASSOCIATION FOR FINNIE LTD

The following are the rules for running this company:

1. The authorised share capital of this company consists of 500,000 ordinary shares of €1 each.
2. Meetings
   (a) 28 days' written notice must be given in advance of all annual general meetings.
   (b) All votes shall be held by secret ballot.
3. Directors
   (a) All directors must own shares in the company.
   (b) A director can be removed from office at the annual general meeting by simple majority vote or during the year by 75% majority vote.

Form A1

The founders must fill in this form. It requires them to give details of:

- The company's name and registered office.
- Details of the secretary and the directors.
- Signatures of the secretary and the directors, showing that they agree to be the secretary and directors in this company.
- Details of the amount and type of shares the company intends to sell.
- A statement promising that the company will obey all the rules laid down for companies in the Companies Act.

Public Limited Company

A public limited company (PLC) is a business owned by at least seven owners, called **shareholders**. There is no upper limit on the number of owners.

The shareholders have limited liability. This means that if the company fails, all they lose is the money they invested in it. The last word in the name of the company must be plc (public limited company).

The company can raise capital by selling its shares to the public.

Examples of public limited companies include Bank of Ireland plc, AIB plc and Aer Lingus plc.

Advantages of Public Limited Companies

1. The shareholders in the company have limited liability.
   This means that if the company goes bankrupt and owes a lot of money, the shareholders are *not personally liable* for paying back the company's loans.

   If, after selling the company to repay the loans, debts are still owed, the shareholders do not have to sell their own personal assets, such as their houses, to pay back their share of the loans. All they lose is the capital they put into the company.

2. Public limited companies find it easier to raise the capital they need. The company can raise large amounts of capital by selling shares to the public on the Stock Exchange. Public limited companies also have a good credit rating. This makes it easier to borrow money to expand the business.

3. Public limited companies attract a lot of free publicity. They are constantly written about in the newspapers and mentioned on TV. This high profile combined with the prestige of working for large public limited companies helps a PLC to attract the best managers to come work for it.

4. Public limited companies pay less tax on their profits than either sole traders or partnerships. The rate of Corporation Tax that companies pay on their annual business profits is much less than the rate of Self Assessment Income Tax that sole traders and partnerships have to pay.

Disadvantages of Public Limited Companies

1. It is complicated to set up a public limited company. The owners cannot begin trading until they receive a certificate of incorporation *and* a certificate of trading from the Registrar of Companies. Furthermore, they must also pay a fee for this service.

2. A public limited company must publish its accounts in great detail. Therefore, it is not a very confidential type of business. Customers, competitors, employees and anyone else who is interested can see the company's financial position in great detail and may use this information to their advantage.

3. It is very expensive to sell shares to the public. Brochures (called **prospectuses**), which detail the history of the business so far, have to be designed and printed. Advertisements have to be placed in newspapers. Lawyers and stockbrokers have to be hired to handle the sale of the shares.

4. A public limited company may become the target for a hostile takeover bid because its shares can be freely bought and sold on the Stock Exchange. This means that anyone can approach the shareholders and ask to buy their shares. If enough shareholders sell, the company is taken over. This can happen even if the directors don't want it to happen.

    Despite many fans' protests, Malcolm Glazer succeeded in taking over Manchester United plc. Ryanair tried (and failed) to take over Aer Lingus in 2006, despite protests from many quarters.

People Involved in Companies

As we have seen, there can be up to 50 owners in a private limited company and any number (even hundreds, thousands or millions) in a public limited company. How is it possible to run a business with so many owners?

In many ways, a company is run like a country. The millions of people who live in Ireland vote in a government to run the country for them. In a company, the shareholders vote in a Board of Directors to run the company on their behalf.

In Ireland, the head of the government is An Taoiseach, who is in overall charge of running the country. In a company, the managing director fulfils this role.

Irish people elect a president to act as a figurehead for the country. A chairperson does a similar job in a company.

We now look at each of the people involved in running a company.

Shareholders
- Shareholders are the owners of the company.
- They invest their money in the company in return for shares (part-ownership) in the business.
- They receive a share of the company's profits each year, called a **dividend**.
- They can vote at the company's Annual and Extraordinary General Meetings. Each share they own entitles them to one vote.
- They vote in a Board of Directors to run the company for them.

Board of Directors
- The Board of Directors is voted in by the shareholders of the company to run it for them.
- The Board of Directors makes all the major decisions in the company.
- The Board is responsible for ensuring that the business is successful. The directors set strategic goals for the company to achieve and makes sure it accomplishes them.
- The directors must report back to the shareholders on how their company is progressing. This is done at the company's Annual General Meeting.
- The directors decide the share of the company's profits that each shareholder will receive at the end of the year. This is called a dividend.

Managing Director/Chief Executive Officer
- The managing director (MD), also known as the chief executive officer (CEO), is appointed by the Board of Directors to run the company on a day-to-day basis.
- The CEO/MD is in overall charge of the company. It is her job to see that the business achieves its objectives.
- The CEO/MD is the leader in the business who sets out a vision and a direction for the business and must motivate all the employees to follow her and work

together to make the business a success. She must spot problems in the business and opportunities that it can avail of and then take action to deal with them.

○ For example, Michael O'Leary, CEO of Ryanair, turned the company into one of the world's most successful airlines.

○ The CEO/MD hires the senior managers in the business and delegates duties to them, such as marketing, production, finance and Human Resource Management (HRM). She evaluates their performance to make sure they are doing a good job and must sack those who are not performing.

○ The MD/CEO is answerable to the Board of Directors.

Chairperson

○ The chairperson is a director elected by the Board of Directors to be in charge of running the company's meetings.

○ The chairperson also acts as a figurehead for the company.

Company Secretary

The company secretary is responsible for administration in the company. His functions include:

○ Keeping an up-to-date register of all the company's shareholders.

○ Sending the company's annual return to the Companies Registration Office.

○ Sending out the notice and agenda for all company meetings.

○ Taking the minutes (record) at the company's meetings.

Auditor

An auditor is an accountant who does not work for the company. The auditor is independent and has no connection with the company whatsoever. Her job is to check the company's accounts. The auditor's job is to:

(a) Make sure that the company has kept proper accounting records.

(b) Write a report stating whether the accounts are complete and accurate.

All companies must have their accounts audited by law.

Co-Operative

A co-operative (co-op for short) is a business set up by a group of people, who come together and establish an enterprise with the aim of helping (co-operating with) one another.

For example, a group of farmers might be annoyed at the low prices that the local dairies offer them for their milk. They decide to cut out the middleman and set up

their own business selling their milk under
one brand name, directly to the
supermarkets.

There must be at least seven owners in the
co-op. There is no upper limit to the
number of owners the co-op can have.

The owners apply to the Registrar of Friendly Societies for permission to set up the co-
op by submitting a copy of the rules they intend to use to run the business. If the
Registrar is satisfied with the application, she issues a certificate of registration to
them. The co-op now exists legally.

The owners of the co-op have limited liability.
The co-op cannot sell its shares to the public on the Stock Exchange.

Examples of Co-Operatives

Producer Co-op
A group of producers (for example, farmers) set up a business together. They sell their
produce to the co-op and it in turn sells the produce on to the public.
Kerry Co-op is an example of this.

Worker Co-op
This is a co-op owned and controlled by those who work in it.
Greencaps in Dublin Airport was a co-op set up by people from Ballymun. It offered a
left luggage and luggage porter service in Dublin Airport.

Credit Unions
A credit union is similar to a bank. It consists of a group of people (with a common
interest, such as having the same job or living in same area) who save together and
lend to each other at a reasonable rate of interest. Most communities in Ireland have a
credit union.

Advantages of Co-Operatives

1. The owners of the co-op have limited liability.
    This means that if the co-op goes bankrupt, they will lose only the capital they
    put into the business. They will not have to sell any of their personal assets to
    repay business loans.

2. Co-ops are run on the principle of **one member**, **one vote** and not **one share**,
    one vote, as is the case in companies. This means that they are a very
    democratic type of business. Each member has an equal say in the running of the
    business. No one person can dominate decision-making just because she has
    made a large investment.

3. There is an incentive for members to do business with the co-op. For example, the more the members of Drumcondra Credit Union save with Drumcondra Credit Union, the more loans it can give out to local people, the more interest it can make and the more profits it will make to share out among the members.

Disdvantages of Co-Operatives

1. It is complicated to set up a co-op. The founders must apply for permission from the Registrar of Friendly Societies. Furthermore, every year they must send in an annual report to the Registrar.

2. Profits must be shared between all the members.

3. A co-op must publish its accounts. Therefore, it is not a very confidential type of business. Customers, competitors, employees and anyone else who is interested can see the co-op's financial position in great detail and may use this information to their advantage.

4. Because each member has an equal say, there is less incentive for members to contribute more capital to the co-op. Thus, a co-op may find it difficult to raise additional capital to expand. This may be one reason why a lot of Irish co-ops changed their status and became public limited companies.

State-owned Enterprises

State-owned enterprises are businesses owned by the Irish government on behalf of the people of Ireland. They are run by professional managers who are appointed by the government. They are also called state-sponsored bodies or semi-state bodies. There are many state-owned enterprises in Ireland.

Transport	Training	Production	Energy	Services	Help Business
Iarnród Éireann	FÁS	Bord na Móna	ESB	RTÉ	Enterprise Ireland
Bus Éireann	Tourism Ireland	Coillte	Bord Gáis	VHI	IDA Ireland

You may be wondering what the Irish government is doing owning businesses, especially when there are other more pressing problems that need solving. There are arguments in favour of and against the government owning business.

Advantages of State-owned Enterprises

1. State-owned enterprises create employment in Ireland. Many Irish people work in state-owned enterprises. This means that there are less people claiming social welfare and more people earning a wage. Thus, state-owned enterprises help provide a better standard of living for Irish people.

2. State-owned enterprises provide essential services such as postal delivery (An Post), electricity (ESB) and public transport (Bus Éireann) to *all* people in *all* parts of Ireland. Private entrepreneurs would not service the less populated parts of the country because they wouldn't make a profit on it.

3. State-owned enterprises have played a major role in developing the Irish economy. IDA Ireland is responsible for attracting many foreign companies to set up here. Enterprise Ireland has helped many Irish people to set up their own businesses.

4. State-owned enterprises that make a profit (such as ESB) pay a dividend to the government every year. This means that the government has more money to spend on improving roads, hospitals, schools and so on.

Disadvantages of State-owned Enterprises

1. Many state-owned companies make a loss (including CIÉ). They do not make enough money from sales to pay their expenses. The government has to give them **subsidies** to keep them in operation. For example, CIÉ got almost €300 million from the Irish government in 2006. This money would be better used improving hospitals and schools.

2. Commercial businesses (such as AIB or Tesco, for example) are judged on the profits they make, so there is an incentive to keep costs to a minimum. *Non-commercial* state-owned companies (for example, Bord Iascaigh Mhara) are not judged by profit, so there is less incentive to keep costs to a minimum. Therefore, they may be inefficient and waste taxpayers' money.

3. The Board of Directors of the state-owned enterprises is appointed by the government. The directors may therefore be appointed because of their support for a particular political party rather than because of their business expertise. They may not have the skills needed to make good decisions for the state-owned enterprise. Furthermore, the government may interfere with the running of the state-owned company. For example, CIÉ and VHI must ask the government's permission to increase prices.

4. Many state-owned enterprises have large loans because their owner, the government, won't or can't (under EU Competition Policy rules – *see Chapter 25*) give them the money they need to expand.

Privatisation

Because of the disadvantages we have just read, some people believe that the government should sell its state-owned enterprises and let entrepreneurs and businesspeople run them instead. Selling state enterprises in this way is called **privatisation**.

Privatisation is when the government sells a state-owned enterprise to private individuals or companies. The government can offer its shares in the state-owned enterprise for sale to the general public (as happened in the case of eircom). Or it can sell its shares to one business, which happened when the government sold its shares in the state-owned shipping company B&I Line to Irish Continental Line, now called Irish Ferries.

The Irish government has privatised a number of state-owned enterprises:

- ❍ It sold the state-owned telephone company, called Telecom Éireann, on the Stock Exchange. Today, the company is known as eircom.
- ❍ It privatised the state-owned sugar manufacturing company, Cómhlucht Siúicre Éireann Teoranta, which became Greencore plc.
- ❍ It sold the state-owned insurance company called Irish Life, which later merged with Irish Permanent to form Irish Life and Permanent.
- ❍ In 2006, the Irish government privatised its Great Southern Hotel chain and the national airline Aer Lingus.

Advantages of Privatisation

1. The government receives cash from the sale of the state-owned enterprise. This cash can be used to improve the economy by paying for tax cuts, improving roads and infrastructure and/or paying back some of the national debt.

2. It frees the company from political control and interference. Decisions are no longer made by politicians but by business managers whose main goal is profit. The company will be freer to develop new products and enter new markets. This will result in increased profits.

3. It allows the company to raise finance for development and expansion. The company no longer has to rely on a government unwilling or unable to invest in it. It can raise money by selling shares to the public.

4. Privatisation offers Irish people an opportunity to invest their money and make a decent return.

Disadvantages of Privatisation

1. The experience of privatisation around the world and in Ireland has been one of job layoffs, cutbacks in the quality of service and increased profits.

    For example, privatised rail companies in the UK provide a worse service now than the old state-owned British Rail.

2. The directors of the privatised company will make decisions for the good of the company and not necessarily for the strategic interests of Ireland.

    Aer Lingus was privatised in 2006. In 2007, the company announced that it was cutting its Shannon–Heathrow route. Many business leaders and politicians in the mid-west asked the company not to do this, arguing that the air link with Heathrow was vital for business in the mid-west. The company ignored these concerns and cut the route.

3. The government loses the annual dividend it received from the company. Instead of the government using these dividends for the benefit of all Irish people, the company's profits will fall into the hands of a few select investors.

4. Only the profitable state-owned companies can be privatised. This means that the government will be left with all the loss-making state-owned companies.

Franchises

Franchising is a business arrangement whereby one person (**franchiser**) sells the right to use her name, idea or business to others (**franchisees**) and allows them to set up an exact replica of that business.

Examples of franchise businesses operating in Ireland include Domino's Pizza and Spar.

The franchisee must pay the franchiser a large once-off fee for permission to open up the franchise business. Every year after that, the franchisee must pay the franchiser a percentage of the profits he makes. Therefore, setting up and running a franchise is a costly business.

The franchisee must obey the rules and conditions laid down by the franchiser. These may include store layout, staff uniforms, buying raw materials from approved suppliers and so on. The franchiser does this to make sure that her business reputation is not harmed by a franchisee making a mistake.

Advantages of Franchises

1. **Reduced Risk**

    There is less risk of the business failing as it has already proved to be successful. The name is well known. It is a tried and tested formula. Customers are more readily attracted to the business because they already know the name of the business.

2. **Economies of Scale**

    Because the head office buys the stock for all the franchisees, it will get a good discount. This means that the franchisee gets the stock at a low cost. Lower costs give the franchisee an advantage over his competition.

3. **Training and Ongoing Support**

    The franchiser gives the new business owner training and guidelines in all aspects of the business, including site location, staff training, management of a business and so on. The franchiser provides ongoing support to the franchisee with accounts, running the business and with marketing.

4. **Advertising**

    The franchisee benefits from national advertising that she could never afford on her own. For example, Domino's Pizza sponsors *The Simpsons* on Sky One. All Domino's franchisees benefit from this. Very few independent pizza delivery businesses could afford this sponsorship.

Disadvantages of Franchises

1. **Cost**

    The franchisee must pay an initial fee to buy the franchise and an annual payment thereafter. If she set up her own business, these fees would not have to be paid, thus saving a lot of money.

2. **Restrictions**

    The franchiser imposes restrictions and conditions on the running of the business. This leaves the entrepreneur with very little room for individual flair and freedom in her own business. The franchisee is under a lot of pressure to meet the very high standards of the franchiser.

Alliances

A strategic alliance is an arrangement where two businesses agree to co-operate with each other on a single business project. It is sometimes called a **joint venture**. The businesses *remain* separate from each other.

This co-operation has benefits for both businesses. The businesses benefit from sharing the costs of the venture between them and sharing their expertise and skills to come up with the best ideas possible.

An example of a strategic alliance is the one between the watch company Swatch and the car manufacturer Mercedes. They worked together to make the "smart" car. (SMART stands for Swatch Mercedes Art.)

Both companies co-operated on a joint venture to make the car. By working together, they could share ideas. They combined the styling and design ideas of Swatch with the technological knowledge of Mercedes to produce a radically different car. By working together, they could split the costs of designing and producing the car.

Another example of a strategic alliance is Postbank. It is a joint venture between An Post and Fortis, a major international bank.

By co-operating on this joint venture, Fortis has expanded its business throughout Ireland without the cost of setting up branches nationwide. It simply operates from An Post's existing post offices. An Post benefits from having more customers using its post offices to do their banking.

Advantages of Alliances

1. An alliance is a temporary agreement between two businesses. Alliances are much easier to form and get out of than a merger or takeover.

2. Both businesses benefit from the alliance. They grow bigger by sharing ideas, expertise, costs and risks. For example, Swatch and Mercedes's strategic alliance to produce the smart car allowed both businesses to split the enormous costs involved in designing a car between them. Engineers and designers from both companies shared ideas to produce the best car possible.

3. Alliances can open up new markets to both businesses. For example, *The Irish Independent* has an alliance with the Institute of Education in Dublin whereby they jointly produce the Leaving Certificate guide, *Exam Brief*. Secondary school students who might never buy a broadsheet newspaper might stick with *The Irish Independent* after buying the *Exam Brief Supplement* issues.

Disadvantages of Alliances

1. The two parties to the alliance may have a disagreement if one feels that it is not getting as much out of the alliance as the other. Smaller businesses may feel that their identity is hidden by the higher profile of the bigger businesses in the alliance.

2. Customers may be unhappy with the alliance because they may feel that they have a restricted choice. For example, An Post customers might prefer a different bank to Fortis but Fortis is the only bank available in the post office.

Transnational Companies

A transnational company is a business with a head office in one country and branches or factories in many different countries. The head office controls the entire business, while the branches around the world usually carry out different jobs. Examples include Dell and Intel.

Transnational companies that set up in Ireland have a major impact on the economy, mostly positive but there also can be some negative aspects to them.

Advantages of Transnational Companies

1. Transnational companies create thousands of jobs in Ireland. This leads to lower unemployment in the country and a higher standard of living for Irish people. For example, Intel employs 5,000 Irish people in its plant in Leixlip. Dell employs 4,500 Irish people in its plants in Limerick and Dublin.

2. They bring *new* technologies, *new* products and *new* management skills and ideas into Ireland. Dell and Intel bring the latest computer technology into Ireland and train their Irish employees in the latest computer skills.

3. They bring competition into the Irish market. This is good for Irish consumers because it leads to lower prices and better quality. For example, Lidl and ALDI have increased competition in the Irish grocery market, leading to lower prices for Irish consumers.

4. They pay Corporation Tax on the profits they make in Ireland to the Irish government. This money can be used by the government to improve Ireland's economy through lower taxes and better infrastructure.

5. Transnational companies operating in Ireland may buy their raw materials and other supplies from local Irish businesses. Thus, they help many Irish businesses to increase their sales and profits. For example, Tesco buys vegetables, milk and meat from Irish farmers.

Disadvantages of Transnational Companies

1. A number of transnational companies have taken the grants and low taxes offered by Ireland. They then closed down with very little notice and left Ireland in order to go to cheap-labour countries. This leads to unemployment in Ireland. For example, Fruit of the Loom, a US transnational, closed down its factory in Donegal to move to Morocco, where wages are cheaper.

2. Many are so big that they can put pressure on the government to give them their own way. They may be even too powerful. If the government were to introduce a law that the transnationals didn't like, they could threaten to pull out of Ireland, taking all the jobs with them.

3. They often repatriate most of their profits. This means that they send most of the profits they make in Ireland back home. So the money they make in Ireland doesn't necessarily benefit the Irish economy.

4. Most decisions are taken by the head office abroad and they may not take Irish interests into account.

Indigenous Firms

Indigenous firms are businesses set up, owned and managed by *Irish* people. Their main place of business is Ireland. They make their products here in Ireland and may sell them here also. And they may export their products from Ireland to other countries.

Examples of indigenous firms include the chocolate company Lily O'Briens and the fast-food restaurant Supermac's. Pat the Baker is an indigenous bakery located in Granard, Co.Longford. It employs over 400 people.

Indigenous firms are helped and encouraged by Enterprise Ireland, the state-owned enterprise. It provides them with advice on setting up and running a business. It gives them grants to help them buy the things they need.

Advantages of Indigenous Firms

1. They create thousands of jobs in Ireland, thus reducing unemployment and improving the standard of living of many people.

2. They remain loyal to Ireland. They tend not to leave Ireland when the economy goes through a bad patch.

3. They foster and encourage an enterprise culture in Ireland. When Irish people see successful Irish businesses, it encourages them to set up their own business.

4. They keep their profits in Ireland. They reinvest their profits to expand their business in Ireland or put it into Irish banks where it can be loaned out to help other Irish entrepreneurs.

Changing Trends in Ownership and Structure

We have now looked at all the different types of business organisations in Ireland. Like everything else in Ireland, business organisations have undergone and continue to experience major changes. Among the main changes taking place in business ownership in Ireland are:

1. Co-operatives Becoming Public Limited Companies

Many co-operatives have changed their organisational structure and become public limited companies. Examples include Kerry Co-op, which is now Kerry plc, and Avonmore Co-op and Waterford Co-op, who merged to form Glanbia plc.

The main reasons why many co-ops have become public limited companies are as follows:

1. As a plc, the businesses can sell its shares on the Stock Exchange. This means that the former co-op can raise large amounts of money and use this to expand the business.

2. As a plc, the businesses can attract the very best managers to come work for it, because these managers would be more likely to work for a plc than a co-operative.

3. As a plc, the business attracts a lot of free publicity. Public limited companies are constantly written about in the newspapers and feature on the radio and TV as well. This publicity provides the former co-op with PR, which helps in the promotion of its products.

2. Privatisation of State-owned Enterprises

In recent years, the Irish government has sold off more and more of the companies it owns to private owners. In 2006 the government privatised Aer Lingus and Great Southern Hotels.

3. Irish Businesses Becoming Transnational Companies

A number of Irish businesses have become transnational companies. Examples include Smurfit Kappa, which is a paper and packaging company. It has branches in Europe, the USA and South America. Allied Irish Banks (AIB) has branches in the UK, USA and Poland. These businesses have become transnational companies because of our membership of the EU, increasing free trade worldwide and because of the small size of the Irish market.

3. Increasing Popularity of Franchises in Ireland

There has been a large increase in the number of Irish people setting up franchises. Examples include Starbucks, O'Briens Sandwich Bar, Domino's Pizza, Four Star Pizza, Days Hotels and so on. Irish people wishing to set up their own business have taken to franchising because there is a lower risk of their business failing.

4. Increasing Popularity of Alliances in Ireland

In recent years, there has been an increase in the number of Irish firms forming alliances with other businesses. This allows them to share costs, ideas and markets with their alliance partners. An Post and Fortis formed Postbank, an alliance to provide banking services in Irish post offices.

Why Businesses Change their Organisational Structure

Many businesses change their structure over time. For example, a sole trader might change her business to a private limited company. There are a number of reasons why a business changes its structure:

1. To Raise Capital

A major reason why a business would change its structure is the ability to get its hands on more money with a new structure. The more people that can invest in the business and better credit ratings enjoyed by some businesses make them an attractive choice when the entrepreneur needs more money to finance her business.

A private limited company, a state-owned enterprise or a co-operative would change its structure to a public limited company because this enables them to sell their shares on the Stock Exchange. The money raised from selling shares in this way can be used to finance the further expansion of the business.

Kerry Co-op became a public limited company so that it could sell shares to the public to raise money. It used this money to expand the business.

2. To Lower the Risk Faced by the Owners

Businesses may change their structure so as to reduce the risk the owners face. Certain businesses give the owner the advantage of limited liability. This means that if her business goes bankrupt, all she would lose is the money she invested in the business. All her other private assets are safe.

A sole trader has unlimited liability. She is personally liable for all the debts of her business. But, by changing her organisation structure to that of a private limited company, she protects her home and other private assets because they are no longer at risk, as they were when she was a sole trader.

3. To Increase Sales and Profits

If a business forms a strategic alliance with another business, this can give it the ability to sell more products. For example, An Post has a strategic alliance with Fortis whereby Fortis provides banking services in post offices around the country. This has lead to increased business for both.

Similarly, the Institute of Education's strategic alliance with *The Irish Independent* newspaper to produce the *Exam Brief* study supplement has given the Institute of Education increased publicity and has given the *Independent* increased sales.

If a business changes its structure to become a public limited company, it will enjoy increased publicity. Public limited companies are constantly written about in newspapers and referred to on radio and TV programmes. This gives the new business a better image and reputation, which will help it increase sales.

4. To Acquire Skills

A business may change its structure so as to acquire new skills. For example, a sole trader might enter into a partnership with others who have the skills she needs to expand and improve her business.

Ordinary Level Questions

EXAM SECTION 1 (25%) – SHORT ANSWER QUESTIONS [10 marks each]

1. List four different types of business organisations.

2. Explain the term "unlimited liability".

3. Outline two disadvantages of a sole trader as a type of business organisation.

4. What type of business organisation is a partnership?

5. List three reasons why a sole trader might expand to become a partnership.

6. Distinguish between a memorandum of association and articles of association.

7. What is a public limited company? Give two examples.

8. Outline two disadvantages of a public limited company as a type of business organisation.

9. Identify two differences between a public limited company and a private limited company.

10. Column 1 is a list of business terms. Column 2 is a list of possible explanations for these terms. Match the two lists by placing the letter of the correct explanation under the relevant number below. One explanation has no match.

Column 1	Column 2: Explanations
1. CEO	a) Invests capital in the company in return for shares in it
2. Shareholders	b) Acts as a figurehead leader for the company
3. Board of Directors	c) Prepares the company's financial accounts
4. Auditor	d) Sends out notice for and takes minutes of all company meetings
5. Company Secretary	e) Chief Executive Officer
6. Company Chairperson	f) Elected by shareholders to run the company for them
	g) Checks the company's accounts to make sure that they are correct

1	2	3	4	5	6
E					

11. Indicate whether each of the following (A, B, C, D and E) is true or false.

	Sentence	True or False
A	A private limited company can have only one shareholder.	
B	A public limited company can have only one shareholder.	
C	The rules for forming companies are contained in the Companies Formation Act, 2005.	
D	Companies pay a higher percentage of tax on their business profits than sole traders.	
E	The accounts of a company are more confidential than those of a sole trader.	

12. Explain what is meant by a co-operative and give two examples of co-operatives.

13. List four state-owned companies.

14. Name three companies that the government has privatised.

15. Define "franchising".

16. Outline two advantages of franchising as a type of business organisation.

17. Explain what is meant by a business alliance and illustrate your answer with an example.

18. Outline two advantages of an alliance as a type of business organisation.

19. Explain what is meant by a transnational company.

20. Outline two advantages of indigenous firms for Ireland.

EXAM SECTION 2 (75%) – LONG QUESTIONS

1. Explain three reasons why you would recommend that a friend set up her business as a sole trader. (15 marks)

2. Your friend has been invited to set up a business as a partnership with four other people. Outline three reasons why you think he should not do this. (15 marks)

3. Outline two differences between a sole trader and a private limited company. (10 marks)

4. Name the law that lists the rules for setting up a private limited company. Describe the steps involved in setting up a private limited company. (20 marks)

5. Discuss the advantages of a public limited company. (15 marks)

6. Explain the role of the "company secretary" and the "auditor" in a company. (20 marks)

7. Describe three types of co-operatives operating in Ireland. (15 marks)

8. Outline two advantages and two disadvantages of co-operatives. (20 marks)

9. Discuss the important role that state-owned enterprises play in Ireland. (20 marks)

10. Using examples, explain the term "privatisation". (10 marks)

11. Outline three reasons for privatisation.   (15 marks)

12. Define the term "franchising".   (10 marks)

13. Discuss two disadvantages of franchising.   (10 marks)

14. Explain, using examples, what is meant by the term "business alliance".   (15 marks)

15. Describe two differences between transnational and indigenous businesses.   (10 marks)

16. Describe three trends taking place in business ownership in Ireland.   (15 marks)

Higher Level Questions

EXAM SECTION 1 (20%) – SHORT ANSWER QUESTIONS [10 marks each]

1. A sole trader is a popular choice of business organisation in Ireland. List three other business organisations and explain any one of them.

2. Complete this sentence: Limited liability helps businesses because it…

3. Define the term "memorandum of association".

4. Illustrate your understanding of the term *ultra vires*.

5. What is a public limited company? Name two public limited companies.

6. Outline two differences between a co-operative and a public limited company.

7. Column 1 is a list of business terms. Column 2 is a list of possible explanations for these terms. Match the two lists by placing the letter of the correct explanation under the relevant number below. One explanation has no match.

Column 1	Column 2: Explanations
1. Deed of Partnership	a) Document that sets out the internal rules and regulations for running a company
2. Memorandum of Association	b) Document that sets out the internal rules and regulations for running a partnership
3. Articles of Association	c) Document that sets out the auditor's opinion as to the accuracy or otherwise of the company's accounts
4. Certificate of Incorporation	d) Document that sets out details of the company's secretary and directors
5. Form A1	e) Document that establishes a company in law
	f) Document that sets out the objectives of a company

1	2	3	4	5

8. What is a state-owned enterprise? Name two state-owned enterprises.

9. Distinguish between the terms "private limited company" and "privatisation".

10. Explain the term "franchising".

11. Complete this sentence: An alliance involves…

12. Illustrate your understanding of the term "transnational company".

13. What is an indigenous firm? Name two indigenous firms.

14. The following table shows three types of business organisation and four features. For each feature, tick (✔) the type of business organisation that is *most* likely to match that feature.

	Sole Trader	Private Limited Company	Co-op
Unlimited liability			
No maximum number of owners			
No official permission needed to set up the business			
Financial accounts are confidential			

EXAM SECTION 2 (20%) – APPLIED BUSINESS QUESTION – 80 MARKS

Erica Butler

After graduating from college with a diploma in computers, Erica Butler started working for a large transnational computer company called Replos, which makes computer parts in its factory in a town in the south of Ireland and employs almost half the people in the town. Thanks to her hard work in Replos, Erica now owns her own home, a new car and a holiday cottage on the coast.

Erica has seen the town transformed since Replos came. There are new restaurants, shops and houses. A number of factories have opened to supply Replos with materials. A new motorway makes the town more accessible and locals believe it will encourage further businesses to set up there.

The success of other businesses in the town inspired Erica to leave Replos to set up her own computer firm as a sole trader, six months ago. The local bank loaned her most of the money she needed because they were very impressed with all the experience and skills she had gained from working in Replos. However, Erica is finding it hard to cope with the demands of running a business. She is unsure how to go about marketing her products. She is running seriously short of money. The business needs a capital injection but the bank is unwilling to lend her any more. The stress of this combined with the long hours is making her question her choice.

(A) Discuss a sole trader as a suitable type of business organisation for Erica.   (25 marks)

(B) Recommend, with reasons, a more suitable form of
     business organisation for Erica.   (25 marks)

(C) Evaluate the importance of transnational companies,
     such as Replos, for Ireland.   (30 marks)

EXAM SECTION 3 (60%) – LONG QUESTIONS

1. Compare a sole trader and a partnership as types of business organisations.   (15 marks)

2. Contrast a partnership and a private limited company as types of
    business organisation.   (20 marks)

3. Outline the stages in the formation of a private limited company.   (15 marks)

4. Distinguish between a memorandum of association and
    articles of association.   (20 marks)

5. Discuss why many Irish co-operatives have expanded to become
    public limited companies.   (20 marks)

6. Differentiate between the role of shareholders and directors in a company.   (20 marks)

7. Discuss the arguments for and against state-owned companies.
    Use examples to illustrate your answer.   (30 marks)

8. Evaluate the impact of privatisation on the Irish economy.
    Use examples, where appropriate.   (30 marks)

9. Explain why you would recommend franchising as a type of
    business organisation for a new business venture.   (20 marks)

10. Contrast an alliance and a co-operative as types of business organisations.   (20 marks)

11. Contrast the importance of transnational and indigenous firms to Ireland.   (20 marks)

12. Discuss the changing trends in business ownership and
    structure in the Irish economy.   (25 marks)

13. Explain the reasons why businesses change their organisational structure
    over time. Use relevant examples to illustrate your answer.   (25 marks)

Categories of Industry

Over the last 15 years, Ireland has become a very wealthy country. How did Ireland make its money? Was it from potatoes or crystal glassware or computers or banking? In truth, all the different types of industry made a contribution to the country's economy.

The three categories of industry in Ireland are as follows:

1. Primary sector – extractive industry.
2. Secondary sector – manufacturing and construction industries.
3. Tertiary sector – services industry.

Primary Sector of the Economy

The primary sector of the economy is also called the extractive industry. It comprises all those businesses that are engaged in taking **raw materials** from nature. In Ireland, extractive/primary industries include:

- Agriculture – farmers take potatoes, carrots and so on from the ground.
- Fishing – fishermen catch cod, ray and so on from the sea.
- Forestry – foresters cut down trees.
- Mining – miners dig coal, zinc and so on from the ground.

Importance of Primary Sector to the Economy

1. Many people in Ireland work in agriculture, fishing, forestry and mining. They pay taxes on their wages and this gives the government more money, so it can improve Ireland's economy by reducing taxes, increasing grants and improving infrastructure.

2. Primary industries are a major consumer of Irish products, so they pump money into the economy. Farmers buy a huge amount of farm machinery, fertilisers, chemicals and so on. Fishermen buy boats and nets. Forestry and mining use lots of equipment.

Therefore, the primary sector increases the profits of Irish businesses involved in selling these products.

3. Primary/extractive industries export massive amounts of raw materials from Ireland, thus improving Ireland's balance of payments (*see Chapter 24*). This brings lots of money into the country. This money makes Irish farmers, fishermen, miners and those involved in forestry wealthier and the country richer.

4. Some primary industries provide food for the country. This reduces our need to import foreign food, thus improving our balance of payments.

Changing Trends in Primary Sector

1. The European Union (EU) has a big impact on Irish farmers' and fishermen's income. EU rules put a limit on how much food can be produced and how many fish can be caught. These limits are called **quotas** and are designed to stop over-production of food in the EU. By limiting how much they can produce, the EU is limiting how much Irish farmers and fishermen can earn. The EU fines farmers and fishermen if they go over their quotas.

2. A major trend in the primary sector is consumers' concerns about the quality of the food they eat. The demand for **organic foods** is increasing and many farmers are now starting to produce organic foods to cater to this market. All farmers must address the issue of disease, pesticides, pollution and genetically modified foods if they want consumers to continue to buy from them.

3. Extracting our own **natural resources** is helping Ireland to reduce its dependence on foreign oil. The country's natural gas reserves off the south and west coasts provide some of the energy we need. Wind farms are also becoming increasingly common. They harvest the wind and turn it into electricity.

4. Some farmers' incomes have reduced in recent times, because of EU changes and increased foreign competition. This is causing many farmers to look at alternative uses for their land. Many farmers are turning their land into **forests**. The government offers grants and tax exemptions if they do so. Thus, forestry is on the increase in Ireland.

Secondary Sector of the Economy

The secondary sector of the Irish economy consists of the **manufacturing** and **construction** industries.

Manufacturing Industry

Manufacturing takes the output from the primary industry and changes it into a totally different finished product. For example, Tayto is part of the manufacturing industry. It takes potatoes and uses them to make crisps. A carpenter takes wood and uses it to make furniture.

The Manufacturing Industry in Ireland includes:

- **Agri-businesses** – these take farm produce and transform it into food for consumers. Glanbia plc buys milk from farmers and uses it to make Yoplait yoghurt. Denny buys pigs from farmers to make rashers and sausages.

- **Indigenous firms** – these are Irish businesses set up by Irish people that make their products here in Ireland. For example, Lily O'Briens is an indigenous firm that makes chocolates.

- **Transnational companies** – these are foreign businesses that set up factories in Ireland to manufacture their products here. For example, Dell is a transnational company that manufactures computers here. Similarly, Intel makes computer parts here.

Importance of Manufacturing to the Economy

1. A lot of Irish people have jobs in manufacturing. They pay taxes on their wages and this gives the government more money, so it can improve Ireland's economy by reducing taxes, increasing grants and improving infrastructure.

2. Ireland exports a lot of the products that are manufactured here, which improves Ireland's balance of payments.

3. Manufacturing is a major consumer of raw materials. Manufacturers buy the output of the primary industry and turn it into finished goods to sell. This means that it provides a lot of income to those involved in the primary/extractive industry.

    Ribena buys 95% of all the blackcurrants grown in Ireland. Thus, Ribena increases the income of Irish farmers.

Tayto buys all its potatoes from Irish farmers (over 20,000 tonnes a year) and is one of the biggest users of potatoes in Ireland. It is therefore a major customer of Irish farmers and provides many of them with an income.

Changing Trends in Manufacturing Industry

1. Manufacturing industry is becoming more **capital intensive**. This means that it uses more and more machines (e.g. Computer Aided Design, Computer Aided Manufacture, robots and so on) and fewer employees. Therefore, fewer Irish people are now employed in manufacturing.

2. A lot of transnational manufacturing businesses have set up in Ireland to make their products here in order to gain access to EU markets. For example, Dell makes computers in Ireland.

3. Many labour-intensive clothes manufacturing companies have closed down because of competition from low-wage countries. For example, in May 2006, Fruit of the Loom closed its factory in Donegal and moved to Morocco, where it now manufactures its clothing.

Construction Industry

The construction industry consists of all those businesses involved in designing, producing and maintaining the built infrastructure of the economy. It includes those involved in building houses, schools, roads, factories, bridges and so on.

Importance of Construction Industry to the Economy

1. The construction industry is a labour-intensive industry; this means that it uses more people than machines. Therefore, the construction industry provides thousands of jobs in Ireland. Construction workers pay taxes on their wages and this gives the government more money, so it can improve Ireland's economy by reducing taxes, increasing grants and improving infrastructure.

2. Construction is a major consumer in the Irish economy. Builders buy a huge amount of sand, gravel and wood from the primary sector. Therefore, construction helps businesses involved in selling these products.

3. The construction industry builds the infrastructure (such as roads, airports, ports and so on) that is essential for Irish businesses to transport their products quickly and cheaply.

Changing Trends in Construction Industry

1. The late 1990s and early 2000s saw huge growth in the construction industry in Ireland, with a particular increase in the demand for new homes. There were not enough Irish builders to do all the work needed. This led to an influx of immigrant builders to satisfy the demand. However, there are signs of a slowdown starting in the construction industry.

2. The country is engaged in major infrastructural projects such as extending the M50 and joining up the two Luas lines in Dublin. These projects have provided a huge boost to the construction industry.

Tertiary Sector of the Economy

The tertiary sector comprises all those businesses that provide a service to consumers and to other businesses. These businesses do not take things from nature or make a physical product.

For example, DHL provides a courier service to Irish businesses, delivering their packages all over the world for them.

In Ireland, there are lots of service businesses. Banks (*see Chapter 13*) provide financial services (such as cheque books, laser cards, ATM cards and so on) to their customers. Meteor, eircom, and Vodafone provide communication services. Theatres, cinemas and TV stations such as RTE and TV3 provide entertainment services.

Importance of Tertiary Sector to the Economy

1. The services industry is by far the biggest employer of Irish people. The huge number of jobs it provides leads to lower unemployment in the economy. Employees pay taxes on their wages and this gives the government more money, so it can improve Ireland's economy by reducing taxes, increasing grants and improving infrastructure.

2. Ireland exports financial and software services (**invisible exports** – *see chapter 24*), thus improving our balance of payments. This means that the

tertiary sector brings lots of money into the country. This money makes Irish service providers wealthier and the country richer.

3. A well-developed service industry is essential to attract transnational companies to Ireland. Ireland's telecommunications and transport services play a vital role in this.

Changing Trends in Services Sector

1. There has been huge growth in the services industry. One reason for this is that Irish people have more money to spend than ever before. This wealth has led to increased demand for personal services such as tourism (weekend hotel breaks in Ireland) and entertainment (cinema, theatres and so on).

2. Ireland is exporting more and more services (such as software development and call centres). This brings in lots of money into the country. This money makes Irish service providers wealthier and the country richer.

3. Ireland has a thriving financial services sector. Half of the world's top 50 banks and half the top 20 insurance companies have located in the Irish Financial Services Centre (IFSC) in Dublin. Thousands of people work in the IFSC and it deals with investments worth over €500 billion.

Factors of Production

Manufacturers take raw materials and convert them into a totally different finished product. In business, we say that a manufacturer uses the four **factors of production** to make that product.

The factors of production are the four essential resources that entrepreneurs combine to make a product or service:

1. Land

Land refers to physical land and other **natural resources** used to make the products.
- Tayto use potatoes to make crisps.
- Cadbury uses milk to make chocolate.

2. Labour

Labour refers to the **human effort** (both physical and mental) used to make the products.
- A cake factory uses bakers to make the cakes.

3. Capital

Capital refers to **human-made goods** that are used in the production process, such as buildings, machinery, equipment, tools and so on.

● A factory making cakes uses ovens to bake the cakes.

● Tayto uses packing machines to pack its crisps into bags.

4. Enterprise

Enterprise is the skill of **combining** all these factors together to make the product. It involves an entrepreneur thinking of an idea, combining the factors of production and taking a risk to make the product.

● Joe Murphy thought of the idea for Tayto in 1954 when he spotted a market for flavoured crisps in Ireland.

Ordinary Level Questions

EXAM SECTION 1 (25%) – SHORT ANSWER QUESTIONS [10 marks each]

1. List the four primary industries in the Irish economy.

2. Outline two reasons why agriculture is important for the Irish economy.

3. What is an indigenous firm? Name an indigenous firm involved in manufacturing.

4. List two reasons why manufacturing is important to the Irish economy.

5. Distinguish between primary and secondary industries.

6. Identify three businesses in the service industry.

7. Column 1 is a list of business terms. Column 2 is a list of possible explanations for these terms. Match the two lists by placing the letter of the correct explanation under the relevant number below. One explanation has no match.

Column 1	Column 2: Explanations
1. IFSC	a) Natural resources that are used to make a product
2. Tertiary Industry	b) Involves an entrepreneur combining the factors of production to make a product
3. Land	
4. Labour	c) Human-made goods, such as machinery, that are used in the production of products
5. Capital	
6. Enterprise	d) Services industry
	e) Irish Financial Services Centre
	f) Limit on the amount of food that a farmer can produce
	g) Human effort involved in making products

1	2	3	4	5	6
E					

8. Indicate whether each of the following (A, B, C, D and E) is true or false.

	Sentence	True or False
A	A farmer operates in the primary/extractive sector.	
B	Tayto is an example of a business involved in the manufacturing industry.	
C	A hairdresser works in the extractive sector.	
D	A miner digging for coal is an example of a manufacturing industry.	
E	Taxi drivers are in the tertiary sector.	

9. Indicate, by means of a tick (✔), the category of industry to which each business belongs.

	Primary	Secondary	Services
Cadbury			
A cinema			
Dublin Bus			
A farmer growing potatoes			
Aer Lingus			

10. Indicate, by means of a tick (✔), the factor of production to which each item belongs.

	Land	Labour	Capital	Enterprise
Water				
Employees				
Bill Gates				
A factory				
A photocopier				

EXAM SECTION 2 (75%) – LONG QUESTIONS

1. Discuss the importance of the primary sector to the Irish economy. (15 marks)

2. Explain, using two examples, what is meant by the secondary sector of the economy. (15 marks)

3. List two benefits of a growing construction industry for the Irish economy. (10 marks)

4. Outline two changing trends taking place in Irish manufacturing. (10 marks)

5. Describe three benefits of the services sector for the Irish economy. (15 marks)

6. Describe the changes taking place in the Irish services sector. (15 marks)

Higher Level Questions

EXAM SECTION 1 (20%) – SHORT ANSWER QUESTIONS [10 marks each]

1. Illustrate your understanding of the term "primary sector of the economy".

2. Name a business involved in manufacturing. Explain two reasons why manufacturing is important to Ireland.

3. Illustrate your understanding of the term "agri-business".

4. Explain the term "construction industry". Illustrate its impact on the development of the Irish economy.

5. Distinguish between the secondary and tertiary sectors of the economy.

6. Column 1 is a list of business terms. Column 2 is a list of possible explanations for these terms. Match the two lists by placing the letter of the correct explanation under the relevant number below. One explanation has no match.

Column 1	Column 2: Explanations
1. Labour Intensive	a) A limit placed on the amount that can be produced
2. Capital Intensive	b) The roads, railways, bridges and so on that are required for an industrial economy to function
3. Infrastructure	
4. Quota	c) An industry that uses more workers than machines
5. Factors of Production	d) An industry that uses more machines than workers
	e) Natural resources used in the production process
	f) Four resources that are combined to make a product

1	2	3	4	5

7. Indicate, by means of a tick (✔), the category of industry to which each business belongs.

	Primary	Secondary	Services
Esso drilling for oil			
A carpenter making a chair			
An insurance company			
A coffee shop			
A factory making jeans			

8. Complete this sentence: In the context of production, land means…

9. Distinguish between labour and capital as factors of production.

10. Complete this sentence: As a factor of production, enterprise involves…

EXAM SECTION 2 (20%) – APPLIED BUSINESS QUESTION – 80 MARKS

> **John Connolly**
>
> John Connolly graduated with a degree in Agricultural Science in 2005. He spent a number of years working in farming abroad before returning to Ireland to buy and run his own farm. With the help of a government grant, he bought a small farm in the mid-west.
>
> John is a mixed farmer. He grows crops and rears cattle for dairy and beef purposes. His business has proved fairly successful in recent years. He has been so busy that he has had to hire a number of local people to work for him. He sells most of his milk to the local dairy and the rest of his produce to a food manufacturing company located some 5 miles away. John spends a whole afternoon each week travelling to and from the factory on bad roads to deliver his produce.
>
> John faces other problems in his business. Competition from other EU farmers is fierce and John is often shocked at the amount of foreign milk and vegetables that he sees for sale in the supermarket. Things are tough in farming and John knows he could not survive without ongoing grants and payments from the Irish government. Without this government money, he does not know how he could buy all the farm equipment and fertilisers and chemicals his business requires.

(A)   Discuss the importance of businesses in the primary sector, like John's, to the Irish economy.   (20 marks)

(B)   Evaluate how a downturn in the secondary sector could impact on John's business.   (20 marks)

EXAM SECTION 3 (60%) – LONG QUESTIONS

1. Describe the categories of industry in the Irish economy.   (20 marks)

2. Evaluate the impact on Ireland of a downturn in the primary sector.   (20 marks)

3. Analyse how changing trends are impacting the primary sector.   (20 marks)

4. Compare the importance of the construction and manufacturing sectors to the Irish economy.   (20 marks)

5. Describe important changes taking place in the secondary sector of the economy.   (20 marks)

6. What is the services sector? Explain its role in the development of the Irish economy.   (20 marks)

7. Evaluate the importance of the Irish Financial Services Centre to the Irish economy.   (10 marks)

8. Discuss three changes taking place in Ireland's tertiary sector.   (15 marks)

9. Describe, for a business of your choice, the factors of production it uses to make its product or service.   (25 marks)

CHAPTER 21

Business, The Economy and Government

Business is extremely important to Ireland. It creates millions of jobs for Irish people and it generates a lot of tax revenue for the government to spend on essential services such as schools, hospitals, roads and gardaí.

Because the government knows how important business is, it tries to create the right climate for business to flourish. However, the government also regulates business activities to ensure that businesses do not damage the environment, or treat employees or customers badly.

Government's Role in Creating a suitable Climate for Business

The government tries to help business in the following ways:

1. Government Economic Planning

The government agrees **national pay deals** (also known as national agreements) with the **social partners**. The social partners include the Irish Business and Employers Confederation (IBEC), the Irish Congress of Trade Unions (ICTU), the Construction Industry Federation (CIF) and the Irish Farmers Association (IFA). The social partners agree a *reasonable* pay rise for Irish workers over the next few years in return for the promise of lower taxes and more jobs.

STRONGER TOGETHER
CONGRESS
Irish Congress of Trade Unions

These national pay deals create a suitable climate for a business enterprise in a number of ways:

- Reasonable wage increases help to keep a business's **costs low**. Lower costs mean that the business can charge a lower price for its products. Charging lower prices helps Irish businesses to sell more goods at home and abroad, thus increasing their sales and profits.

- National agreements have led to **better industrial relations** in Ireland. Employers and employees have fewer disagreements about pay because wage increases are agreed in advance for the next number of years.

- Businesses can **plan for the future** more accurately because they know in advance the pay increases they will have to give their workers.

The current national agreement is called *Towards 2016*.

2. Government Expenditure

Government expenditure is the money that the state spends every year. It is divided into **current spending** on wages of state workers and **capital spending** on the country's infrastructure. This expenditure helps business as follows:

- The government buys billions of euro worth of products and services from businesses every year (Garda uniforms and school desks, for example). This leads to increased sales and profits for business enterprises in the economy.

- The government spends money improving Ireland's infrastructure (roads, airports, sea ports and so on). This makes it easier, quicker and cheaper for businesspeople to transport their goods around the country.

3. Government Agencies

The government has set up a number of state-owned enterprises to help businesspeople.

Enterprise Ireland
Helps indigenous (Irish) businesses to set up in the following ways:
- Helps an entrepreneur to draw up her business plan.
- Provides the entrepreneur with grants to pay for machines, buildings, workers' wages and so on.
- Provides equity investment for the business (i.e. it buys shares in the business).

IDA Ireland
Attracts transnational companies to come to Ireland, by offering them grants and promoting Ireland as a low-tax country with plenty of highly educated and skilled workers.

Fáilte Ireland
Provides advice to businesses involved in the tourism industry. It trains people to work in the tourism sector. And it spends money developing tourist projects around the country.

FÁS

- Trains an entrepreneur's workers in the skills needed for the business.
- Finds workers for the business (by providing a free recruitment service).

Bord Bia

Helps Irish food and drink companies to sell their products abroad by promoting Irish food and drink at trade fairs throughout the world.

Údarás na Gaeltachta

Provides grants and advice to entrepreneurs setting up a business in Gaeltacht (Irish-speaking) regions of Ireland.

4. Government Taxation

The government can lower taxes to create a suitable climate for a business enterprise.

- ◑ When the government lowers the taxes on wages (PAYE and PRSI – *see Chapter 12*), workers have more **disposable income** (money) to spend in shops. Thus, lower taxes lead to an increase in businesses' sales and profits.

- ◑ Lower business taxes increase the profits to be made from running a business. This encourages enterprise and investment in Ireland. For example, the government lowered corporation tax from 16% in 2002 to $12\frac{1}{2}$% in 2003.

5. Government Grants

Grants are money that the government gives to businesspeople to help them pay for things that they need, such as machines, computers, training and so on. The money does not have to be repaid if the business satisfies all the conditions of getting the grant.

Grants create a suitable climate for business enterprises as follows:

- ◑ Grants make it cheaper to set up a business. The government pays for part of the costs involved.

- ◑ Grants attract transnational companies to set up in Ireland. These transnationals buy from Irish businesses, thus increasing their sales and profits.

Government's Role in Controlling Business (Govt. Regulation)

Although the government seeks to encourage business in Ireland, it does not allow it to act unchecked. It **regulates** business for the good of society.

The government has passed many laws to control the activities of business and to protect employees, consumers and society from the actions of businesses.

Law	Effect on Business
Companies Act, 1990	This law ensures that companies are correctly set up and regularly monitored by the Registrar of Companies.
Data Protection Act, 1988	Businesses that keep information about others on computer have a number of responsibilities, including ensuring they get that data fairly, keep it safe, use it only for the purpose given, give the person a copy and so on.
Sale of Goods and Supply of Services Act, 1980	Businesses *must* give refunds to customers if the products they sell them are not of merchantable quality (fit for their purpose, as described or the same as the sample shown).
Consumer Information Act, 1978	Businesses must give consumers truthful information about their products, prices and in advertisements. If not, they will be taken to court by the National Consumer Agency.
Industrial Relations Act, 1990	Businesses cannot stop official striking workers from peacefully picketing outside the business. Nor can they sue the workers for losses suffered as a result of the strike.
Unfair Dismissals Act, 1977/93	Businesses cannot sack employees without a just reason.
Employment Equality Act, 1998	Businesses cannot discriminate against workers on the grounds of gender, age, sexuality, disability, family status, marital status, membership of the travelling community, beliefs or race.

How Government affects the Labour Force

The **labour force** comprises all those people in Ireland who are either in work or are looking for work (i.e. all those available for work). The government can affect these people as follows:

1. National Agreements

The deals agreed between the government and the social partners keep wage costs relatively low. This allows businesses to sell their goods at low prices, which leads to higher sales. More workers are then needed to make the products to satisfy this increased demand. Thus, the national agreements help to increase the number of jobs available for people in the labour force.

2. Lower Taxes on Wages

By reducing the rates of PAYE and PRSI taxes it takes from employees' wages, the government increases the amount of disposable income that employees have to spend. This enables employees in the labour force to have a higher standard of living and buy more goods and services, which also helps to increase the number of jobs available to people in the labour force.

3. Government Expenditure

The Irish government spends a lot of money buying goods and services from businesses. This helps to create and maintain jobs in these businesses, thus increasing the number of jobs available to people in the labour force. Similarly, the government's infrastructure projects (such as building new Luas lines in Dublin, extending the M50 and so on) help to increase the number of jobs available to people in the labour force.

4. Government Regulation

Government regulation is the laws the government has passed to control the activities of business and to protect people from the actions of businesses. The National Minimum Wage Act ensures that all employees in the labour force earn a basic wage. Other laws dealing with discrimination and unfair dismissal give employees in the labour force guaranteed rights and protection from bosses who might otherwise treat them badly.

5. Government as Employer

The Irish government is the biggest employer in Ireland. It employs people in the **civil service** (those who work in the various government departments), the **public service** (such as doctors, nurses and teachers) and in **state-owned enterprises** (such as CIÉ). Thus, the government helps to increase the numbers of jobs available to people in the labour force.

Impact of Economic Variables on Business

The state of Ireland's economy can be judged under a number of headings: inflation, interest rates, unemployment, exchange rates and the levels of tax in the country. Each one of these affects business in different ways.

Inflation

Inflation is the annual percentage increase in the level of prices in the economy. It is measured using the **Consumer Price Index**, whereby the price of an average family's shopping is checked every month. When the price of that shopping goes up, this is called **inflation**.

When inflation is high and prices are increasing in the economy, this is bad for business because:

1. Workers ask for higher wages to enable them to afford the higher prices in shops. Higher wages increase a business's costs and reduce its profits. If a business refuses the pay rise, the workers may go on strike, leading to bad industrial relations.

2. Consumers don't buy as much in shops because they can't afford to pay the higher prices. This leads to lower sales and profits for businesses.

3. The cost of the business's materials increases. This increases the business's costs and lowers its profits.

> **Ireland's current inflation rate is** _____

Interest Rates

Interest rates are the cost of borrowing money expressed as a percentage of the amount borrowed. Interest rates in Ireland are determined by the European Central Bank (ECB). When interest rates rise, so too do loan repayments, with the following consequences for business:

EUROPEAN CENTRAL BANK

EUROSYSTEM

1. Businesses can't afford the higher loan repayments and don't take out loans to expand.

2. The repayments on the business's existing loans increase. This leads to higher costs and lower profits for the business.

3. Higher mortgage repayments leave consumers with less income to spend buying goods and services. This leads to lower sales and profits for businesses.

Unemployment

The rate of unemployment is the percentage of the labour force (all the people in Ireland who could work) who do not have a job.

When unemployment is increasing in the economy, this affects business as follows:

1. The government increases taxes to pay for the extra social welfare it must give to the unemployed. Higher taxes taken from business profits reduce the profits left for the business owners to invest.

2. Unemployed people do not have a lot of money. More unemployed people means less money spent in shops, which lowers businesses' profits.

3. Higher unemployment makes it easier for businesses to find employees to fill vacancies. It can also lead to lower wages because some people will be willing to work for low wages rather than stay on the dole.

4. Higher unemployment may lead to more crime in society. This increases a business's insurance costs and decreases its profits.

> **Ireland's current rate of unemployment is** _____

Exchange Rates

The exchange rate for the euro tells you how much €1 is worth in terms of another currency. In other words, it tells you how much of a foreign currency you will get for €1.

Example
■ An Irish business sells whiskey for €100 a bottle.
■ When it sells the whiskey in the USA, the business must convert the price into US dollars. This is done by multiplying the €100 price by the rate of exchange.
■ If the rate of exchange is €1 = $1.20, the whiskey sells in the USA for $120 a bottle.
■ If the rate of exchange *increases* to €1 = $1.35, the whiskey will now sell for $135 a bottle.

■   Because the whiskey is now dearer in the USA, the Irish company will sell less of it in the USA.

The exchange rate for the euro impacts on Irish business in a number of ways.

1.   When the euro *increases* in value, the price of Irish products sold in non-euro countries (such as USA and UK) *increases*. This means that Irish exporters will sell fewer products in non-euro countries. Irish exporters' sales and profits fall.

2.   When the euro increases in value, the price of foreign (non-euro) goods sold in Ireland decreases. This means that Irish people buy more foreign goods. This leads to lower sales and profits for Irish businesses.

3.   When the euro increases in value, the price of foreign (non-euro) goods sold in Ireland decreases. This means that Irish businesses pay less for imported goods. An Irish restaurant will pay less for the New Zealand lamb it buys, for instance. This lowers the costs for Irish businesses that import and it increases its profits.

Taxation

Tax is the compulsory payment that must be made to the government in return for the benefits of living or doing business in Ireland.

When taxes are increasing in the economy, this is bad for business because:

1.   Businesses have to give more of their profits away to the government as self-assessment tax or corporation tax and so have less left for themselves for expansion.

2.   If PAYE and PRSI taxes on employees' wages increase, employees have less disposable income to spend in shops. Businesses' sales and profits fall as a result.

3.   Higher VAT added to the price of products sold in shops makes them more expensive. Consumers can't afford the higher prices and so buy less. Businesses' sales and profits fall.

Impact of Business on the Economy

Not only does the state of the Irish economy affect Irish business, but business affects the economy. Business can have a positive and a negative impact on the Irish economy.

Positive Impact of Business on the Economy

Businesses **create jobs**. This leads to lower unemployment in the economy. Dell and Intel alone employ thousands of people in their Irish factories.

Lower unemployment means the government spends less on welfare and receives more taxes from all those at work. This gives the government a lot more money to spend on improving the economy by increasing grants, improving roads and lowering taxes.

Businesses **buy materials and services** from other businesses, such as suppliers and service providers. This leads to the creation of more businesses to supply them and hence more wealth in the economy. For example, Ribena buys a huge amount of fruit from Irish farmers.

Competition between businesses forces them to keep prices low to compete. Low prices lead to **low inflation** in the economy. Ryanair is an example of a business helping to lower inflation. The competition that it created in the Irish airline industry means that flights are cheaper now than they were 20 years ago. Similarly, Dunnes Stores and Tesco have had to keep prices low to compete with Lidl and ALDI.

Businesses **create wealth** for the entrepreneur (profits) and the employees (wages). Entrepreneurs and employees spend their wealth buying from other businesses (pubs, restaurants, hotels, department stores and so on). This leads to more businesses and more wealth in the economy.

Negative Impact of Business on the Economy

Competition between businesses can lead to firms having to **close down**. Many Irish factories have closed down because they cannot compete with the prices that low-wage economies can sell their products for. This causes an increase in **unemployment**, which leads to lower tax revenue and higher unemployment benefit bills for the government. The result is that the government has less money to spend improving the economy.

To increase profits, businesses may **increase prices**. This will lead to an increase in inflation, which is harmful to the economy.

In order to make large profits, businesses may **damage the environment** (by dumping waste instead of paying to have it safely disposed of, for example). This will harm the economy, especially the food and tourism sectors because people will not buy Irish food or holiday here if Ireland is considered to be polluted.

Successful businesses lead to **pressure on infrastructure**. (For example, traffic jams on the M50 may be due in part to the number of shopping centres located just off the motorway.) This slows down the transporting of goods and increases the costs of doing business.

Ordinary Level Questions

EXAM SECTION 1 (25%) – SHORT ANSWER QUESTIONS [10 marks each]

1. Outline two ways in which government expenditure can help business.

2. List four state-owned enterprises that help Irish business.

3. What is a grant? Explain how grants help business.

4. Name three laws that the government has passed to regulate the activities of business.

5. Outline two ways in which the Irish government affects the labour force.

6. List three economic variables.

7. Outline two ways in which low inflation can affect business.

8. Explain the term "unemployment".

9. Indicate whether each of the following (A, B, C, D and E) is true or false.

	Sentence	True or False
A	Higher inflation may cause workers to ask for a pay rise.	
B	When interest rates increase, consumers tend to buy more from businesses.	
C	High unemployment in the economy leads to higher taxes.	
D	When the euro increases in value, Irish products become cheaper in the USA and we sell more.	
E	Interest rates in Ireland are set by the government.	

10. Outline two ways in which low interest rates can affect business.

11. Is unemployment in Ireland high or low? Explain how this affects Irish business.

12. Outline two ways in which lower taxes affect business.

13. Distinguish between inflation rate and exchange rate.

14. Outline two ways in which business in Ireland helps the economy.

15. Column 1 is a list of business terms. Column 2 is a list of possible explanations for these terms. Match the two lists by placing the letter of the correct explanation under the relevant number below. One explanation has no match.

Column 1		
1. IBEC	4.	IDA Ireland
2. Government Expenditure	5.	FÁS
3. Enterprise Ireland	6.	Bord Bia

Column 2: Explanations
a)   Attracts transnational companies to Ireland
b)   Percentage of the labour force that does not have a job
c)   Promotes the Irish food and drink industry
d)   Trains Irish workers in the skills needed by business
e)   Irish Business and Employers Confederation
f)   Money that the government spends every year
g)   Helps indigenous Irish entrepreneurs to set up a business

1	2	3	4	5	6
E					

EXAM SECTION 2 (75%) – LONG QUESTIONS

1. Describe three measures taken by the government to help Irish business.   (15 marks)

2. Outline the role of Enterprise Ireland.   (10 marks)

3. Explain the term "labour force". Describe three ways in which the Irish government affects the labour force.   (20 marks)

4. What is inflation?   (10 marks)

5. Give three reasons why high inflation is bad for business.   (15 marks)

6. List three benefits of low unemployment for Irish business.   (15 marks)

7. Identify two disadvantages of the euro increasing in value against the US dollar for Irish business.   (10 marks)

8. Describe the impact of an increase in taxes on business.   (15 marks)

9. Outline four effects (two good and two bad) of business on the Irish economy.   (20 marks)

Higher Level Questions

EXAM SECTION 1 (20%) – SHORT ANSWER QUESTIONS [10 marks each]

1. Distinguish between Enterprise Ireland and IDA Ireland.

2. Complete this sentence: Government expenditure helps a business to…

3. Explain the term "government grant". Evaluate the impact of grants on the development of the Irish economy.

4. Outline two ways in which the government affects Irish business.

5. Define "labour force".

6. Illustrate your understanding of the term "government regulation".

7. Distinguish between inflation and interest rates.

8. What do the letters ECB stand for? Explain the impact of the ECB on Irish business.

9. Explain why a high unemployment rate is bad for Irish business.

10. Define "exchange rate".

EXAM SECTION 2 (20%) – APPLIED BUSINESS QUESTION – 80 MARKS

Julie's Jewels Ltd.

Julie Crowley owns and runs her own jewellery manufacturing business, Julie's Jewels. Enterprise Ireland helped her pay for the expensive equipment she needed and advised her to set the business up as a private limited company. This proved to be good advice because Julie finds this type of business leaves her with more profits to pay for expansion.

Julie's designs have proved so popular that she has had to hire a number of full and part-time staff to help out. Recently, she managed to beat a number of high-profile jewellers with her superior designs and lower prices to win a major contract to supply the government with jewellery as presents for visiting dignitaries. She now exports to a number of countries worldwide but is proud of the fact that she still sources all her materials from indigenous Irish suppliers.

Julie's business has encountered problems, though. The increasing cost of materials from suppliers has put a dent in her profits. Finding good design staff is not as easy as she had hoped because almost all the design graduates in Ireland have jobs lined up before leaving college. A number of Irish customers have cancelled orders for large items of jewellery, citing excessive loan repayments as the reason. One American department store cancelled a €100,000 order at the last minute, complaining bitterly about the price increase. Julie cannot understand this, as she has always charged the store €100,000 for such orders. On a more positive note, IBEC has advised Julie that wage increases for the country have been agreed at 10% over the next three years.

(A) Analyse how assistance from the government has helped Julie's business.   (25 marks)

(B) Evaluate the impact of the economic variables (factors) on Julie's business.   (30 marks)

(C) Evaluate the impact of Julie's business on the Irish economy.   (25 marks)

EXAM SECTION 3 (60%) – LONG QUESTIONS

1. Evaluate the role of the Irish government in creating a suitable climate
    for business in this country.   (25 marks)

2. Explain the various ways in which government affects the labour force.   (25 marks)

3. Outline the impact of exchange rates and taxation on business.   (20 marks)

4. Contrast the effects of higher inflation and higher grants on Irish business.   (20 marks)

5. Illustrate the importance of low interest rates for Irish business.   (10 marks)

6. Discuss the significance of business activity for the Irish economy.   (20 marks)

CHAPTER 22

Community Development

Although Ireland is one of the wealthiest countries in the world, many communities in Ireland still face problems of disadvantage. However, rather than just putting up with these problems or waiting for others to solve them, a lot of communities attempt to solve their problems themselves.

Community Devlopment

Community development is when local people come together to identify the main problems in their area and develop a plan to solve these problems themselves.

It involves local people regenerating their area in a number of ways, often by starting a local community business.

For example, local people in Rathgormack, Co. Waterford built a community centre for their village. To help pay for its upkeep, they convert the centre into a tourist hostel every summer. The money they make from the hostel enables the community to use the centre for its own social and cultural needs during the winter.

Importance of Community Development

1. It creates **jobs** and businesses for local people. The wages or profits they receive give them a higher standard of living than they would have had if they stayed on social welfare.

2. Local people spend the **money** they make from their job or business in their local shops, pubs, restaurants, banks, hotels and so on. This helps these businesses to succeed as well. Thus community enterprise has a spin-off effect.

3. It creates a new breed of **entrepreneurs** in the local area. People in the community see their friends and neighbours set up businesses and this motivates them to set up a business themselves. This leads to more enterprise and wealth in the community.

4. The government receives **taxes** from the new businesses and also has to pay out less on social welfare benefits because fewer people in the community are

unemployed. This increases the money the government has available to spend on local hospitals, schools, gardaí and roads.

5. The **infrastructure** in the local area improves. Shops open because people now have money to spend. New houses are built to house the workers. Roads are improved to make it easier to do business. The entire local economy is transformed.

Community Development Organisations

Many organisations have been established to help local people to set up a community business:

1. Area Partnership Companies

Area Partnership Companies (APCs) are organisations that help local people to set up a business in their area. Each APC develops an Area Action Plan to help its community address the problems of disadvantage that it faces.

Examples include Galway City Partnership, Dublin Inner City Partnership (DICP) and Waterford Area Partnership.

Area Partnership Companies provide the following assistance to local community businesses:

1. They provide community businesses with **grants** to help pay for setting up the business. These grants are used to purchase the computers, machinery and equipment that the business needs.

2. They organise **workshops** to train local people in all the skills needed to run a community business successfully, such as business plans, marketing, accounts and taxation. They also provide ongoing advice for community businesses to help them deal with the day-to-day problems of running a business.

3. They provide the community business with **premises** to operate from, called "enterprise incubation units". Some also offer secretarial assistance such as meeting rooms, and call answering and message taking services.

4. The APC assigns a **mentor** to work with the community business. The mentor is

an experienced businessperson. If the business has any problems, it can contact the mentor, who can give practical advice based upon experience, to solve these problems. He also suggests improvements needed in the overall running of the business.

2. County and City Enterprise Boards

County and City Enterprise Boards (CEBs) were set up by the government to help small local businesses with the aim of creating a strong local economy.

Examples include Wexford County Enterprise Board, Donegal County Enterprise Board, Dublin City Enterprise Board and Limerick City Enterprise Board.

County and City Enterprise Boards help local community businesses in the following ways:

1. They provide **advice** and information to local people on how to go about setting up a business. This includes advice regarding business registration, patenting (protecting an idea) and company law requirements. They also provide access to a large range of business newspapers and magazines and the Internet to help local people find out as much information as possible before setting up a business.

2. They offer a whole range of **grants** to help the community business to start up, develop and expand. Feasibility grants are provided to help the community business to establish whether its idea is likely to be successful. Capital grants are available to pay for the machinery and equipment the community business needs. Employment grants are given to help with the costs of employing workers.

3. County and City Enterprise Boards run **workshops** and courses to train local people in all the skills needed to successfully run a community business, such as sales and marketing, financial management and information technology.

4. They provide the community business with a **mentor**. A mentor is an experienced businessperson. If the business runs into any problems, it can contact the mentor, who will offer impartial and expert advice on how to solve these problems.

3. The Community Services Programme

The Community Services Programme is a community development scheme set up by the Department of Community, Rural and Gaeltacht Affairs. Its aim is to help not-for-profit community businesses to address disadvantage in their area and create local employment. The programme is run by Pobal, an organisation that manages various programmes on behalf of the government and the EU.

The types of business it supports include community childcare services, rural transport for isolated rural communities, rural tourism, managing community halls, community radio and recycling and environmental projects.

The Community Services Programme helps such businesses in a number of ways:

1. It provides **grants** for three years to community businesses that provide services and employment to particularly disadvantaged groups in society such as members of the travelling community, disabled people, the elderly, ex-offenders and recovering substance abusers.

2. The grants are given to pay for the **costs** of running a business, staff training and buying fixed assets (such as computers, equipment and so on).

3. The Community Services Programme pays the **wages** of the manager and workers in the community enterprise (up to certain maximum limits). At least 70% of the workers must come from a particularly disadvantaged group.

4. It provides the community business with **advice** and training in general areas of business management, but especially in managing its finances.

Ordinary Level Questions

EXAM SECTION 1 (25%) – SHORT ANSWER QUESTIONS [10 marks each]

1. Explain the term "community development".
2. List four benefits that a community business can bring to a local area.
3. Name three organisations that help local community development.
4. What is the role of a mentor in business?

EXAM SECTION 2 (75%) – LONG QUESTIONS

1. Outline three benefits of local community development.   (15 marks)
2. Describe three ways in which an Area Partnership Company assists community development.   (15 marks)

3. A friend of yours is thinking about setting up a business but is unsure how to go about it. Describe three ways in which a City or County Enterprise Board will help your friend to set up his business.   (15 marks)

4. Describe the aim of the Community Services Programme run by Pobal.   (10 marks)

Higher Level Questions

EXAM SECTION 1 (20%) – SHORT ANSWER QUESTIONS [10 marks each]

1. Illustrate your understanding of the term "community enterprise".

2. Outline two reasons why local business is important to a local community.

3. What do the letters CEB stand for? Explain the role of a CEB in business.

4. Complete this sentence: Being a mentor involves….

5. Distinguish between capital grants and feasibility grants.

6. Explain the objective of the Community Services Programme. Identify two types of business that it helps.

EXAM SECTION 2 (20%) – APPLIED BUSINESS QUESTION – 80 MARKS

Sandyrock

Sandyrock is a disadvantaged area in one of the big cities in Ireland. It suffers from a number of social problems including unemployment, poverty, crime, poorly designed high-rise council tower blocks and a lack of adequate shops and facilities for local people. Justin Daly grew up in Sandyrock. After being unemployed for a number of years, he recently decided to set up his own business in the area. His business manufactures frames for photographs and pictures.

The success of Justin's business has inspired his friend Barbara to think about setting up her own business in Sandyrock. Although she has not conducted any market research, she is convinced that her idea of bus tours of Sandyrock will be a winner. She intends to eventually hire local people from the area. She asked Justin for advice about setting up a business and he told her to contact one of the local community development organisations in the area.

Barbara is worried that her lack of any business experience will hold her back. She realises that she can't keep asking Justin for advice and is unsure how to proceed.

(A) Analyse the likely impact of Justin's business on Sandyrock if it continues to succeed.   (30 marks)

(B) Describe how the services provided by one community development organisation of your choice can assist Barbara.   (20 marks)

EXAM SECTION 3 (60%) – LONG QUESTIONS

1. Define "community development". Explain its importance for
    local communities throughout Ireland.   (30 marks)

2. Evaluate the role of Area Partnership Companies in assisting community
    development.   (25 marks)

3. In the context of community development, compare the services provided
    by any two community development organisations.   (20 marks)

4. Martina is setting up a not-for-profit community childcare business
    in Tralee. Describe how the Community Services Programme run by Pobal
    can help her.   (20 marks)

Social Responsibility

The main purpose of a business is to make a profit. The entrepreneur is primarily responsible for generating this profit because she sets up the business and makes all the major decisions.

But the entrepreneur depends on many people to help the business succeed. She relies on **employees** to work hard and make excellent products that people will want. The entrepreneur also needs loyal **customers** to buy the products, **investors** to provide the finance needed and the **government** to give grants and tax breaks.

All these people contribute to the business's success. So, as well as concentrating on its main goal of profit, a business also has to look after these people. Treating them well is essential and is called a business's **social responsibility**.

Social Responsibility of Business

The social responsibility of a business is its duty to treat all those it comes into contact with honestly and fairly. The business has an obligation to do good and make a *positive contribution* to the lives of the people and the environment it affects.

- ▶ For example, Vodafone fulfils its social responsibility by giving time off to its employees who volunteer for charity work and by co-operating with the National Council for the Blind of Ireland to make text-to-speech mobile phones for blind people.

- ▶ O2 Ireland has published a guide to dealing with mobile phone bullying and a parents' guide to mobile phones as part of its commitment to child protection.

- ▶ Bank of Ireland actively recruits people with a disability. Its "Bank of Ireland – I can" scheme tries to help people with a disability to get a job.

Businesses have a social responsibility to a number of stakeholders.

Investors

Investors provide the capital that the business needs to set up and expand. The business therefore has a responsibility to its investors to give them honest financial information about how the business is doing and to pay them a reasonable dividend (share of the profits).

> A US company called WorldCom deliberately falsified its accounts to present a good picture of the business so that people would continue to invest in it, even though, in reality, it was going through a very bad patch. The company subsequently went bankrupt and most of the investors lost all their money. It was not fair to the investors to lie to them. The business owed them the truth.

Employees

Employees are the people who work in the business and carry out the tasks needed to make it a success. The business has a responsibility to its employees to pay them a fair wage for the work they do, to provide them with safe working conditions and not to discriminate against them.

> In 2006, a subcontractor working for the ESB in its Moneypoint, Co Clare station paid Polish workers considerably less than the going rate for the job. This is not fair to these workers. The company owes them a decent rate of pay for a decent day's work.

> The board of management of an all-boys primary school in Co Wicklow refused to hire a woman teacher for the job of principal because they though that a man would be better in an all-boys school. This is not socially responsible behaviour.

Customers

Customers are the people who buy the business's products and services, thus providing it with a profit. The business has a responsibility to its customers to provide them with good quality products and services at a reasonable price, to deal with their complaints fairly and to advertise to them in a legal, decent, honest and responsible way.

> A Tipperary car dealer was found guilty of tampering with the milometer on a car he sold to a customer. He certainly did not fulfil his social responsibility to his customers.

Government

The government helps businesses in many ways, including giving them grants, improving Ireland's infrastructure and lowering taxes. Because the government does so much for the business, the business has a responsibility to the government to obey all the laws of the country and to pay its taxes in full and on time.

National Irish Bank was found to have encouraged Irish people to evade tax in the 1990s by opening bogus non-resident accounts, whereby people pretended that they didn't live in Ireland so that they wouldn't have to pay the tax on the interest earned on their savings.

Local Communities

The community consists of all the people living in the area around a business. All businesses must protect the local environment and help the community by buying from local suppliers and hiring local people.

As part of its social responsibility, Tesco Ireland claims that it tries to buy the maximum possible amount of Irish-made products.

Coca-Cola has been heavily criticised for causing extreme water shortages in developing countries where supplies are scarce. It had to close its factory in Kerala, India after it was alleged to have contaminated the local water supply.

Advantages of Being Socially Responsible

1. **Consumers** like socially responsible businesses. Most consumers care about the environment and about society and prefer to buy from businesses whose ethics and social responsibility programmes they agree with.
    - For example, The Body Shop enjoys high sales because of its stance on human rights issues and buying materials from poorer communities.

2. **Employees** like to work for businesses that are socially responsible, i.e. ones that pay decent wages and offer good conditions. This makes it easier for such firms to recruit and keep workers.

3. Socially responsible businesses find it easier to attract **capital**. An increasing number of investors care how and where the capital they provide is used. They would not want their money funding illegal or harmful activities. For example, there are many "green" investment funds that attract billions of euro of capital for socially responsible businesses.

4. The business saves **money** in the long run. If a business behaves properly now, no one will have a reason to sue it in the future for bad business practices. Thus the socially responsible business will save money by avoiding costly law suits and consumer boycotts in the future.

   ○ For example, Shell would have saved money if it had disposed of an old oil rig properly instead of dumping it in the North Sea. This socially irresponsible act led to a consumer boycott that cost the company millions in lost sales.

Business Ethics

Business ethics is a set of moral principles that guide businesspeople regarding how they should act in business situations. It tells business people what is the right thing to do and what is the wrong thing in a given situation.

Ethical business practice means conducting business according to a set of moral principles. This ensures the business behaves in an honest, fair and legal manner. It means doing the right thing in all situations, regardless of the effect on profit.

○ The Body Shop behaves ethically. It refuses to test its products on animals, it pays a fair price to its suppliers and it supports human rights campaigns.

○ Many businesses are now selling products with the FAIRTRADE mark. Fairtrade is an organisation that promotes ethical trade with Third World countries by ensuring that producers and workers get a fair price or wage and better conditions.

How to Improve Business Ethics

1. Managers Must Lead By Example

If managers want their business to be ethical, they must set a good example for their employees. They have to behave ethically themselves at all times. They must disapprove of and punish unethical behaviour and reward ethical behaviour. This shows employees how seriously ethics is valued in the business and motivates them to behave ethically.

For example, if a shop manager sees an employee treating foreign-national customers badly, she must reprimand that worker and let him know that such behaviour is unacceptable. Otherwise, the unethical behaviour will continue.

2. Managers Must Encourage Employees to Report Others

If managers want their business to be ethical, they must know about unethical practices in their business so that they can then take steps to stamp them out. They have to encourage employees to report any instances of unethical behaviour they witness. This is called **whistle-blowing**.

- ◐ AIB runs a confidential phone helpline whereby concerned employees can report to the top managers any examples of unethical behaviour in the bank.

- ◐ The Irish government set up a similar helpline to allow people to report examples of foreign workers being exploited in Ireland.

3. Managers Must Draw Up a Code of Ethics

If a business wants to be ethical, managers and employees must know exactly what ethical and unethical business practices are. The business should draw up a code of ethics.

A code of ethics is a written document that sets out guidelines for employees and managers to follow when making decisions. It tells them the correct way to behave and the right thing to do in a given situation. The code of ethics should be included in staff training so that all staff know how to behave ethically.

CODE OF ETHICS FOR A SCHOOL

1. Teachers should not give grinds to one of their students.
2. Teachers should not discuss personal information they know about a student with anyone else (except in the case of a real danger to the student or where legally required to do so).
3. Teachers should not accept gifts from students.

CODE OF ETHICS FOR A BUSINESS

1. Employees will keep all information confidential.
2. Employees will treat all customers fairly and equally.
3. Employees will not work for rival businesses.
4. Employees will help and support their colleagues.

---

4. Ethical Audits

If managers want their business to be ethical, they should get their business assessed by an independent outsider called an **ethics auditor**. The auditor examines every aspect of the business – how it is managed, where it buys its materials, what it sells and how it treats employees, customers, suppliers, society and other stakeholders.

The auditor then sends a report to the managers, highlighting those areas where the business behaved unethically. The business can then take steps to eradicate this bad behaviour. However, the ethics auditor cannot issue legally binding recommendations. An ethics audit is a voluntary measure that a business takes to improve its ethics. It hires the auditor and pays her.

The Environment

We have seen that businesses have a responsibility to do the right thing. This is especially true when it comes to the environment. Businesses must make themselves aware of the main environmental issues and make sure that they take positive steps to minimise their harmful effect on the environment. They must also remember that environmental issues can have a major impact on their business.

Environmental Issues/Responsibilities for Business

1. **Climate Change**

    Climate change is recognised as one of the most serious environmental threats in the world. Businesses use fossil fuels (petrol, diesel, coal, peat, gas and so on) to provide heat and run machinery and vehicles. This leads to the "greenhouse gas" carbon dioxide being released into the earth's atmosphere. Greenhouse gases trap heat in the atmosphere and cause the earth's temperature to rise, leading to storms, floods and droughts.

    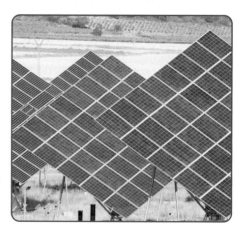

    Therefore, business has a responsibility to use these fossil fuels as efficiently as possible and to switch to renewable sources of energy, such as solar and wind power. These do not cause greenhouses gases, so they will not damage the environment for future generations.

2. **Waste Management**

    Businesses create a huge amount of waste (packaging, chemicals and so on). This waste must be disposed of in a way that does not harm the environment. In Ireland, most of the waste is buried in the ground (this is called landfill), but there are fewer **landfill** sites available in Ireland.

Therefore, business has a responsibility to minimise the amount of waste that it produces. It can do this by reducing, reusing and recycling. A business can **reduce** waste by sending e-mails instead of written memos and by reducing the amount of packaging it uses in its products. It can **reuse** shredded paper for packaging and so on. It can **recycle** glass bottles and jars, cardboard and paper and so on.

The government has a policy to deal with waste management, called the **Polluter Pays** principle. The more waste a business produces, the more it costs to dispose of it.

3. Pollution

Pollution involves humans introducing substances into nature that have a harmful effect on the environment. Ireland is luckier than most because it is not yet as badly polluted as other developed countries, but pollution has been on the increase here.

Businesses must minimise (and hopefully eliminate) harmful polluting emissions into the air and water.

4. Sustainable Development

Sustainable development is defined as development that meets the needs of the *present* without compromising the ability of *future* generations to meet their own needs.

In other words, businesses have a responsibility to protect and preserve the environment so that future generations can live and prosper. If businesses take something from nature, they should replace it.

They should use wood from sustainably managed forests, whereby for every tree chopped down, a new one is planted. To avoid wasting vital resources, businesses should use recyclable materials. They should substitute less harmful ingredients for any toxic or hazardous materials they currently use. They should choose renewable energy sources (such as wind and solar power) over fossil fuels where possible.

Effects of the Environment on Business

1. A major environmental issue is **waste management**. The cost of disposing of waste is increasing and this increases a business's costs and lowers its profits.

2. Consumers are increasingly concerned about the environment. The demand for **environmentally friendly products** is increasing (for example, washing powders that don't pollute the sea). This provides businesses with an opportunity to develop new "green" products, thus increasing sales and profits.

3. Businesses that are not environmentally friendly can incur **negative publicity** and boycotts. This leads to a decrease in their sales and profits. For example, Shell Oil suffered a consumer boycott when it attempted to dump an old oil rig into the North Sea.

4. The Irish government has passed many **laws** to protect the environment. These laws impose a lot of rules and regulations that businesses must follow. Obeying these laws can increase the business's costs, but breaking them will result in the business having to pay hefty fines and penalties.

Characteristics of an Environmentally Conscious Business

A business that truly cares about the environment displays the following characteristics:

1. Sensitive to the Environment

An environmentally conscious business will minimise waste and pollution by reducing, reusing and recycling.

- It **reduces** its waste by photocopying on both sides of the paper, sending e-mails instead of memos, using rechargeable batteries and storing data on computer rather than printing it, for example.

- It **reuses** paper clips and rubber bands, gives workers ceramic mugs to reuse (thus eliminating the need for polystyrene cups), reuses shredded paper for packaging and so on.

- It **recycles** its waste by recycling glass bottles and jars, cardboard and paper and so on.

2. Honest about Environmental Matters

If the business has an industrial accident (for example, accidental pollution of a local river), it tells the appropriate authorities immediately. This enables the authorities to repair the damage as quickly as possible.

3. Open to New Ideas

A business that cares about the environment learns about environmental issues so that it can become as environmentally friendly as possible. It regularly attends waste workshops and waste seminars run by the local council. In this way, the business can learn to manage its waste even better.

4. Environmentally Aware

An environmentally conscious business carries out regular environmental audits to assess the impact it is having on the environment and then takes steps to reduce any harmful effects it has on the environment.

- ○   For example, the Spar Supermarket in Clonskeagh, Dublin had a waste audit carried out, which showed that the shop produced 90% (recyclable) cardboard, 5% (recyclable) plastic and only 5% non-recyclable waste. Once it knew these facts, the shop began to separate its waste and pay a waste management company to take it and recycle it. Only 5% of its waste goes into landfill, whereas before the audit 100% did.

5. Consults Others

The business communicates with all interested parties before it makes any decisions that may affect the environment. It invites them to comment on planned projects and their possible environmental effects. The business takes these views into account before starting the project. For example, an environmentally conscious property developer would listen to what locals, interest groups and the local council have to say before building a new housing estate.

- ○   Tesco listened to complaints about abandoned shopping trolleys from local residents near its Nutgrove Shopping Centre in south Dublin. Each week, 120 trolleys were taken from the centre, ending up in laneways, gardens and rivers. This led the company to introduce a system that prevents a trolley leaving the centre. The wheels lock electronically if someone tries to bring it outside the car park. A month after the system was introduced, only one trolley had been removed.

Businesses may also prepare an **Environmental Impact Assessment** before starting any project. This involves assessing the likely impact of the business's plans on the environment and taking steps to minimise any bad effects they may have.

Impact of Meeting Ethical, Social and Environmental Responsibilities

Being socially responsible brings advantages and disadvantages for a business. The main disadvantages are higher costs in the short term. However, many businesses believe that the higher costs are more than offset by higher sales, a better public image and increased goodwill in the longer term.

Effect on Costs

1. An ethical business pays a **fair wage** and provides safe working conditions to its workers. This increases the business's costs because, to meet its social responsibilities, the business offers its workers a higher rate of pay and better conditions than the minimum legal requirements.

2. An ethical business engages in **Research and Development** to develop new "green" products that are recyclable and don't harm the environment. This increases a business's costs because the business has to pay a research team to do this.

3. A business that acts ethically buys **recyclable materials** and machines that do not pollute the environment, to use in its manufacturing process. This increases a business's costs because it costs the business a lot of money to replace its old polluting and environmentally unfriendly machines. Also, recyclable materials tend to be more expensive than old-fashioned materials that may harm the environment.

4. A business that acts ethically does not dump its **waste** in a manner likely to harm the environment or society. It disposes of it in an environmentally friendly way. This increases a business's costs because the business has to pay to have its waste disposed of safely. Dumping waste costs nothing, but it is not the right thing to do.

Effect on Revenue

1. Consumers like businesses that behave ethically. Most consumers care about the environment and about society. In the future, they will only buy from businesses that are socially responsible and that behave ethically.

2. Consumers buy more products from ethical businesses. Thus, ethical behaviour leads to higher sales and profits. The Body Shop enjoys high sales because of its stance on human rights issues and buying materials from poorer communities.

3. There is a growing demand among consumers for "green" products. These are products that do not harm animals, the environment or society and do not depend upon the exploitation of poor people and countries in their production. A business's sales will increase if it develops such "green" products to satisfy consumer demand.

>   ○   Boeing designed its 787 Dreamliner jet using materials to make the plane lighter and therefore more fuel-efficient. It uses 20% less fuel than other planes. The prospect of lower fuels costs is very attractive to many airlines and the company has received a huge number of orders as a result.

Ordinary Level Questions

EXAM SECTION 1 (25%) – SHORT ANSWER QUESTIONS [10 marks each]

1. Name four stakeholders that a business has a social responsibility to.

2. Outline two benefits for a business of being socially responsible.

3. Explain the term "business ethics".

4. Name a business that is considered to be ethical.
   Outline one reason why this business is ethical.

5. List two rules that might be contained in a business's code of ethics.

6. List four major environmental issues facing Irish business today.

7. Indicate whether each of the following (A, B, C, D and E) is true or false.

	Sentence	True or False
A	The social responsibility of a business is its duty to do make a positive contribution to the lives of its stakeholders.	
B	A business can help solve the problem of waste disposal by reusing and recycling.	
C	An ethical audit is when an accountant checks a business's books to make sure that the profit figure is correct.	
D	A code of ethics is a written document that tells all those in a business the correct way to behave.	
E	Ethical business practice means conducting business in a way that ignores the effects the business has on others.	

8. List three environmental responsibilities of business.

EXAM SECTION 2 (75%) – LONG QUESTIONS

1. List three reasons why being socially responsible is good for a business.   (15 marks)

2. Explain what is meant by "ethical business practice".
    Give two examples of ethical business practice.   (20 marks)

3. Mary runs her own business and is concerned with the effect it has on others.
    A friend suggested that it is important that Mary draw up a code of ethics.
    What is a code of ethics?   (10 marks)

4. Define the term "sustainable development".   (10 marks)

5. You have just read that a transnational company has applied for
    planning permission to set up a factory in your area. Local people are in favour of it
    because it means jobs and more money for the area, but you are concerned
    about its impact on the local environment. Describe three environmental
    responsibilities of the factory that you would consider important
    before granting it permission.   (15 marks)

Higher Level Questions

EXAM SECTION 1 (20%) – SHORT ANSWER QUESTIONS [10 marks each]

1. Illustrate your understanding of the term "business social responsibility".

2. Define the term "business ethics".

3. Distinguish between ethical business practice and social responsibility of business.

4. Column 1 is a list of business terms. Column 2 is a list of possible explanations for these
    terms. Match the two lists by placing the letter of the correct explanation under the
    relevant number below. One explanation has no match.

Column 1	Column 2: Explanations
1. Business Ethics	a) How the actions of a business affect its stakeholders
2. Fairtrade	b) A person who reports unethical behaviour
3. Whistle-blower	c) A document setting out the correct way to behave in business
4. Ethical Audit	d) Concerned with right and wrong in business
5. Code of Ethics	e) An examination of every part of a business to assess its ethical impact
	f) An organisation that promotes better treatment of workers in the third world

1	2	3	4	5

5. What is ethical business practice? Name two businesses that practice ethical business.

6. Describe the role of management in improving a business's ethics.

7. Complete this sentence: An ethical audit requires…

8. Complete this sentence: A code of ethics helps a business because it…

9. Which environmental responsibility of a business do you feel is the most important one? Explain why.

10. Illustrate your understanding of the term "green business".

EXAM SECTION 2 (20%) – APPLIED BUSINESS QUESTION – 80 MARKS

DOS Hotels Ltd.

Doris O'Sullivan owns a large chain of budget hotels operating throughout Ireland. Doris expects her employees to work very hard, and they do. She pays them the legal minimum wage and obeys all employment laws, but she still finds it hard to recruit and keep good employees.

Doris's business strategy emphasises low costs. Doris uses a foreign supplier of beds, furniture and towels. While they are not the best quality and have to be replaced frequently, they are cheap. The business uses a huge quantity of oil each year. Doris is looking for cheaper energy sources to cut the hotels' heating bills.

Doris has not paid any dividends for the last few years, preferring instead to use the company's profits to pay for further expansion. She has her eyes on a prime site in the west of Ireland and has been promised grant funding from Enterprise Ireland to build a hotel there. Doris has hired a UK firm to design and build the hotel and intends to relocate her best employees to run it.

No stranger to controversy, Doris rubbished a recent TV report showing how her business harms the environment. However, the bad publicity led to a substantial drop in the number of guests staying at the chain. The report claimed that the chain's use of washing powders containing phosphates has caused fish kills in local rivers.

(A) Evaluate the business's success in meeting its social responsibility.   (30 marks)

(B) Describe the environmental responsibilities of DOS Hotels.   (20 marks)

(C) Evaluate the effect on Doris's business if she tries to meet her ethical, social and environmental responsibilities better.   (30 marks)

EXAM SECTION 3 (60%) – LONG QUESTIONS

1. Discuss the main social responsibilities of a business.   (20 marks)

2. Define the term "business social responsibility".
    Illustrate the importance of socially responsible business for the success of a business enterprise.   (30 marks)

3. "Ethical business practice is essential for the success of a business enterprise".
    Do you agree with this statement?
    Support your answer with reasons and examples.   (20 marks)

4. Outline and illustrate a method for improving a firm's business ethics. (15 marks)

5. Describe the environmental responsibilities of a business.   (20 marks)

6. Demonstrate how environmental issues can impact on a business.   (20 marks)

7. Explain, using examples, the characteristics of an
    environmentally conscious company.   (25 marks)

8. Evaluate the effect on a firm's costs of meeting its social, ethical and
    environmental responsibilities.   (20 marks)

9. Evaluate the benefits for a firm of meeting its social, ethical and
    environmental responsibilities.   (20 marks)

CHAPTER 24

International Trade

International Trade – Exports and Imports

International trade is commerce between different countries. It involves **exporting** and **importing**.

When Irish businesses *sell* products and services to foreign countries, this is called exporting. For example, Waterford Crystal exports glassware to the USA.

When Irish businesses and people *buy* products and services from foreign countries, this is called importing. For example, Dunnes Stores imports fruit from South Africa.

Exports and imports are either **visible** or **invisible**.

Visible Exports	Ireland sells *products* to foreign countries. Examples of visible exports include: ■ Waterford Crystal sells vases to American shops. ■ Dell sells computers made in Ireland to countries in the Middle East.
Invisible Exports	Ireland sells *services* to foreign countries. Examples of invisible exports include: ■ British tourists stay in a hotel in Dublin. ■ An Irish music group tours Australia.
Visible Imports	Ireland buys *products* from foreign countries. Examples of visible imports include: ■ Dunnes Stores buys fruit from South Africa. ■ Brown Thomas buys Ralph Lauren clothes from America.
Invisible Imports	Ireland buys *services* from foreign countries. Examples of invisible imports include: ■ An Irish family stays in a hotel in Paris. ■ An American singer puts on concerts in Ireland.

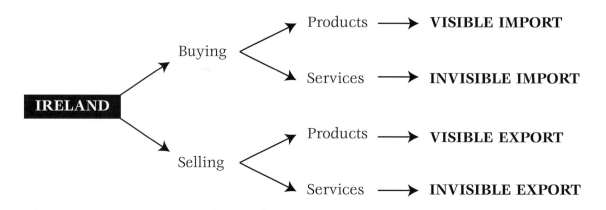

Balance of Trade and Balance of Payments

The **Balance of Trade** and the **Balance of Payments** are sets of accounts that measure how successful a country is at international trade.

The Balance of Trade is the difference between the value of all the *products* Ireland exports and imports.

Balance of Trade	**=**	**Visible Exports**	**–**	**Visible Imports**

It shows only visible trade – Ireland's exports and imports of products.
If Ireland's exports are bigger than its imports, it is called a Balance of Trade **surplus**.
If Ireland's imports are bigger than its exports, we say that there is a Balance of Trade **deficit**.

The Balance of Payments is the difference between the value of all the products *and* services that Ireland exports and imports.

Balance of Payments	**=**	**TOTAL Exports**	**–**	**TOTAL Imports**

The Balance of Payments shows both visible and invisible trade. Visible trade is the import and export of products. Invisible trade is the import and export of services. If Ireland's exports are bigger than its imports, it is called a Balance of Payments **surplus**. This means that more money is coming into the country than is going out and Ireland is getting richer. If Ireland's imports are bigger than its exports, there is a Balance of Payments **deficit**.

Example
Compute the Balance of Trade and Balance of Payments for Ireland using the following figures. State whether each is a surplus or a deficit.

Visible Imports	€30,000 million	Invisible Imports	€15,000 million
Visible Exports	€25,000 million	Invisible Exports	€50,000 million

Balance of Trade	=	Visible Exports	– Visible Imports
	=	€25,000 million	– €30,000 million
	=	€5,000 million Balance of Trade **deficit**	

Balance of Payments	=	TOTAL Exports	– TOTAL Imports
	=	(Visible + Invisible)	– (Visible + Invisible)
	=	(€25,000m + €50,000m)	– (€30,000m + €15,000m)
	=	€75,000 million	– €45,000 million
	=	€30,000 million Balance of Payments **surplus**	

Why Countries Import

Most countries engage in international trade. The main reasons for importing include:

1. Lack of Natural Resources

A country might not have the natural resources that it needs for businesses and consumers, and therefore has to import them.

For example, Ireland does not have enough oil and must import it from Saudi Arabia. Similarly, Saudi Arabia has too much desert to breed cattle and therefore imports beef from Ireland.

2. Unsuitable Climate

A country might not have the correct weather conditions to grow certain crops and will therefore have to import them.

This is the reason why Ireland imports coffee and bananas.

3. Lack of Skills

Some countries have a tradition of being highly skilled in making certain products and they become the best in the world at making them. If other countries want the best, they have to import them.

Although we could make watches here in Ireland, it would take many years for them to be as good as Swiss watches. Many Irish people buy Swiss watches for this reason.

4. Bigger Choice for Consumers

Some countries want to give their consumers more choice over the products they buy. So, even though Ireland produces more than enough potatoes, we can still buy potatoes from many countries in our shops.

Why Countries Export

The main reasons why businesses export include:

1. Survival

The home market in some countries may be too small for a business to make a profit there. Therefore, to make money, the business must export to other countries.

For example, the only way that an Irish aircraft manufacturer could survive is by exporting its planes. The Irish market for planes is too small to make any money.

2. To Increase Sales and Profits

Businesses sell their products and services to foreign countries to increase their sales and profits.

U2 sell their CDs all over the world for this reason.

3. Diversification

A business that depends solely on one country for its sales and profits takes a big risk. If that country's economy goes through a bad patch, the business could suffer.

To *spread* the risk, the business may sell to other countries. If one economy goes through a bad patch, sales in the other countries should keep the company profitable.

Even if the Irish economy faces a downturn and sales of Bailey's fall in Ireland, its sales abroad will keep the company in profits. Bailey's does not solely depend on the Irish market.

Significance of International Trade

International trade is very important to the Irish economy. Irish exports account for a large percentage of Ireland's entire national income. Our biggest customers include the UK, the USA and Belgium. Our biggest exports are pharmaceuticals, chemicals and computers.

Significance of International trade to the Irish Economy

1.   The Irish market consists of only 4 million people. By engaging in international trade, Irish businesses can sell their products to **billions of customers** all over

the world. This leads to increased sales and
profits. Waterford Crystal exports its glassware all
over the world, for this reason.

2. Making more products to export to the world
    gives **economies of scale** to Irish businesses.
    This means that the more they make, the
    cheaper it becomes to make each product. (For example, the more materials they
    buy, the bigger the discount they get.) This makes Irish products cheaper to
    make. Thus, international trade reduces Irish businesses' costs and further
    increases their profits.

3. When Irish businesses sell goods to non-euro countries, they receive **foreign
    currency**. For example, when we sell goods to the USA, they pay us in dollars.
    This foreign currency is important because, with it, we can pay for the foreign
    products we need to import. Irish businesses can buy foreign materials that don't
    exist in Ireland and use them to make finished goods to sell.

4. Increased sales arising from engaging in international trade means that
    businesses have to **hire more employees** to make enough products to meet
    international demand. Thus, international trade leads to job creation in Ireland.
    This decrease in unemployment gives the government more money to invest in
    infrastructure and other important improvements, such as higher grants and
    lower taxes.

5. Irish businesses face a lot of **competition** from foreign firms. This forces them to
    keep their costs low and their prices low so that they can compete. Dunnes Stores
    keeps its prices low to compete with Lidl and ALDI. Ryanair keeps its costs and
    prices low to compete with foreign airlines. Thus, international trade makes Irish
    businesses more competitive.

Free Trade and Protectionism

Free trade means that countries can buy and sell products with other countries
without any barriers or restrictions placed in their way. The countries in the EU
practice free trade with each other.

Protectionism means that countries try to stop foreign imports coming into their
country or help their own businesses to export their goods. They can do this by using
different barriers to trade.

Barriers to Trade

1. Tariff

A **tariff** is a tax that a country adds to the price of foreign imports. This makes
them dearer and they will not sell as well in that country.

Example:

- Say that the USA wants to protect its drinks industry by reducing the amount of Irish whiskey sold in the USA.
- At the moment, a bottle of Jameson (Irish) sells for $20 and a bottle of Jack Daniels (American) sells for $20.
- The US government could add a tariff of $30 to every bottle of Jameson.
- Now Jameson costs $50 a bottle in the USA.
- As a result, American people will buy less Jameson and therefore more Jack Daniels. The US tariff has helped US businesses.

2. Quota

To reduce the number of foreign imports and to help indigenous businesses, a country puts a limit (called a **quota**) on the amount of foreign imports it will allow. Once this limit has been reached, no further imports are allowed. Consumers have no choice then but to buy from indigenous businesses.

Example:

- The USA wants to protect the US car industry from Japanese imports.
- It imposes a quota saying that only 100 Japanese cars will be allowed into the USA each year.
- Once these 100 Japanese cars are sold, no more are allowed into the USA. Therefore, if Americans want to buy a car, they have to buy a US car.
- The US quota on Japanese cars helps the US car industry.

The EU has a quota on how many Chinese garments it will allow into the EU.

3. Embargo

To reduce the number of foreign imports and to help indigenous businesses, a country puts a complete ban (called an **embargo**) on all foreign imports (or imports from a specific country) into the country. Its consumers have no choice then but to buy from indigenous businesses.

The USA has a trade embargo with Cuba. It does not allow any Cuban imports.

4. Subsidy

A **subsidy** is money that a government gives to its own domestic (indigenous) businesses to allow them to sell their products or services more cheaply. In international trade, it can help businesses to export more.

Example:

- Seat sells cars in Spain for €25,000.
- Toyota sells cars in Spain for €25,000.
- If the Japanese government gives Toyota a €10,000 subsidy for every car it sells in Spain, Toyota could drop its price by €10,000 and sell each car for only €15,000.

- Spanish people would buy more Japanese cars and fewer Spanish cars.
- Thus Japanese subsidies help Japanese companies to sell their products abroad.

Changes in International Economy

The world of international business is constantly changing. Because Ireland is an open economy (we buy and sell with many countries around the world), these changes have a major impact on Irish businesses. The major trends in international commerce include the following.

1. Globalisation

A big trend in international trade is the increasing number of **global businesses**. These are businesses that operate throughout the entire world. Examples include Coca-Cola, Toyota, McDonald's, Microsoft and so on. Global businesses treat the whole world as one big market. They sell the same product all over the world. They make their products in various locations in the world (often in countries with low labour costs).

Globalisation provides an opportunity for Irish businesses. If these global companies set up in Ireland, they may buy materials from Irish businesses, thus increasing sales and profits. However, it is also a threat for Irish businesses because competition from global businesses can wipe them out.

2. Improved Information and Communications Technology

Many businesses are using the Internet for international trade. They can sell their products all over the world on their website without having to set up shops all over the world. Customers everywhere can see and buy the business's products from its website. This means that even the smallest Irish businesses can engage in international trade.

3. Increasing Number of Trading Blocs

Many countries in the world are co-operating with each other by forming trading blocs together. A trading bloc is a group of countries that agree to freely buy from and freely sell to each other without any barriers to trade (such as tariffs, quotas, embargoes or subsidies). However, they may impose a tariff on all imports coming in from non-member countries.

- An example of a trading bloc is the North American Free Trade Agreement (NAFTA), which is a trading bloc consisting of Canada, the USA and Mexico.

○ Another example is the European Union (EU). The EU is the world's largest trading bloc. It comprises many countries in Europe, including Ireland. There is totally free trade between all the members of the EU.

The EU allows Irish businesses to sell their products in all the member states without any restrictions at all. This gives Irish businesses an opportunity to increase their sales and profits by selling to a market of 500 million people. However, it is also a threat for Irish businesses because of the competition from EU businesses that can sell here without restrictions.

4. Deregulation of International Trade

Deregulation is the process of removing all the government rules and regulations (barriers to trade) that prevent free trade between countries.

WTO OMC

The World Trade Organisation (WTO) is a body consisting of over 150 countries, including Ireland. Its job is hold negotiations between countries and reach agreements to remove barriers to international trade. These agreements form the legal ground rules for international trade. The WTO is also a place where countries can go to sort out the trade problems they face with each other.

Deregulation presents Irish businesses with the opportunity to increase their sales and profits by exporting their products more freely all over the world. However, it is also a threat for Irish businesses because of competition from other businesses that can sell here with fewer restrictions.

5. New Markets

In the past, communist countries did not trade with the West. However, communism has collapsed in many countries, including Russia, Poland, Latvia, Lithuania, the Czech Republic and so on. These former communist countries are now starting to grow and develop and are importing and exporting. This provides an opportunity for Irish businesses to sell more products to these countries.

However, Ireland now faces increasing competition from low-wage economies, such as the Philippines. It is impossible for Ireland to compete with these countries in low-skill manufacturing jobs because Irish workers expect much higher wages than people in developing countries do for this type of work. This has led to the closure of many factories in Ireland.

A major new market is China. It has the biggest population on the planet. Up until relatively recently, it did not trade with the rest of the world. The Chinese government now allows international trade. This provides Irish businesses with the opportunity to increase sales. The Irish government has put a lot of emphasis on building good trade relations with China. However, competition from Chinese factories poses a major threat to Irish manufacturers. China is known as the factory of the world and can make its products far more cheaply than Irish businesses can.

Ireland's Opportunities in Developed and Developing Markets

1. Increased Sales

Ireland's membership of the European Union allows Irish businesses to sell their products and services anywhere in the EU without any barriers to trade. Furthermore, deregulation by the World Trade Organisation has removed many worldwide barriers to trade and allows for freer international commerce. Both of these give Irish businesses the opportunity to increase their sales and profits by exporting their products more easily all over the world.

2. Lower Costs

Irish exporters have to make lots of products to satisfy international demand. This gives them economies of scale. The more products they make, the cheaper it costs to make each one. Thus, international trade helps Irish businesses to lower their costs and become more competitive.

3. Diversification

International trade gives Irish businesses the opportunity to spread their risk (diversify). By selling in other countries, the Irish business does not rely solely on the Irish market. If the Irish economy goes through a bad patch, the business's sales in other countries will keep it in profit.

4. Earn Foreign Currency

When Irish businesses export to foreign countries, they receive foreign currency. They can use this money to pay for goods and services that they need to import. They can use these imports to make better products. For example, an Irish yoghurt manufacturer can export yoghurt to the USA and use the dollars received to pay for fruit from Florida, which he can use to improve the variety of flavours he offers.

5. Overcome Trade Barriers

Irish businesses can set up branches in other countries as a way to overcome barriers to trade. For example, if an Irish business sets up a manufacturing plant in Mexico, all products made there could be freely sold throughout Canada, USA and Mexico because they are all NAFTA members.

6. English

Irish people speak fluent English. English is the international language of business. This means that all Irish people can automatically converse with other businesses worldwide in the international language of business.

This helps Irish businesses to do business more easily abroad.

7. Educated Workers

Ireland has a well-educated workforce. Most young people go to college. Many study Science. Their excellent education helps Irish entrepreneurs invent new products that can be sold all over the world to make a lot of money for Ireland. Our biggest "knowledge-based" exports are medicines, chemicals and computers.

8. Green Image

Ireland has a good image around the world as a clean, green and unspoilt country. This image makes it easier for us to sell food to other countries as they can trust our food to be of top quality. It also helps to attract foreign tourists. Both these industries bring in billions of euro to the country.

Ireland's Challenges in Developed and Developing Markets

1. Foreign Languages

Although English is the international language of business, many foreign customers obviously prefer to deal in their own language. This poses a number of communication problems for Irish exporters. They have to make their websites available in many languages. The name of the product may have to be changed. Contracts and other documents have to be translated. This costs time and money.

There are many famous examples of businesses having problems because of their poor foreign language skills.

- When Coca-Cola was first launched in China, the company printed thousands of signs with Chinese characters spelling out "ke-kou-ke-la", which means "bite the wax tadpole" or "female horse stuffed with wax", depending on the local dialect.

- KFC accidentally translated its slogan "finger-lickin' good" into "eat your fingers off" in Chinese.

- When Parker launched a new pen in Mexico, it wanted to use the slogan "It won't leak in your pocket and embarrass you". When translating this, it incorrectly thought that the Spanish word "embarazar" means "embarrass". It doesn't. The ads ran all over Mexico with the slogan "It won't leak in your pocket and make you pregnant".

2. Exchange Rate Changes

Ireland's currency presents a problem for Irish businesses engaging in international trade. If the euro increases in value, the price of Irish products in non-euro countries increases. Therefore, foreigners buy fewer Irish products and our exports fall. This leads to lower sales and profits for Irish exporters. If the euro decreases in value, the price of foreign materials imported into Ireland increases. This increases costs for Irish businesses that have to import materials from non-euro countries.

3. Distribution Problems

Ireland is an island. It is one of three EU
countries without a land link to other EU
countries. (Cyprus and Malta are the only other
two). This makes transporting goods more
difficult and more expensive for Irish businesses.
Goods can only be exported from Ireland by ship
or plane. However, the goods can be transported
only according to shipping and airline
companies' timetables and the weather. Almost
every other business in the EU can simply load
up its lorry at the factory and drive it straight to
the destination anywhere in the EU at any time,
day or night.

4. Cultural Differences

Different countries have different cultures, i.e. different notions of what is
acceptable behaviour and what is not.

Up until very recently, Ireland was almost an entirely homogenous society (white
and Catholic). Therefore, a major challenge for Irish businesses is to learn the
cultural norms of our trading partners so that we do not offend them and hence
lose their business.

Many businesses have made embarrassing and costly cultural mistakes. Revlon
tried to launch a perfume in Brazil that smelled of camellia flowers. It didn't
realise that camellias are funeral flowers in Brazil and, predictably, the perfume
was not a success.

5. Competition from Low-Wage Economies

The rate of pay in Ireland is considered to be quite high. To cover this expense,
Irish manufacturers must charge a relatively high price for their products. Other
countries have much lower wages and therefore their products are always cheaper
than Ireland's. It is almost impossible for Irish manufacturers to compete against
these low-wage economies when it comes to simple, low-technology products. The
challenge for Irish businesses is to develop advanced, high technology,
knowledge-based products that these low-wage economies do not have the skills
to make.

6. Payment Problems

Irish firms may have difficulties getting paid for the goods they export. If a foreign
customer does not pay, there may be little that the Irish business can do to
recoup its money. Different countries have different legal systems and the rules
for recovering money from a customer may be harder to enforce abroad than here
in Ireland.

Role of ICT in International Trade

New Information and Communications Technology (ICT) has made it easier and cheaper for businesses to engage in international trade. Businesses can communicate with customers, suppliers and subsidiaries around the world quickly and cheaply.

ICT has many benefits for International Trade.

1. Increased Sales

The Internet enables businesses to engage in **e-commerce**. A business can showcase its products on its website and customers from any part of the world can order the products by clicking on an item and sending their credit card details over the Internet as payment.

Even small businesses that cannot afford their own website can use e-commerce to sell their products to the world. eBay enables individuals and small businesses to sell their products in online auctions to buyers throughout the world, for a small fee.

In this way, Irish businesses can sell their products all over the world without having to set up shops all over the world.

2. Advertising

Businesses can use the Internet to advertise their products globally. They can pay a well-known website such as MSN or Yahoo to display an advertisement on its website. These websites are used by millions of people worldwide and hence the business's ads will be seen all over the world.

3. Faster and Cheaper Communications

E-mail enables you to send a typed message (and other information such as pictures, sounds or movies) directly from your computer to another via the Internet.

A business can send as many e-mails as it wants to its customers, suppliers and employees all around the world for one flat monthly fee. This reduces the cost of communication in international trade.

E-mail is a quick form of communication. Messages are sent and received immediately by computer. This enables a business to respond immediately to customers' queries from around the world.

4. Decision-Making

The WWW (Web) is a vast collection of information on millions of topics accessed via the Internet.

It enables businesspeople to get information about foreign countries, markets and opportunities. This helps the business to make better-informed decisions.

5. Reduced Costs

Video-conferencing is a virtual meeting held between people who are in different locations. Live pictures and sound of each person are sent via the Internet to screens in all the other locations so that all participants can see and hear each other as if they were in the same room.

Video-conferencing makes international trade easier. The chief executive officer (CEO) of an international business does not have to travel to each overseas branch for meetings about sales figures in that country, for example. He can meet with managers and staff worldwide through video-conferencing. There is no need for foreign travel or hotel accommodation. Thus video-conferencing reduces the time and expense of travelling to a business's international branches.

Government help for Irish Exporters

The Irish government provides a range of organisations to help Irish businesses export.

Enterprise Ireland

Enterprise Ireland helps Irish firms to export their products by providing:

- Market research information on opportunities in foreign countries.
- Low-cost loans to Irish businesses to help them export.
- Grants to help them export.
- Training courses to teach them what they need to know about exporting.
- Advice on everything to do with foreign trade, including all documentation, how to get paid, labelling of goods and so on.

Enterprise Ireland is running a major campaign in the UK to get British industry to use Irish building firms and materials to construct the infrastructure for the 2012 Olympic Games in London. A total of €15 billion is expected to be spent on the infrastructure.

Department of Enterprise, Trade and Employment

This government department helps Irish businesses to export their products by:

- ● Giving advice on the documents used in foreign trade and in the regulations that must be obeyed.
- ● Providing Export Credit Insurance for certain industries.
  This is where the Irish government promises to pay the Irish exporter if a foreign customer does not pay him.

Diplomatic Services

The Irish diplomatic service helps Irish exporters by:

- ● Promoting Ireland abroad to maintain and increase Irish exports.
- ● Lobbying foreign governments and companies to trade with Ireland.
  They resolve any problems that Irish businesses may have in foreign markets. For example, when mad cow disease broke out in the UK, many countries banned Irish beef. Ireland's ambassadors and diplomats abroad explained to the foreign governments that Ireland was not affected and they succeeded in reopening these markets to Irish farmers.
- ● Helping to organise trade missions.
  Irish businesses go abroad to make foreign contacts, often accompanied by the President of Ireland on a state visit. For example, following the largest ever trade mission to China led by President McAleese in 2003, participating Irish companies reported winning new business contracts worth over €40 million.
- ● Helping to organise trade fairs.
  Ireland puts on an exhibition of its products in a foreign country. This is done to take orders at the fair and to attract publicity for Ireland.

Ordinary Level Questions

EXAM SECTION 1 (25%) – SHORT ANSWER QUESTIONS [10 marks each]

1. Explain the term "international trade".
2. Explain the term "imports" and give two examples of Irish imports.
3. Distinguish between visible exports and invisible exports. Illustrate with an example of each.

4. Indicate by means of a tick (✔) the category to which each good or service belongs:

	Visible Exports	Invisible Exports	Visible Imports	Invisible Imports
An Irish consumer buys a bottle of French perfume.				
An Irish family stays in an Italian hotel.				
An American music band tours Ireland.				
An Irish company services a South African Airways plane.		'		

5. Compute the Balance of Trade and Balance of Payments for Ireland using the following figures. State whether each is a surplus or a deficit.

Visible Imports	€18,000 million	Invisible Imports	€11,000 million
Visible Exports	€12,000 million	Invisible Exports	€19,000 million

6. Compute the Balance of Trade and Balance of Payments for Ireland using the following figures. State whether each is a surplus or a deficit.

Visible Exports	€45,000 million	Visible Imports	€40,000 million
Invisible Exports	€16,000 million	Invisible Imports	€15,000 million

7. List two reasons why Irish businesses import and two reasons why they export.

8. Column 1 is a list of business terms. Column 2 is a list of possible explanations for these terms. Match the two lists by placing the letter of the correct explanation under the relevant number below. One explanation has no match.

Column 1	Column 2: Explanations
1. EU	a) Money received from the government to help a business pay for fixed assets such as machinery and computers
2. Tariff	b) Limit placed on the number of foreign imports allowed into a country
3. Quota	
4. Embargo	c) Money received from the government to help a business sell its products more cheaply
5. Subsidy	
6. Free Trade	d) Countries engage in international trade without any barriers or restrictions
	e) European Union
	f) Tax added to the price of foreign imports
	g) Total ban on all foreign imports

1	2	3	4	5	6
E					

9. Indicate whether each of the following (A, B, C, D and E) is true or false.

	Sentence	True or False
A	The EU is a trading bloc.	
B	Deregulation involves countries putting up barriers such as tariffs and quotas to prevent free trade.	
C	A global business sells its products in only one country.	
D	WTO stands for Worldwide Trading Ombudsman.	
E	Protectionism involves countries removing barriers such as tariffs and quotas to improve free trade.	

10. Outline two ways in which the Internet helps Irish businesses engaged in international trade.

EXAM SECTION 2 (75%) – LONG QUESTIONS

1. Define "international trade". Explain three reasons why Ireland trades with other countries. (20 marks)

2. Describe three benefits of exporting for Irish businesses. (15 marks)

3. Distinguish between "balance of trade" and "balance of payments". (20 marks)

4. Outline three benefits of international trade for Ireland. (15 marks)

5. Distinguish between "free trade" and "protectionism". (10 marks)

6. Identify three barriers to free trade that countries can use. (15 marks)

7. Explain the term "trading bloc". (10 marks)

8. What is "deregulation" and how does it help Irish businesses? (10 marks)

9. Describe three changes taking place in the international economy. (15 marks)

10. Explain three opportunities facing Irish business in international trade. (15 marks)

11. Explain three challenges facing Irish business in international trade. (15 marks)

12. Explain how video-conferencing and e-mail help Irish businesses engaged in international trade. (20 marks)

Higher Level Questions

EXAM SECTION 1 (20%) – SHORT ANSWER QUESTIONS [10 marks each]

1. Illustrate your understanding of the term "international trade".

2. Compute the Balance of Trade for Ireland using the following figures. State whether it is a surplus or a deficit.

Balance of Payments	€10,000 million surplus
Total Exports	€75,000 million
Visible Exports	€55,000 million
Invisible Imports	€25,000 million

3. Compute the Balance of Payments for Ireland using the following figures. State whether it is a surplus or a deficit.

Invisible Imports	€6,000 million
Total Exports	€100,000 million
Balance of Trade	€22,000 million deficit
Visible Exports	€75,000 million

4. Differentiate between Balance of Trade Surplus and Balance of Trade Deficit.

5. Illustrate your understanding of the term "trading bloc".

6. A tariff is one barrier to trade that governments can use to protect indigenous firms. List three other barriers to international trade and explain any one of them.

7. Explain the term "globalisation". Illustrate its impact on the development of the Irish economy.

8. Complete this sentence: Deregulation requires…

9. What do the letters WTO stand for? Explain the role of the WTO in business.

10. Outline two impacts of a fluctuating euro on Ireland's international trade with non-euro countries.

11. In the context of international trade, outline two functions of Enterprise Ireland.

EXAM SECTION 2 (20%) – APPLIED BUSINESS QUESTION – 80 MARKS

Agricola Foods Ltd.

Agricola Foods is an Irish agri-business involved in milk processing. It has received a lot of funding from Údarás na Gaeltachta because its factory is situated in the Kerry Gaeltacht. It produces butter, cheese and yoghurt for the home market, under the brand name "Ciarraí Abú".

Its main customers are supermarkets operating in Ireland. A recent order from a global hotel chain with a large number of hotels in Ireland helped the company to boost sales. In order to boost profits further, the company is currently planning an export drive into Europe and the United States.

Agricola has recently faced increasing competition from cheaper foreign firms, not only from other EU food manufacturers but also from firms in Asia. The company was concerned how a trade dispute between the EU and the US (which saw the US place an embargo on all EU foodstuffs) would affect its plans. But this dispute was resolved last week.

The firm's IT expert has advised management that Agricola must invest heavily in ICT if it is to remain competitive. She puts the success of Agricola's international competitors in stealing its market share down to their clever use of the Internet for marketing and other purposes.

(A) Evaluate how changes in the international economy are impacting
on Agricola Foods Ltd.   (30 marks)

(B) Discuss the opportunities and challenges provided by
international trade for Agricola Foods Ltd.   (30 marks)

(C) Outline how the Irish diplomatic service could help Agricola Foods Ltd.   (20 marks)

EXAM SECTION 3 (60%) – LONG QUESTIONS

1. "Ireland is a small open economy." Explain what this means and
discuss the reasons why Ireland has no choice but to be an open economy.   (30 marks)

2. Analyse the importance of international trade for the Irish economy.   (25 marks)

3. Outline the measures that governments can take to protect
their domestic businesses from international competition.   (20 marks)

4. Describe the impact of trading blocs and deregulation on Irish business.   (20 marks)

5. Explain the aims and objectives of the World Trade Organisation.   (10 marks)

6. Discuss the challenges provided by international trade for Irish business.   (25 marks)

7. Evaluate the increasing importance of information technology (IT)
in international trade for Irish businesses.
Use relevant examples to illustrate your answer.   (20 marks)

European Union

The European Union (EU) is a **trading bloc** of 27 countries in Europe, including Ireland. The countries are called **member states**. There is free trade between all the member states. This is called the **single market**. But the EU is more than just a free trade area. It is also working towards closer political co-operation (working together on defence, policing and international events).

The 27 member states are listed below:

Austria	Belgium	Bulgaria	Cyprus	Czech Republic	Denmark
Estonia	Finland	France	Germany	Greece	Hungary
Ireland	Italy	Latvia	Lithuania	Luxembourg	Malta
Netherlands	Poland	Portugal	Romania	Slovakia	Slovenia
Spain	Sweden	UK			

Importance of EU Membership for Ireland

The European Union is very important to Ireland. Our membership of the EU played a part in making Ireland the wealthy country it is today. The EU has helped Ireland in a number of ways.

1. The **Single European Market** provides Irish businesses with the opportunity to increase their profits by allowing them to sell their products and services freely to a market of over 480 million people.

2. The EU has given Ireland **grants** to improve its infrastructure, such as motorways, airports, ports and so on. This has helped Irish businesses to transport their products more quickly and more cheaply.

3. Ireland's membership of the Single European Market attracts **transnational companies** here, such as Dell and Intel. These transnational companies provide thousands of jobs in Ireland. They also buy materials from Irish businesses, which helps to increase their sales and profits.

4.   The EU **Common Agricultural Policy (CAP)** and the **Common Fisheries Policy (CFP)** have helped Ireland's primary industries of agriculture and fishing by giving those who operate in these sectors a decent standard of living and by helping to modernise and improve these industries with grants.

EU Institutions

The EU has established a number of organisations or institutions to look after the running of it. Among the most important are:
1.   The European Commission
2.   The European Parliament
3.   The Council of the European Union
4.   The European Court of Auditors
5.   The Court of Justice

European Commission

The European Commission is the institution that runs the EU. It consists of commissioners. Each **commissioner** is in charge of a different area of responsibility within the EU, such as transport, the environment, education, health, agriculture and trade.

The main functions of the Commission are:
1.   **To propose new European laws**
      The Commission thinks up new ideas for laws that are needed in the EU. Therefore, the Commission has to be aware of problems in the EU. The Commission then drafts a law that it thinks will solve the problem.

      These new laws, when passed, will have a direct influence on Ireland. For example, the Commission thought of the idea for the **minimum wage**. This law had a direct effect on the lives of Irish workers. It improved the standard of living for many of them. It also had a direct effect on Irish businesses because it increased their costs.

2.   **To enforce EU laws**
      The Commission supervises the EU to make sure that everyone obeys EU laws. If it finds any EU country not obeying an EU law, the Commission takes that country to the Court of Justice to force it obey the law.

      The Commission is responsible for making sure that EU policies are carried out properly.

For example, the EU Competition Policy states that all businesses must follow the principles of fair competition. To make sure this is adhered to, the Commission keeps an eye on all mergers and takeovers that take place in the EU. It can stop any mergers or takeovers if it thinks they will harm free competition.

In 2007, the Commission did not allow Ryanair to take over Aer Lingus, stating that such a takeover was a threat to consumer choice and a recipe for higher fares.

3. **To draft the EU budget**

The Commission is responsible for drawing up the EU budget. This means that it makes the initial decision as to how much money each country should get back from the EU.

This is important for Ireland because the Commission decides how much money Ireland will get from the EU. This money is important to Ireland because it is used to build our infrastructure and develop the poorer parts of the country.

European Parliament

The European Parliament is the institution that is directly elected by the citizens of the EU to represent their interests in discussions with the other EU institutions. Elections to the parliament are held every five years. There are over 700 Members of the European Parliament (MEPs) representing people in all the member states. Their job is:

1. **To debate and approve new European laws**

The Parliament considers laws proposed by the Commission. The MEPs discuss the advantages and disadvantages of the law and suggest changes to make it better.

Under the co-decision principle, the Parliament has to agree to a proposal for a new law. Otherwise, it will not become law in the EU.

2. **To supervise the EU**

MEPs keep an eye on what the Council of the European Union is doing. It calls the President of the Council (the prime minister of whichever country holds the EU presidency) into the Parliament to answer questions from the MEPs about its work.

The Parliament interviews all the candidates for the European Commission. It then votes on whether to accept the new Commission or not. The Commission cannot be appointed without Parliament's approval. Parliament also has the power to sack the entire Commission if it is unhappy with it.

3. **To approve the EU budget**
    The Parliament has the power together with the Council of the EU to approve of or reject the entire EU budget. Therefore, it can influence how the EU spends its money.

Council of the European Union

This is the most important decision-making body in the EU. It represents the member states and its meetings are attended by one minister from each of the EU's national governments.

If the Council is meeting to discuss the environment (Environment Council), each country will send its government Environment Minister to represent it. If the Council is meeting to discuss finance issues, each country will send its government Minister for Finance.

The main functions of the Council are:

1. To pass European laws. The Council is the institution (together with the European Parliament) that has the final say on what becomes EU law. This is called co-decision.

2. To conclude international agreements between the EU and other countries or organisations. Every year, the council officially signs such agreements on behalf of the EU. These agreements often cover areas such as trade with non-EU countries or organisations, fisheries, science, technology and transport.

3. To approve the EU's budget. The Council has the power together with the European Parliament to approve of or reject the entire EU budget. Therefore, it can influence how the EU spends its money.

4. To allow member states to work together in the areas of foreign policy, security and defence. For example, to enable it to deal with international crises, the Council of the European Union created a **Rapid Reaction Force**, consisting of soldiers from each EU army who work together to carry out humanitarian, rescue and peacekeeping duties in the world. In 2004, the EU began a peacekeeping operation in Bosnia and Herzegovina.

European Court of Auditors

The European Court of Auditors is responsible for ensuring that the EU budget is managed properly.

Its job is to check that EU funds, which come from EU taxpayers, are properly collected and that they are spent legally, economically and for the intended purpose. Its aim is to ensure that the taxpayers get maximum value for their money.

The Court has one member from each EU country. It can audit any country or organisation that received EU funding to make sure that the money was not wasted and was spent for the purpose intended. This means that it investigates the paperwork of the organisation and carries out on-the-spot checks to make sure that everything was done correctly.

The Court writes a report on its findings and this draws the attention of the Commission and the member states to any problems.

Court of Justice

The role of the Court of Justice is to make sure that EU laws are applied the same way in all EU countries so that EU law is the same for every EU citizen. The Court is made up of one judge from each EU country.

The functions of the Court of Justice are as follows:

1. The Court of Justice gives **advice** to member states' national courts to help them understand EU laws and how they apply to their country. It makes sure that different countries do not give different rulings on the same issue.

2. The Court of Justice makes sure that each country and institution in the EU **obeys** EU law and does exactly what EU law requires. It has the power to settle disputes between EU countries, EU institutions, citizens and businesses.

    For example, the politician Gerry Adams took a case to the Court of Justice when the UK government denied him access to mainland UK. He claimed that the UK government was breaking EU law, which says that all EU citizens have the right to travel freely throughout the EU. The Court investigated his claim and Mr. Adams won his case. The Court then ordered the UK government to let him into mainland UK.

3. The Court of Justice can **strike down** any EU law that is illegal.

    If any of the member states or institutions of the EU believe that a particular EU law is illegal, they may ask the Court to annul it.

    EU citizens can also ask the court to cancel a law if it directly affects them in a negative way.

    If the Court finds that the law in question breaks the rules that govern the EU (called the Treaties), it will declare that law null and void.

Decision-making in The EU

The EU tries to benefit all the people in each member state by passing laws to protect and help them. The process of passing a law that suits each country is a complicated one and involves a number of steps.

1. The European Commission thinks of ideas

2. The European Parliament debates it and sends amendments back to

3. The European Commission, which amends idea and sends to

4. The European Parliament and Council of the EU, who have final say

1. The first step in EU decision-making involves the European Commission. Its job is to identify problems in the EU and then to think of laws that will solve these problems. The Commission sends its idea for a new law to the European Parliament.

2. The European Parliament debates the proposed new law. It discusses the law's advantages and disadvantages, and suggests how it could be improved. The Parliament then sends its suggestions to improve the law (called **amendments**) back to the Commission.

3. The European Commission then modifies the proposed new law after it has listened to the debate in the Parliament. It incorporates the amendments suggested by the European Parliament and excludes what the Parliament thought was wrong with the law. The Commission then sends the amended law on to the Council of the European Union and the European Parliament.

4. The Council of the European Union and the European Parliament jointly have the final say. This is called co-decision. They decide whether the proposal will become law in the EU. If either disagrees with it, it does not become law. If both accept it, it becomes law in the EU and is implemented by regulation (applies immediately in all countries), directive (all countries must obey it within a given time limit) or decision (applies to only one country, business or citizen who must obey it immediately).

Role of Special Interest Groups in EU Decision-making

An **interest group** is an organisation of people who come together to fight for a common goal. By joining forces, they have more power, more money and more talents at their disposal and hence are more likely to be listened to by the decision-makers.

There are thousands of these special interest groups in the EU, including Amnesty International, the Irish Business and Employers Confederation (IBEC), the Irish Farmers Association (IFA) and businesses such as Intel, IKEA, Ford and British Nuclear Fuels (which runs Sellafield).

The aim of these special interest groups is to pressurise EU decision-makers into making decisions that they want to achieve their aims. For example, IBEC will try to get the EU to make decisions that help Irish businesspeople. IBEC has an office in Brussels. It uses this to meet with, write to and phone EU decision-makers so that they can put forward the case of Irish businesspeople.

Special interest groups will do the following to achieve their aims.

1. **Lobby Members of the European Parliament (MEPs)**
   Special interest groups will phone, write to and meet with MEPs to try to persuade them to vote a certain way. They will send a petition to the European Parliament about an issue they feel strongly about in order to pressurise the MEPs into doing something about it.

2. **Lobby the European Commission and individual commissioners**
   Before it can think up ideas for new laws, the Commission has to be aware of problems in the EU that need to be solved. This is where special interest groups come into their own. They meet with the commissioners and make them aware of the particular issues they are concerned about and tell the commissioners what to do to sort it out.

3. **Set up an office in Brussels**
   Many EU decisions are made in Brussels, so special interest groups use their Brussels offices to lobby decision-makers on a regular basis. For example, IBEC and the IFA have offices in Brussels close to the Commission and the Parliament.

EU Directives

An EU directive is a law that all EU member states *must* obey. It sets out a desired result that each country must achieve **by a given date**.

Member states must change their own national law to implement the directive, but they can change it whatever way they want to, so long as they achieve the desired result by the deadline.

An EU working time directive issued in 1996 stated that EU workers were to get 20 days paid holidays by 1999. In 1996, Irish employees got only 15 days holidays. Over the next three years, the government added 5 holidays onto Irish workers' entitlement.

The Waste Electrical and Electronic Equipment (WEEE) Directive states that Irish retailers must allow customers to leave back their old WEEE for free when they buy new equipment from the shop. The shop has to bring it to a proper disposal facility. The shop has to make its customers aware of this law.

The WEEE Directive has increased Irish businesses' costs. They have to pay to print posters and leaflets telling their customers about the directive. And they have to arrange storage for customers' old WEEE and they have to transport the WEEE to approved disposal sites.

EU Policies

EU policies are major programmes that are designed to help specific categories of people in the EU. There are EU policies for EU farmers (called the Common Agricultural Policy), the EU fishing industry (called the Common Fisheries Policy), EU workers (called the EU Social Charter), EU consumers (called the Competition Policy) and EU businesses (called the Single European Market and the Euro).

Common Agricultural Policy (CAP)

The CAP was established to give all farmers in the EU a decent standard of living. It achieves this in a number of ways.

1. EU farmers are allowed to sell their produce anywhere in the EU **without any barriers** or restrictions. There is a totally free market. This gives Irish farmers a much bigger market (over 480 million people) to sell to and therefore the opportunity to increase their sales and profits.

2. The CAP gives grants to all farmers to guarantee them a basic minimum wage. This is called the **single payment scheme**. The EU makes these payments to farmers to help them survive but only if they obey food safety and environmental standards. These payments are important to Irish farmers as they help ensure that

farming in Ireland remains viable. The grants supplement the income made from agriculture to ensure that Irish farmers make a decent living.

3. To help farmers improve the **quality** of their produce and therefore sell more, the CAP gives EU farmers grants to spend on improving their land and animals. This helps Irish farmers to grow better quality crops and rear better quality animals, which helps them to sell more and thus increase profits.

4. To protect EU farmers from competition from other countries, the CAP adds **tariffs** to non-EU food imports to make them dearer. This will encourage consumers to buy more EU produced food.

If, for example, Irish potatoes sell for €3 per kilo and South African potatoes sell here for €2 per kilo, Irish farmers won't sell too much. But, if the CAP adds a €4 tariff onto South African potatoes, they will now cost €6 per kilo. Irish potatoes are now cheaper, so Irish farmers sell more.

Common Fisheries Polity (CFP)

The Common Fisheries Policy (CFP) was devised to give those involved in the EU fishing industry a decent standard of living and to conserve fish stocks (making sure there is enough fish for everyone for years to come).

It tries to achieve this in the following ways:

DECENT STANDARD OF LIVING	PREVENT OVER-FISHING
1. Prices for fish are fixed at the start of the year to guarantee Irish fishermen a decent income.	1. Every country is given a quota, setting out the maximum amount of each type of fish it can catch each year.
2. To improve the quality of fish caught and thus to help EU fishermen sell more, the CFP gives grants to EU fishermen to buy better boats and modern fishing technology.	2. The CFP sets down limits for the size of the holes in nets to stop immature fish being caught.
3. To increase fishermen's sales and profits, the CFP pays for marketing campaigns to encourage consumers to buy more fish.	3. The CFP helps member states to patrol their waters and catch those involved in illegal fishing.

EU Social Charter

The EU Social Charter is the EU's social policy. Its aim is to improve working and living conditions for EU citizens. It gives all EU workers the following rights:

1. EU citizens have **freedom of movement**. This means that they have the right to work in any EU country they want and be treated the same as nationals of that country.

    This can be good for Irish businesses because, if they are short of workers, they can hire more from the other EU countries without the need for visas or work-permits. The Irish economy, particularly the construction industry, depended very heavily on immigration from the EU states to fill job vacancies, in recent years.

    However, it could be bad for Irish businesses because Irish people may decide to live and work elsewhere in the EU, leaving Irish businesses short of Irish workers.

2. EU workers have the right to a **fair wage** that will give them and their families a decent standard of living. All EU countries must set a minimum wage.

    The minimum wage increases costs for some Irish businesses. They have to pay more wages to workers than they otherwise might.

3. EU workers can work only a maximum of **48 hours a week**. They also have the right to public holidays with pay and four weeks' paid annual holiday.

    This too can be bad for Irish businesses. In businesses that rely on a lot of overtime (such as security, hospitals and so on), they will have to hire more employees to cover busy periods as they are not allowed to ask existing staff to work more than the legal limit.

4. EU workers have the right to be **consulted** by their employer and to take part in decision-making in their company. They must be kept informed regularly by their boss of the financial situation the business is in. They must be consulted in plenty of time about any decisions their employer plans to make that will affect them and their jobs.

    This forces Irish employers to become more democratic.

Competition Policy

The EU Competition Policy is a set of rules intended to ensure free and fair competition between businesses in the EU. Its aim is to ensure that EU consumers get quality products at reasonable prices. It contains a number of rules.

1. Businesses cannot form **cartels**. A cartel is an illegal secret agreement between competitors in which they agree to restrict competition. The Competition Policy

states that businesses cannot work together to rip off consumers by agreeing that they will all charge the same high price for their products. Businesses must compete against each other.

Examples
- It would be illegal if all the B&B owners in a town met before the start of the summer season and agreed that they would all charge €100 per person per night.
- There have been a number of cases in Ireland of car dealers forming illegal cartels and all charging the same high price for cars.

This rule is important to Ireland because it ensures that Irish businesses compete under conditions of fair competition.

2. Businesses in a dominant position in the market (ones that control a large percentage of the market) cannot abuse their power by increasing prices or trying to stop new competitors from entering the market.

This means that smaller Irish businesses – the vast majority of Irish businesses are small and medium sized enterprises (SMEs) – are protected against being bullied out of the market by bigger businesses.

Example
- The Court of Justice found HB Ice Cream guilty of abusing its dominant position when it gave free freezers to shopkeepers around Ireland on the condition that they were only to be used to stock HB ice cream and no other brand. The court saw this as HB trying to prevent other ice cream from being sold in Irish shops.

3. EU competition policy ensures that Ireland's state-owned enterprises cannot enjoy a monopoly position. This means that they cannot be the only business selling a particular product. They must be open to competition.

This gives Irish entrepreneurs the chance to set up businesses in areas previously off limits to them. If they offer a better service than the government's business, they will make a profit.

For this reason, the old state monopolies of VHI, RTÉ and CIÉ now face competition from Quinn Healthcare, TV3 and Aircoach respectively. This leads to greater competition in these sectors, which should ensure better service and lower prices for consumers.

4. EU competition policy prohibits mergers and takeovers that would reduce free competition. Any proposed merger or takeover must seek and obtain permission from the European Commission to go ahead. Permission is denied if the Commission believes that the merger would seriously damage competition.

This means that Irish entrepreneurs will be prevented from expanding their business by merger or takeover if the European Commission believes that such a merger or takeover would be bad for competition.

In 2007, the European Commission blocked Ryanair's takeover of Aer Lingus. It felt that this would lead to less choice and probably higher prices for EU passengers.

Single European Market (SEM)

The Single European Market (SEM) – part of Economic and Monetary Union (EMU) – makes the EU the world's largest free trade area. There are no barriers to trade between the EU countries.

There is free movement of goods, labour and capital throughout the EU.

Goods	Businesses can sell their products anywhere in the EU without any restrictions (such as tariffs, quotas or embargoes).
Labour	EU workers can live and work anywhere in the EU.
Capital	EU citizens and businesses can invest their money anywhere in the EU.

Significance of the SEM for Ireland

1. Irish businesses can **sell their products** anywhere in the EU just as easily as they can sell them here. There are no barriers to trade between the countries. This is a major opportunity for Irish businesses to increase their sales and profits. They can now sell their products freely to a market of 480 million consumers.

2. Irish businesses can bid for **government contracts** of other EU countries. National governments are not allowed to show favouritism to their own country's businesses. They must choose the best quote they get from within the EU. This gives Irish businesses the opportunity to win lucrative contracts from other EU governments and hence increase their sales and profits.

3. The SEM has made trade within the EU easier. There are no customs checks or border controls anymore. This means that Irish goods are not physically inspected by government officials when they enter an EU country.
    Before the SEM abolished border checks, 60 million customs clearance documents were required every year. These are no longer needed.
    This means that there are no delays for Irish businesses when they transport their

products to EU countries. Fewer delays mean quicker transportation and hence lower costs.

4.   Ireland's membership of the SEM provides another opportunity for Irish businesses. It is a major tool in attracting **transnational companies** to Ireland. They come here to get free access to the EU market.
When they come here, these transnational companies may buy their raw materials from Irish businesses. This leads to higher sales and profits for Irish businesses. Furthermore, they bring to Ireland the latest technologies, products and skills. Therefore, Irish businesses that deal with them acquire the latest skills.

5.   The SEM allows for the **free movement of capital**. This means that EU citizens can invest their money anywhere in the EU. This makes it easier for Irish entrepreneurs to raise the capital they need to set up, run and expand their businesses. They can sell shares in any EU stock market and borrow from any EU bank.

Challenges of the SEM for Ireland

1.   The SEM has brought challenges for Irish businesses. In the same way that we can sell our products all over the EU, other EU businesses can set up here and sell their products in Ireland.
For example, Irish chemists face major **competition** from Boots (UK). RTÉ faces major competition from Sky and ITV (UK).
This increased competition may force some Irish businesses out of business if they cannot cope with the threat from big EU competitors.

2.   The free movement of labour means that EU citizens have the right to travel and work in any EU country. This could have a negative impact on Irish business because Irish people may decide to live and work elsewhere in the EU, leaving Irish businesses **short of workers**.

3.   Irish firms can no longer rely on contracts from the Irish government for sales and profits. Under SEM rules, all **government contracts** must be advertised to allow all EU businesses apply. The Irish government *must* give the contract to the best applicant, regardless of which country it comes from.

Monetary Union - The Euro

Monetary union (part of EMU) involved establishing one single currency (the euro) for some countries of the EU and the setting up of the European Central Bank (ECB).

15 countries have the euro as their currency. These are:
Austria, Belgium, Cyprus, Finland, France, Germany, Greece, Ireland, Italy, Luxembourg, Malta, Netherlands, Portugal, Slovenia and Spain.

Advantages of The Euro

1. **It reduces businesses' costs**

   Irish businesses no longer have to pay bank charges to change currency when they are buying from and selling to the other eurozone countries.

   Furthermore, they don't need to worry about the exchange rate going up or down because they pay and are paid in euro.

2. **Interest rates in the eurozone countries are set by the ECB**

   So far, the ECB has set interest rates lower than those previously charged in Ireland. These low interest rates mean lower loan repayments for Irish businesses. This reduces their costs and increases their profits.

3. **It increases trade between the eurozone countries**

   A major barrier to trade (exchange rate fluctuations) has gone. This gives Irish businesses the opportunity to sell more to these countries and thus increase their profits. It will increase tourism. People in eurozone countries will be more willing to come to Ireland because they won't have to change their money to come here.

4. **It has led to greater transparency in prices in the eurozone**

   Customers can now directly compare the prices of different goods in all the eurozone countries because they are all priced in the same currency. This leads to similar prices all over Europe. This means that many products in Ireland will cost less. This reduces inflation, which is good for Irish business because it keeps their costs down.

Disadvantages of The Euro

1. **The UK has not adopted the euro as its currency yet**

   The UK still uses the pound sterling. A large part of Ireland's international trade is with the UK. Irish businesses still face the costs of changing money and the risks of fluctuating exchange rates when it comes to buying from and selling to the UK.

2. **Ireland has no control over its interest rates**

   They are set by the ECB. If Ireland's economy falls out of sync with the rest of the eurozone countries, Ireland could suffer. The ECB might decide to help the rest of the eurozone countries by changing interest rates to suit them rather than Ireland.

3. **Irish businesses may face increased competition**
    Irish consumers can now compare prices directly because products are priced in euro in all the eurozone countries. They may decide to buy goods from foreign businesses.

Ordinary Level Questions

EXAM SECTION 1 (25%) – SHORT ANSWER QUESTIONS [10 marks each]

1. List three interest groups that try to influence EU decision-making.

2. Explain the term "EU directive" and give one example.

3. Column 1 is a list of business terms. Column 2 is a list of possible explanations for these terms. Match the two lists by placing the letter of the correct explanation under the relevant number below. One explanation has no match.

Column 1	Column 2: Explanations
1. EU	a) Directly elected by the people of Europe to speak for them in the EU
2. European Parliament	
3. Council of the EU	b) Consists of commissioners whose job is to run the EU on a day-to-day basis
4. European Court of Auditors	c) EU policy designed to help farmers
5. Court of Justice	d) Gives advice to the courts of EU countries about EU law
6. European Commission	e) European Union
	f) Most important decision-making body in the EU
	g) Makes sure that the EU budget is spent correctly

1	2	3	4	5	6
E					

4. Outline two functions of the European Commission.

5. What do the following letters stand for?   EU   MEP   CAP

6. Name three EU policies.

7. What is the function of the Common Agricultural Policy?

8. Outline two advantages of the euro for Irish business.

9. Indicate by means of a tick (✔) the EU policy which each sentence describes.

	Competition Policy	Social Charter	Common Agricultural Policy	Common Fisheries Policy
Helps farmers achieve a decent standard of living				
Tries to preserve fish stocks				
Gives grants to farmers				
Gives EU citizens the right to work anywhere in the EU				

10. Indicate whether each of the following (A, B, C, D and E) is true or false.

	Sentence	True or False
A	The European Commission decides whether a law is passed in the EU.	
B	The Common Fisheries Policy pays grants to fishermen to buy better boats and equipment.	
C	Under the EU Social Charter, EU workers must be consulted by their boss about decisions affecting their jobs.	
D	The EU Competition Policy allows businesses to form cartels.	
E	Ireland can stop any EU businesses selling its products here if that might put Irish firms out of business.	

EXAM SECTION 2 (75%) – LONG QUESTIONS

1. List the steps involved in EU decision-making.   (20 marks)

2. What is the European Parliament? Outline three of its functions.   (20 marks)

3. Explain the role of the European Court of Auditors.   (10 marks)

4. The EU Competition Policy tries to make sure there is free and fair competition in the EU. Outline three ways it achieves this.   (15 marks)

5. Describe three rights that EU workers enjoy under the EU Social Charter.   (15 marks)

6. Distinguish between the Common Agricultural Policy and Common Fisheries Policy.   (20 marks)

7. State three benefits of the Single European Market (SEM) for Irish business.   (15 marks)

8. Outline three challenges of the Single European Market (SEM) for
    Irish business.   (15 marks)

9. Describe three disadvantages of the euro for Ireland.   (15 marks)

10. Identify three reasons why EU membership is important to Ireland.   (15 marks)

Higher Level Questions

EXAM SECTION 1 (20%) – SHORT ANSWER QUESTIONS [10 marks each]

1. Illustrate your understanding of the term "EU directive".

2. Distinguish between the European Court of Auditors and the Court of Justice.

3. Which EU institution do you feel is the most important? Explain your choice.

4. What do the following letters stand for?   SEM   EMU   CAP   ECB   EU

5. The Competition Policy is an important EU policy. List three other EU policies and
    outline the purpose of any one of them.

6. Complete this sentence: The EU Competition Policy requires…

7. Column 1 is a list of business terms. Column 2 is a list of possible explanations for these
    terms. Match the two lists by placing the letter of the correct explanation under the
    relevant number below. One explanation has no match.

Column 1	Column 2: Explanations
1. Co-decision	a) Sets out EU workers' rights
2. Single Payment Scheme	b) European Commission proposes laws and the European Parliament debates them
3. Cartel	c) Business that controls a large percentage of a market
4. Dominant Firm	d) Council of the European Union and the European Parliament jointly pass laws in the EU
5. Social Charter	e) Income grants paid to farmers every year
	f) An illegal agreement between competitors to restrict competition

1	2	3	4	5

8. One of the benefits of the EU is that it allows for "the free movement of goods, labour
    and capital". Briefly outline what this means.

9. Differentiate between economic union and monetary union in the EU.

10. What do the letters SEM stand for? Explain the importance of the SEM to Irish business.

EXAM SECTION 2 (20%) – APPLIED BUSINESS QUESTION – 80 MARKS

O'Dea Electrical

Mary O'Dea runs her own electrical shop in Waterford, selling all manner of electrical goods to the general public. The business is situated in an out-of-town retail park that also has many transnational factories. She imports all her stock from the UK and Germany. A new motorway, paid for with the help of EU grants, from the city to the port has improved delivery times dramatically.

However, the business has encountered a number or problems recently, not least the ever-increasing number of rules and regulations coming from the EU that have resulted in a reduction in Mary's annual profits. Competition from other electrical retailers in the city is so intense that Mary organised a meeting to come to an arrangement whereby they would all stop selling at rock bottom prices and cut back on costly advertising. Reports that a major UK electrical chain is to open a branch in the city led those present to express the fear that this UK store would put them out of business. One retailer proposed they merge their businesses in order to fight back.

The high cost of wages is another factor causing the drop in Mary's profits. To survive, Mary plans to introduce compulsory overtime with no extra pay. While industrial relations have never been good at O'Dea Electrical, Mary knows that the employees have no alternative but to accept these changes. She has approached a number of local investors without success for capital to help her through the current situation.

(A) Describe how one EU directive and one EU institution has impacted on
Mary's business.   (30 marks)

(B) Evaluate the effects of the Single European Market for O'Dea Electrical.   (20 marks)

(C) Explain how the provisions of EU Competition Policy and
the EU Social Charter apply to Mary's business.   (30 marks)

EXAM SECTION 3 (60%) – LONG QUESTIONS

1. Explain the decision-making process of the EU.   (20 marks)

2. Outline the role of special interest groups in EU decision-making.   (20 marks)

3. Evaluate the impact of the European Commission on Irish business.   (20 marks)

4. Contrast the role of the European Parliament with that of
    the Council of the European Union.   (20 marks)

5. Illustrate the impact of EU Social Policy on Irish business.   (20 marks)

6. Using examples, analyse the role of the EU Competition Policy
    in creating a suitable climate for business enterprises in Ireland.   (25 marks)

7. Evaluate the significance of the Single European Market for Irish business.   (25 marks)

8. Discuss the opportunities and threats for Irish business arising from
    the single currency (the euro).   (25 marks)

CHAPTER 26

Global Business

Many businesses expand into other countries to increase profits. If they sell their goods in a few countries, they are called **transnational companies** and, if they sell around the world, they are called **global companies**.

This chapter looks at transnational and global companies and examines how to sell a product all over the world.

Transnational Companies

A transnational company is a business with a head office in one country and branches or factories in a number of other countries.

The head office controls the entire business, whereas the branches around the world may carry out different jobs.

- ▶ Examples include Dell, Intel, Marks & Spencer, Lidl, ALDI and Zara.
- ▶ CRH is a building materials company. It has its headquarters in Ireland and operates in 28 countries around the world.

Reasons for the Development of Transnational Companies

There are many transnational companies today. The reasons for this include the following:

1. Businesses expand into different countries to **spread their risk**. They don't want to become too dependent on one market. For example, Dell (a US transnational) expanded into Europe. If there is a downturn in the US economy and sales of computers fall in the US, European sales may keep the business in profit.

2. Businesses expand into different countries to **increase their sales** and profits. By expanding overseas, they can sell their products to many more customers than if they concentrated solely on their home market.

3. Advances in transport and in **communications technology** have made it easier for businesses to run overseas branches. Video-conferencing enables managers to run a transnational business without having to travel. They can hold meetings with branches all over the world from their office.

4. Expansion into different countries is a way of overcoming **trade barriers**. Japanese car manufacturers set up factories in the EU (for example, Nissan set up a car manufacturing plant in Sunderland, England) to get round EU quotas on car imports from Japan.

Transnational companies that set up in Ireland have a major impact on the economy, mostly positive but there also can be some negative aspects to them.

Advantages of Transnational Companies

1. Jobs
They create thousands of jobs in Ireland. This leads to lower unemployment in the country and a higher standard of living for Irish people. For example, Dell and Intel employ almost 10,000 people in their Irish plants.

2. New Technology
They bring new technologies, new products and new management skills and ideas into Ireland. Dell and Intel bring the latest computer technology into Ireland and train their Irish employees in the latest computer skills.

3. Competition
They bring competition into the Irish market. This is good for Irish consumers because it leads to lower prices and better quality. Lidl and ALDI have increased competition in the Irish grocery market, leading to lower prices for Irish consumers.

4. Taxes
They pay a lot of tax to the Irish government on the profits they make in Ireland. This money can be used by the government to improve Ireland's economy through lower taxes and better infrastructure.

5. Buy Irish
They buy raw materials from Irish businesses, thus increasing the sales and profits of these indigenous businesses. Tesco Ireland buys a lot of Irish-produced food to sell in its stores, thus increasing Irish food businesses' sales and profits.

Disadvantages of Transnational Companies

1. They leave

They can close down with very little notice and leave Ireland in order to move to countries where wages and other costs are lower.

Fruit of the Loom, for example, closed its factory in Donegal to set up in Morocco because the wages it has to pay employees there are much lower than in Ireland.

2. Too much power

Many are so big that they can put pressure on the government to give them their own way. They may demand changes in the law that suit them and might threaten to leave the country if the government fails to comply. They may be too powerful in this regard.

3. Repatriate profits

They often repatriate most of their profits. This means that they send most of the profits they make in Ireland back home. So the money they make in Ireland doesn't necessarily benefit the Irish economy.

4. Decisions taken abroad

Most decisions are taken by the head office abroad and they may not take Irish interests into account.

Global Companies

Global companies are businesses that operate all over the world. They sell their products and services worldwide.

Examples of global companies include Coca-Cola, Toyota, McDonald's and Nike.

They treat the world as if it were a single country. They buy their materials from the cheapest place in the world they can find them.

Global companies make their products anywhere in the world, particularly in cheap-labour countries. They borrow money from the cheapest banks in the world. They transfer managers from one country to another.

An example of this can be found in the US car industry. When one typical US car was analysed to see how "American" it was, it turned out that many countries were involved in some aspect of its production or sale.

○   The car was assembled in South Korea.

○   Its electronic parts were bought from Japan.

○   It was designed in Germany.

○   The ad campaign for the car was developed in the UK.

Reasons for the Development of Global Companies

There are a number of reasons why there are so many global businesses operating today.

1. Businesses become global to **increase sales** all over the world. This leads to higher profits. Also, making enough products for the whole world leads to economies of scale for the business and lower costs.

2. It is now possible to **mass produce** enough products to satisfy global demand. Technological advances, such as Computer Aided Manufacture and robots, have improved mass production techniques. These technologies can make enough products to satisfy world demand.

3. **Communication** and transport advances have made it easier to run a global business. Video-conferencing enables managers to run a global business without having to travel. They can hold meetings with branches all over the world from their office.

4. **Deregulation** by the World Trade Organisation has made global business possible. Businesses can now enter markets previously denied to them thanks to freer world trade. For example, one of the biggest markets in the world, China, did not trade with the rest of the world until relatively recently.

Global Marketing

Global marketing means selling the same product all over the world using a global marketing mix (4Ps). When a global business uses the same marketing mix in each country, this is called a **standardised marketing mix**. The global business concentrates on the similarities across world markets. One example of this is Coca-Cola.

However, sometimes a global business will change elements of the product, price, promotion and place to suit local tastes, cultures and so on. For example, a company will produce right-hand drive cars in Ireland and UK. This is called an **adapted marketing mix**. This leads to additional production, advertising and packaging costs.

Global Product

This is a product that is sold throughout the world. Coca-Cola is an example of this. This is the one element of the global marketing mix that is most likely to stay the same all over the world.

To help with global recognition, most businesses will try to use the same product brand name throughout the world. In Ireland, Cif used to be called Jif, Snickers used to be called Marathon, Oil of Olay used to be called Oil of Ulay and Starburst used to be called Opal Fruits. Each company changed its product's brand name so that it would be the same all over the world. This makes it easier for customers to recognise it when they travel and it helps the company to save money by enabling it to use the same advertisements all over the world.

However, global businesses must take local needs and cultures into account if they want their product to succeed.

- For instance, McDonald's does not sell beef burgers in India as the cow is considered a sacred animal there.

- Mattel was mystified that sales of its "Barbie" doll were very low in Japan, despite constant advertising. It conducted market research that revealed that Japanese girls couldn't relate to Barbie. She didn't look Japanese. Mattel made changes to the doll for the Japanese market and it then became a best seller in Japan.

Global Price

The price that the company charges for its product may vary around the world. This is due to a number of factors including:

- The **standard of living** varies in different countries. Prices will normally be higher in wealthy countries because people can afford to pay more.

- Extra **transport costs** may be involved. The further the global business has to transport the product, the higher the price will have to be to cover the extra transportation costs.

- **Taxes and tariffs** may have to be paid. Countries that the global business exports to may add different taxes to its price.

- **Local rival firms** charge different prices. The level of competition in the market will also determine the maximum price the global business can charge for its product in different countries.

Global Promotion

If a global business can use the same promotion methods all over the world, this will save it a lot of money. Global companies love global events such as the Olympic Games and the World Cup because sponsorship of these events reaches a truly global market.

However, it is not always possible to use the same promotion throughout the world. Promotion may change in different countries to take account of differences in language, culture and advertising laws. If global businesses do not take these differences into account when promoting their product, they may offend locals and lose sales.

Proctor & Gamble (a global business that sells beauty and household cleaning products) aired a popular ad showing a European woman bathing. In the ad, her husband entered the bathroom and placed his hand on her shoulder. The ad was received very badly in Japan. Many Japanese people considered such behaviour inappropriate for television.

Global Place

In global marketing, getting the product to customers all over the world can be a daunting process. Many global businesses rely on *local* agents and distributors to deliver their product for them.

Coca-Cola enters into agreements with local businesses and allows them to bottle and distribute Coke under licence.

- In Israel, Coca-Cola products are produced and sold by the Central Bottling Company (CBC), the company's authorised bottling partner. CBC is an independent, privately owned company based near Tel Aviv.

- In Nigeria, the company's main bottling partners include the Nigerian Bottling Company.

Importance of Global Marketing

Global marketing is important for global businesses for the following reasons.

1. By selling the same product throughout the world, the global business can enjoy lower costs. It makes so many products to satisfy global demand that it enjoys massive **economies of scale** – the more products the business makes, the

cheaper it becomes to make each one. This allows the global business to sell the products at a very competitive price and enjoy even higher sales and profits.

2.   Selling the same product all over the world requires making it in **huge quantities**. The global business becomes an expert in making the product and, through practice, better than anyone else at making it. Furthermore, the global business can afford to invest in research and development on the product to make it the best in the world. Both of these factors mean that the global business can supply a world-class product. This leads to increased sales for the global business. For example, the global business Sony is one of the best electrical goods manufacturers in the world.

3.   Global businesses must realise that a truly **standardised marketing mix** may not always be appropriate or even possible. If local tastes are ignored, the global business may alienate local people and lose sales. For example, sales of Barbie dolls were low in Japan because the doll looked too Western. The company changed the doll to make her look more Japanese and sales increased rapidly.

4.   Global businesses must consider **cultural differences** when advertising its global products. For example, ads shown in Western countries depicting women in a certain way might cause offence in some other countries. Furthermore, global businesses must be aware of the backlash against globalisation. Many people vehemently oppose the imposition of one culture – for example, the "McDonald's fast food American culture" – on the world. Global businesses have to change their promotion methods to reflect local cultures. Otherwise, they risk negative publicity, boycotts and loss of sales.

Ordinary Level Questions

EXAM SECTION 1 (25%) – SHORT ANSWER QUESTIONS [10 marks each]

1.   Explain the term "transnational company" and give one example.
2.   List two advantages of transnational companies.
3.   Outline two disadvantages of transnational companies.
4.   Define the term "global business".
5.   Identify two factors that explain why a global business charges a different price in different countries.

EXAM SECTION 2 (75%) – LONG QUESTIONS

1.   Identify three reasons why a business might decide to become a
     transnational company.   (15 marks)
2.   Describe three reasons why Ireland encourages transnational companies
     to set up here.   (15 marks)

3. Outline three disadvantages of transnational companies for
    the Irish economy.   (15 marks)

4. Distinguish between a transnational company and a global company.
    Illustrate your answer with one example of each.   (20 marks)

5. "Globalisation is a major trend in business."
    Outline two reasons why there now are more global companies than ever.   (20 marks)

6. Explain the term "global marketing".   (10 marks)

7. Describe two advantages of global marketing for a business.   (10 marks)

Higher Level Questions

EXAM SECTION 1 (20%) – SHORT ANSWER QUESTIONS [10 marks each]

1. Illustrate your understanding of the term "transnational company".

2. Distinguish between transnational companies and global companies.

3. Define the term "global marketing".

4. What is a global brand?

5. Explain what is meant by the term "adapted global marketing mix". Illustrate your answer
    with an example.

EXAM SECTION 2 (20%) – APPLIED BUSINESS QUESTION – 80 MARKS

Nevin Glass

Vincent Nevin founded his own business, making a range of crystal glasses and vases
over 30 years ago. The business grew rapidly and has expanded to a number of
European countries. Vincent's glassware is now sold and made under licence in France,
Poland and Latvia.

In recent years, though, competition from a number of global companies has harmed
Vincent's business and profits have fallen. Customers have revealed that the competitors'
glassware is cheaper and of a better quality. This has prompted Vincent to turn Nevin
Glass into a global brand.

He believes that his designs have a universal appeal and that customers throughout the
world will like them. The Christmas season is his busiest and most profitable, so he wants
to launch the brand globally right before this crucial period. To save money on
marketing, he plans to use his existing advertising campaign, which has proved very
successful in Europe. It features a range of Christmas scenes, including one with Santa
Claus, one with a family sitting down to Christmas dinner and a scene featuring children
praying before a crib in a church.

(A) Evaluate the implications of global marketing for Vincent's business.   (25 marks)

EXAM SECTION 3 (60%) – LONG QUESTIONS

1. Discuss the reasons for the growth in the number of Irish businesses
    becoming transnational companies.   (20 marks)

2. Evaluate the impact, both positive and negative, of foreign
    transnational companies on the Irish economy.   (25 marks)

3. Outline the factors contributing to the increasing number of
    global companies.   (20 marks)

4. Define the term "global marketing". Illustrate its importance to the success
    of a global enterprise.   (25 marks)

Note: Cross-referenced terms are shown in bold.

Term	Definition
4Ps	The four tools of marketing: Product, Price, Promotion and Place.
absenteeism	Frequent absence from work without good reason.
acceptance	A person agrees to all the terms of a contract.
accrued expenses	Bills for services that are used now and paid for later. The cost of phone services are accrued expenses because you can use the phone now and pay for the service later.
acid test ratio	A calculation that tells a business how much real cash it has, when stock is ignored. The formula is (Current Assets – Closing Stock) ÷ Current Liabilities. The calculation shows the business's **liquidity**.
acquisition	See **takeover**.
adapted marketing mix	A **marketing mix** that may be changed when marketing in different countries and cultures.
advertising	The paid, non-personal communication of information about a product or service through various media.
agenda	Document listing items to be discussed at a meeting
AGM	Annual General Meeting. All companies must have an AGM every year.
agri-business	A business that converts farm produce into food.
alliance	See **strategic alliance**.
amalgamation	See **merger**.
AOB	Any other business. Last item to be discussed at a meeting.
APC	Area Partnership Company. An organisation that helps local people set up businesses in their area.
APR	Annual percentage rate. It shows the cost of a loan, including the interest and any other charges.
arbitration	The use of an independent third party to settle **industrial relations** conflicts.
Area Action Plan	A plan drawn up by an **APC** to enable a local community to set up businesses.
articles of association	A list of internal rules a **private limited company** and a **PLC** draw up to oversee how the company is run.
asset stripping	An offensive reason for business expansion. A business takes over a company in order to sell that company's assets at a profit.
autocratic leadership	A style of leading where the manager makes all decisions without consulting the employees.
average clause	A rule applied when you under-insure an item. If you insure an item for only a fraction of what it is worth, the insurance company will pay out only the same fraction of the compensation.
backward vertical integration	A defensive reason for business expansion. A business takes over its supplier in order to protect its supplies.
bad debts	Debts that have to be written off because the customers cannot pay them.
Balance of Payments	The difference between the value of all the products and services that Ireland exports and imports.

Balance of Trade	The difference between the value of all the products that Ireland exports and imports.
Balance Sheet	A financial statement showing everything the business owns and all the money it owes.
bank overdraft	A source of finance whereby the bank allows a household or business to pay for things by writing cheques up to an agreed limit, even though they don't have enough money in their current account to cover these cheques.
bar chart	A chart that uses bars to display information. Bar charts are useful for showing the relative sizes of things.
batch production	A business makes a large amount of identical products in one production run.
benefit-in-kind	A non-cash payment (such as a company car or subsidised meals) made to an employee.
brainstorming	A technique used to generate business ideas. A group of people list all the relevant ideas they can think of. After they have generated enough ideas, they start analysing them.
brand name	A name, symbol, design or logo used by a business to distinguish its products from others.
breakeven price	The minimum price a business can charge to cover the cost of making and selling a product.
breaking bulk	A purchasing strategy. A wholesaler buys large quantities of a product direct from the manufacturer and then sells smaller quantities to the retailers.
business ethics	A set of moral principles that tells businesspeople what is the right and wrong thing to do in a given situation.
business plan	A document that outlines a business's objectives and strategies. It is used to attract investors.
CAD	Computer Aided Design. Computer software that is used to design new products.
CAI	Consumers' Association of Ireland. An **interest group**.
CAM	Computer Aided Manufacture. Computer software that controls factory machines.
CAP	Common Agricultural Policy. An EU policy designed to give all EU farmers a good standard of living.
capacity to contract	An essential element of a contract. It means you have the legal ability and authority to make a legally binding contract.
capital	Money used to set up a business.
capital spending	Money the government spends to maintain the country's infrastructure.
capital-intensive industry	An industry that uses more machines than employees. Manufacturing is a capital-intensive industry.
cartel	An illegal secret agreement between businesses to restrict competition.
cash flow forecast	A document that outlines how much money the business (or household) expects to spend and receive in the future.
CAT	Capital Acquisitions Tax. A tax you pay if you receive a gift or inheritance.

caveat emptor	The principle of "buyer beware".
CEB	**County Enterprise Board** or **City Enterprise Board**.
CEO	Chief Executive Officer. The person in overall control of a business.
Certificate of Incorporation	A document sent by the Registrar of Companies to the shareholders of a **private limited company**. It enables the company to start trading.
Certificate of Trading	A document sent by the Registrar of Companies to the shareholders of a **PLC**. It enables the company to start trading.
CFP	Common Fisheries Policy. An EU policy designed to give all involved in the EU fishing industry a good standard of living. It also aims to conserve fish stocks.
CGT	Capital Gains Tax. A tax you pay if you sell an asset and make a profit from the sale.
channel of distribution	The means by which a business distributes its products to its customers. For example, a manufacturer might sell to a wholesaler, who then sells to a retailer, who then sells to the customer.
City Enterprise Board	A government body that helps small local businesses in a city.
civil service	Employees of government departments.
climate change	Changes to Earth's climate caused by the use of **fossil fuel**.
closed shop	The situation where workers have only one choice of union to join.
code of ethics	A document outlining the moral behaviour and expectations of an organisation. It shows managers and employees exactly what is regarded as ethical or unethical behaviour.
co-decision principle	An EU decision-making principle. The **European Parliament** and the **Council of the European Union** jointly decide what becomes EU law.
collateral	An asset that is used as security on a loan.
collective agreement	An agreed settlement after negotiation.
commercial rates	A tax that businesses pay to their local council every year.
community development	The process where a local community identifies the problems it faces and develops plans to solve these problems.
Community Services Programme	A **community development** scheme that helps not-for-profit community businesses.
comparability claim	A claim for a pay rise, based on pay rises given to those who perform similar work.
comparative advertising	A type of advertising. A business advertises how much better its product is than its competitors' products. For example, a supermarket might advertise that its products are better value than its competitors' products.
competitive relationship	A business relationship where two or more **stakeholders** fight against each other.
conciliation	An independent outsider helps two disputing parties to talk out their differences and reach a mutually acceptable solution.
consent to contract	An essential element of a contract. It means that you give your permission willingly to enter the contract.
consideration	An essential element of a contract. It is the payment one party gives to another as part of the contract.

constructive dismissal	The situation where an employee is forced to resign because of unfair treatment (such as bullying) by her employer.
consumer	A person who buys goods or services.
Consumer Information Act, 1978	An act that protects consumers from false or misleading information about goods or services.
consumer panel	A group of consumers who are monitored to get their opinions on a product.
Consumer Price Index	A measure of the level of prices in the economy. It is calculated by monitoring the cost of an average family's shopping each month.
contract condition	A fundamental part of a contract. If you break a condition of a contract, the contract is terminated.
contract warranty	A term of a contract that is not fundamental to it. If you break a warranty, the contract is not terminated.
contribution	An insurance principle that applies when you insure an item with a number of insurance companies.
contribution per unit	The price of a product less its variable cost.
controller manager	A manager who tells employees what to do and expects them to do it without question. A controller manager makes decisions without consulting the employees.
controlling	The management activity of ensuring that a business stays on target to achieve its goals.
co-op	See **co-operative**.
co-operative	A business set up by a group of people who want to co-operate with each other.
co-operative relationship	A business relationship where two or more stakeholders work together to help and benefit each other.
corporation tax	A tax that companies pay on their annual profits.
cost of living claim	A claim for a pay rise, based on increases in the cost of living.
Council of the European Union	An EU decision-making body, comprising the government ministers from the member states.
counter offer	A new contract, which replaces an existing contract. If you change the terms of a contract, you are making a counter offer.
County Enterprise Board	A government body that helps small local businesses in a county.
Court of Justice	An EU court that ensures the EU laws are applied the same way in all member states.
credit control	A management control that aims to eliminate **bad debts** and encourages customers to settle their debts promptly.
credit rating	A person's or business's reputation for paying back loans. Someone with a poor credit rating will find it difficult to get a loan.
creditor	Someone you owe money to.
current spending	Money the government spends to pay state workers.
customs duty	A tax paid on imports from a non-EU country.
CV	Curriculum vitae. A document summarising a job applicant's qualifications, experiences and interests.
Data Protection Act, 1988	A law that deals with information held about people on computer.
Data Protection Commissioner	A government official who checks how computer data is used and investigates claims of data misuse.

debenture	A long-term loan that has to be paid in one lump-sum in the future. In the meantime, the company pays a fixed rate of interest on the loan every year.
debt capital	Money an investor lends to an **entrepreneur** for a business. The investor expects the loan to be repaid with interest.
debt/equity ratio	A calculation that shows how a business is financed. The formula is Debt Capital ÷ Equity Capital.
debtor	Someone who owes you money.
deed of partnership	A contract between business partners to set up a business.
deficit	Shortage of money.
delegation	A manager gives some of his work to an employee to do for him.
democratic leadership	A style of leading where the manager involves the employees when making decisions.
dependent relationship	A business relationship where two or more **stakeholders** need each other.
deregulation	The removal of government rules and regulations that restrict free trade.
desk research	Using existing research in marketing.
differentiation strategy	A business strategy where a company makes products that are so different, they stand out from the competitors' products.
direct debit	A system where an account holder instructs her bank to regularly pay money from her account into someone else's account. The amount can change each time. Many people pay phone and ESB bills by direct debit.
DIRT	Deposit Interest Retention Tax. A tax paid on the interest earned on savings.
dividend	A share of a business's profits, which is paid to shareholders.
dynamic relationship	A business relationship where two or more **stakeholders** have a constantly changing relationship.
e-commerce	The use of Internet technology to conduct business.
economic variables	Factors that affect a country's economy. They include **inflation**, **exchange rates**, interest rates and tax rates.
economies of scale	A phenomenon whereby the more products a business produces, the less it costs to produce each individual product.
EDI	Electronic Data Interchange. A system that links the computers of two different companies so that they can exchange standard documents without any human intervention.
EGM	Extraordinary General Meeting. This is a company meeting called to discuss a specific urgent issue.
embargo	A ban on all foreign imports or a ban on imports from a specified country.
emergency tax	A tax paid by employees until they complete the **Form 12A**.
employee empowerment	Giving employees the power to make decisions for the good of the business.
employee participation	Involving employees in the running of a business.
Employment Appeals Tribunal	An independent body that investigates infringements of employee rights in a quick, informal and inexpensive way.

Employment Equality Act, 1988	Law that bans discrimination at work under nine grounds.
Endowment Policy	A life assurance policy where the insurance company pays out when the insured person reaches a specified age or dies, whichever occurs first.
enterprise incubation unit	A community business premises that local businesses can operate from. It is set up by the local **APC**.
Enterprise Ireland	A **state-owned enterprise** that provides advice and grants to indigenous Irish businesses.
entrepreneur	Someone who sets up a business.
Environmental Impact Assessment	An assessment of how a business's plans are likely to affect the environment.
Equality Authority	A government body that works to prevent discrimination in the workplace.
equity capital	Money the owners (and shareholders) have invested in a business.
equity finance	Money an investor gives to an **entrepreneur** for a business. In return, the investor receives a share in the business and gets an annual **dividend**.
ethical business practice	Conducting business according to a set of moral principles which ensures that the business does the right thing in all situations.
ethics auditor	An independent outsider who examines every aspect of a business to see whether the business is behaving ethically.
EU Competition Policy	A set of rules that aims to ensure free and fair competition between businesses in the EU. It also bans the formation of a **cartel**.
EU decision	An EU law that might apply to only one country, organisation or citizen. An EU decision must be implemented immediately.
EU directive	An EU law that must be implemented within a set time by all member states.
EU regulation	An EU law that applies immediately in all member states.
EU Social Charter	The EU's social policy. It aims to improve working and living conditions for EU citizens.
European Commission	The EU body that runs the EU. It proposes new EU laws and enforces them if they become law.
European Court of Auditors	The EU body responsible for ensuring that the EU budget is managed properly.
European Parliament	The EU body that supervises the EU. It debates proposed laws and approves the EU budget.
exchange rates	How much of a foreign currency you can get for €1.
executive summary	A summary of the major findings and conclusions of a report.
Export Credit Insurance	A guarantee given by the government that it will pay an Irish exporter if its foreign customer does not pay up.
exporting	Selling products and services to foreign countries.
extractive industry	See **primary sector**.
facilitator manager	A manager who consults the employees and encourages them in their work.

factoring	A short-term source of finance. A business sells it debtors to a bank for cash. The bank charges a fee for the service.
factoring with recourse	A type of **factoring**. If any of the debtors fail to pay up, the business must reimburse the bank.
factoring without recourse	A type of **factoring**. If any of the debtors fail to pay up, the business does not have to reimburse the bank.
factors of production	The essential items needed to make a finished product. They are land, labour, **capital** and enterprise.
FÁS	The national training and employment authority.
feasibility study	A study to assess the practical implementation of an idea.
field research	Carrying out new research in marketing.
financial statements	Documents drawn up by a business to compute its annual profit (**Profit and Loss Account**) and its assets and liabilities (**Balance Sheet**).
fixed rate loan	A loan that charges the same rate of interest every year for a specified number of years.
flexitime	An employment arrangement where a business is flexible about what time employees start and finish work.
focus group	See **consumer panel**.
Form 12A	A form that employees complete when they start working for the first time. They return the completed form to **Revenue**.
form A1	A form completed by the owners of a **private limited company**. It outlines the company name, registered offices, directors and secretary.
forward vertical integration	A defensive reason for business expansion. A business takes over the firm that distributes its products in order to guarantee distribution.
fossil fuel	Fuel derived from fossils. It includes petrol, diesel, coal and peat.
franchise	A business expansion strategy. A business allows another **entrepreneur** to copy its business exactly, in return for a fee.
franchisee	An **entrepreneur** who opens a business by buying a **franchise**.
franchiser	An **entrepreneur** who sells a business idea as a **franchise**.
free trade	The ability of a country to buy and sell products with other countries without any restrictions.
functional organisation structure	An organisation structure that splits a business up into major jobs (or functions) to be done, such as Marketing, Production and so on.
gearing	The ratio of borrowings and investments used to finance a business. Low gearing means that the owners have invested more money than they have borrowed. Neutral gearing means that the owners have invested the same amount as they have borrowing. High gearing means that the owners have borrowed more than they have invested.
generic advertising	A type of advertising. It is used to advertise an entire industry, rather than just a specific brand.
geographic organisational structure	An organisation structure that splits a business up into the major geographic regions that it operates in.
global company	A company that sells its products all over the world.

global marketing	Selling the same product all over the world using a global **marketing mix**.
globalisation	The trend for businesses to operate throughout the entire world.
green investment fund	An investment fund that invests only in socially responsible businesses.
gross profit	The profit made from the sale of goods, after subtracting the cost of making or buying the goods.
gross profit percentage	A calculation that shows what percentage of sales is **gross profit**. The formula is (Gross Profit ÷ Sales) × 100.
Hierarchy of Needs	A theory developed Abraham Maslow. It argues that people have a hierarchy of physiological, safety, social, esteem and self-actualisation needs.
Hire Purchase	A medium-term source of finance. A person or business buys an item, collects it and pays for it in installments over an agreed period of time.
HRM	Human Resource Management. The process of managing employees in a business.
IBEC	Irish Business and Employers Confederation. An **interest group**.
ICMSA	Irish Creamery Milk Suppliers Association. An **interest group**.
ICT	Information and Communications Technology. Any technology that enables communication in the business.
ICTU	Irish Congress of Trade Unions. An **interest group**.
IFA	Irish Farmers Association. An **interest group**.
illiquid	Lack of the ready cash needed to pay short-term bills.
import substitution	An indigenous version of an imported product.
importing	Buying products and services from foreign countries.
indemnity	An insurance principle that states that you cannot make a profit from an insurance claim.
indigenous firm	An Irish business set up by Irish people that makes its products in Ireland.
industrial action	Action taken by employees when conflicts with employers cannot be resolved.
industrial democracy	See **employee participation**.
industrial relations	The state of relations between employers and employees.
Industrial Relations Act, 1990	An act that legislates on **industrial relations** issues, such as **industrial action**.
inflation	The percentage increase in the general level of prices in Ireland in a year.
informative advertising	A type of advertising. A business gives its customers specific information about the product. A business might advertise that the latest version of its product will be available on 1 March.
INO	Irish Nurses Organisation. An **interest group**.
inorganic growth	The quick expansion of a business using a **merger**, a **strategic alliance** or a **takeover**.
insurable interest	An insurance principle that states that you can only insure something you own.

intention to contract	An essential element of a contract. It means that the parties to the contract understand that it is a legally binding contract.
interest group	A group of people who campaign for a common goal.
international trade	Commerce between different countries. It involves **importing** and **exporting**.
intrapreneur	An employee who presents business ideas to his employer.
invisible exports	Services sold to foreign countries.
invisible imports	Services bought from foreign countries.
invitation to treat	An advertisement, a price tag or a shop display. It is an indication of the price someone is prepared to accept for goods of services. It is not a legally binding contract.
invoice	A bill for goods sold on credit.
ISME	Irish Small and Medium Enterprises. An **interest group**.
ISO	International Organisation for Standardisation.
ISO 9000	A mark of quality awarded to businesses by the **ISO**.
jargon	Technical language used by a specific group.
job production	A production option. A business makes one product at a time. Hand-made suits use job production.
joint venture	See **strategic alliance**.
just-in-time	A **stock control** strategy where the business aims to have exactly the right amount of stock (no more and no less) needed at any time.
labour court	An organisation set up by the government to solve industrial disputes.
labour force	All the people in Ireland who are in work or are available for work.
labour turnover	The rate at which employees leave a business.
labour-intensive industry	An industry that uses more employees than machines. Construction is a labour-intensive industry.
laissez faire leadership	A style of leading where the manager does not interfere with how employees do their work.
leading	The ability to direct people, give them instructions and make them follow and obey you.
leaning on the trade	Keeping your suppliers waiting for payment of goods you receive. This affects your **credit rating**.
legality of form	An essential element of some contracts, such as mortgage agreements. It means that the contract must be drawn up in a certain way.
legality of purpose	An essential element of a contract. It means that contracts are legally binding only if they are used for legal purposes. For example, a contract to commit a crime is not legally binding.
limited liability	A legal term. If a **private limited company**, **PLC** or a **co-operative** goes bankrupt, shareholders lose only the capital they invested in the business. They do not have to sell any of their personal assets in order to repay the business's debts.
line graph	A chart that uses lines to show how values change over time.
liquidation	Closing down a business and selling its assets.
liquidity	The ability of a business to pay its short-term bills.

loading	An extra charge added to insurance premiums to cover higher risks.
lockout	An **industrial action** where the employer excludes employees from work.
loss leader	A pricing strategy. A business sells a product below cost in order to attract customers into the store. It is hoped that the customers will then buy other products as well.
low cost leadership strategy	A business strategy where a company keeps costs low so that it can sell its products cheaply.
LRC	The Labour Relations Commission. A government body that aims to promote better **industrial relations**.
manpower planning	Ensuring that the business has the right number of employees with the right combination of skills.
margin of safety	The difference between a business's forecast sales and its breakeven point.
market segmentation	Dividing the overall market for a product into different groups of customers. The market for toiletries is divided into men's and women's segments.
marketing concept	The principle that the customer is the most important person in the business.
marketing mix	The four tools used in marketing. See **4Ps**.
marketing strategy	A written plan outlining a business's marketing objectives and how it aims to achieve them.
mass production	A production option. A business makes the same product continuously. Chocolate bars use mass production.
matrix organisation structure	An organisation structure that combines a **functional organisation structure** with a project team structure.
memorandum of association	A list of rules that govern how a **private limited company** and a **PLC** deal with the public.
mentor	An experienced businessperson who assists local businesses that are set up by **community development**.
merchantable quality	Under the **Sale of Goods and Supply of Services Act, 1980**, goods bought must be of acceptable standard, taking into account their price and purpose.
merger	A form of **inorganic growth** of a business. Two separate businesses voluntarily agree to join together to form a new business. Also known as an amalgamation.
minutes	A summary of what was said at a meeting and what decisions were made.
mission statement	A statement of a business's principal objective.
mortgage	A long-term loan used by a household to buy its house.
motivating	The manager energises employees and provides them with incentives so that they co-operate and work harder for the business.
NAFTA	North American Free Trade Agreement. A **trading bloc** comprising the USA, Canada and Mexico.
National Consumer Agency	A government agency that protects consumers' rights.

National Pay Agreement	An agreement between the government and **social partners** on pay issues.
net profit	The profit made after business expenses have been subtracted from the **gross profit**.
net profit percentage	A calculation that shows what percentage of sales is **net profit**. The formula is (Net Profit ÷ Sales) × 100.
niche market	A subset of the **target market**.
niche strategy	A business strategy where a company aims to satisfy a **niche market**.
offer	A person asks another to enter into a contract with him.
off-the-job training	Training employees outside of the normal working situation by sending them on training courses and conferences.
Ombudsman	A person who investigates complaints against public bodies.
on-the-job training	Training employees while they are performing their jobs. They learn by practical experience and observation.
open economy	An economy that trades with most countries.
ordinary share capital	See **equity capital**.
organic growth	The slow, natural growth of a business.
organising	The management activity of arranging a business's resources in the best way to help it achieve its goals.
P21	A form sent by **Revenue** to an employee, showing the employee the balance of income tax he owes or is owed for the year.
P45	A form given to an employee when he leaves a job. It outlines the pay earned and the **PAYE** and **PRSI** paid by the employee from the start of the year to the date he left.
P60	A form given to an employee at the end of the tax year. It outlines the pay earned and the **PAYE** and **PRSI** paid by the employee in that tax year.
partnership	A business owned and managed by 2 to 20 people.
patent	Legal protection for an idea.
PAYE	Pay As You Earn. An income tax that employees pay on their wages.
paypath	A payment system where an employee's salary is paid directly into his bank account.
performance appraisal	An evaluation of how an employee is performing her job.
persuasive advertising	A type of advertising. A business tries to persuade its customers that they must have its product.
pictogram	A chart that uses pictures to convey information.
pie chart	A chart that uses pie slices to illustrate the relative sizes of things.
PLC	Public limited company. A business owned by at least seven owners. It can sell its shares to the public.
planning	The management activity of setting goals for the future and devising strategies to use to achieve them.
Pobal	An organisation that manages various projects on behalf of the government.
political strike	An **industrial action** where employees go on strike to protest against government action.

Polluter Pays principle	A **waste management** principle that says that polluters must pay for the cost of disposing the waste they produce.
positive discrimination	A policy to ensure that protected groups achieve full equality in the workplace.
preference shares	A long-term loan, similar to a **debenture**.
price discrimination strategy	A pricing strategy. A business charges different customers different prices for the same product. For example, a newspaper might have a discount price for students.
price penetration strategy	A pricing strategy. A business charges as low as possible for its products in order to win customers from its competitors.
price skimming strategy	A pricing strategy. A business initially charges a high price for a product to recoup the money spent developing it as quickly as possible.
primary picketing	An **industrial action** where employees picket outside the employer's business.
primary sector	The section of the economy involved in extracting raw materials.
private limited company	A business set up by between 1 and 50 shareholders.
privatisation	Selling a **state-owned enterprise** to a private **entrepreneur** or business.
PRO	Public Relations Officer. The person responsible for handling a company's relations with the public and the media.
product life cycle	The stages in the sales history of a product. It comprises introduction, growth, maturity, saturation and decline.
product organisational structure	An organisation structure that splits a business up into departments, each of which is responsible for a product the business makes.
product screening	Assessing the ideas for new products and deciding which ones to pursue and which ones to reject.
production run	See **batch production**.
productivity claim	A claim for a pay rise, based on an increased workload or changes to work.
Profit and Loss Account	A financial statement showing how much profit or loss a business has made in a given year.
profitability ratios	Calculations that evaluate the profit made by the business.
protectionism	A means of preventing or limiting foreign imports coming into a country. It can be achieved by an **embargo**, a **quota** or a **tariff**.
prototype	The first working model of a new product.
PRSI	Pay Related Social Insurance. A tax that employees pay on their wages. Paying this tax entitles them to social welfare benefits.
psychological pricing	A pricing strategy. A business uses its price to appeal to customers' emotions. A business might charge a high price because its customers associate high prices with quality.
public service	Those employed by the government to provide a service to the public. The public service includes doctors, nurses and teachers.
Quality Circle	A group of employees who work to solve quality issues in a business.

quality control	The management activity of ensuring that the business's products meet consumers' expectations.
quorum	The minimum number of people needed to attend a meeting in order for the meeting to take place.
quota	A limit. It can refer to: • The limit placed on the number of imports allowed into a country. • The limit on the amount of food that can be produced. • The limit on the number of fish that can be caught.
reality perception	The ability to see things as they really are, and not just as you would prefer them to be.
recruitment	Finding suitable candidates to apply for a job vacancy in the business.
Registrar of Friendly Societies	The organisation that is responsible for the registration of, among others, a **co-operative**.
relativity claim	A claim for a pay rise, based on a pay rise achieved by a linked group. For example, a TD's salary is linked to civil service salaries.
reminder advertising	A type of advertising. A business uses advertising to remind customers that its brand is still available.
reserves	See **retained earnings**.
retained earnings	Profits that the owners have reinvested in the business.
Revenue	A government body that ensures that all citizens pay the correct tax.
Rights Commissioner	A member of the **LRC** who investigates certain disputes between an individual employee or a small group of employees and the employer.
risk management	Taking steps to reduce the risks a business is exposed to. Businesses hire security guards to minimise the risk of theft.
ROI	Return on Investment. The percentage profit made on the money invested. The formula is (Net Profit ÷ Capital Employed) × 100.
Sale of Goods and Supply of Services Act, 1980	An act outlining the rights that consumers have when buying goods or services.
sales promotions	Incentives a business offers consumers to encourage them to buy more of its products.
sampling	A **quality control** strategy where inspectors examine samples in different batches of products. If the sample fails to meet quality standards, the entire batch is rejected.
secondary picketing	An **industrial action** where employees picket outside another employer's business.
secondary sector	The section of the economy involved in converting raw materials into products. It includes manufacturing and construction.
selection	Choosing the best candidate for a job vacancy from all those who applied.
Self-assessment Income Tax	An income tax paid by a **sole trader** or a **partnership**.
semi-state body	See **state-owned enterprise**.
service screening	Assessing the ideas for new services and deciding which ones to pursue and which ones to reject.

share options	Shares that can be bought by employees at a reduced price.
shop steward	A **trade union** representative who acts as a liaison between a trade union and employees.
SIPTU	Services, Industrial, Professional and Technical Union. An **interest group**.
Small Claims Court	A court dedicated to judging consumer claims quickly and cheaply without involving solicitors.
social partners	Interest groups concerned with economic and wage issues. They include **IBEC** and **ICTU**.
social responsibility	A business's duty to treat people (employees, customers, investors and so on) and the environment well.
sole trader	A business owned and managed by one person.
span of control	The number of employees that directly report to a manager.
specific performance	A remedy for breach of contract whereby the person who breaks the contract is forced to carry it out exactly as originally agreed.
spreadsheet	A computer programme used for basic accounting calculations.
stakeholders	People who are affected by how a business is run.
standardised marketing mix	A **marketing mix** that is not changed when marketing in different cultures.
standing order	A system where an account holder instructs her bank to regularly pay money from her account into someone else's account. The amount is the same each time.
state-owned enterprise	A business owned by the Irish government on behalf of the Irish people. Also known as a semi-state body or a state-sponsored body.
state-sponsored body	See **state-owned enterprise**.
statutory meeting	The initial meeting of a **private limited company**.
stock control	The management activity of ensuring that the business has the right amount of stock at all times.
stockout	When a business runs out of stock.
strategic alliance	A form of **inorganic growth** of a business. Two separate businesses agree to co-operate on a project, but remain two separate businesses. Also known as a joint venture.
strategic plan	A major long-term plan for a business.
subrogation	An insurance principle that states that once you receive full compensation, that is all you are entitled to.
subsidy	Money given to a business so that it can charge a lower price for its products.
surplus	Money left over.
sustainable development	Development that ensures that present needs are met without compromising the ability of future generations to meet their needs.
SWOT	Strengths Weakness Opportunities Threats. An analysis of the challenges and opportunities facing a business.
sympathetic strike	An **industrial action** where employees go on strike in sympathy with another group.
tactical plan	A short-term plan for a particular section of a business.

takeover	A form of **inorganic growth** of a business. One business buys another business outright, with or without the other business's consent. Also known as an acquisition.
target market	The segment of the market that a business aims its product at.
tariff	A tax imposed on imports coming into a country.
tax relief at source	A portion of **mortgage** repayments that is paid by the government.
term loan	A loan from a bank that is paid back in installments over five years.
tertiary sector	The section of the economy involved in providing services for business and consumers.
test marketing	Launching a product on a small "test" segment of the market.
Theory X manager	A type of manager who believes that employees do not want to work. Theory X managers use a combination of supervision and threats in order to make sure employees do their jobs.
Theory Y manager	A type of manager who believes that employees enjoy working. Theory Y managers use a combination of encouragement and promotion in order to make sure employees do their jobs.
time management	Getting all the important jobs done in the time available.
TQM	Total Quality Management. A **quality control** technique that aims to ensure 100% perfection and 100% customer satisfaction.
trade credit	A short-term source of finance for a business. The business receives goods and pays for them later. The payment amount is included in the **invoice**.
trade union	An **interest group** that represents employees' interests.
trading bloc	A group of countries that agree to trade freely with each other. **NAFTA** and the EU are trading blocs.
transnational company	A company with a head office in one country and branches in a number of other countries.
uberrimae fidei	See **utmost good faith**.
ultra vires	Beyond the terms of a contract. A director who exceeds her authority is acting *ultra vires*.
Unfair Dismissal Act, 1977/93	An act that protects employees from unfair dismissal.
unlimited liability	A legal term. If a sole trader or partnership goes bankrupt, the owners are liable for paying back all the business's debts. If selling the business does not cover the debts, the owners have to sell some personal assets as well.
USP	Unique selling point. A product feature that favourably distinguishes the product from competitors' products.
utmost good faith	An insurance principle that states that people must be truthful when completing an insurance proposal form. They must provide accurate information and volunteer any relevant information that they are not asked for.
variable rate loan	A loan that charges a varying rate of interest every year for a specified number of years.
VAT	Value Added Tax. A tax added to the price of goods and services.
visible exports	Products sold to foreign countries.

visible imports	Products bought from foreign countries.
waste management	How a business deals with the waste it produces. Businesses should aim to reduce, reuse and recycle waste.
whistle-blowing	Reporting unethical behaviour within an organisation. For example, employees are encouraged to report any unethical behaviour they witness.
Whole Life Policy	A life assurance policy where the insurance company pays out only when the insured person dies.
wildcat strike	An **industrial action** where employees go on strike without giving any notice. This is an illegal strike.
worker director	An employee who is a member of the Board of Directors.
working capital ratio	A calculation that shows how much money a business has for every €1 it owes. The formula is Current Assets / Current Liabilities.
works councils	Groups of employees who are elected by their fellow employees and have a say in the business's plans and strategy.
WTO	World Trade Organisation. It negotiates the trading agreements that form the basis for **international trade**.